Reconciling Difference

Praise for *Reconciling Difference: Beyond Collective Violence in India*

'Rudolf Heredia makes a compelling case for dialogue as a process to end the collective violence of today. Drawing on India's history, the Constitution and even contemporary initiatives, he shows us how we can bring a healing touch to close the faultlines in our society.'—C. Rammanohar Reddy, Editor, *The India Forum*

'*Reconciling Difference*, written by one of the foremost thinkers and writers in India today, is his most important work to date. It is also the most urgent, for its theme is collective violence, which is threatening to send India, this great civilization, spiralling down to becoming a mirror image of Pakistan, perhaps even something worse. That would be a tragedy for not just India, but all of humanity. A must-read for those who want to know what is happening in the country, and what to do about it.'—Kiran Doshi, author of *Jinnah Often Came to Our House*

'A passionate advocate for peace, communal harmony, and the equal rights of all citizens, Rudolf Heredia has spent half a century bringing a moral conscience to the social sciences, and scholarly rigour to social activism. *Reconciling Difference* is the culmination, both of his long years of service among the most deprived communities of India, and of his painstaking research in many of the greatest libraries of the world. Heredia asks us to return to Gandhian non-violence in a time of escalating religious nationalism, sectarian strife and majoritarian violence. He explores India's multiple traditions of religious and philosophical thought in search of resources to revitalize our damaged polity and heal our fraying social fabric. This book will rally all those who truly care about the survival and flourishing of Indian democracy.'—Ananya Vajpeyi, author of *Righteous Republic: The Political Foundations of Modern India*

'*Reconciling Difference* is an anguished and troubled citizen and scholar's attempt at understanding the present predicament of collective violence in modern India. It is a thoughtful, reflective, and dialogic engagement which explores possible ways of restoration of peace and harmony via Gandhi's method of ahimsa, and within a framework true to the founding Constitution.'—Virginus Xaxa, Professor of Eminence and Bharat Ratna Lokapriya Gopinath Bordoloi Chair at Tezpur University (2016–2018)

RECONCILING DIFFERENCE

Beyond Collective Violence in India

RUDOLF C. HEREDIA

SPEAKING
TIGER

SPEAKING TIGER BOOKS LLP
4381/4, Ansari Road, Daryaganj
New Delhi 110002

First published by Speaking Tiger Books in paperback in 2021

ISBN: 978-93-90477-51-7
eISBN: 978-93-90477-52-4

10 9 8 7 6 5 4 3 2 1

Typeset in Adobe Garamond Pro by SÜRYA, New Delhi
Printed at Shree Maitrey Printech Pvt. Ltd., Noida

CONTENTS

PREFACE

A GANDHIAN CLAIM

Within/Without – The Wolf at the Door – A Gandhian Claim – Our Present Predicament – Overview of the Argument

Within Without

Violence has no borders. It is like a forest fire which once lit, even if by an accidental spark, in a dry, hot summer drought burns out of control, fanned by the wind until the entire forest is gone. It must then wait for the next rains to restore it. If the rains fail, desertification will inevitably follow. But first the crisis must be recognized before it can be addressed; the problem understood, before a resolution can be attempted. The urgency of the present emphatically suggests that collective violence in India, with its brutalizing horrors, is now becoming the new normal, to judge by the way it is rationalized by its perpetrators, supporters and ideologues.

After India and Pakistan came out of their nuclear closets, the Director of the CIA (America's Central Intelligence Agency) in 1993 warned: 'The arms race between India and Pakistan poses perhaps the most probable prospect for future use of weapons of mass destruction, including nuclear weapons.' (*Economist* 20 May 1999)

Now that both nations are armed with nuclear weapons, the premonition seems well on track. Nuclear weapons do make possible a world of Mutually Assured Destruction (MAD), in which the option of total war is mutually unacceptable. But in such a MAD world, an accident or a miscalculation may set off an Armageddon, as happened with the First Great War. But that was in the pre-nuclear era. Since then nuclear weapons have been used twice, both times by the same super power on the same disabled enemy within a few days of each other. And its justification is still contested by peace activists though forgotten by the great powers.

Some years after the CIA report of 10 March 2000, the then president of America, Bill Clinton, expressed grave concern regarding South Asia: 'The most dangerous place in the world today, I think you could argue, is the Indian subcontinent and the line of control in Kashmir.' But a few days later on 21 March, the then Indian president K.R. Narayanan was dismissive: 'These alarmist descriptions will only encourage those who want to break the peace and indulge in terrorism and violence.' (23 March 2000, http://news.bbc.co.uk/2/hi/south_asia/687021.stm) Notwithstanding these brave words, Kashmir still remains a flashpoint at the time of writing this book. Indeed, nuclear deterrents are designed not for hopes of peace but against threats of war, however remote. And here again, perceptions count for more than the reality, which follows like a self-fulfilling prophecy in its wake.

The ongoing hostility between these two nuclear-armed neighbours is kept constantly on the boil by their own internal compulsions. Meanwhile, spiralling internal violence is tearing apart these societies. Hindu-Muslim violence is a deliberately engineered ethnic cleansing in India. In Pakistan, religious violence is fratricidal terrorism, often politically sponsored by the state. The only lasting diffusion and reversal of this subcontinental collective violence lies in the reconciliation and healing of the warring factions between these two countries and within these societies.

The Wolf at the Door

The Native American Cherokee people have a folk tale about two wolves struggling for supremacy in a person's soul: one is good and righteous, and strives to live in peace; the other evil, full of anger, and thrives on conflict and violence. Cherokee wisdom concludes: the one we feed is the one that gets stronger and wins. The confrontation between the two can get fierce and a compromise could be sought: feeding both wolves in a pragmatic accommodation for peace. But that is only to postpone the inescapable choice. It will come back to haunt us. From the collective level of the nation down to the local community, the protagonists make the issues far more complex and dangerous, as happens when rival wolf packs feud over territory with other packs and fight for dominance within their own.

Social Darwinism leaves to natural selection the choice of which wolf to feed. Adam Smith, the Scotish economist (1723–90), in his *Wealth of Nations* (1976) leaves the outcome to 'the invisible hand' of the free-market. Thomas Hobbes, in his *Leviathan* (1651), subcontracts it to an absolute sovereign power. In *Science and Human Behavior* (1953) by the American psychologist B.F. Skinner (1904–90), stimulus and response become an infinite regress since every response would be to an earlier stimulus. The American sociobiologist, E.O. Wilson's (b. 1929) *On Human Nature* (1978) bases human behaviour in biology and attributes choice to the inherited altruistic or selfish genes. For the 18th-century utilitarian Benthamites, 'the greatest good for the greatest number' is what matters, ignoring the smaller numbers of more vulnerable people at the margins of society and the discriminated-against minorities, ghettoized outside the scope of these majoritarian calculations. Neoliberalism's rational actors with their bounded rationality often show themselves up as 'rational fools'. (Amartya Sen 1997)

All of these and more have had their heyday, and all projected, if not the best of all possible worlds, then at least worlds that would allow for as much good as possible and as little evil. However, the contradictions and tensions do not go away. From the debris of failed gods and broken worlds what seems to survive is a pragmatic default 'non-option' as an everyday survival technique: a balance of contradictions and tensions we must live with. For ultimately, 'people everywhere, are capable of both respect and aggression, of both democratic mutuality and anxious domination.' (Nussbaum 2007: x)

A Gandhian Claim

To move forward into a peace-building process, the initiative must be taken by the more powerful, larger partner, who can afford to be more generous and take more risks. However, internal political compulsions stymie reconciliation and peace processes before they even begin. Hence, 'at a deeper level…is the Gandhian claim that the real struggle that democracy must wage is a struggle within the self, between the urge to dominate and defile the other and a willingness to live respectfully on terms of compassion and equality, with all the vulnerability that such a life entails.' (Nussbaum 2007: ix)

The standpoint of this monograph is precisely this Gandhian understanding that begins with ahimsa, commonly translated as non-violence. This is a double negative etymologically: 'a', a negation, of 'himsa', the desire to do harm. Gandhi never seemed to tire of emphasizing that his concept of ahimsa was not a passive one: 'In its positive form, Ahimsa means the largest love, greatest charity.' (*Harijan*, 11-8-'40 p. 245) Moreover, Gandhi's understanding is premised on the ancient wisdom of ahimsa as satya (truth/reality), of peace as harmony and justice as mercy. This runs counter to the realpolitik of our times, whose only answer to violence is more violence, thus setting us off on a carrousel from which we cannot get off as it turns faster and faster, spinning us to our doom.

Human collectives are generally identified by a common characteristic, or rather a 'family resemblance' (Wittgenstein 1998: 14) between the members. In this monograph, ethnicity is ascribed to 'those human groups that entertain a subjective belief in their common descent because of similarities of physical type or of customs or both, or because of memories of colonization and migration; this belief must be important for the propagation of group formation; conversely, it does not matter whether or not an objective blood relationship exists.' (Weber 1978: 389)

Horowitz (1985: 41–44) is more succinct. The 'term ethnic group includes groups based on all such indicia of ascriptive differences.' (Horowitz 2001: 1, nt1, and 1985: 41–84) This is then a more inclusive term, embracing communities that identify by caste, creed, race or language, or indeed any distinguishing characteristic. In India, collective ethnic violence is prominent between religious and caste groups; linguistic conflicts are on the wane, though racial violence targeting our peoples from our northeastern states is sporadic but real.

Moreover, this endeavour is not meant to be a compendium cataloguing the atrocities and riots in the subcontinent. Single events can add up to a cumulative crisis, but before we reach there, indicative events already point to such ominous possibilities in the future. Numerous reports can bring an ennui with an information overload and a certain emotional fatigue. Violence against women, minors, minorities, Dalits, and mob lynchings are now shamefully frequent—a new normal, it would seem. The Nirbhaya tragedy stirred the conscience of the nation, and the very politicians who expressed such self-righteous outrage at the people in power at the time have now failed to deliver on the promises, made so readily at the time, of drastic remedies and preventative measures and zero tolerance they are now suffering from post-electoral amnesia. Their response to the Kathua and Unao rape atrocities expose how reluctant they are to face down their own party patriarchs, refusing to compromise their favoured vote banks. Offenders and public approvers are even given political protection! Mob lynchings are perceived as deserved, or at most accidental.

Our Present Predicament

Today our polarized society cannot escape the question staring us in the face: will India follow the ethnic nationalist trajectory of other South Asian nations? For seven decades, the Preamble to our Constitution has inspired the collective dream of our tryst with destiny. Now ethno-nationalism has become our nightmare. Indeed such jingoism has become a global phenomenon now. Soon this becomes a Hobbesian war of all of us against all of them. Cultures are polarized, and religions instrumentalised to serve partisan causes in the political arena, thus alienating them from their original purposes. Cultural and religious differences become grounds for aggressive mobilization against the other. They lose their humanizing potential and cease to be domains of exciting discovery and creativity, and mutually enriching experience.

They become cynical instruments for the pursuit of power and pelf. Culture no longer serves as a creative and ethical critique of society. Religion is hollowed out of meaning and motivation; and the quest for the ultimate purpose of life is replaced by suspect ideologies and devotions meant to protect us from our insecurities and unacknowledged fears.

Reducing the great epics like the Ramayana and the Mahabharata to literal historical documents is to squander and impoverish the great literary beauty and power of these monumental sagas, and marginalize and ignore the social insight and challenge their 'mythic history' represents. To reduce an epic to a fixed text with a single point of view is to miss the enormous diversity, its rich multi-valences, the numerous perspectives it brings to bear on the narrative discourse—all of which allow for a multitude of interpretations. An encounter with an epic is meant to be a rich and rewarding experience that brings to life the mythomoteur of a people, their constitutive myth.

A.K. Ramanujan wrote of 'Three Hundred Ramayanas' but that is only a beginning. Every tribe and people of this subcontinent have their own take on the story. Buddhist versions of the legend predating the Valmiki account are found in Southeast Asia, for instance in Cambodia. The Indira Gandhi Centre for the Performing Arts in Delhi has hundreds of Ramayana texts in its archives, each different in its own way; all with diverse understandings of the characters and roles therein. Ram and Ravana are very different in north India and in Sri Lanka. Sita and her agni pariksha have been differently, even oppositely, interpreted by women and patriarchs.

Such unity in diversity was the unique characteristic of Indic civilization down the ages and it has proved to be its richness and strength. Majoritarian ethno-nationalism in India would paint all this with the same saffron brush and trap us all into a neoliberal market economy. The traditional caste-class dominance and modern free-markets are proving to be not such strange bedfellows. The fundamental flaw here is to premise unity on uniformity, which ultimately kills the creative spirit and sharpens the destructive sword as the quest for ethnic 'purity' gains momentum. This is surely a revolution that is waiting to eat up its children.

The discussion here falls back on my earlier work and draws on it where pertinent. Many of the topics and themes, issues and problems, recommendations and remedies are similar if not the same. However, the critical urgency of the present situation is that it seems to mark a turning point: away from the 'idea of India', forged in the freedom struggle and expressed in our Constitution; and the move towards an exclusive ethno-nationalism, premised on Hindu majoritarianism, thus polarising the population and alienating the minorities and marginalized. This fosters a politics of divisiveness and conflict, of violence and hate. Many new democracies have gone down this path to end in collective violence and respond with authoritarian rule. We have examples of this in South Asia and beyond.

Surely moderates on all sides of the many divides in our country would not want this to happen here. However, without an open and equal dialogue to come to terms with, and heal our past hurt, to reach out to the different other in the present, to keep our future true to our founding Constitution, without reconciliation and peace, we cannot remain liberal and democratic but will become increasingly majoritarian and authoritarian, and as we have seen, inevitably violent and oppressive as well. The rich diversity of a multicultural, pluri-religious society that could boast of being 'the world's largest democracy', the very uniqueness of Indic culture would be compromised and finally lost.

Our hope is that the moderate majority will read the situation, and heed the call to reconcile differences, with tolerance and dialogue, for peace. The alternatives are too frightening and too real to risk.

Overview of the Argument

The focus of this study is on collective, not individual or interpersonal violence. There is an obvious relationship between the individual and the community, and one impinges on the other, but each has its own specificities. Gender violence is clearly both structural and cultural, gender divides are not so much between, as within communities; hence it will not be within the main ambit of this study. It would require a study of its own.

Moreover, this is a grounded rather than an abstract study. Its scope is India contextualized in South Asia; though in a globalizing world, isolating contexts is not always feasible or desirable. However, limiting the scope thus will hopefully add some measure of depth. A comprehensive study would require several volumes and many specializations. This limited endeavour attempts an understanding of this collective violence and its aftermath as a prelude to reconciliation and peace, perhaps a Utopian dream but surely one worth pursuing, considering the alternative can only be more of the same and eventual self-destruction.

Broken promises and hopes betrayed litter the tragic trajectory of our inability to constrain the enemy within. Our better angels have been overwhelmed by our bad ones, leaving us engulfed in a sea of violence which has become the new normal. The colonialists' 'divide and rule' policy has morphed into a politics of polarization, replaying Partition with mounting Hindu-Muslim violence. The India we dreamed of once has now been co-opted by neoliberal free-marketeers and populist ethno-nationalists, precipitating caste and religious violence. We cannot rely on a 'Great Leader' to address upstream causes of these downstream effects. Whatever the tentative explanations of our predicament, only a long march will reverse the spiral of violence we have set off.

Rediscovering our history against a new normal of intolerance being set is now a priority. Untangling two nations on the subcontinent seems unviable without coming to terms with the wounded memories and unhealed traumas of violence that led up to and followed in the aftermath of the Partition. The freedom movement left a legacy in the 'idea of India', premised on Tagore's humanism, Gandhi's swaraj, Nehru's discovery of India and Ambedkar's republicanism. We are now engaged in a struggle between revivalism and transformation. Envisioning our future as a liberal republic is now challenged by an ethno-nationalist state.

The clash is within, between imposing uniformity and choosing an alternative future with the rich diversity of Indic civilization.

By religionizing violence, secular rationalists make it the principle cause of collective conflict, leaving the role of secular ideologies unexamined. Religious extremism and violent ideologies tend to absolutize demands bringing barbaric horrors with them. Moreover, religionising terror does not stand up to factual data. A religious or secular tradition needs both charisma and institution; the first, founded on experience is more inclined to humanize a tradition; the second, premised on reason, rationalizes it and is more open to co-optation by other interests and concerns. This dynamic can be traced through the various religious traditions of India: Hinduism and Hindutva, Islamic diversity and Wahabism, Religious Buddhism and Buddhist Nationalism, traditional Buddhism and Ambedkar's Navayana, Christian origins and colonial distortions, through the long trajectory of Christianity and its encounter with other religions. This myth of religious violence obfuscates the secular roots of violence in our world today.

In comprehending violence in contemporary India, the Gujarat model of neoliberal development, and the Gujarat model of communal polarization works in tandem to underscore how the tensions of growth without social equity are contained and obfuscated by community conflict and collective violence. The failure of neoliberal development increases the reliance on identity politics to trump interest politics. The consequent communal conflicts set a new normal for the banality of violence in society. Clarifying concepts helps analyze causes and motivations, especially terrorisms, now reinscribed as a cosmic war. Defusing terrorism with violence has led to genocide. Addressing the root causes and sensitizing the collective conscience is more effective. But there are levels of analysis—socio-psychological, eco-political, socio-cultural, socio-religious—to be considered in their historical context. The anatomy of a lynching illustrates this. Hence the imperative of a finely nuanced response.

Interlocuting Gandhi will help in building non-violent initiatives, even in a communally polarized community. Such initiatives imply historicizing ahimsa into the socio-political domain, as Gandhi did from an individual dharmic ascetic practice. Contextualizing Gandhi draws us into conversing with him and his *Hind Swaraj*. This sets the main themes for his freedom struggle: his opposition to colonial imperialism, industrial capitalism and rationalist materialism. Gandhi's relevance cannot be gainsaid today. Gandhi's critique is drawn into sharper focus by the neo-colonialism, post-industrialism, post-modernism prevalent today. A new hermeneutic is required to dialogue with Gandhi's counter-culture and its basic themes of swaraj, swadeshi and satya. In reinterpreting Hinduism for our world today with its post-socialism, globalization, violence, Gandhi's synthesis suggests a cultural transformation which demands a response of creative alternatives to his 'Constructive Programme'.

The spiralling violence must be contextualized in the atrocities and the hate crimes which an exclusive ethno-nationalism visits on those who are different, driven by politics of hate rather than a patriotic love of the country. We are faced with a critical choice between Hindu Rashtra and the pluralist nation of our Constitution. But populism rather than constitutionalism seems to prevail. So instead of celebrating our diversity in a constitutional social democracy we have a saffron neoliberalism with increasing inequality, and growth without equity.

Bridging the divides in our fractured society requires that the ambiguities of political passions be sorted out, endorsing the positive in the public domain and disavowing the negative. (Taylor 2008: pp. vii–viii) In the aftermath of collective violence, the Truth and Justice Commission of South Africa demonstrated a path through reconciliation intended to heal the hurt and hate Apartheid had generated. Drawing on African Ubuntu culture, the focus was on restoration, not retribution. The Ubuntu model is not so much to be replicated as contextualized, drawing on the rich resources of our Indic cultural heritage: universalism, pluralism, tolerance. Unconscionably the divide-and-rule policy of colonial times has been replicated as 'polarize and prevail'. We need greater agency for civil society since the political quest for power is failing to make reconciliation a process for the acceptance of pluralism and minority rights; failing therefore to reconcile difference. Rather it is sacralising the state as uniformiser for unity.

CHAPTER ONE

PROMISES BROKEN, HOPES BETRAYED

Tragic Trajectory – Enemy Within – Better Angels, Bad News? – Sea of Violence – Banality of Violence – Divide to Rule – Politics of Polarization – Replaying Partition – Subcontinental Nightmare – Dreaming India – Free-markets and Populism – Navigating the Conundrum – Saffron Agenda – Domains of Collective Violence – Upstream Causes, Downstream effects – Great Leader, Little Wo/ Man – The Long March – Tentative Explanations – Reversing the Spiral – Open-ended Encounter

Tragic Trajectory

The Kathua horrors are monstrous in their stark reality: an eight-year-old girl, drugged, starved, gang-raped by eight men over five days in a temple, after they performed rituals there. All done to panic her tribe of Muslim Bakarwal nomads to vacate the area so the settlers could usurp their land. Her father had reported her missing on 12 January 2018 but there had been a police cover-up so it was a week by the time people recovered the little girl's mutilated body in the forest. And yet there was an orchestrated support for the rapists: the Bar Association openly and violently demonstrated against the police registering the case; and the Hindu Ekta Manch, formed by the main accused on 23 January 2018, organized aggressive public protests locally. The women of the village, who knew and indulged the little girl, cried over the corpse when it arrived, but later joined the protestors.

Two state cabinet ministers, whose party was in the coalition with state government and in power at the centre, vociferously supported the protests and demanded the investigation be turned over to the CBI (Central Bureau of Investigation), a central government institution, which has been described by the Supreme Court as a caged parrot. (Reuters 13 May 2013) The silence of the government in Delhi was deafening, and disingenuously broken only days after the uncovering of the crime caused an outrage by decent citizens nationwide and even beyond. As the backlash became politically threatening, worn-out tokenism by the prime minister only added insult to injury: justice will be done, the law will take its course, the guilty punished.

We have heard that before and we know what course our law takes. However, the Punjab High Court, to which the case was transfixed, in June 2019, found six of the seven accused guilty, and sentenced three of them to life imprisonment and the other three to five years in jail.

In Unnao, a mofussil town in Uttar Pradesh, just outside Kanpur city and not far from Lucknow, a well-connected Member of the Legislative Assembly (MLA) from the Bharatiya Janata Party (BJP) raped a seventeen-year-old minor, then wiped her tears and promised her a good job. Her father, who went to register a complaint, was detained by the police and interrogated. He was released later, but died of 'shock' soon after, with fourteen major injuries on his body as per the postmortem report. The police refused to arrest the MLA as required by the law, while the chief minister insisted that the state policy of zero tolerance was still in place. The MLA flaunted his immunity from the law in public and demanded that the real perpetrators be punished. Again, only after a threatening public outcry and a High Court order was the MLA finally charged and arrested.

The central government has passed an ordinance to mandate death penalty for the rape of a minor under the age of twelve, as if to demonstrate the government's seriousness. But increasing the severity of the punishment does not reduce the rate of the crime, especially when the conviction rate is so dismal. At the most it assuages public outrage. Rather it is the certainty and legitimacy of the punishment that does this. Furthermore, there are other issues that must be addressed as well: prevention, competent investigation, due process for a convincing judicial outcome. But instead, the alternatives we seem to have fallen back on are police 'encounter killings' and custodial deaths. Increasingly common too are cover-ups in politically sensitive cases, including 'accidental' deaths of key witnesses, or 'persuading' them to turn hostile. In Madhya Pradesh, the Vyapam scam of the State Examination Board for Admission and Recruitment, and state investigations into the Gujarat pogrom of 2002 are damning evidence of this.

From time to time, the courts have expressed concern over such extrajudicial measures but the criminalization of society continues unabashed. Obviously, political patronage prevails even in the courts which now seem compromised at the highest levels. What such case studies demonstrate is that when the law fails to protect citizens, criminals and those who sponsor them, and rioters and those who patronize them, have a free hand. Society is thus set off on a trajectory of collective violence.

Kathua is part of a process of genocidal ethnic cleansing in which rape becomes an instrument against the minorities and the marginalized, and the most vulnerable among them, like the pastoral nomads in this case. Ethnic cleansing happened in the Balkans; it is happening in India. The end-point of this trajectory is partition and secession. It happened in the Balkans; it happened here between Hindus and Muslims during the independence struggle resulting in the Partition. The terror visited by Pakistan on its Bengali eastern half did not anticipate the birth of Bangladesh and a truncated Pakistan in 1971. All this is now surely an ominous warning to our present government which is in a rush to establish a Hindu Rashtra even at the cost of others in their way—the minorities and even Hindus of different persuasions.

Unnao, and the way the UP government of Yogi Adityanath—born Ajay Mohan Bisht—handles such cases, is a stark illustration of caste hierarchies, and male power and privilege that preys on vulnerable women. According to a report in *The Times*, 'More than 100 rapes every day are reported across India, 40 per cent of them attacks on children. The true figure is certain to be many times higher.' (Tomlinson 2018) The frequency of rape has got

Indian society the reputation as the most misogynistic country in the world. A Thomson Reuters poll in 2018, 'ranked India the most dangerous country for women in terms of human trafficking, including sex and domestic slavery, and for customary practices such as forced marriage, stoning and female infanticide.'

Our common response to atrocities against women is to blame the victim, doubt their integrity and ask them to take preventive, cautionary measures. The violators are given the benefit of our doubt. This is but a reflection of the macho, casteist culture that is now being politicized in saffron hue.

Enemy Within

Wali Muhammad Wali (1667–1707), known as Wali Gujarati and considered the father of the Urdu ghazal, was truly the pride of literary Gujarat. In the melee of the February–March 2002 communal pogrom in Gujarat, his 300-year-old grave was vandalized and razed. Overnight, it was paved over to become a road and even removed from the local revenue records. In August 2002, an infructuous petition to rebuild it was filed in the Supreme Court. However, in 2005, a literary award was introduced in his name. In 2016, based on a petition submitted in the Gujarat High Court, the shrine was restored with other damaged religious structures. The state government now admitted before the court that a shrine did exist at the erased grave site. That same year a lesson on Wali Gujarati was included in the eleventh-standard textbook of state schools, together with that of K.K. Shastri, the founder of the Vishwas Hindu Parishad (VHP) (*Times of India* 4 May 2016), which has now mutated into an extremist organization as part of the Sangh Parivar (family).

It seems even when such a concession is made for a Muslim poet, it must be neutralized by doing the same for a prominent Hindutva person. A simple admission as to existence of a popular shrine had to be extracted in court.

Wali Gujarati loved Gujarat and was honoured by both Hindus and Muslims. The attempt to eliminate his memory is a sad comment on the Gujarati asmita (pride) of the day. As he left Gujarat for Delhi, Wali wrote:

My heart is thorn-filled with longing for Gujarat;
Restless, frantic, flame-wrapped in the spring;
On earth there exists no balm for this wound;
My heart is split asunder by the dagger of separation.

Almost three centuries later in 2014, another Gujarati left the state for Delhi, intent on his state model being replicated throughout the country. We can only conjecture about his feelings on that occasion.

The contours of the Gujarat model of communal polarization would be a matter for humorous satire and ridicule of such stereotypical prejudice, but for the monstrous brutality in which it finds expression. After the party and its ideology captured power at the centre as well as in many states, the Gujarat model of communalization has become the template for communal violence across the country, particularly in the many states it rules: precipitate and politicize a conflict in a community, escalate it, polarize it along religious faultlines and consolidate the majority community for further political advantage.

Such barbarism is de-civilizing India, and this at the hands of the very same saffron brigade of the Sangh Parivar, whose boastful agenda is to restore the ancient glory of a lost Hindu civilization, through their imagined version of history, where myth becomes fact and pride turns into prejudice. Such a narrative has been convincingly deconstructed and dismissed by competent historical experts in this field, but its hold on the saffron faithful still prevails.

Many places of worship have been desecrated and demolished and each has its own tale to tell, like the shrine to Wali Gujarati, and the most significant being the demolition of the Babri Masjid by a mob of 'Ram bhakts' of the Ram Janma Movement. This only further polarized Hindus and Muslims.

Here history is challenged by faith, and commissions and courts obfuscate and postpone redress ever further. Now the Supreme Court has set up a mediating committee, and after the submission of their report has taken up more formal court proceedings. We can only be amazed by the intensity of negative feelings, no doubt politically instigated, that seeks to rewrite history and eliminate memory.

The Supreme Court's final judgement on 11 November 2019, granting that the demolition was illegal, still handed over the disputed site to a Hindu trust to build a temple and allotted 5 acres for a mosque to be built elsewhere.

Of course, all this did not begin in Gujarat nor has it stopped there. Our claim of a tolerant, pluralist India now seems a forgotten dream, thanks to those who thrive on this de-civilizing violence for their own partisan ends. We see this spilling over to other domains beyond communal polarization, in caste, in gender, even in everyday street violence. The violence we visit on the 'other' is now internalized in a more violent self, in ways in which we may never have intended and are unable to reverse easily. The very beast we let loose on 'the other' has found other violent expressions in ourselves. We internalize our enemies to become mirror images of them.

Thus instigating a group of frustrated and insecure people, and turning them into violent mobs is not uncommon and politically very expedient. There is an unacknowledged lynch law at work; summary justice scapegoating on the vulnerable. The Supreme Court's judgement of 17 July 2018, and its directive to the Government of India to enact a law against lynching seems to imply it is a law and order problem. However, 'lynching is not something that happens on the spur of the moment or is just another breakdown of law and order. Rather, it is primarily a tool for maintaining the status quo. That it is supposed to remind oppressed communities of the price they will pay for attempting to move ahead of their station in life.' (*EPW* 21 Jul 2018) In fact, lynching is a stratagem used to put and keep people in their place, whether it be the racist lynchings of blacks by whites, the casteist lynchings of Dalits and tribals by savarnas (upper castes), or the gau rakshaks' (cow protectors) lynchings of cattle traders—all this has a 'performance element' and in actuality often has the tacit approval of the state.

The 'beef ban' seems designed to target Muslims and ruin their dairy business and meat trade. The biggest exporters of buffalo beef, however, are Hindu traders claiming to be gau-mata protectors. 'Love-jihad' is yet another instrument to harass Muslims, and control women's right to choose in the bargain. Moral police are similarly targeting young persons in public places, while major sexual atrocities go unchecked, and at times the same policemen have been guilty of the more perverse crimes. The gender divide is getting further polarized in our misogynistic society between sexually frustrated men and mortally vulnerable women. Of the few that reach the courts an abysmally small proportion are found guilty. Marital rape is just too much to consider criminalizing in our patriarchal society. Judicial judgements show the shocking gender insensitivity of the male-dominated judiciary.

The list is endless, for the politics of hate used at the hustings only deepens and embeds this free-floating violence and hate in the hearts and minds of people. Such a crisis adds up to a breakdown in civil society and a perversion of citizenship. Only the rich and their corporations, the political and socially dominant elites, with a safe exit strategy, can profit unconcerned. It is imperative that people comprehend and come to terms with how we got here, and search for a way forward from, and out of the mess we have got ourselves into, before an Armageddon consumes us all. Manipur and Rajasthan introduced anti-lynch laws in 2019, January and November respectively. But besides such legal activism, a policy to prevent collective hate crimes must be put in place.

Unfortunately, there are people still in denial. For, 'it is difficult to get a man to understand when his salary depends on his not understanding it'; whether this is paid in cash or kind or social and/or political capital. Or are people too fearful of understanding it, preferring the false consciousness of security, to the challenge of an honest introspection? And too many of us rationalize an uncritical and false loyalty with not wanting to be a 'namak haraam', a betrayer of one's benefactors. For the consequences may unravel our comfort zones, disturb our way of life or disrupt profitable businesses. Unwittingly this makes us prisoners unto ourselves and ignorance becomes bliss.

Better Angels, Bad News?

Can we thus rationalize away, our responsibility to choose by leaving it to fate—que sera, sera? Are we then trapped in the

Buddhist dukkha of this world, Virgil's 'lacrima rerum', the tears of creation? Are we condemned to a fateful karma by some pitiless, unforgiving deity? Steven Pinker's confidence that *The Better Angels of Our Nature* explains *Why Violence Has Declined* (Pinker 2011) seems at best like an intellectual 'comfort guru' reassuring his anxious flock, unable to cope with the violence visiting their societies and impacting their lives, but who never interrogate their own role in the violence which their histories have left behind, never face the question of whether they are part of the problem or part of the solution. It is a desperate expression of American optimism, or more generally colonial imperialism in denial. They are unconcerned about its upstream causes and downstream protraction. Only what touches them concerns them.

Pinker seems to be oblivious of the violence the worst angels of his own country and the West have precipitated during the two worldwide wars in the last century. These are estimated to have exceeded 105 million deaths, including 62 million civilian ones. Moreover, 'Genocidal wars, firebombed cities, nuclear explosions, concentration camps, spreading plagues of private blood-letting: this century has seen more than its share of planned and unplanned violence, with prospects of still more to come.' (Keane 1996: 3).

So much for the privileged-blind, suffering from 'affluenza' and self-righteous self-pity. They wonder: why do 'they hate us so much?' Such touching innocence opportunistically forgets that what's sent around, comes around. Living in a comfortable bubble sealed off from the violence of the world outside with its brutalized social environment, to which in many direct and indirect ways they have contributed by fault and default. They fail to do a reciprocity of perspectives with those unfortunate, condemned to live outside the comfort zone of the rich and privileged. The immigration crises are such telling examples of this—those who precipitated the catastrophe disown responsibility for its victims.

Granted bad news makes better copy than good news, and so gets far more prominent attention in the media. For 'compared to war the idea of peace seems uninteresting', (Kumar 2007: 55) especially for those who need stronger medicine to wake them up. Harmony is reported only in the context of violence, as a counterpoint, as a positive outcome of an earlier conflict now in a precarious truce. This is neatly captured in the aphorism: war certain if no peace, peace certain if no war. The protagonists become mirror images of each other, locked in a race to the bottom. Thus violence precipitates counter-violence, aggressive violence provokes defensive violence, and the escalating spiral seems to have untraceable beginnings, lost in history, and uncertain ends hidden in some future.

Bin Laden's execution, 'termination with extreme prejudice' in CIA euphemism, did not end the war on terror, but scattered it far and wide, compounding the problem of terrorism and escalating the war against it: after Afghanistan, then Iraq, next Syria, and ISIS. Who is next and where will it happen? Europe and the West? The remedy seems worse than the disease. Terrorism is no longer a leader-dependent movement but a hydra-headed monster with lone ranger extremists near at hand.

The collateral damage caused by this war on terror has strengthened grassroots support in distant locales, and extended its geographic reach globally, even into cyberspace. State-sponsored violence against terror is making it more and more like its opponents, the terrorists.

This reiteration of action-reaction was used to rationalize the Gujarat pogrom of 2002 by the Chief Minister. (*Times of India*, 2 March 2002, https://timesofindia.indiatimes.com/india/Newton-Modi-has-a-lot-to-answer/articleshow/2599766.cms) The counter-terror state becomes a terrorist state, whose violent reaction is equal and opposite to the terrorists' action. If terror is the weapon of the weak opponent, then technology is steadily evening the balance. What could happen if these weapons of mass destruction fell into the hands of some terrorists is unthinkable.

The United Nations Educational, Scientific and Cultural Organization (UNESCO) was created with the 'objectives of international peace and of the common welfare of mankind for which the United Nations Organization was established and which its Charter proclaims'. The UNESCO Constitution endorsed by the General Assembly in 1948 in its Preamble declared 'that since wars begin in the minds of men, it is in the minds of men that the defences of peace must be constructed'. It is within our minds and in their hearts, that evil is first born and nurtured and then set off on a rampage without. (http://www.unesco.org/education/pdf/UNESCO_E.PDF)

The UNESCO Constitution flags several causes of war. They are well applied to collective violence in general: 'ignorance of each other's ways and lives', 'suspicion and mistrust between the peoples', 'denial of the democratic principles of the dignity, equality and mutual respect'. It also makes some constructive suggestions: 'wide diffusion of culture, and the education of humanity for justice and liberty and peace'.

This same wisdom is as relevant to all collective violence: between nations collective violence is war; within a society it begins as civil disturbances which can escalate to civil war as in the case of the Bangladesh war of 1971, and the Sinhala-Tamil ethnic violence in Sri Lanka. Terrorism too has precipitated a kind of low-intensity guerrilla war between state and non-state actors and even among terrorist groups in a struggle for dominance.

Sea of Violence

Violence now seems to have become the normal stasis of our people and our world. It seems to be always latent, lurking in the shadows. The ease with a lynch mob can be mobilized is telling evidence of this. The insecurity and fears of the weak and vulnerable in our society confirms this: women must go out properly covered and stay home after sunset, lest they be responsible for provoking the lust of macho men on the streets, who are not expected to exercise self-control; Dalits and tribals must demonstrate suitable submissiveness to upper dominant castes, lest they be aggressively debunked of their aspirations for rightful equality as citizens; minorities must submit to majority sensitivities like the 'beef ban', and to temple music before their places of worship lest there be lynchings and riots. For the majority community matters of faith must be above the law, and must prevail even when they are in contradiction with fairness and fact, lest mosques be demolished and churches vandalized; minorities must acquiesce to majority sentiments and even fancies and foibles, or they will be shown their place with violent riots and pogroms; racial differences are mocked, even punished with street violence; dissenters and deviants are pilloried as anti-national by a political party which has only recently discovered the convenience of nationalism for its partisan purposes.

The list is endless. It all adds up to a severe indictment on those indulging in and approving such violence and aggression, actively or passively. This over-sensitivity to one's supposed honour, especially community and collective honour, together with an aggressive willingness to exaggerate one's hurt feelings by hurting others in revenge, would in political psychology terms best make sense as the narcissism of grandiosity and the narcissism of victimhood. It amounts to the 'right to feel hurt' and play for payback time. This must be honestly and courageously confronted or it may become part of our national character and heritage, a nationalism of insecurity and inferiority. Self-righteous superiority wallowing in past glory further exacerbates this wounded pride. Moreover, to uncritically escape into the past is to betray the present. Such romanticizing has been more an elitist, nationalist interpretation, a history 'from above'. However, subaltern approaches to a history 'from below' have been better at critiquing such elitist nationalism, than at constructing alternative interpretations in viable and adequate measure.

Ashis Nandy (Nandy 2013) argues that narcissism and despair, as polar contradictions, are symptoms of an anomic and alienated society, where insecurity leads on to anxiety, and this to fear, which turns into anger that morphs into rage with a little help from players with overt and covert vested interests. If not addressed and defused, this subconscious violence can have a dangerous fallout. It is all too readily co-opted and focused on a scapegoat. This suppressed internalized violence finds external expression in interpersonal violence, then gets up-scaled to communal violence on the national stage and eventually to the international scene as well.

However, such violence is certainly not the monopoly of any single community or country in South Asia or elsewhere: whether it is insurgent tribals in the Northeast, the separatists in Kashmir, the Shia-Sunni violence in Uttar Pradesh and Pakistan or the other religious groups there, the Bangladeshi suppression of the Chakma tribals in Chittagong and the Rohingyas of Myanmar, the caste wars in Bihar, the Shiv Sena's machismo in Maharashtra, the Naxalite movement in Andhra and elsewhere, the Tamils and the Sinhala civil war in Sri Lanka as well as the continuing atrocities against outcastes and women everywhere. Each of these is distinctive in its own way, and the response, whether by state or non-state actors, has been particular to the varying contexts.

Governments appoint judicial commissions, which take years to submit their reports that are then tabled in Parliament, if at all, and finally filed away. Action-taken reports are hardly ever forthcoming because little, if any, action is taken. The big fish instigators go free, a token number of the hands-on dispensable operators are symbolically punished and acquitted later as and when convenient. Inevitably lessons are learnt that the collusions and even protection of the law is available to perpetrators but not to victims. And so the stage is set for upping the ante the next time. After each outbreak of this escalating violence, a new normal for violence and polarization falls in place, backing the victims into a dead end and lifting the perpetrators to their victory stand.

Banality of Violence

In such a sea of violence, what can tolerance or peace mean, let alone rights and justice? Religious fundamentalists perpetrate violence in the name of their religion with their battle cry: 'religion in danger'; nationalist extremists do the same by identifying their community with the nation: 'nation dishonoured'. Gujarat was considered a laboratory for the Sangh Parivar. Now the experiment is being reproduced in the rest of the country. Where does this leave mainstream religious traditions and political ideologies on the question of tolerance or the quest for peace? Is communal intolerance displacing these?

The Hindu-Muslim polarization during the freedom struggle culminated in the Partition that witnessed a subcontinental genocide. The horrors of politicized religious violence shocked the world. It is still being played out today in India with every communal riot, where the main religious other is the minority Muslim community inside the nation. In Pakistan the 'other' as enemy is now outside their nation, i.e., Hindu India. The possibility of another genocide is never very far away. In 1971 it was the Bengali speakers in Pakistan who suffered and seceded to become Bangladesh. Pakistan is still facing the issue of Baluch ethno-nationalism. (Sheikh 2019) In Sri Lanka a twenty-year civil war wreaked havoc on both sides. In India to mention a few of the worst more recent ones, there was the Nellie massacre of Muslims in Assam in 1983, the slaughter of Sikhs in Delhi in 1984, the massacre of Muslims across the state in Gujarat in 2002. Nor are more defenceless tribal Christians spared, as in the Dangs beginning in November 1998 and continuing sporadically into 1999; and again, in Kandhamal, Orissa, in 2007 and once more in 2008.

Not uncommon are the increasing atrocities against Dalits and tribals for any claim, even symbolic ones, to constitutional guaranteed equal status, including merciless public thrashings for minor or imagined offences. And now the Supreme Court, in its concern for the non-SC/ST citizen, in March 2018 diluted the stringent Scheduled Castes and Tribes (Prevention of Atrocities) Act, 1989. Only after nationwide protests by SCs, STs and their supporters, did the government file a review petition, and the court admit its error and reversed its ruling in October 2019. Similarly, to protect men from misuse of the Dowry Prohibition Act, 1961, the act was diluted; once again on purely anecdotal evidence before the court, rather than on formal reports by a constituted commission. Patriarchal men could not accept the access given to women as protection against dowry deaths.

Beatings and lynchings of scheduled castes and tribes, of Muslims and minorities are used by resentful dominant upper castes to enforce community boundaries and panic the vulnerable into fearful submission, to 'show them their place', sometimes provoked merely for wearing a distinctive dress, like a skull cap, or for looking different as with our fellow-citizens from the

Northeast. Moreover, there is a spreading progression of sponsored and spontaneous violence across the regional states, from urban to rural, from larger to smaller minorities, against political dissidents and social deviants, against the otherly-abled to the differently/alternatively gendered.

Gujarat has become the most acutely defined context of such collective violence. Earlier instances of horrific collective violence have gone under the radar. When these surface in debates in the media, the level of discourse sinks to a pitiful, if not disgusting, low: 'Your massacre was worse than ours; if you target us for Gujarat 2002, then we will fling Delhi 1984 at you.' Historical reconstructions of communal violence are now beyond the Masjid versus Mandir conflict with its toll in blood, go all the way back to Muhammad Ghazni's sacking of Somnath and its temple in 1024. That historical narrative of Somnath, which has several voices relating its complex history, (Thapar 2004) is opportunistically skewed and rolled out only to further politicize and polarize the already precarious faultlines between communities.

There is little effort towards a truth and reconciliation movement. The few beginnings at healing and reconciliation that are made are deliberately stymied, usually to the advantage of the perpetrators of the violence regardless of the cost to the victims. There is a method in this madness, for there is generous payoff from these at the voting booths at a low-cost investment by the violators. The price the victims pay is not considered. The whole brouhaha in 2017 over the dishonour to Rajput women occasioned by the film the *Padmavati* (later changed to *Padmavat*) proved to be a teacup-storm and petered out after the regional by-elections there. We should now be asking: who started it and why? Who sponsored the Karni Sena that created the controversy? Was this about proud Rajput honour or saffron election strategy? Why was the Ram Mandir controversy rolled out at election time until it lost traction when Supreme Court took up the matter comprehensively? There are numerous instances of such hate politics that have still not reached the point of diminishing returns.

The normalization of violence in society by rationalizing it into a banality, which is excused or ignored, is a mechanism to protect oneself from its real-life horror: 'I did not do this, I am not responsible for this, I'm not to be blamed for it.' We do the same with other inconvenient in-your-face realities, like the beggars on our streets. We don't notice them anymore, they become invisible to us. Until of course it begins to hurt us where it counts. However, as the situation careers out of control the passivity of those who allowed this drift into such chaos makes them helpless bystanders, even as others who first caused it now exploit it. As the 18th-century liberal, John Stuart Mill, presciently warned: 'For bad men need nothing more to compass their ends, than that good men should look on and do nothing.' (John Stuart Mill 1867: 36)

In other words, there may well be no direct involvement, but there is a broader social connection that we cannot escape. In his book, *Protecting the Vulnerable: A Reanalysis of Our Social Responsibilities* (1985), Robert Goodin argues coherently about our social responsibilities and expanding our circle of obligation to include larger sections of society, especially those dependent on us, the vulnerable and the marginalized, instead of just our immediate circle of family and friends. When the state fails to meet its obligations, it is the duty of rights-bearing citizens to step in and do the little they can for the disenfranchised. (1964) This solidarity is expected of a republic of liberty, equality, fraternity. This is what 'citizen' must mean if there is to be any semblance of a national community, a fellowship of rights and duties, of commitments and compassion.

Marion Young helps us to distinguish individual personal guilt from collective social responsibility: guilt as 'blame, fault, or liability'; and 'political responsibility as a duty of individuals to take public stands against actions and events that affect the broad masses of people and try to organise collective action to prevent massive harm or foster institutional change for the better', (Young 2011: 76) for 'many share responsibility without being guilty'. (Young 2011: 78)

Thus, I may not be to blame for the homeless and destitute, but can I escape responsibility for them as human beings and fellow citizens? If I am not part of the riot or the lynch-mob, do I not have a responsibility as part of the larger social and political fabric to respond as best I can, and support others who do, or can I leave such resistance to others and stay disengaged while this is happening and even escalating? Can rationalizing such things away as one-off exceptions, and waiting for the 'law to take its course' be an acceptable option for a just and fair society? We may feel helpless with the little we are able do, but can we weigh in on the side of the solution by doing what we honestly can, and not become part of the problem by passively doing nothing or worse actively rationalizing it—none of my business, I don't want to get involved, they had it coming—merely for the partisan patronage I may gain from the fallout, while those who precipitate such situations flourish, and those who suffer them go under?

Divide to Rule

All colonial governments thrive on a divide-and-rule agenda. The trauma of what the British called the Indian Mutiny of 1857 had lessons from barbarisms on both sides: Hindus and Muslims can unite in a national cause; there are limits to the colonial exclusion of local elites and alienated colonized peoples. This was the most important revolt against Western imperialism in modern times (Devji 2008: 127) and it left a lasting and bitter impact in its aftermath.

With the Indian renaissance and religious revival that began in the last quarter of the 19th century there was another surge of nationalist feeling. The British were taking no chances of another Hindu-Muslim alliance against the government. With the forced abdication and exile of *The Last Mughal* (Dalrymple 2007) emperor, Shah Bahadur Zafar, they swept away what they perceived to be a dangerous symbol of Hindu-Muslim unity. Later, even the national freedom movement could not find a unifying symbol or narrative powerful enough to overcome the differences of the Muslim League and the Indian National Congress (INC).

The colonial census began identifying people by their religious tradition, and the colonial government followed and legitimized this with codified personal laws based on one's religious tradition, supposedly for more efficient governance. Not surprisingly, the on-going religious revivalism was strengthened by this identification with one's religious community and made it so much easier to mobilize communities on the basis of religious identity. Muslim community leaders, fearful of being marginalized by the Hindu majority, lobbied for and demanded separate electorates as serving their interest best. This suited the colonial policy of divide and rule.

Separate electorates for Hindus and Muslims were first introduced in the 1890s as a temporary measure and restricted to the Punjab. (Barrier 1968: 538) The Government of India Act of 1909, known as the Morley-Minto Reforms, extended this across the country in response to Muslim demands. The Lucknow Pact of 1916 gave a third of the seats in the Imperial Legislative Council to Muslims. In 1919, 'although the Montagu-Chelmsford report is vehemently critical of separate electorates, it does not follow the logic of its recommendations through' and scrap separate electorate in favour of joint ones. (McMillan 2005: 25) Instead, the report also known as Government of India Act, 1919, extended the provisions to Sikhs, Indian Christians, Anglo-Indians and Europeans.

The polarization of communities made fertile ground for the Machiavellian divide-and-rule policy of the colonial government, fearful of a united front of Hindus and Muslims in the national freedom movement that was rapidly building up against colonial rule. As communal divisions got embedded, they reinforced the faultlines in society, thus setting off a trajectory that eventually precipitated the Partition of the subcontinent. Religious nationalists mobilized their followers on either side of the divide and extremist leaders pushed their divisive agenda to consolidate their base. The Indian freedom movement led by the Indian National Congress was uncompromising on the unity and integrity of India but failed to contain this divisiveness; the Muslim League was apprehensive of Hindu dominance in a united India and remained adamant. The British exploited this antagonism to their advantage rather than play a reconciliatory role. Ironically, a century after the Great Revolt of 1857, when Hindus and Muslims had fought together against the colonial rule, freedom from it was won with the Partition of the subcontinent in 1947.

The horrors of the genocide that led up to and followed this tragedy were visited on the people, not by an alien government but by the Hindus and Muslims on each other. This has not been forgotten or forgiven, by either side. Every communal riot re-enacts the same traumas, and feeds the same communal hatreds—each time deepening them further. Surely, not all are involved in this politics of hate, but too many are indifferent, if not positively complicit. It is this critical mass of uncertain moderates that hold the balance between the polar extremes of revenge and reconciliation.

Ideologues and provocateurs keep alive the alienation and antagonism between the protagonists to exploit it to their partisan advantage, inciting vengeance and resisting reconciliation, to keep hatred and fear on a slow boil to be politically available as and when needed. In a communally polarized nation, it is a heady resource, which is used by chauvinist politicians to mobilize the electorate, consolidate their power, and meld their followers into a dependable vote bank. Very few leaders and their parties can resist this temptation for short-term gains at the cost of more substantial change. This is the basis of a patronage politics that is now the dominant form in most developing countries, and India is no exception.

Moreover, a partisan political agenda did not help towards a resolution of the vicious hostilities that preceded and followed Partition. Only the shock of Gandhiji's assassination forced a truce between the warring protagonists but that did not hold for long either. For, the enormous burden of unhealed memories and wounded histories is still being carried over to the next generations, not just within but even across national borders. Today, there is no Gandhi daring enough to do a Noakhali satyagraha and bring some minimal peace between the protagonists; no Mandela to enable a Truth and Reconciliation Commission to bring some measure of healing and closure to the traumas of a wounded past. Too few who will dare to cross communal borders in a Karwan-e-Mohabbat (Caravan of Love). (Mander et al 2018)

Rather, increasingly there is a closing of the mind and an unwillingness to consider alternatives that challenge our hardening hearts, to enlighten our darkened mindsets, to call us out from our comfort zones of familiarity and security, to create a freedom beyond this unfortunate inheritance which is seeping into our DNA. This is a prescription for a future disaster. When old enemies are eliminated, new ones will have to be found. For when the sources of violence and hate within us, collectively and individually, are not effectively addressed and defused, resolved and healed, they fester and are driven to find scapegoats. We need more than ever Gandhiji's 'swaraj', the transformation of our inner-self as the necessary condition for an ethical transformation of our society; Nehru's egalitarian social democracy to contain gross inequalities; Ambedkar's Republic to defuse prejudice and foster fraternity across differences; and Tagore's humanism to give us cultural depth. The crude cultural nationalism promoted today is innocent of such sensitivities.

Politics of Polarization

Where is the present polarization in South Asia grounded and where is it headed? No country in postcolonial South Asia seems to have escaped the ethnic tensions that have embroiled their peoples. This polarization of communities along religious communal divisions that once were far more fluid and porous is endemic in the new postcolonial nation-states. Rather it complicated them in both the nations: first a truncated India and soon a 'moth-eaten Pakistan'—each at war within itself and with its neighbour.

Neither side has come to terms with Partition; the blame game continues and with it the search for appropriate scapegoats. Now the chickens were coming home to roost, throwing the roosters, who spawned them, out of kilter. The old religious identity politics, reconstructed and mobilized anew, began a gradual escalation which has now climaxed in continuing orgies of collective violence.

Certainly, this is not what the Indian freedom movement intended. To come to terms with the fallout, a sustained process of healing and bonding is needed. The secular Right and the Left presumed the Partition traumas would be defused in the new progressive agenda. But when this faltered, religious radicals and political extremists were quick to exploit the discontent of people disoriented by the rapid change overtaking them.

Even without the Partition of 1947, the temptation of popular leaders to precipitate such a polarization would be almost irresistible. Such chauvinist politics always appeals to opportunistic politicians in times of crisis. The violence between India and Pakistan has thrice erupted into wars: 1948, 1965 and 1971. The border engagement at Kargil in 1999 was almost another war. Cross-border intrusions of trained 'freedom fighters' from Pakistan, and India's responses, euphemistically called surgical strikes, could at any moment spiral out of control into another war between these nuclear-armed neighbours. Moreover, the continuing ethnic cleansing with Hindu-Muslim riots in India could well escalate into a civil war.

Pakistan's Islamic state has failed to constrain its religious fundamentalism from erupting violently, nor has it been able to contain and channel its ethno-linguistic nationalism. The secession of its Bengali East could be a presage of more to come in its west, with the Baluch freedom movement. In Bangladesh too, among Muslims, religious and political differences are becoming polarized between extremist Wahabi Islam and a more moderate Indic Islam, while secular liberal Muslims are increasingly marginalized. Buddhist nationalism in pre-Independent Ceylon, peaked in post-Independent Sri Lanka. The serendipity island was projected as destined to be the light to Buddha's dhamma in the sea of subcontinental darkness (dukkha). Beginning in the 1950s with the privileging of Sinhala as state language and the consequent marginalization of Tamil, this chauvinist exceptionalism began a tragic slide into a full-blown civil war by the 1980s, ending with a bloody massacre in 2007. There has been little healing and reconciliation since. Religio-ethnic strife are not absent in Nepal and even in little Bhutan.

Replaying Partition

The defining moment for India after the trauma of the Partition was the founding of the Republic, described so evocatively in the Preamble to its new Constitution, as sovereign, socialist secular, democratic. This was a promising start with enormous goodwill on all sides. The new Constitution sought a social transformation for its people. The idea of India of the freedom movement was surely its principal inspiration. But along the way national democratic politics got co-opted by vested interested into a politics of patronage and dynasty, but which failed to meet the rising expectations of the masses.

Moreover, in not giving the Directive Principles of State Policy the priority they deserved, we lost the plot. These set inspirational goals for State policy to pursue in law. They set the context for the exercise of constitutional rights within the overall pursuit of a welfare state and social democracy. Though they are not justiciable, like constitutional rights, they express the spirit of the Constitution. They set the guidelines: 'a just society by just means'. (Nehru to Malraux 1968: 160)

Unresolved contradictions were neglected and necessary institutions and their structures corrupted by a chauvinistic politics of pragmatism. Interest politics was trumped by identity politics. Stereotypes were sharpened, distancing communities each from the other. The inclusive Ganga-Yamuna tehzeeb (culture) of the sant-kavis, of Kabir and Guru Nanak, as also of Tukaram and Mirabai, of Thiruvalluvar, and Tyagaraja and so many others, is becoming a permanent casualty. The devotional popular religiosity is being transformed into a vehicle of exclusion and intolerance.

In contemporary India, the Partition ordeal is constantly replayed in a slow-burn civil strife of ethnic cleansing for Muslims, and of traumatizing minorities. The Muslims are blamed for Partition and have not yet been forgiven by Hindu nationalists. 'Pakistan ya Kabrastaan' (to Pakistan or the graveyard) is the rallying cry of these extremists.

Subcontinental Nightmare

Pakistan was founded as the land of the pure, a homeland for all the Muslims of the subcontinent, a shining light in the Umma of the Islamic world. It began with secession from undivided India but its religious Islamic faith could not hold it together. The Punjabis were more dominant, the others more dormant. Resentments simmered below the surface and emerged in secessionist movements, the precedent being set by Pakistan's own secession from undivided India. Urdu as the national language, was a foreign one, but could not play a neutral mediating role. Linguistic loyalties were too strong, especially with the majority Bengali Muslims in the east. Ultimately, Islamic identity could not hold Pakistan together, and with India's intervention in 1971, the country was dismembered and East Pakistan seceded to be born anew as Bangladesh.

An aggressive Islamization that followed with Mohammad Zia-ul-Haq's rule (1978–88) became a defence against further fragmentation. However, all this has not united the country, but further divided its people. With Saudi Arabia's help, Wahhabism, a puritanical, fundamentalist regressive Islam became the dominant religious doctrine. Other Islamic sects, like Shias, were considered heretical and subject to violence; marginal ones like the Ahmadiyas were declared to be non-Muslims by the 2nd Constitutional Amendment (1974) under prime minister, Zulfikar Bhutto. General Zia-ul-Haq in 1984 passed an ordinance forbidding the Ahmadiyas from calling or posing as Muslims. He Islamised Pakistan's laws to align them closer to the Sharia. Religious minorities and others were victimized by this. Extremists have been murderously paranoid when blasphemy laws are involved; there have been extra killings of the accused or the critic. Such laws have been grossly misused, even inviting international criticism. Secular and liberal Pakistanis have been pushed into a corner.

The Pakistan-sponsored militant Islamist Taliban may have seemed useful to Pakistan's interests in Afghanistan, but now these militia are lodged within its own borders, bringing home a faction-ridden religious extremism. The only common denominator holding the country together is its enmity towards India and its own military establishment. The Muslim nationalism on which Jinnah's movement was founded has been disastrous for the country's faltering economy and its rich and diverse religio-cultural traditions. This could all presage a failing state, a danger to itself and its neighbours. What might have begun as Jinnah's Muslim homeland dream has turned out to be a subcontinental national nightmare for itself and others.

Dreaming India

The 'idea of India' put together in the freedom struggle was articulated in the freedom movement and elaborated and promulgated in the Constitution. It is so movingly expressed in the Preamble of the Constitution on 26 November 1949:

> We the people of India solemnly resolved to constitute India into a sovereign democratic republic and to secure to all its citizens:
>
> JUSTICE, social, economic and political;
> LIBERTY of thought, expression, belief, faith and worship;
> EQUALITY of status and of opportunity;
> and to promote among them all,
> Fraternity assuring the dignity of the individual and the unity and integrity of the Nation.

An early authority on the Indian Constitution, Granville Austin, insisted that it 'is first and foremost a social document. The majority of its provisions are either directly aimed at furthering the goals of the social revolution or attempt to foster this revolution by establishing the conditions necessary for its achievement'. (Austin 1966: 50)

The Nehruvian consensus of the early years of our Republic sought to institutionalize this 'social revolution' in deliberate contrast to models of democratic capitalism of the First World and the autocratic communism of the Second. Nehru's democratic socialism with its mixed economy clearly foregrounded its priorities: economic growth with social equity in a planned agenda, political participation within a regime of democratic rights and civil liberties, national integrity with cultural and religious diversity in a secular society, a scientific temper, an ethic of tolerance as the way to peace and harmony in Indian society, a principled nationalism that allowed dissent, not a refugee for jingoistic politicians, a polity committed to its own people, but not at the cost of the community of nations.

The commitment and energy of the first decades after the founding of the Republic waned, as vested interests and electoral compulsions compromised these constitutional ideals. 'The bourgeoisie influence at the centre—in spite of an adverse political culture there—and the peasantry, increasingly, was powerful in State governments.' (Corbridge and Harris 2000: 66) Nehru's 'democratic socialism' mutated into 'post-office socialism', 'a way of describing a commitment to public enterprise at no profit, and hopefully no loss, with no particular efficiency, and no other clear purpose in mind'. (Galbraith 1963: 43) The rich profited, the poor paid the price.

Eventually this spawned a dysfunctional licence permit raj and stymied growth but brought little equity, and left rising and unfulfilled expectations churning below the surface. Rather than turn this 'post-office socialism' around into a democratic socialism as foregrounded in the Constitution, especially 'The Directive Principles of State Policy', successive governments gradually dismantled Nehru's legacy, including Indira Gandhi, his own daughter, with the imposition of an 'Emergency' in 1975, and later Rajiv Gandhi, his grandson with the liberalization of the economy. With globalization, this has accelerated. Now it has become a headlong rush into a free-market in an emphatically saffronized neoliberal version. With the closer alignment with the West in expectation of greater capital investment from there, 'the policy of non-alignment had become a sham. Domestically, the way of conciliation, compromise, and consensus, had given way to confrontation, and casteism, communalism and violence were on the increase.' (Corbridge and Harris 2000: 68)

The present government is committed to dismantling Nehru's legacy completely and replacing it with Deendayal Upadhyaya's (1916–68), the ideologue of the Rashtriya Swayamsevak Sangh, integral humanism. But does it have the breadth and depth to inspire beyond the faithful of the flock? Rather it seems that it is being used as symbolic tokenism. In actuality the RSS's Hindutva is an ideology straight from Savarkar, who draws basically from Mazzini (1805–72) not Deendayal.

Free-markets and Populism

Free markets disproportionately advantage the rich and disadvantage the poor. When the contradictions of the system reach the tipping point, market failure and social unrest threatens to bring the system down, as happened with the Great Depression in the aftermath of the Great War of 1914–18. People look for strong leaders and readily fall prey to authoritarian demagogues who 'save' them by binding them in a combative unity against their enemies. These enemies must be found or imagined by these leaders, and scapegoats are always available. In such times of frustration and desperation, an authoritarian demagogue, with a simplified ideology will have an immense, almost irresistible, popular appeal.

There are numerous avatars of this 'jealous populism that is utterly intolerant of rival populist mobilizations and hence violently repressive'. (Chatterjee 1997: 25) In Italy in the 1920's, it was Mussolini's National Fascist Party with its slogan: 'Il Duce ha sempre ragione' (The leader is always right); in Germany it was Hitler's Nationalsozialistische Deutsche Arbeiterpartei (The National Socialist German Workers' Party) with: 'Ein Volk, ein Reich, ein Führer' ('One People, One Nation, One Leader').

In India we have the RSS with its aggressive promotion of Hindu nationalism: Hindi, Hindu, Hindustan. Its political sponsored party, the Bharatiya Janata Party, with its exclusive cultural nationalism deliberately provokes the Muslim minority with: 'Hindustan mein rehna hoga, Vande Mataram kehna hoga' (If you want to live in India, you must chant Hail to Mother India). At times, this becomes a chant for the strong man: 'Hindustan mein rehna hoga, Modi, Modi kehna hoga' (You must chant, Modi, Modi if you want to live in India).

Before the point of no return is reached, drastic intervention is needed to contain and manage the situation of social crisis. In the United States, the Great Depression brought the New Deal. After the crash of 2008, the global meltdown crisis was only contained with a multi-trillion bailout. But the subterranean slide into authoritarianism continued, dismissed by liberals, only to surface with Donald Trump in the United States, and the imbroglio of Brexit in the United Kingdom. In India in 2017 bank recapitalization by a saffronized neoliberal government had rescued failing banks from precipitating a national economic meltdown.

Such massive public bailouts leave private profit untouched by socializing the costs of the rescue. The rich get richer, the poor remain relatively poor or are left worse off.

However, populism, whether in extreme fascist form or a lesser authoritarian majoritarianism also fails to defuse the upstream causes of the downstream crisis. Its unravelling may be violent and traumatic, as with fascism in 1945, with unconditional surrender after losing the war; or non-violent and reconciliatory, as with the flower revolution in the Philippines in 1986; or democratic and divisive as after the Indian Emergency in 1977. But if the root causes of the contradictions that precipitated the crisis are not resolved, there will surely be a fall-back again, and the next time it could well be far worse: as has happened with the Arab Spring, or in the Philippines with Rodrigo Duterte, in Russia with Vladimir Putin, in Turkey with Endogen. And as is happening in contemporary 21st-century India with what is increasingly turning out to be an undeclared Emergency, a parliamentary government morphing into presidential form.

Navigating the Conundrum

Polarized, conflict-riddled states at an impasse, weak states, failing states—all such polities invite the authoritarian leader, who promises to reverse the drift and set things right swiftly. This would mean reneging on the democratic dividend because we are overwhelmed by the democratic deficit, and falling into the majoritarian syndrome of right-wing nationalism, a global phenomenon today.

In addressing this conundrum, our Constitution enshrined in the fundamental rights, linguistic and religious minority rights as the statutory expression of a minimum protection for individuals and vulnerable linguistic and religious communities. Fundamental rights were temporarily suspended during the Emergency but were restored later and further protected. The Supreme Court judgements have affirmed minority rights together with secularism as part of the basic structure of the Constitution, the most authoritative being the eleven-judge bench in 2002. This is a baseline for a pluralism meant to protect and preserve our diversity.

The Constitution guarantees state protection of minorities, so that as vulnerable communities they are not marginalized by the larger majority community, but it does not mandate state promotion for them. Rather, the state must position itself as equidistant from all communities. In a democracy minority rights are a protection against the 'tyranny of the majority' (Tocqueville 1862) but they can be abused when community identities become isolationist and exclusivist, or worse antagonistic and hostile to other communities. Diversity describes the context in which identity politics must function. But the transition from old hierarchies and powerful hegemonies to an egalitarian and enriching pluralism does not go uncontested; it is still a work in progress. To renege on this through political short-sightedness and opportunism is to risk deepening contradictions rather than celebrating complementarities.

Indeed, the test for a functioning and just democracy is not how the majority prospers, but how the minorities fair and how secure they feel. So too the authentication for justice is not how this is accessed by the rich and privileged, but how available and protective justice is made for the poor and vulnerable. Today our polity is hurtling into a free-fall authoritarian free-market economy. Electoral waves have seen a swing from Left to Right and back again. The dance of democracy is morphing into a dance of death of our republic mutating into a Republic of Fear, where promises are broken and hopes betrayed. (Mehta *Indian Express* 16 Aug 2018, https://indianexpress.com/article/opinion/hope-and-fear-independence-day-narendra-modi-speech-red-fort/)

Moreover, there has been a continuing advance of an aggressive, majoritarian religio-nationalist extremism, as also of a defensive, minority religious fundamentalism. These become mirror images of each other, and covert antagonism and hostility inevitably spill over into overt conflict and violence. Such religious fundamentalism is a 'militant piety' (Armstrong 2000: ix) that transforms anxiety into fear, and then fear into anger, and anger into rage. It is a defensive reaction that constructs the other as a threatening and dangerous enemy and the self as threatened and suffering victim. However, unless we can address the upstream causes of these downstream effects, we will compound this aggressive militancy, not contain it.

Politicizing the nation on the basis of majority and minorities could easily lead to a majoritarianism that overrides democratic rights and infringes on civil liberties of minorities as well as other dissenters. For when minorities as the different 'other' are excluded or marginalized as subversive deviants, then all dissenters are perceived as subversive too. Dissent itself is delegitimized. This is the very antithesis of an inclusive, participatory democracy. Such a politicization around negative ideologies and exclusive identities will, in the end, polarize society to the tipping point, and precipitate a formal separation for a compromised unjust peace—Apartheid—or a final solution of genocide—the Holocaust. History has examples of both for us to learn from.

Thus in the British Isles, Ireland's separation of Northern Ireland from the Republic precipitated decades of 'The Troubles'. In the Levant, Israel carved out of Palestine, was premised on creating two neighbourly states. It has resulted in Israeli dominance and ethnic cleansing of Arabs on the wrong side of the border with continuing bloody strife across their borders, disempowering and humiliating the Palestinians who became increasingly hostile, setting off a cycle of terrorist attacks and vengeful violence. The Partition of British India has its own horrors and as yet unresolved history.

Only post-Apartheid South Africa, relying on its tradition of Ubuntu, has so far succeeded in its transition to a 'rainbow nation' from a racist one. Political reform was premised not on Western retributive justice but the African traditional restorative justice. This meant dealing with political reform on the basis of an egalitarian ideology and minority protection within a democratic praxis, premised on its Constitution and the Truth and Justice Commissions it instituted that defused the bloodbath that was widely feared.

In India, a politics of hate is getting more deeply embedded, and this cannot augur well for the future of our 'sovereign, socialist, secular, democratic' Republic which we as, a united people, constituted ourselves into, when we began this saga of our 'nation in the making', or rather a multi-nation state in the making. For, a Hindu Rashtra as envisaged by the saffron brigade is not compatible with the basic structure of the Constitution of India.

Saffron Agenda

As the economy falters and unemployment sharply rises, farmers' agitations boil over, the legacy of the government's failed promises create an enormous credibility deficit. The commitment was to 'sabka vikas, sab ke saath' (the development of all, with all). This has shown to be 'billionaire raj' in the economy. (Chancel and Piketty 2017) When this neoliberal development is thwarted under the weight of its own tensions and contradictions and overgenerous electoral promises, then the Hindutva agenda takes an even firmer hold on the party's agenda, and communal polarization comes to its rescue. Disturbingly, we are becoming a Hindu majoritarian polity.

However, the once successful strategy of panicking Hindus into Islamophobia, and polarizing people with a divisive hate politics is less convincing now, at least to the moderates across the political spectrum. Moreover, when the Opposition stands united, the vote share of the BJP and its allies are unable to swing the elections. The Bihar Mahaghatbandan for the state assembly elections trounced the BJP and its allies in 2015. In the face of economic realities the failed promise of the much-touted Gujarat model of development exposed the vulnerability of the BJP. But then, not unexpectedly, they failed to hold together as their own contradictions and compulsions unravelled before the parliamentary elections in May 2019.

After the shock in the Gujarat assembly elections of December 2017, when BJP's vote share slumped to 49 per cent from 60 per cent in 2014, the Congress gained from 33 per cent in 2914 to 41.4 per cent in 2017. However, it would seem lessons have not been learnt by both protagonists: the BJP still depending on a polarizing agenda to distract from its failed development promises; while the Congress and the Opposition are unable to hang together so as not to hang separately. In subsequent state elections, especially those in the Northeast, it was not just polarization that worked for the BJP but also bringing over or buying out disgruntled politicians from other parties, including the Congress. Desperately clobbering up patchwork alliances, only degrades the political discourse all round.

The new India promised in 2014 is looking more and more like the old one, dressed in saffron, as the BJP get 'Congressified'! Coalitions are cobbled together by chicanery and skulduggery, with obfuscations and defections. It is the very thing the BJP had accused the Congress of, when in the Opposition and boasted of being a party with a difference. The Prime Minister's Office (PMO) is once again the court of the 'king' as once there was that of a Congress 'queen'. And courtiers are never wanting. It now seems that 'the new India is Modi and Modi is the new India', echoing the sycophancy of a very similar period during the Emergency, which it would seem is now being replayed but as an undeclared one.

In 1980, the BJP got only two seats in Parliament. To gain wider acceptance and moderate its Hindu extremism, at its first plenary convention in Bombay on 28 December 1980, the party affirmed 'Gandhian socialism' as one of its five commitments but its National Executive abandoned it in October 1985, though its National Council restored it formally. The saffron brigade talks with many voices and speaks in many tongues; if some find one inconvenient there are always other voices and tongues at hand to co-opt uncritical people. But then, 'What's in a name? That which we call a rose / By any other word would smell as sweet;…What's true for roses, is true for rogues—only the scent differs!'

Domains of Collective Violence

There are two main domains of collective violence in India: the first is between religious communities, particularly the majority and minority communities; and the second between hierarchical castes with their embedded patriarchy and now coalescing with class divisions.

Regarding the first: when collective identities are imagined as singular and totalizing, they collapse other individual identities into this common one. This gets projected onto the community and internalized in the individual. These identities tend to define and determine the community, and become inflexible and rigid; community boundaries become fixed and nonporous, leaving increasingly homogenized communities within exclusive boundaries. They are no longer diversified in inclusive openness and complementarity to the 'other'. Such communities are readily mobilized for socio-political causes and movements, much to the short-term advantage of their leaders but less for the long-term real interests of their communities. Thus the emotive politics of identity trumps the more rational politics of interests, and community identities are mobilized for alien interests even against their own, and the common good.

These identities are complicated by the majority-minorities divide. All collective identities are 'imagined' and constructed around demographic numbers. A democratic election of 'one man, one vote', (Const. Ass. Debates Ambedkar 26 Jan 1950, V. 12) becomes an electoral game of numbers: a homogenous majority will always be winners against a fragmented minority which will always be losers. Inevitably, the game of numbers becomes authoritarian and oppressive, a 'tyranny the majority'. (Tocqueville 1862)

On the other hand, a democracy premised on 'one man, one value' (Ambedkar ibid.) must provide the protection of an effective regime of rights to each and all. Or else a hapless minority may have no recourse but to turn to desperate measures, even violent ones. The tardy government response to atrocities against minorities and marginalized is a deafening silence. Often insecure minorities become forced non-voluntary migrants and refugees. This is how ethnic cleansing escalates into genocide.

Regarding the second domain, caste conflict is precipitated by the 'graded inequality' (Ambedkar Constituent Assembly Speech 27 Nov 1949) of the hierarchical system, now being challenged by the new egalitarian aspirations and rising expectations from below. This challenge to the caste status quo, not unexpectedly, is vigorously resisted by upper castes who feel their old privileges being undermined. Since by and large upper castes belong to the upper classes, caste hierarchy coalesces with class stratification as upper castes and upper classes at the apex of the social pyramid. This dominant hegemony is very difficult to dislodge because it is structurally and culturally supported.

The saffron brigade of the RSS-led Hindutva movement is, by and large, an upper caste one, more so is its leadership. Other Backward Classes (OBCs) are more prominent in other Sangh Parivar organizations, like the Bajrang Dal and the VHP. Now the BJP is trying to co-opt aspiring upwardly mobile OBCs and even Dalits and tribals (SCs and STs) into the movement as its foot soldiers, and even Muslims who can provide the 'token face', as and when needed. However, with escalating atrocities being committed by the dominant and even the middle castes/classes against these most vulnerable in our society, and the parlous response of the BJP government, the game seems to be up. The ambiguities and contradictions of the Hindu Rashtra agenda and its Manuvad caste hierarchy cannot be hidden forever.

Upstream Causes, Downstream Effects

The upstream origins of such collective ethnic conflicts can have devastating downstream consequences in pogroms and genocides. When religion and caste are politicized along communal divides, it can have a disastrous and lasting impact on social conflicts because of its enormous emotive and motivating power. This gains traction from popular religiosity and caste prejudice, community barriers and gender stereotypes, so widely ingrained in society and so readily exploited politically. This religionizing of politics, militarizes religion and adds an ominous, sinister dimension to national politics, raising the violence to another level even as it becomes increasingly endemic in the very DNA of society.

For the consequent response against the vulnerable ruptures and eventually destroys the very the social fabric, which sustains any human community. When this spirals out of control, we have a 'failed state', which may be beyond repair and have to be reimagined and rebuilt, all over again. We have numerous examples of this in history, and premonitions of it in South Asia today, even resulting in civil war, where a demographically constructed majority-minority divide is politicized into a majority versus minority polarization to gain and keep power. Where powerful communities are divided, the alternative to conflict and hostility can be through a 'consociation' arrangement i.e., various communities through their leaders sharing power proportionately. (Lijphart, 1984)

Furthermore, the recent mainstreaming of the neoliberal free-market in the economy is a blatant promotion of upper-class interests, in spite of its precipitating greater socio-economic inequalities and widening the relative poverty gap between rich and poor. Neoliberal saffronization is now racing out of control, inviting populist remedies from authoritarian demagogues. This is happening in affluent democracies as well. While in the West neoliberalism is at best secular, at worst racist, mostly premised on a racist white supremacy and the compradors this co-opts, in India neoliberalism is getting saffronized. It makes strange bedfellows with the Hindutvavadis of the Sangh Parivar, for neoliberalism is meant to be globalized with inclusive markets, while Hindutva is located in India and exclusive to Hindus.

There are further ambiguities and contradictions among Hindus themselves: between the more traditional upper castes and the new arrivals from other castes; between the more traditionally religious middle classes and the more secular upper ones, between the enterprising businessman and the devoted religious bhakt. This leaves alienated and anomic individuals with divided hearts and spilt personalities. There is also the tension within the caste-class hegemony between the globalization internationalist agenda of neoliberalism and the localization of the nationalist one of Hindutva, between the market and Manu. Eventually, the clash of globalization and localization could leave in its wake, a global chaos and fractured national societies. It is already happening in the advanced capitalist countries of the West, especially in the Anglo-Saxon neoliberal ones, the United States of America (America first, Make America Great!) and the United Kingdom (I want my country back, Take back control!).

However, there are no impermeable 'cultural boundaries' in a plural society, no 'neatly bounded and mutually exclusive bodies of thought and customs, perfectly shared by all who subscribe to them, and in which their lives and works are fully encapsulated'. (Ingold 1994: 330) This gives rise to 'fuzzy communities', (Kaviraj

1992: 26) and allows for multiple or layered identities for group members. For communities subjected to rapid social change, this can be an especially problematic area. However, since the first colonial decennial census of 1871 began enumerating religion and caste, the 'fuzzy boundaries' between communities, which allows for multiple or layered identities for group members, (Kaviraj 1992: 26) began to be replaced by more rigidly defined 'enumerated communities' as categorized by the Census.

With universal franchise in Republican India these 'enumerated communities' have been increasingly consolidated around such constructed identities and further politicized and mobilized for electoral gains. For, electoral democracy in India functions on the basis of communities, not individuals. They make up the 'vote banks' that all political parties are riveted on for winning political power at the hustings. Electoral politics with its rhetoric and campaigns displaces substantive democracy with its real issues and concerns. For an aspirational class with oversized expectations of upward mobility, campaign promises of leaders and politicians are more enthralling than their actual performance subsequently.

Empty promises consumed now, only end with polluting hot air later. Dissenting community leaders and opinion makers are targeted, and party cadre get the vote out. If the media owned by corporate interests fails in its watchdog role, and political leaders are bonded to powerful lobbies, then even a stunning victory on an electoral wave, all too often brings only a 'circulation of elites', (Pareto 1966: 108) replacing one set of rascals with another. Political patronage enthrals voters and entrenches the system; the actors may change, the script does not. Only a critical and alert citizenry, and a civil society to match can expose hegemonic interests, and conscientize voters to their real issues and concerns. However, substantive democracy can make incremental gains and ratchet up a process of inclusive and participative democracy. Otherwise the patronage politics of such an electoral democracy invites a populism which begins a dance of death for substantive democracy.

Great Leader, Little Wo/Man

Patronage politics opens the door to decisionism, (Hirst 1988) the political theory that Carl Schmitt (1888–1985) used to justify the Third Reich. Bold decisions were lauded as self-legitimating, drawing their validity from their form not their content, as long as they are taken by the right political authority. The sudden decision on 'demonetisization' and 'lockdowns' are precisely examples of this 'shock and awe' decision-making. It projects a decisive leader, regardless of the decision and what is achieved and who pays the price. For 'as far as most essential issues are concerned, making a decision is more important than how the decision is made'. (Schmitt 1985: 55–56)

Pandian and Roy (2014) elaborate this: 'The Decisionist dream of the subalterns is that the leader is one like us, yet could decide/do what we cannot…such perception leads the common people to identify with the idealised leader as the compensation for the lack in their lives.'

Implied here is a messianism that gives unquestioned authority to the leader to deliver on the utopian expectations of the followers. Inevitably, greater trust is placed in the leader than in the institutions of governance. It is possible for strong leaders to shore up democratic institutions, but they can undermine them as well, especially when checks and balances are not in place. Hence the crucial role of a free and critical media, an impartial judiciary, the supremacy of Parliament and a formally recognized and effective 'loyal opposition'. Otherwise an authoritarian leader can readily lead to a majoritarian democratic dictatorship, and selective violence scapegoating on the minorities and marginalized.

In this form of leadership, at first the leader is projected as 'great little man', a person who embodies both the greatness the followers long for and littleness with which he can identify with them and they with him. Mussolini and Hitler, once lionised by the RSS, are textbook examples of this. From office boy to the White House, is the American saga for a people's president. Ours now is 'Chaiwala to PM'. This affirms ordinariness of our everyday lives even as it opens them to extraordinary expectations with unreal promises. The neo-middle class is particularly prone to this kind of appeal. Consumerism makes passive citizens receptive to such communications, with their addictions to comfort zones, they demand for instant everything: I want it all and I want it now, syndrome.

Indian democracy has never quite recovered from the damage done to the constitutional institutions nurtured by Nehru and hollowed out by his daughter. The standards Nehru set for constitutional proprietary and parliamentary debate have been displaced by money power and political muscle. The fragmentation of the polity and the pragmatic compulsions of coalition politics have come to dominate governments. We are now trapped in an authoritarian governance, an undeclared Emergency—the worse for being unofficial and promoted by a pliable judiciary and an even more submissive and complicit bureaucracy, by criminals and corrupt law enforcement agencies, while watchdog media become echo-chambers of their masters' voices. All courtiers in the court of the king.

The Long March

The official statistics on violent conflicts, euphemistically called 'civil disturbances', are shocking and getting ever worse. They indicate only the tip of the iceberg of the death and destruction of so many promising lives cut short by violence. But we are rather blasé about our predicament. It is like not being alarmed by numerous murders because so many people are still alive. When tragedy strikes nearer home, we suddenly awake from our slumbers.

If this is where we are, how do we get to where we want to be? Having lost our way, we are very far from the tryst we made that midnight of our awakening to freedom. But, as a Chinese proverb has it: a journey of a thousand miles begins with one small step. So does getting back on track begin with the first step; but it has to be taken in the right direction. This necessitates not just 'sincerity'—a reflection in our words and deeds of what we think and mean—but also 'honesty'—a self-transparency so we can honestly know our true selves to the extent we can. Too often we 'sincerely', though unknowingly, deceive ourselves. This is a failure of transparency, a dishonesty that cheats our own selves before it does others.

Our behaviour faithfully reflects our perceptions and perspectives, perhaps even quite 'rationally'. But often we are all too self-righteous to critically examine the unconscious origins of these, nor do we sensitize ourselves to their unintended effects. And so our culpable negligence leaves behind the trail of the brute in its wake. Extremists and fundamentalists, dogmatists and decisionists, ideologues and rationalists are often persons of deep and sincere conviction. But often extremely and radically deceived because of a closing of the mind to alternatives too dangerous and threatening to their present ego to consider. Their still small inner voice is smothered by the sound and fury within themselves, or by the confusion and contradictions without, and consequently the alienation and anomie all this precipitates.

This 'honesty' will demand a ruthless self-interrogation, both of persons and collectives. What makes ordinary people capable of perpetrating extraordinary violence? (Chitralekha 2012) What are the motivational structures that inspire and support such savage killings of innocent people and then leave no trace of regret? Rather the murderers are feted as heroes. Sometimes even neighbours they lived with for years are thus brutalized. What are the pathologies that allow the demonization of the 'other' to the point of complete dehumanization and erasure? What ideological worldview gives such motivational and structural support that makes everyday persons like you and me perpetrators of such 'extraordinary violence'? What makes them feel justified in killing innocent persons, often their own neighbours and more often people they never knew or ever had any contact with?

Tentative Explanations

What is difficult to comprehend is that such inhumanly horrific behaviour, full of blood and gore, of barbarity and vindictiveness seems to leave no trace on the perpetrators' conscience. How do they return to their 'ordinary' lives unscathed by what they have done to their victims, even as the devastated survivors of the horrors struggle to get their lives back together, and cope with the post-traumatic stress and wounded memories that haunt them still? How can they mock and pillory their victims in the aftermath of the violence they have subjected them to? How can they strut around before survivors in their neighbourhoods in the very clothes they have looted from them?

Some explanations have been attempted: Mancur Olson's 'rational actors' theory calculates the tipping point when individual actors coalesce into to a mass movement (Olson 1965); Ted Gurr's (1970) politicization of discontent and its actualization in violence; Charles Tilly's (1978) focus on psychological and ideological causes to the purposive revolutionary movement; Dipak Gupta (2001) on the complexity of the motivations involved in genocide and mass murder; Stathis Kalyas's (2003) interaction between political and private identities; and Theda Skocpol's (1979) five stages of a revolutionary movement changes in society giving rise to grievances, disorientation, new interests, a mass movement, an ideology and an organization. However, such theories need to be integrated into a continuous narrative of collective violence in India.

The explanatory power of any analysis is necessarily limited to the horizons of the discourse in which it is set. And the churning of explanations must happen in the public domain where these can be tested and challenged by competing ones. India has a long tradition of such public debate going back into the first millennium BCE. (Parekh 2015: 3-33) In the Buddhist Sanghas such internal discussions and public debates were very much alive. There were schools of thought that debated publicly through the Puranic period and in the Mughal Court. Akbar engaged in interreligious debates in his Ibadatkhanna, while Europe was into Inquisition, persecuting heretics and burning witches during the Reformation on both sides of the religious divide there.

The 'Argumentative Indian' was very much part of our Indic tradition. (Sen 2005) The freedom movement inherited this tradition of public debate. There were many simultaneous and parallel debates, often with Gandhi at the centre: Tagore on nationalism; Jinnah on Hindu-Muslim unity; Ambedkar on Dalits; between Nehru and Sardar Vallabhai Patel on governance among others. Not all reached resolution in unanimity but a collective consensus was reached in the Constituent Assembly debates, in which all sides participated. This was a process of maturing public opinion and support, not dumbing it down to co-opt people to one's own side while rubbishing the other, as is happening today in our political discourse, with trading insults and pillorying dissenters, showmanship and spin. A prime example being the performance in TV debates led by anchors whose interest in TRPs (Television Rating Points), on which the channels' advertising revenue depends, trumps their principles, if any, and do not credibly and critically inform viewers.

Reversing the Spiral

Modern society has no solution to the problem of violence, either at the individual or the collective level, except to answer it with more violence. In our world today the final arbitrator in human disagreements is still violence: whether this is perpetrated by individuals, terrorist groups, or by the law and order machinery of the state, often resulting in legalized violence, staged police encounters and extra-legal terror. At the end of the day the ultimate argument used by kings and now by presidents and prime ministers is war against external enemies and deliberate violence against internal dissenters. At times declarations of 'total' wars and subtle structural violence, at others undeclared low-intensity conflicts and institutional prejudice; from the use of military might and oppressive state machinery, to the threat of violent intervention and pogroms. But even when a practical, realist politics does temporarily contain and restrain violence, it can never really remedy and heal the wounds left behind, or wipe away the scars that remain.

Hence the only result at worst is to add to, or at best postpone the continuing spiral of violence. For 'The practice of violence, like all action, changes the world, but the most probable change is to a more violent world.' (Arendt 1970: 80) What have we learnt from our violent world? How did we get here and where are we going?

To reverse this, some neutral space for mediation and resolution must be created for the protagonist in the conflict. This can be complicated, and the parties to the conflict may be too entangled to do this themselves. A violent conflict may result in the victor imposing a resolution. But even when accepted by the protagonists, if this does not address underlying and upstream causes of the conflict, if it does not engage with the real needs and concerns of the victims, it cannot be lasting or stable.

For peace is the fruit of justice. However, what is imperative today is justice as restorative, not retributive. Justice needs must be premised on truth, or else it can only be manipulative never fair. Such truth must be oriented to reconciliation, not revenge. And there's the rub. For all the parties actively or passively involved, especially for individuals and communities who have borne the brunt and brutality of the violence, the traumas of conflict leave unhealed hurt and wounded memories. These form a subterranean residue that easily turns into hate and even revenge. It is not possible to return to the status quo ante.

The challenge will be to find new possibilities and create new futures. But for communities deeply involved in hospitality and hate, there can be '*No Future Without Forgiveness*', (Tutu 2000) only more of the same to the point of exhaustion. This is what blood feuds are all about. (Stathis N. Kalyvas 1999) Cultural faultlines that have been politicized to polarize peoples, must be bridged with new narratives, with inclusive symbols and motivating myths. For such political violence always adds to a wanton senselessness.

Within a national society the role of the state becomes crucial to such conflict mediation, to contain, resolve and reverse it. However, the partisan implication of the state itself in such collective violence makes any resolution or reconciliation extremely problematic. Vested interests lobby against change that may adversely affect them, regardless of the consequences of the contradictions and violence that have been precipitated. When the state fails in its function as a just and fair mediator, other actors in civil society must play a critical role, for ultimately, the polity reflects society and vice versa.

But here again there must be more than 'narcissistic compassion', a consciousness of kind that restricts fellow-feeling to one's own or similar people. We need a critical 'reciprocity of perspectives' to counter any self- or group-centeredness coming from hidden prejudice, so as to include 'the other', the stranger, the last and the least. Only a genuine pluralism can adequately meet this challenge at the crucial levels needed. We must have both a critical passion of the mind, and genuine compassion of the heart.

All this demands a reciprocity of perspectives, we see the world from where we are placed. For instance, to Pope John Paul's request for his intervention on behalf of the US hostages taken by the Islamic Republic, Ayatollah Khomeini asked, why none was made for the victims of the Shah.

Open-ended Encounter

We must steer our narrative between the rationalism of a positivist approach, and the relativism of the alternative facts of post-truth nihilism, between the devil and the deep blue sea, between Scylla and Charybdis, lest the story gets landed on the rocks of hard facts, or beached in the shallows of ridiculous caricature. This requires a hermeneutic approach able to problematize both the modernist's grand narrative of rationality, as well as the post-modernist's multiple fragments of polysemy, situating the problematique in its life-situation (sitz-im-leben) for a contextual comprehension and then seeking a fusion beyond both horizons.

This implies four steps: hermeneutic suspicion, proclamation, remembrance, creative actualization. (Grey 2010: 106) To begin with, a hermeneutic suspicion that the accepted explanations are inadequate to the complexity it considers, that the phenomena, what appears, the phonomena, hides more, than reveals what's real, the noumenna, that lie deeper, and hence needs to be explored. The second step is announcing the dissonance, recalling the historic origins of this from the past, deconstructing this, by comparing similarities and differences of other such instances across the spectra where these occur. Thirdly, helping memory to disentangle and analyze, reconstructing the narrative and then, making creative and imaginative actualizations in response. Finally, thinking out of the box and the daring to risk must carry along as many as possible towards building a critical mass that will precipitate a new and more human normal.

However, different interpreters within their different horizons of understanding may well clash, especially over basic issues on which there can be fundamental and even prejudiced differences. All interpretations can only be within the limited horizons of the interpreter's understanding. Only an adequate hermeneutics can address such basic issues underlying this controversy by setting our historical 'texts' in their present 'contexts', and indicating the horizons of understanding within which a dialogue can lead to a 'fusion of horizons' and not a clash of perspectives. For dialogue is pedagogic, when each side learns from the other, meeting on common ground to journey together to a higher ground. This 'fusion of horizons' will complete the hermeneutic circle that begins with a suspicion and dialogues to a resolution, tests it on the ground, and then sets off again to reiterate the process. This is the praxis of action-reflection-action.

We are caught in a spiral of escalating violence at multiple levels and in numerous arenas. To turn this back will demand a new narrative framed in an alternative discourse, open to all people of goodwill. It must be an open-ended encounter with our past for an understanding that is empathetic, i.e., Weber's empathetic understanding, 'versethen' (Weber 1946) and tolerance that is compassionate (Panikkar 1983: 20–36), to endure into our future. This is a journey on which we can expect to be surprised, even shocked, by what we encounter with other dialogue partners, and what we discover within ourselves in engaging with them. As Wendy Doniger presciently writes: 'India is a country where not only the future but even the past is unpredictable'. (Doniger 2010: 668)

CHAPTER TWO

REDISCOVERING OUR HISTORY

New Normal – History as Prophecy – Untangling Two Nations – The Idea of India – Tagore's Humanism – Gandhi's Swaraj – Nehru's Discovery – Ambedkar's Republic – Bharat Resists India – Revivalism and Transformation – Envisioning Our Future – An Ethno-nationalist State – Indic Civilization

New Normal

On 22 May 2018, a twenty-three-year-old Muslim boy was spotted with a nineteen-year-old Hindu girl near the Garjiya Devi temple near Ramnagar, Uttarakhand. A mob gathered 'to teach the young couple a lesson'. (*Indian Express* 23 May 2018)

It seemed clearly another instance of 'love jihad', a stratagem used to accuse Muslims of alluring innocent Hindu women into marriage and converting them. This could have led to another instance of Muslim lynching, no longer uncommon in our land, and reported only tangentially, if at all in the media. Public lynching is part of the targeted, purposeful violence that is becoming a very real stratagem to put Muslims in their place by making them vulnerable and insecure.

The Ramnagar incident would have been another instance of the same but for the selfless bravery of twenty-eight-year-old police sub-inspector Gagandeep Singh. He rushed to the spot and made himself a human shield, holding the man to his chest and taking the blows for him. Eventually the frustrated mob dispersed and the couple was taken into the police station and handed over to their parents.

Such exceptional bravery can hardly be expected from our public servants anymore, certainly not from political leaders with their elaborate state security detachments, who are more focused on protecting and promoting themselves than their people. The image of Sub-inspector Singh protectively holding the endangered youth to his chest is a symbol of the large-hearted compassion we once privileged. As a response for his bravery, he got so many threat calls that he had to switch off his mobile. (News India 31 May 2018) Today, leaders with power and pelf and puffed up chests are strutting around with shrunken hearts.

In a village in Bulandshahr in western Uttar Pradesh a police officer, Subodh Kumar Singh, was trying to pacify a mob enraged over reported cow carcasses found in a field and brought to the police station. He was lynched, shot dead and two others injured, after which the mob went on a rampage, burning vehicles and pelting stones. (*Indian Express* 4 Dec) Later the chief minister described this as not a murder but an accident. The police then went on to investigate the alleged cow slaughter and not the police office's murder. This seems such a telling obfuscation of perspectives and priorities. Where does it come from? What does the silence of the government mean?

The heroism and self-sacrifice once so deeply embedded in the freedom movement seems part of our lost history now. That was an epic struggle over many decades for an India that drew on our civilizational resources, with an openness for the best wherever it was found. An India free to be herself, inclusive and tolerant, multicultural and pluri-religious, democratic and egalitarian. It was inspired by an idea of India, articulated by our leaders, internalized by our people and encapsulated in our Constitution.

Those early years of our Republic were exciting years of great promise and even greater hopes. But we have not stayed the course. Along the way we lost the plot, and are now are careering towards a majoritarian and intolerant India, increasingly authoritarian and autocratic. This is a betrayal of the founders of our Republic and those who sacrificed themselves for our freedom, of those who gave their yesterday for our tomorrow. Our struggle for freedom was premised on non-violence, but it did have its inevitable underbelly of bloody, communal conflict. When independence from colonial rule was finally won in 1947, it came to a truncated India, partitioned between Hindus and Muslims. It left us with an as-yet unhealed trauma from which neither of the antagonistic sides have recovered completely. In India we still carry the burden of that unhealed memory, and relive it with every communal conflict, each terrorist attack, the repeated mob lynchings, derogating Muslims with slogans such as: Pakistan ya kabrastan (to Pakistan or the graveyard).

The subcontinent has still not come to terms with the tragedy of the Partition. Hindu nationalists dream of reversing history, of turning the clock back to an undivided India, with some convenient ethnic cleansing, no doubt, and tamed and subservient minorities communities. Others, more moderate and sensible, prefer to move beyond the status quo in which we are still mired now. But wounded memories are all too easily manipulated by religious fundamentalists and political chauvinists to precipitate violent expressions of their brooding, unsatisfied rage and dangerously unreasonable fears.

History as Prophecy

An authentic historical consciousness can best be described as a passionate concern with the present, a compassionate interpretation of the past and taking both into a creative anticipation of the future. It is about discovering where we came from, so as to realize who we are and how we got here as we reach out to construct our future. We mine the archives of the past, not just to get at the 'facts of history', but also to find our origins in them, discover our roots there, and inspire hope for our future. Coming to terms with our past is a sine qua non for healing memories and rebuilding dreams. In this sense, all history as remembrance is necessarily contemporary, that is, interpreted from the present for the future. Thus in helping us to understand the present and read the signs of the times, history can also be prophecy.

A genuine historical memory must be faithful to the facts. We do not create the past nor can we recreate it. The uncritical glorifying of the past is but an escape from the challenges of present realities. Such romanticizing has been more an elitist, nationalist interpretation, a history 'from above' that supported the idea of a homogenous community of peoples that were identified as 'Hindus' in the colonial census. Subaltern approaches to a history 'from below' have been better at critiquing such elitist perspectives than at constructing alternative interpretations in viable and adequate measure. Yet the past is never quite dead, it lives in the present and has implications for the future. This is precisely why history has an explosive potential for the future. However, the selection we make of the facts and the meaning we give to them will demand an honest and sensitive transparency that preconceived prejudice does not permit.

A positivist approach to history presumes to base itself on a 'hard core of facts' following the popular wisdom of 'facts speak for themselves'. But historical facts, such as they are, come to us refracted through the observer, the recorder, the transmitter. 'Facts' can hardly remain 'pure' on a journey of so many possible distortions, like a game of 'Chinese whispers' down the ages, across the globe. E.H. Carr insists that 'the facts speak only when the historian calls on them: it is he who decides to which facts to give the floor, and in what order or context'. (Carr 1996: 11) Without a judicious selection, it is possible to drown in an ocean of detail.

Our survival response to 'information overload', finally settles us into a comfort zone of oversimplified stereotypes, catchy sound-bites and enhanced media images. For Carr, history is 'a continuous process of interaction between the historian and his facts, an unending dialogue between the present and the past'. (Carr 1996: 30) Ultimately, 'any reliable meaning derives from the interpretation of facts rather than the facts themselves.... Any interpretation moves from the illusive history to the engaging story.... History is accessible only through tradition and comprehensible only through interpretation.' (Charlesworth 2007: 461)

A persevering Indophile and Indological scholar of great repute, A.L. Basham is severely critical of projecting the present into the past 'to fit traditional Indian conceptions into the framework of twentieth century democracy'. (Basham 1975: 490) However, our world of alternative facts created for partisan purposes and post-truths relativize and obscure any grounding in impartiality. As recently as 6 March 2018, Reuters reported that an official committee of some fourteen persons was constituted with an annual budget of about $400 million. (Jain and Lasseter 2018) It 'aims: to use evidence such as archaeological finds and DNA to prove that today's Hindus are directly descended from the land's first inhabitants many thousands of years ago, and make the case that ancient Hindu scriptures are fact not myth'. The purpose of this predetermined objective 'to shape the national identity to match their religious views, that India is a nation of, and for Hindus'.

The theory of an influx of people from Central Asia 3,000 to 4,000 years ago was embraced by mainstream academia the world over. This is the foundation of the pluralism of Indic civilization, as old as the *Indica* that Megasthanes, the Greek, wrote about in the 3rd century BC. India as a multicultural tapestry was born of migrations, invasions and conversions, and is a bewildering diversity in unity. Scientific evidence from 'The Genomic Formation of South and Central Asia' (March 2018) tells us 'the story of our ancestors and where we came from'. It confirms the Harappan peoples as distinct from the Arya ones who came later. After their decline other migrants followed over the centuries, settled, mingled and mixed so that Joseph concludes: 'we are a multi-source civilisation, not a single-source one, drawing our cultural impulses, traditions and practices from a variety of heredities and migration histories. We are all Indians. We are all migrants. And we are all mixed'. (*The Hindu* 13 Sept 2019)

But to assert their own primacy, Hindu nationalists need to claim descent from ancestors and a religion that is indigenous. They reject the idea that India was forged from mass migrations. And this idea requires a rewriting of history to forge the story of our subcontinent in saffron colours. Thus the Hindu epics are being promoted as historical documents, and the search is on for the mythical Saraswati river of Vedic times. Eventually, the intention is to introduce this 'Hindu first' version of Indian history into the school curriculum, a process that has already begun.

However, the sensitive historian must find and select facts, interpret and draw out their meaning and relevance. Of course, one's own subjectivity impinges on this and so an objectivity check against other selections and interpretations must also be put in place. None of this must displace the hermeneutical doubt with which we must begin this encounter. The underlying historicity of truth and the need to deal with this critically and meaningfully must not exclude a similar approach to the obverse of this, the historicity of error. Navigating between the two is a delicate yet necessary task for any historical contextualization.

In attempting to sketch this in broad outline, what we leave out may be as important as what we include, for silence can speak louder than words, if we but listen to the silence. However, a fulsome wealth of inconsequent detail can obfuscate the bigger picture just as too superficial an exposé leaves the door open to other charges. The full picture cannot be completed in just a single venture. It must be an ongoing endeavour on which we set out now with small steps but great expectations.

Untangling Two Nations

The insanity of the genocidal paroxysms, which happened with the Partition is depicted in Sa'adat Hasan Manto's tragic story of 'Toba Tek Singh'. In the aftermath of millions of refugees caught on the wrong side of the Indo-Pakistan border scrambling for safe havens, the confused inmates of a mental asylum are also being relocated according to religion. But they have no idea where Pakistan is. That is why they are all at a loss whether they are now in India or in Pakistan. If they are in India, then where is Pakistan? If they are in Pakistan, how come that only a short while ago they were in India? How could they have been in India a short while ago and now suddenly in Pakistan? How come the change when they had not moved? Bhishen Singh, once a land owner in Toba Tek Singh, resists relocation but is forcibly taken and left on the border. (http://www.sacw.net/partition/tobateksingh.html) The irony of the certified insane defying the insanity of the supposedly sane is starkly illustrated with a searing image that Manto leaves us: the wild and ferocious-looking, but harmless, Toba Tek Singh as he was called in the only home he had for the last fifteen years, crumpled on the narrow strip of no man's land, refusing to cross over.

After the horrific genocide during the Partition, the shock at the assassination of the Father of the Nation seemed to presage a saner and more realistic approach in coming to terms with the aftermath of the brutalizing trauma. Resettlement and rehabilitation were moved into place and new adjustments made and new futures opened. This was the immediate necessity and had to be the first priority at the time. But traumatized memories have not yet been allowed to heal. Today, the faultlines of conflict between peoples living in the Indian subcontinent are being drawn ever more sharply and deeply.

Yasmin Khan's *The Great Partition: The Making of India and Pakistan* attempts at 'untangling two nations' to conclude that Partition 'stands testament to the follies of empire, which ruptures community evolution, distorts historical trajectories and forces violent state formation from societies that would otherwise have taken different—and unknowable—paths'. (Khan 2007: 210) However, this was not just an unfortunate folly. Rather it is inherent to the colonial legacy of divide and rule, a Machiavellian politics irresistible to any empire since Roman times and before: 'divide et impera' (divide and rule).

Jinnah's cussed intransigence and Nehru's unholy fatalism played into the hands of a determined Mountbatten to have the British exit before the gathering storm. Gandhiji was right when he wanted the colonialist to go and leave our problems to us. Even if it took a civil war to bring some sanity to bear on the protagonists, it would have been preferable to the unending hostilities the Partition has left on the subcontinent. For, however impartial they may seem, if at all outsiders resolve contested issues between protagonists, they are likely to do so to their advantage, rather than seek a real resolution. Colonial imperialists are not the best third-party mediators.

British imperialists have left a legacy of similar festering wounds from Ireland to the Middle East and beyond. British India was just one more instance of this, but on a subcontinental scale. However, we cannot disagree with Nisid Hajari's plea, with which he ends his book, *The Deadly Legacy of Partition*: 'It is well past time that the heirs to Nehru and Jinnah finally put 1947's furies to rest'. (Hajari 2051: 261) Tragically this has not happened. Rather the trauma has been carried forward through generations by both protagonists in slow motion, erupting into war periodically, and driven by chauvinist politics on both sides. For Jinnah's Pakistan, even though 'moth-eaten', as he complained, Partition was the birth of their new nation. Tragically it has broken its promise of a homeland for all the Muslims of the subcontinent, riven as it is by internal religious violence. Nehru's India, though left truncated, has betrayed the hopes of its 'tryst with destiny', and is now hijacked by religious fundamentalists and nationalist extremists. It would seem the two protagonists are well on their way to becoming mirror images of each other. Little wonder then, that the Pakistani version of this history is hardly recognizable in India and vice versa. Only contemporary leaders thrive on the conflict, people on both sides pay the price; not just the cost of the unhelpful antagonisms, but the enormous opportunity cost of a failed peace, a lost reconciliation, a shared prosperity, saving thousands of lives lost in conflict.

Stanley Tambiah's *Leveling Crowds*, (1996) which records the horrors of *Ethnonaionalist Conflict and Collective Violence in South Asia,* would seem to confirm our worst fears of a 'clash of civilizations' (Huntington 1996) engulfing the subcontinent. The two nations born in the trauma of the Partition were already three by 1971. Insurgencies and ethnic conflicts continue to contest, and threaten to unsettle the borders of the nation-states here. India's Northeast and Kashmir are seen by the locals as territories garrisoned by the Indian Army, but by Indians as land appropriated by the insurgents. Pakistan's North West frontiers are convulsing in suicidal terror that is engulfing the whole country and spreading beyond. Bangladesh has yet to contain its religious extremists, besides its own home-grown ethnic conflicts with the Chakma, also known as the Changma, hill tribe, and other non-Muslims, which spill over its borders.

And elsewhere, in the rest of South Asia, unrest continues.

The brutality with which the government put an end to almost thirty years of civil war in Sri Lanka only leaves future violence gestating in the resentment of outraged Tamils and the chauvinism of the victorious Sinhala. The ethnic tensions in the mountainous interiors of Myanmar are being suppressed by a ruthless military dictatorship but the Rohingya and the Karen and other tribes are not quite subdued as yet. Nepal has growing differences between the Khas people in the hills and the Madhesi in the Terai. Little Bhutan has ethnic tensions between the Bhutanese and Nepalis there.

In a large country like India, internal ethno-religious conflicts leave the minorities wounded and traumatized. The poisoned legacy of the divide-and-rule policy of the colonial government seems to have acquired a new dynamic with a momentum of its own. The 'deadly ethnic riot' (Horowitz 2001) has become a means to polarize a community for electoral gains of extremist leaders on both sides. Enforcing majority dominance precipitates minority consolidation. Such polarized communal violence becomes an instrument of appropriating public space for essentially communal group purposes. (Freitag 1990) Among the 'competing nationalisms in South Asia' (Brass 2002) the most volatile tectonic faultline is between the Hindu and Muslim communities. Little wonder that 'the production of Hindu-Muslim violence in contemporary India' (Brass 2003) becomes one more systematic manipulation of electoral politics within a procedural democracy. However, religious violence is not confined just to these communities. In 1984, the Sikhs in Delhi and in 2007–08 the Christians in Kandhdamal, Orissa, were subjected to pogroms by Hindu extremists and other lumpen elements.

Yet, however much we may blame the colonial divide-and-rule policy for the majority-minority divide, we must own responsibility for the continuing communal violence after Independence, which so dramatically underscores the unresolved issues of Partition. The deepest roots of the communal divide between Hindus and Muslims lie in the sense of treacherous betrayal that each still attribute to the other for the Partition and its aftermath. As a people we have not yet come to terms with that trauma. Its festering memories and contested history are carried forward over generations. The subliminal antagonism readily plays into a politics of hate that mobilizes vote banks and consolidates hostile identities.

As with the origins of many nation-states, especially multinational ones, 'history is a source of resentment and division between national groups, not a source of shared pride.... To build a sense of common identity in a multination state probably requires an even more selective memory of the past'. (Kymlicka 1995: 189)

For wounds fester if they do not heal. Today the faultlines of conflict between peoples living in the Indian subcontinent are being drawn ever more sharply and deeply, between Pakistan and India, the two heirs of British India, and within both states as well. In Pakistan, between Islamic sects, in India between the Hindu majority and other minorities, especially the Muslim community.

In Pakistan religious fundamentalism and extremism is careering into violence that is turning the country into a failed state at home and a terrorist threat abroad; in India, majoritarianism is creating a new category of second-class citizens, among the minorities and the marginalized, particularly Muslims. This category of people is defenceless and insecure, unsure of their constitutional guarantees. The blame game between the two countries, as also the warring ethnic factions within them, only deflects responsibility for what each can do to resolve its own internal contradictions and the consequent internal tensions that eventually are externalized and scapegoated on the vulnerable 'other'.

With minorities forming a substantial proportion of India's billion-plus population, this cannot augur well for our future. Minorities too have their own internal contradictions and anomalies which must be addressed. According to the Census of India, 2011 data, India is home to 966.3 million Hindus, who make up 79.8 per cent of the population. But there are 172.2 million Muslims (14.2 per cent of the population); 27.8 million Christians (2.3 per cent) and 20.8 million Sikhs (1.7 per cent). Ethnic cleansing of such large numbers will amount genocide.

However, blaming one's own difficulties on the majority and

retreating into defensiveness, even aggression, only mirrors the majoritarianism of the other with a 'minorityism' of one's own. This can set off a downward spiral in which the weaker antagonist still suffers the worst. Hindu nationalists are now on the upswing with a reconstructed history of the last thousand years as a subjugation to an invading Islam. This narrative is used to rationalize the communal violence against Muslims in India today, to 'teach them a lesson' with the cruel narcissism of the hurt Hindu's wounded pride.

In Pakistan the battle cry is chillingly familiar: Islam in danger! The underlying paranoia is promoted and exploited for the most chauvinist political ends. This accelerates the downward spiral into collective carnage. Our contemporary imbroglio has its more immediate origin in the debacle of the Partition, but the unresolved inequalities and anomalies of a society in rapid transition have not been addressed but left to fester and be co-opted by vested interests.

The concern here is not so much the history of violence in India, but to contextualize it in the present, as also in its upstream causes, unravelling its meaning, coming to terms with the personal and community traumas precipitated, healing wounded memories embedded in people's consciousness, understanding the imperative of reconciliation and forgiveness, and hopefully the value of peace and harmony. We have experienced enough and more violence in our world. And our preferred response to violence seems to be to contain it with defensive violence. We must hope now for an Ashokan Kalinga moment or a change of heart, a metanoia. A society that constructs 'the other' as different and threatening needs to experience a fall on the road to its Damascus.

The Idea of India

The Independence movement for a free and undivided India was only half won. It ended with the Partition. Jinnah's version of the two separate nations as expressions of two distinct civilizations resulted in the secession of Pakistan, which soon became an Islamic state. India, free but truncated, constituted itself into a sovereign, democratic Republic. Both sought historical justifications to bolster their nationalist projects. Pakistan's preoccupation was to establish its sovereign authority on their territory and so it traced its origins to Mohamed bin Qasim's conquest of Sindh in 712 CE. However, the secession of Bangladesh in 1971 put paid to its very raison d'etre as a homeland for all subcontinental Muslims.

The 'idea of India' was traced to its earliest history, and articulated in its new republican Constitution. Both narratives projected a utopian future: Pakistan to become an exemplary 'Islamic state'; and India constituted itself into 'a sovereign socialist secular democratic republic', a project still in progress.

Pakistan's quest for the ideal Umma, the community of Muslims bound together by ties of religion, careened into religious extremism and violence. Moreover, with a huge population of Muslims left in India, and after the secession of Bangladesh in 1971, it is no longer viable as the homeland for all subcontinental Muslims, as Jinnah had projected. India, with its complex multicultural, pluri-religious society so bound by tradition, stumbled in its social revolution to become a democratic, egalitarian society, and a modern urban-industrial one. Hindu nationalism began to undermine its secular democracy to establish a Hindu Rashtra, as the mythical 'Ram Rajya', from the 'Indus to the sea' and aimed to 'weld it into a nation'. (Savarkar 1989: 17) V.D. Savarkar's Hindutva version of the two nations theory is the obverse of Jinnah's Islamist one, with a different nuance. Jinnah settled for two separate nations; Savarkar did not. His Hindutva envisioned a single nation-state, as a Hindu Rashtra, with the Muslim minority subordinate to the Hindu majority.

These narratives project a utopian future: ideal Umma, and the mythical 'Ram Rajya'. However, a reality check would disabuse all but the most extreme fundamentalist faithful from such illusions. More crucially, few if any credible historians will buy into such a narrative that uses religious scriptures as an ideology for a modern state, and literary epics as literal historical texts to construct the past. Clearly, this is not an intellectual exercise to imagine a nation's future, but a political one for partisan contemporary purposes.

The 'idea of India', which inspired and mobilized the freedom struggle, was very different: scholarly and open, a search for, and *The Discovery of India*, (Nehru 1985, 1st 1946) buried and smothered under colonial rule. This was an India with a rich social and cultural diversity within an overarching and binding civilizational unity, an Indic civilization, ready to birth the Indian nation-state. The Constitution of India wrote this India into the basic structure of our Republic, and it sketched an agenda for a social transformation, from a tradition of inclusion and tolerance to a modernity of liberty, equality, fraternity. Jinnah's Pakistan was founded on a negation of this India to become an Islamic state, which has become more fundamentalist and extremist driven by its own internal compulsions.

This articulation of the idea of India was mostly the work of some of the foremost leaders of the freedom movement and they mobilized the masses towards realizing it. It is still the great unfinished business of our freedom struggle. Regrettably now, it seems to be losing ground to a Hindu Rashtra, which is a negation of the basic values of our Constitution, though its protagonists pretend otherwise.

Two such different version of our shared past can only perpetuate the conflict that was thought to have ended with a bloody, brutal separation of ways. The complexity of events and the diversity of experiences could interrogate and help nuance conventional understandings, but each side projects itself positively while demonizing the other. As terrorism and collective violence escalate, mutual antagonism and prejudice are further entrenched.

Seven decades and more after the event, Partition still darkens the future of the subcontinent. The consensus of the Nerhuvian years was inspired by the constitutional idea of India as expressed in its Preamble, articulated in a regime or rights and nuanced in the Directive Principles of State Policy. The consensus is fraying and we need now to recapture what so many in the freedom movement struggled and died for.

The post-Independence consensus was constructed on an understanding of our history that grounded the idea of India underpinning the freedom struggle. In stark contrast to the European nation-states, which were premised on creating homogeneous societies and destroying regional cultures and languages. (Fernée 2014) This 'Western model is broken'. (Mishra: 2014) Our movement imagined an idea of India that would celebrate its diversity of language and race, culture and religion. It was to be founded on three basic elements: democratic rights and civil liberties, anti-imperialism, and a priority for the poor masses. (Mukherjee 2015: 38–39)

The struggle for Independence brought various strands of the movement with different political emphases under its umbrella, but wedded them into a common core, i.e., the 'idea of India', a phrase first used by Tagore in 1902, and later popularized by Nehru's *Discovery of India*. (1946) Gandhi's *India of My Dreams* was more utopian. (*Young India* 10 Aug 31) It was a self-understanding or rather an aspiration for a tolerant, peaceful India, where peoples of diverse religions and cultures, ethnicities and languages would find a place, their niche in the social mosaic.

This was 'a prolonged movement, lasting nearly a century, and was based on the mass of people, millions of them, making it perhaps the greatest mass movement in world history'. (Mukherjee 2015: 39) Its best aspirations were convincingly articulated in the Constitution we gave ourselves to be the common foundation on which to build together a 'Sovereign socialist, secular, democratic Republic' as a viable and effective reality for all Indians, especially the poor and marginalized, for Gandhi's last and least Indian, in our quest for a just and decent society, and thus to make the 'idea of India' we fought for in our freedom struggle a reality by drawing on the best in our Indic civilization's syncretic traditions.

To recapture this legacy, we must turn to its principle architects: Rabindranath Tagore, Mohandas Gandhi, Jawaharlal Nehru and Bhimrao Ambedkar.

Tagore's Humanism

Tagore's idea of India was distinctly syncretic: a civilization 'embedded in the tolerance encoded in various traditional ways of life in a highly diverse plural society', welcoming all peoples and cultures. (*Bharatvarsher Itihas*, 1902) Though this was not common among the intelligentsia at the time, 'Tagorean anti-nationalism was almost exclusively borne out of Indian philosophical and theological traditions, and from autochthonous historical experience'. (Collins 2013: 78) However, it was Brahminic Hinduism, which from the middle ages built up 'a system of barriers. Its nature was to forbid and to exclude. The world never saw such a neatly constructed system against assimilation of any kind. This is not a barrier only between Hindus and Muslims. People like you and me who want freedom in conducting our life are also impeded and imprisoned.' (Tagore 1922: 313)

Tagore perceived two organizing principles in society: competition and cooperation. (Nationalism 1966a: 454) This was the contradiction between the humanizing core of a civilization and the pursuit of power for self-aggrandisement. His wish for India was this: 'Let our civilisation take its firm stand upon its basis of social cooperation and not upon that of economic exploitation and conflict.' (Tagore 1996a: 465) This he felt was the genius of Indian civilization. It was a fundamental choice 'between fighting one another, and combining, between their own interest or the common interest of all'. (Tagore 1996: 465)

Tagore was keenly aware of the dangers of nationalist chauvinism (Nationalism 1996, 1st 917) and sharply critical of how European nationalism had turned 20th-century Europe into a 'civilisation of power'. (Tagore 1996: 425) He saw the politicization and commercialization as having broken the wholeness of Western civilization and leaving it deeply flawed. (Tagore 2008a: 60) In an alternative civilization, the idea of sanskriti (culture) would be premised on dharma or sadachar, as a moral force towards perfection. A civilization has 'some guiding moral force' in a society towards 'the object of attaining perfection'. (Tagore 2008b: 269) This was quintessentially human and the basis of our unity across diverse cultures. Gandhi in his *Hind Swaraj* (1909) would be even more emphatic about the moral or dharmic dimension of civilization.

Tagore was apprehensive of the militant nationalism in India and in the freedom movement he remained a critical participant yet always a much valued and respected one. The genius of the India he elaborated was in terms of a spirit of cooperation. He was quintessentially a humanist and an internationalist. Tagore's *The Religion of Man* (1931) affirms his faith in a universal humanism, for all men have honoured the reality of the good. Man can lead a life of self-seeking but he also 'transcends his self-interest'. In 1941, at the end of his last public speech, 'Civilisation in Crisis' he asserts: 'A day will come when unvanquished Man will…win back his lost human heritage.' (cited, Bhattacharya 2016: 29)

Gandhi's Swaraj

Gandhi, like Tagore, rejects competition as an organizing principle for a society, even more emphatically. For Gandhi, 'civilisation is that mode of conduct which points out to man the path duty.' (Gandhi 1909: Ch.13) The basis then of his swaraj could not be just rights, it had to be duties as well. It had to be a person's rule over one's own self in this path of duty, before it could be the collective rule over one's country, swadesh. This was the foundation of his rajdharma. His 'idea of India' is bold and challenging, a utopian reference point to serve as a critique of contemporary society.

Gandhi's *Hind Swaraj* expresses his dream for India. First published in Gujarati in 1909, it was translated by him into English in 1910. It is a foundational text for any understanding of the man and his mission. To dismiss it as quaint and out-of-date is to misunderstand his message and overlook his contribution to our contemporary situation as well. However, a slavish interpretation of the text would simply amount to a kind of Gandhian fundamentalism that is neither creative nor constructive. This was 'a proclamation of ideological independence' (Dalton 1993:16) which he never compromised; his 'confession of the faith', (Nanda 1974: 66) which he never abandoned. In this 'rather incendiary manifesto', (Erikson 1969: 217) he proclaimed his revolution. No wonder the Gujarati edition was banned by the colonial government in 1910 for fear of sedition.

He incisively rejects Western civilization built on colonial imperialism, industrial capitalism, and rationalist materialism, and then presents his alternative for India: unity and diversity, both philosophical and religious; swaraj as rule over the self, both personal and social; swadeshi, as localism and neighbourliness; and finally satya and satyagraha with their imperative of ahimsa or non-violence. In rooting such themes in Indian culture, Gandhi is not just re-interpreting and re-appraising our cultural heritage, he is refreshingly relevant to our cascading contemporary crises, even as he poses a liberating challenge to a deeper self-realization and the achievement of a more humane and humanizing society.

He was very wary lest the freedom movement merely replace 'white sahibs' with 'brown' ones. He feared we might succeed in getting independence, (swantrata), from the British for political and other elites, and fail in achieving freedom, (swaraj), or rather purna swaraj (integral self-rule) for the people of India, especially for the last and least among them. In Gandhian terms this meant going the distance from swatantra to swaraj: 'freedom from', but more so 'freedom for', freely to fulfil one's duties not merely affirming of one's rights. Herein lay true freedom that finally led to moksha via ahimsa and the sevamarg. This was not just an economic-political agenda, but a socio-cultural one for a civilizational revolution.

Today we find his fears have proven all too prescient. In our present context of neo-colonialism, post-industrialism and post-modernism, these need to be re-appraised. Gandhi was visionary in the integrated manner in which he dealt with them. This adds up to a comprehensive perspective on Indic civilization as a contrast to that of the West and very distanced from the cultural nationalism being promoted today in our land.

Nehru's Discovery

Nehru sees India not in exclusive terms, but rather as a multicultural and pluri-religious civilization that was to be the defining basis for its national identity. Nehru traces this right back to the meeting between the Aryans and the Dravidians, and later between the settlers and the Iranians, Greeks, Parthians, Bactrians, Scythians, Huns, Turks (before Islam), early Christians, Jews (and) Zoroastrians. (Bhattacharjee 2015: 21) The basis of such a synthesis was Hinduism's 'astonishing inclusive capacity to absorb foreign races and cultures'. (Nehru 1985, 1st 1946: 73–74) To Nehru, Hinduism thus represents a culture more than a religion. In *The Discovery of India* he writes: '[T]here is a special heritage for us in India not an exclusive one, for none is exclusive and all are common to the race of man.' (Nehru 1985, 1st 1946: 36)

In the Enlightenment rationalist Nehru's 'discovery of India', the country was not bound by religious roots or defined by specific practices. Nehru distinguishes culture and history. For him 'the clash between different cultures was rather fictitious; the real thing was the historical opposition', and contrary to the anthropologists and the historians who postulate the multiplicity of cultures, Nehru affirmed the unity of thought and the universality of science, art and technology. In this universality, he saw the answer to the antagonism of the historical worlds. (Paz 1967: 14)

This is what makes it possible for a diversity of non-exclusive, non-antagonist cultures to be integral to a more expansive, inclusive civilization. This is not a static, conservative understanding of culture; but a dynamic one that allows space for multiple and fluid identities. For Nehru, the interaction of peoples is not confined within their religious traditions, it is a sharing of values and practices of their religious communities. In Nehru's *Discovery of India*, there is both 'continuous growth and often conflict'. (Nehru 1985 1st 1946: 118) The consequent interaction between these identities makes for a larger, inclusive, collective identity, that becomes the basis for a peoples' unity. It is this collective identity that Nehru discovers in our history and carries forward into the freedom movement to make it integral to the idea of India and its future progress:

> She was like some ancient palimpsest on which layer upon layer of thought and reverie had been inscribed, and yet no succeeding layer had completely hidden or erased what had been written previously. All of these existed in our conscious or subconscious selves, though we may not have been aware of them, and they had gone to build up the complex and mysterious personality of India. That sphinx-like face with its elusive and sometimes mocking smile. (Nehru 1985, 1st: 58)

For Nehru, then, collective identities are historical constructions, they are not primordial givens. It is not a matter of 'blut und boden', blood and land, or pritru bhumi and punya bhumi (father land and holy land). This historically contextualized understanding of a people's identity is the very opposite of those who would base such collective identity on ethnic origins or religious belonging or some atavistic throwback. As they have been constructed in the past, they can be deconstructed in the present and reconstructed for the future. But he would want us to preserve our rich and enduring legacy of a composite culture. This would be the basis of our shared identity and unity for the common good.

For Nehru, as our first prime minister, there were two most critical problems to be faced, as he communicated to Andre Malraux in an interview: 'Creating a just state by just means... Perhaps, too, creating a secular state in a religious country. Especially when its religion is not founded on an inspired book'. (Malraux 1968: 160)

For eighteen long years he laboured to do this, nurturing the 'idea of India' in the infant Indian Republic to create a modern, egalitarian state by democratic means and processes, one that was neutral to all religions (dhrama-nirapekshata) in an egalitarian and pluralist society. This was the core of the Nehruvian consensus. In the early formative years of the republic, in a country burdened with mass illiteracy and one that was tradition-bound, poverty-ridden, famine-stricken, this was an enormous challenge against cruelly skewed odds made all the worse by the legacy of Partition. No country has overcome such odds to successfully modernize without a greater rather than a lesser degree of authoritarian force. 'Will India survive?' or Balkanize, was a question that agitated many at the time.

The Constitution that promulgated our Republic, and called for a social transformation, was a leap of faith the Constituent Assembly made in the peoples of India. But a little more than half a century later that tryst with destiny is being challenged, by a supposedly shinning, rising 'new India', an India whose recent leaders are reneging on the constitutional commitment to 'a just state by just means' and 'secular state in a religious society'. The Nehruvian consensus is now broken and will need to be reconstructed to recapture and renew the India the freedom movement fought for so courageously and perseveringly.

Ambedkar's Republic

For Ambebkar, Buddhism originally defined India, but through the ages Buddhism was displaced by a Hinduism that became corrupted beyond redemption by Brahminism. He hoped his neo-Buddhist Navayana would restore the original Buddhist ideal and be the foundation of the newly constituted Republic of India. As he said at the Constituent Assembly on 25 November 1949:

> There was a time when India was studded with republics, and even where there were monarchies, they were either elected or limited. They were never absolute. It is not that India did not know Parliaments or Parliamentary Procedure. A study of the Buddhist Bhikshu Sanghas discloses that not only there were Parliaments—for the Sanghas were nothing but Parliaments—but the Sanghas knew and observed all the rules of Parliamentary Procedure known to modern times. (CAD 25 XI: pp. 336–337)

After Independence was won, the Constituent Assembly debates, over which Ambedkar presided, took two years to hammer out the compact expressed in the final document, 'The Constitution of India'. It represented the broad consensus of the movement led by the Indian National Congress. Despite differences and disagreements this was not a pragmatic political compromise lacking conviction and commitment but a compact based on mutual trust to allow for various underlying approaches and perspectives to be sorted out with sensitivity and understanding.

The Constituent Assembly left a fertile ground for conflict between the political compulsions of the governance and the constitutional propriety of the courts. This area of constitutional propriety and political demands for rights has increasingly become a tug-of-war between the legislature and the judiciary. Thus when a law was struck down it was placed in the 9th Schedule of the Constitution, where they were beyond judicial review. A thirteen-judge bench in 1967 placed fundamental rights in a 'transcendental position' beyond reach of Parliament. In 1973 the nine-judge bench of the Supreme Court restricted Parliament from making laws or constitutional amendments that violated or distorted the basic constitutional structure. In 2007 a five-judge bench ruled that anything in the Ninth Amendment violating the basic constitution would be subject to judicial review. There were 284 such laws in the Schedule in 2007.

And so the tussle goes on between the populist of politicians and the judicial propriety of the court. However, as Parliament must use the 9th Schedule in majoritarian or populist ways, so too must the Court consider the social context and reality before striking down a law or amendment. Or else both would be undemocratic.

Ambedkar, considered to be the father of the Constitution, was acutely aware of this. In his last speech at the closure of the Constituent Assembly on 25 November 1949 he warned:

> The working of a Constitution does not depend wholly upon the nature of the Constitution. The Constitution can provide only the organs of State such as the Legislature, the Executive and the Judiciary. The factors on which the working of those organs of the State depends are the people and the political parties they will set up as their instruments to carry out their wishes and their politics. (CAD 25 XI: 330)

However, the constitutional principles of liberty, equality and fraternity are not to be treated as separate items in a trinity. They form a tri-union in the sense that to divorce one from the other is to defeat the very purpose of democracy. Liberty cannot be divorced from equality, nor equality from liberty, and both must be held together by fraternity. Indeed, 'lived fraternity can redeem liberty and equality. What binds people together is what makes us free and society more just.' (Pabst 2019)

Moreover, not everything in civic and political life envisaged by the Constitution can be spelt out in statutary or legal terms. It requires a commitment to a constitutional ethic as the basis for a constitutional propriety in the pursuit of constitutional ideals and goals. This must be foundational for public discourse in which political and civic culture is forged. Populist mass mobilization for collective self-interest, as competitive politics often dictates, undermines this constitutional propriety by mobilizing extra-constitutional means. For Ambedkar such 'constitutional morality is not a natural sentiment. It has to be cultivated. We must realise that our people are yet to learn it. Democracy in India is only a top-dressing on an Indian soil, which is essentially undemocratic.' (CAD 1989: VII, 38)

Ambedkar's last speech to the Constituent Assembly, on 25 November, laid out three final cautions:

> If we wish to maintain democracy not merely in form, but also in fact, what must we do? The first...hold fast to constitutional methods of achieving our social and economic objectives....
>
> The second...observe the caution which John Stuart Mill has given...not 'to lay their liberties at the feet of even a great man, or to trust him with power which enable him to subvert their institutions.'
>
> The third...not to be content with mere political democracy....Political democracy cannot last unless there lies at the base of its social democracy. (CAD 1989: 336)

The governance of our ancient republics and Buddhist Sanghs had their rules and regulations with its ballot counting and censure motions. However, as Ambedkar warned, 'This democratic system India lost. Will she lose it a second time?...It is quite possible for this new born democracy to retain its form but give place to dictatorship in fact.' (Ambedkar 1989: 337)

We drastically compromised our democracy with the Emergency of 25 June 1975–21 March 1977. There is now is a real danger again and it is alarming. Some would characterize it as a continuing undeclared Emergency in slow motion. A single-party dominance with a single dominating leader. In fact elected dictatorial leaders are not uncommon anymore as Ambedkar so presciently had warned. Hopefully the Argumentative Indian, whom Amartya Sen foregrounds, (Sen 2005) will not allow such a repeat to betray the legacy we have inherited from our freedom struggle and the idea of India.

Bharat Resists India

The roots of the reactionary resistance to Western colonialism in India go back to the 19th-century 'renaissance' which began in Bengal and spread to the Presidencies of Bombay and Madras. At one level this had an 'Orientalist' agenda popularized by Max Muller (1823–1900) and others. In reaction to the colonizing West, it projected an idealized India, unsurpassed in its timeless genius and originality. Thus Swami Vivekananda preached a 'sanatan dharma' (eternal religion), whose universal spirituality surpassed all other religions. In 1903, Bal Gangadhar Tilak (1856–1920), describing the *Arctic Home in the Vedas*, promoted a Vedic civilization as the most ancient and advanced, a resource to regenerate a decaying West.

But besides this revivalist strand, there was another more critical rather than reactionary one, that also originated with this 'renaissance'. This was oriented to change rather than restoration, beginning with the reformists Ram Mohan Roy (1772–1833) in Calcutta and Justice Mahadev Govind Ranade (1842–1901) in Mumbai and becoming more radical with Mahatma Jyotirao Phule (1827–90) in Pune. In Chennai, E.V. Ramaswamy (1879–1973), the Thanthai Periyar's, (noble father) Self-Respect movement of the avarnas founded on Tamil identity was a total rejection of Brahminism.

The perspectives of Vivekananda and Tilak projected a nationalism that was more Hindu than Indian, with a definite inclination towards religious revivalism. Though somewhat subdued in the freedom struggle, it found an echo in the Hindu Right as it gained ground in the post-Nehruvian period. Today this finds effective political expression in the Bharatiya Janata Party (BJP), not to mention the Sangh Parivar, the extended family of numerous front organizations inspired and promoted by the RSS. Their ideology of Hindutva (Hinduness) claims to be a 'cultural nationalism' and seeks to establish a 'Hindu Rashtra'.

The second perspective found expression in the freedom struggle, dominated by the Indian National Congress and its leaders, especially Gandhi with his tolerance and pluralism, and Nehru's liberal secularism and democratic socialism, as enshrined in the Constitution after the Partition. These ideas are different from the ideology of the RSS and Hindutva. Now Hindu nationalists attack Gandhi and Nehru as pseudo-secularists who discriminated against Hindus and appeased Muslims. They privilege the Hindu majority, marginalizing other minorities and making them extremely insecure. Their coming to power at the Centre on an electoral wave in 2014, and in many states in the aftermath has intensified rather than moderated the majority-minority divide, precipitating violent communal conflicts all over the country. Their electoral sweep across the country in the 2019 Parliament elections will promote and consolidate their divisive and polarizing agenda for the country.

It was seen in the passing of the Citizenship (Amendment) Act (CAA), and the abrogation of Article 370, the Bhima-Koregaon incident of 2018 and the arrests of civil rights activists in its aftermath, the North Delhi pogrom of February 2020, the numerous booking of dissenters on trumped up charges, and more. Such polarization may win elections with the majority Hindu vote, but such majoritarianism does not make for decent and just society. Sooner rather later the violence will turn against its own. The Hindutava violence is like all violence, as Hanah Ardent says: 'The practice of violence, like all action, changes the world, but the most probable change is to a more violent world.' (1970: 80)

Briefly then, the difference between these two perspectives can be succinctly described thus:

> There are Indians...who do not fear difference. Who seek peaceful relations with people from other religions and ways of life, and who see democratic institutions as strong enough to provide the groundwork for a future of mutual respect. There are also Indians,...who fear religious and ethnic differences as a deep threat to order and safety, who have learned to hate people who insist on living in a way that sets them off from the majority, and whose anxious desire to control leads them to legitimise violence. These two types of democratic citizens can be found in many if not most modern nations. (Nussbaum 2007: 78)

Our formal education and informal socialization process have failed to cultivate in such persons the capacity for tolerance and empathy, and the curiosity and courage to welcome the strangers and explore their inner world. Rather by default at first, and increasingly now by deliberate fault, there is a surrender to the inner demons of anxious fears and oppressive domination, preferring the comfort of a tired, familiar old world to the challenge of uncertain brave new ones. This is our tragic failure: to transmit our rich Indic inheritance of bewildering complexity and diversity, and compromise it for personal gain, and private profit at the cost of our common good, negating and alienating our constitutional patriotism.

Revivalism and Transformation

There was an inherent ideological tension in the freedom struggle between these two visions: an idealized ancient past prioritizing religious and cultural revival, and a dream of an enabling new future centred on social transformation and concern for Gandhi's last and least Indian. The dominant Nehruvian consensus of the early Independence era was premised on the second, but it never could quite contain or defuse the lure of the first.

In the subcontinent, Muslim religious nationalism has painted itself into a corner. Mohammed Ali Jinnah, the Qaid-e-Azam (The Great Leader) and founding father of Pakistan, was more pragmatically concerned with the secular interests of Muslims than theologically involved with the religious practices of Islam. Addressing the Pakistan Constituent Assembly meeting for the first time on 11 August 1947, Jinnah dreamed of the time, when, 'Hindus would cease to be Hindus and Muslims would cease to be Muslims, not in the religious sense, because that is a matter of the personal faith of each individual, but in the political sense as citizens of the State'. (Jinnah 1948: 10)

Now the dream lies shattered in the religious terrorism that is holding Pakistan to ransom, while its military legitimizes itself as the only effective force restraining the terrorists (as President Musharraf credibly claimed once), though they had earlier encouraged them (as

President Zia-ul-Haq did). Bangladesh, having debunked the two-nation theory for a three-nation one, is still struggling to establish credible, stable secular credentials. There are many distinctly different Muslim communities in the subcontinent and religion is not always the most unifying factor among them. Indeed, it is pan-Islamism rather than Muslim nationalism in the subcontinent that is now the more pressing threat in South Asia. However, today the most threatening challenge to our constitutional compact on 'creating a secular State in a religious country' (Malraux 1968) is from Hindu nationalism pushing for Hindu Rashtra to replace the Indian Republic. Nehru had anticipated this in his interview with Andre Malraux, but secular rationalists never took this seriously and now it has overtaken them.

The first to propound the two-nation theory even before Jinnah did in 1941 was V.D. Savarkar in his presidential address to the Hindu Mahasabha in Ahmedabad in 1937, when he said: 'There are two antagonistic nations living side by side in India.' (Savarkar 1971: 24) But it found no real echo among Hindus then, for they were mostly with the Indian National Congress. Savarkar's Hindu nationalism is not particularly religious. He was himself a rationalist atheist, who wanted his body cremated after his death without any religious ceremonies. Yet he was fanatical about Hindutva or Hinduness, which he first formulated in 1923, and deliberately set in opposition to other religious traditions not originating in India, such as Islam and Christianity. Though this founding father of Hindu nationalism was not particularly religious; he was decidedly ethno-political.

Savarkar's early projection of Hindu-Muslim unity with his *War of Independence of 1857*, published in 1909, was completely reversed during his transportation to the Andamans from 1911–21. His Hindutva was articulated as an ideological nationalism and it embraced culture and race (Savarkar 1989). It was designed to unify and mobilize the inegalitarian classes and hierarchical castes among Hindus under a communal banner. In 1941, his birthday wish was expressed in the slogan: 'Hinduise all politics and militarise all Hindudom'. (cited McKean 1996: 71)

Hinduism refers to a religious faith tradition that is far easier to describe than define. With Savarkar there is an emphatic distinction between Hinduism as a religious system and Hindutva as a political ideology. 'What is Hinduism?' and 'Who is a Hindu?' are questions better answered in inclusive rather than exclusive terms in regard to both culture and religion. Savarkar politicizes these questions, answering them in terms of a nativist, sacred geography to make the answers exclusionary.

Thus for him, 'Hinduism must necessarily mean the religion and the religions that are peculiar and native to this land and people'. (Savarkar 1989: 104) He defined Hindu in terms of 'the three essentials of nation (Rashtra), race (Jati) and civilization (Sanskriti)'. (Savarkar 1989: 101) The first important qualification of a Hindu is that 'the whole continental country from the Sindhu to Sindhu, from the Indus to the Seas', (Savarkar 1989: 82) 'is not only a Pitribhu but a Punyabhu, not only a fatherland but a holyland'. (Savarkar 1989: 111) He spelt this out in his presidential speech to the Hindu Mahasabha at Nagpur in 1938, 'India must be a land reserved for the Hindus.' (Savarkar 1949: 63-64) Others are here on sufferance as lesser citizens. He drew his inspiration from Giuseppe Mazzini (1805–72) and Benito Mussolini's (1885–1945) National Fascist Party. Savarkar is the first and principal ideologue of this extreme Hindu nationalism. The RSS, which he never joined, espoused his ideology.

Dr K.B. Hedgewar (1889–1940) founded the Rashtriya Swayamsevak Sangh in 1925. M.S. Golwalkar (1906–73), its long-time Sarsanghchalak (supremo), from 1940 till his death in 1973, is considered the second founder. He drew on Savarkar but repeated rather than advanced his argument. *We or Our Nationhood Defined* (1939) was the first systematic statement of RSS ideology. Golwalkar (Guruji) later revealed that his booklet was an abridgement of an earlier work on nationalism, *Rashtra Mimansa*, a critical reflection on the 'nation', by Ganesh Damodar (Babarao) Savarkar (1879–1945), first published in Marathi in 1934. Later *A Bunch of Thoughts*, a collection put together first in 1966 and now in its third edition, was intended 'to clarify and understand the true purpose, the exact nature, the ambit and scope of the RSS work…and its activities'. (cited Noorani 2001: 18-21)

In 1978 both were endorsed by the Sarsanghchalak Ragendra Singh.

However, on 9 March 2006, the *Times of India* reported:

> In a major ideological shift, RSS has for the first time officially disowned M S Golwalkar's book *We or Our Nationhood Defined* published in 1939 as 'neither representing the views of the grown Guruji nor of the RSS'....
>
> Former RSS spokesperson M G Vaidya while approving the removal of *We* from the Sangh's pantheon of texts, says the book that is central to 'us is Golwalkar's Bunch of Thoughts since it consists of his views after he became sarsanghchalak on June 21, 1940.'

The textual expressions in the brochures are extremist and awkward, but the substance still continues to be reflected in the praxis of the RSS even today.

Hindutva overlapped and was conflated with Hinduism in the popular projection. Justice J.S. Verma in his remarks in a Supreme Court judgement in 1995 concerning the political use of religion opined an explicit equivalence between the two: Hindutva is nothing but Hinduism. This has been much quoted by the Sangh Parivar to legitimize its intolerant and aggressive ideology. Later, however, shocked by the horror of the Gujarat pogrom in February–March 2001, Justice Verma claimed he had been misunderstood on this account. (*The Indian Express* 3 Jan 2017. A bit too little, and rather too late. Two decades later the same court declined to address a petition to clarify the difference. (*The Hindu* 25 Oct 2016, http://www.thehindu.com/news/national/SC-declines-to-go-into-Hindutva-verdict/article16081556.ece)

Hindutva was for a while projected as Bharatiyata, Indianness, to make it more acceptable beyond the Parivar, an equivalence that Savarkar himself had rejected: 'the term Hindutva cannot be synonymous with Bharatiya or Hindi and mean Indian only.' (Savarkar 1989: 84) The change in name proposed is merely to make it more acceptable to the unsuspecting. Ultimately, as an ideology of religious nationalism, the basic content, the first premises and final conclusions of Hindutva remain the same.

Then in 2006 when the BJP was out of power, the RSS booklet *Shri Guruji and Indian Muslims* (Sinha 2006) was claiming neither the *Rashtra Mimansa* nor *We or Our Nationhood* represented the views of Guruji or the RSS. From 2007, the focus was on 'cultural nationalism'. (Vyas, *Hindu* 1 Apr, 2007) Now with the saffron brigade returning to state power with a bang in 2014 and again in 2019, it is back to basics once more: Hindu Rashtra and Hindutva, openly embraced and promoted.

From its very origins, the project of Hindu nationalism has been to mobilize Hindus into a politicized ethnic group and to construct this into a dominant majority. Non-Hindus would become subordinate minorities or sub-nationalisms, provided they present no threat to the Hindu majority. The apprehensions regarding the CAA is not only about its compatibility with the basic structure of the constitutional propriety but that it will further divide the populace into a more dominant majority and only accept only minorities as second citizens, or non-citizens.

Moreover, the way it implicitly equates 'Hindu' and 'India' is far from being the most significant interpretation, or the most dominant expression of Hindu culture and religious traditions in its long and rich history. Hindutva's preoccupation is to project the pre-eminence of Hinduism as indigenous to the land from Vedic times and even earlier from the dawn of history, as the march of a single people, with its singular culture, in a sacred land.

The waves of migrations from Vedic times and earlier that came and settled, and over centuries, integrated with its people and assimilated by the land, and the consequent diversity in unity are still established in mainstream history. The Hindutva ideologues are trying rather desperately to construct their own narrative to serve their purposes of a glorious unitary Hindu pre-eminence. The Islamic millennium on the Indian subcontinent is simply dismissed as an aberration, a thousand years of brutal oppression, due to the weakness of decadent Hindus at the time. However, the British colonialists were not considered a serious obstacle. The RSS did not participate in the freedom movement though now they seem to be inventing their involvement in it.

Religious nationalisms thrive on religious homogeneity: one

creed, one code, one cult. They then attempt to translate this into a political hegemony: one ideology, one party, one nation. But the inherent diversity among Hindus, of caste and tribe, of language and region, of gods and sages, of scriptures and sects, has proven extremely resilient to any externally imposed uniformity. However, the endemic hierarchies of caste and insoluble inequalities of class need serious commitment to affirmative action for the last and the least, which still not forthcoming.

Indeed, India is far too complex for any imposed uniformity. Even among the reformists there was a diversity from conservative to revivalist. The India of Ram Mohan Roy (1772–1833), who founded the Brahmo Samaj in 1828, was reformist and did not privilege any particular scripture. The Tagore family were prominent members of this Samaj. So was Swami Vivekananda's (1863–1902) Ramakrishna Mission, as was the Theosophical Society. However, there were other players who were more revivalist and focused on the past. Maharishi Dayananda Saraswati's (1824–83) Arya Samaj, established in 1875, wanted to bring back a Vedic Hinduism. The Hindu Mahasabha founded by Madan Mohan Malaviya (1861–1946) in 1915 to protect Hindu rights was politically conservative.

Envisioning Our Future

We are faced with two possible futures. The first is the India that the freedom movement articulated with Tagore, Gandhi, Nehru and Ambedkar, a social transformation now embedded in the Constitution that we gave ourselves with the founding of our Republic. The second is the new India as a Hindu state premised on V.D. Savarkar's Hindutva, which has used political clout to seize centre stage today. The Indian National Congress (INC) as the principal protagonist of, and successor to, the freedom movement espoused the first; RSS, which did not participate in the movement, is committed to the second. The irony of the Sanghis now claiming to be the most emphatically committed nationalists is startling.

The idea of India from the freedom movement is defined in the Preamble to our Constitution as a Sovereign, Democratic,

Secular, Socialist Republic. It is an expansive and inclusive, diverse and complex, a multicultural, pluri-religious nation-state in the making. We have many imagined communities in a single constructed polity; a multi-nation state, very different and far more complex and problematic than even the European Union. Its liberalism struggles to be democratic; its secularism to be neutral, but respectful to all religious traditions and privilege no single one, but keep a 'principled distance' from all; (Bhargava 2013) its socialism would be Fabian with an especial concern for Gandhi's last and least Indian. This was in deliberate contrapuntal distinction from Pakistan as an Islamic state for Muslims of the subcontinent. It was a daring wager for a people abysmally poor and hugely illiterate.

However, the drift of the Congress began after Nehru with the corruption of the party and its government. The Nehruvian years were an enormous struggle to deliver on its reformist agenda, against the growing resistance of conservative lobbies within and outside the party. When the agenda was challenged and faltered, Indira Gandhi's response was to personalize party leadership, building a mass following that dispensed with party cadre on the ground and regional satraps in the states. She centralized state power in the PMO in the early 1970s and controlled the government with loyal henchmen.

Once the Cabinet Secretariat was marginalized by the PMO, it opened the way for authoritarian prime ministers to dominate the Government and the party, while weak ones used it to protect themselves from the Opposition. Unelected bureaucrats answerable only to the prime minister seemed to be running the country with a shadow cabinet, even making it possible for extra-constitutional authorities to dictate the agenda, like Sanjay Gandhi, prime minister Indira Gandhi's son and heir-apparent at the time.

When her position was threatened by an adverse High Court judgement, she declared a National Emergency in 1975, suspended fundamental rights and ruled with an authoritarian iron fist. The consequent sycophancy was best echoed by the Congress Party president at the AICC (All India Congress Committee) meeting in Guwahati in 1976 and cheered by the rest: 'India is Indira and

Indira is India'. Indira Gandhi's silence on this could only mean consent.

This seemed to presage the demise of Indian democracy. Other South Asian nations had already compromised their fledgling democracies even earlier. India no longer looked the exception. However, the lifting of the Emergency in 1977, brought a stunning rejection at the polls and the collapse of her Congress Party. With Indira Gandhi herself losing her election, a new future seemed to have dawned. But with the failure of other stop-gap political adjustments and the paralysis of governance, she bounced back in 1980 with the slogan, 'A government that works'. But now a fractured polity marked the end of single-party rule from Delhi as the political norm. The brief exception of 1984–89 was when a sympathy wave after her assassination swept the Congress back to power with 414 seats out of 515, more than three fourths majority, in the 8th Lok Sabha.

After a succession of coalition governments the Congress was back in power in Delhi as a minority government in 1998 which completed its full term before going into the Opposition once again. It was then back again for two terms between 2004 and 2014 to lead the United Progressive Alliance (UPA) for two successful terms. It then collapsed under its own weight under attack for corruption by a virulent Opposition, supported by a hyped-up media and corporates who owned these media corporations.

In the general election in 2014 out of a house of 543 seats, the National Democratic Alliance (NDA) coalition won 336 seats, an almost two-thirds majority. The BJP made a quantum leap over the threshold of coalition politics, winning 282 seats a clear majority on its own, within their coalition. The United Progressive Alliance (UPA) won just 60 with its allies of which the Congress won 44 seats, the lowest number it had ever won in Parliament. Since then it has been progressively losing power in the states it ruled. Congress no longer seems to be the natural party of governance it once was. Now it is struggling to make a comeback.

The vacuum created by the progressive self-destruction of the Congress Party has been filled in different ways in different parts of the country, though invariably by parties that have depended on the mobilization of the 'lower castes'. (Corbridge and Harris 2000: 137) These parties lacked a cohesive and coherent national agenda and with the Congress Party in retreat, the BJP with its Sangh Parivar has become the dominant party at the Centre and in most states. A disunited squabbling opposition was unable to resist it. Only a convincing new alternative narrative, with a positive agenda will be able to measure up to this.

Ethno-nationalist State

The alternative future now staring us in the face is envisioned as a Hindu Rashtra which draws its inspiration from Savarkar's *Hindutva: Who Is a Hindu?* (Savarkar 1989, 1st 1923) This is an exclusivist and aggressive ethno-nationalism. M.S. Golwalkar takes Savarkar's ethno-nationalism to dangerously new levels with his admiration of Hitler's ruthless quest for racial purity and his 'Final Solution' of genocide of the Jews in Germany. He was inspired by Hitler's anti-sematic racial purity (Jaffrelot 1996: 57). Golwalkar's praise of the Nazi's racism is unambiguous and ominous. In 1938 he wrote:

> To keep up the purity of the Race and its culture, Germany shocked the world by her purging the country of the Semitic races—the Jews. Race pride at its highest has been manifested here. Germany has also shown how well-nigh impossible it is for Races and cultures, having differences going to the root, to be assimilated into one united whole, a good lesson for us in Hindustan to learn and profit by. (Golwalkar *We or Our Nationhood Defined* 1939: 43)

There is also Koenraad Elst's, the intrepid polemicist for the Sangh Parivar, two-volume *The Saffron Swastika: The Notion of Hindu Fascism* (2001), which he describes in his blogs as 'the only book in the world to analyse this much-used line of discourse (except for my sequel from 2006, *Return of the Swastika*), both by foreign India-watchers and by the Indian secularists'. (http://koenraadelst.blogspot.com/2014/02/what-have-i-done-2.html) It has been much appreciated by RSS pracharks, like L.K. Advani, and sundry Sanghis, but scholarly reviews are hard to find. Deen Dayal Upadhyaya is now the saffron flavour being promoted officially, not the old stalwart ideologues, Savarkar and Golwalkar, whose virulent aggression against the other non-Hindu Indians plays well mostly among the faithful but not beyond.

Others, however, are more than just sceptical. On the assassination of Gandhi, Sardar Vallabhai Patel wrote in a letter to Shyama Prasad Mukherjee, dated 18 July 1948: 'As regards the RSS and the Hindu Mahasabha…our reports do confirm that, as a result of the activities of these two bodies, particularly the former (RSS) an atmosphere was created in the country in which such a ghastly tragedy became possible'. (Das 1973: 281)

Indeed, the aggressiveness of the Hindutvawadis (followers of Hindutva) of the majority community is the obverse of the militant Islamists in Pakistan, though any suggestion of a Hindu Pakistan is violently countered. Perhaps it cuts too close to the bone. Such communal polarization is always more to the advantage of the leaders, who use it to mobilize their communities and consolidate their hold over them; it is less beneficial to their followers, who are used as foot soldiers in communal battles, all at the cost of the larger common good of all.

For such aggression escalates into a politics of hate and violence, which in times of crisis become the ultimate resort of desperate and frustrated peoples, and easily can spin out of control. The assassination of the Father of the Nation in the chaos of Partition was inspired by the Hindutva politics of hate, disguised by faux nationalism. Though Nathuram Godse, the assassin, was not a member of the RSS at the time, he was a faithful follower of Savarkar. The RSS was banned in 1947 after that, and many of its leaders were jailed. The ban was lifted in 1948, after a commitment to be a cultural not a political organization and keep a membership register.

Regardless of this, it later sponsored and mentored a political wing, the Jana Sangh (People's Organisation) 1951–77, which was pilloried as a 'shetji-bhatji', a bhramin-bania party. However, after the confusion of unstable coalitions following the lifting of the Emergency, it merged into the Janta Party (People's Party). When the coalition splintered, it emerged in a new avatar as the Bharatiya Janata Party (BJP, Indian People's Party), together with a family of associated organizations, the Sangh's Parivar, which now has a large footprint in the country.

The BJP had had very brief stints in power with its National Democratic Alliance: for sixteen days in 1996 and again twenty-four days in 1998 and then a full term in 1999–2004. However, the people were not buying into its saffron agenda. After the Gujarat pogrom, its 'Shining India' was rejected by the people for the United Progressive Alliance in 2004 for two successive terms. But in 2014, it campaigned very successfully on a 'vikas' (development) manifesto which corporate business supported in a big way with the media they owned. The opposition was quite convincingly trounced. Firmly in the saddle now the saffron slip has begun to show, appointing RSS cadre and Sangh Parivar loyalists to key positions in government and important public institutions, whether in education and research, science and the humanities, thus saffronizing the public domain and civil society. Their landslide re-election in 2019 can only promise more of the same.

Indic Civilization

The violence initiated by colonial powers, suggests a clash of barbarisms rather than anything even remotely civilized. The events of 1857 on this subcontinent, the great revolt and its suppression, were witness to such barbaric violence. Moreover, the wounded memories and unresolved grievances from a long gone colonial and pre-colonial past are all too often deliberately kept alive by vengeful zealots, nursing injured collective egos. These self-selected traumas, self-righteously legitimize brutal horrors in the name of 'my people', to whom loyalty is expressed in revenge.

Hinduism may be a latecomer to these aberrations, but now Hindutva's religious nationalism is driving a politics and culture of hate in the name of wounded Hindu pride. The endeavour to erase a millennium of Muslim presence in India appeals to the same distorted logic of incompatible and hostile worldviews. This madness without method can only mean ethnic cleansing and eventually even lead to genocide.

Even after the founding of Pakistan, Jinnah was committed to a more inclusive secular rather than an Islamist sectarian state. According to Hamsa Alavi, Islamic fundamentalism was a late arrival. (Alavi 2002) The Islamization of Pakistan was used first to contain Bengali nationalism in what was then East Pakistan. This failed and the country was divided. Later, more cynically, Islamization served General Zia-ul-Haq, who controlled the country from 1977 until his assassination in 1988, to shore up the feudal class and the military establishment.

However, this has not meant any greater cohesion for that society, only an endless, proliferation of various extremist groups. The ethnic diversity among Muslims there and the religious differences within Islam itself have not been homogenized. With increasing frequency, it explodes in collective violence, threatening the continuing stability of that country. It is not the non-sectarian magnanimity of Akbar but religious prejudice of Aurangzeb that the country is modelling itself on. Surely this is an aberration from an expansive and inclusive Indic civilization. Transnational Islamism inculturates an Arabization that alienates subcontinental Muslims from their native cultures even more. The increasing use of burqa and the hijab, the growing of beards, replacing the regional mother tongue with Urdu, all this and more are but little indicators of the spread of a new conservatism and orthodoxy, generously patronized by Wahabi Muslims of Saudi Arabia.

All the world's major religious traditions have been able to find a place in Indic civilization with their cultures and languages making Indic civilization diversely and inclusively multicultural and pluri-religious. It was the amazing capaciousness of Hinduism that made this possible. However, the 'divide and rule' of colonialism wedged a division between the two major religious communities of the subcontinent which we failed to contain. The 'discontents of modernity' precipitated a revivalist reaction; our faltering development was further politicized by a corrosive identity politics and chauvinist leaders who leveraged polarized communities for their own advantage and the detriment of the common good of our peoples.

Such inflexible and intolerant projections of cultural and religious identities do not enrich civilizations or make for diversity and unity. Rather it polarizes communities into an antagonistic 'them' versus 'us'. This only furthers conflict and extremism. Certainly we do not want communal violence and religious fanaticism to polarize us to a point where pogroms for a 'final solution' spill over into genocide.

Millennia ago in the 4th century BC to counter this danger in his vast multi-diverse empire, he placed Emperor Ashoka (265–232 BCE) placed his rock edits all over his empire with messages of secular tolerance. His seventh edict reads:

> Beloved-of-the-Gods, King Piyadasi, desires that all religions should reside everywhere, for all of them desire self-control and purity of heart. But people have rious desires and various passions, and they may practice all of what they should or only a part of it. But one who 2 great gifts yet is lacking in self-control, purity of heart, gratitude and firm devotion, such a person is mean. (tran Mark 2020: https://www.ancient.eu/Edicts_of_Ashoka/)

Are we careering into a 'clash of civilizations' on this subcontinent, similar to what Samuel Huntington (1998) was predicating for the 'West versus the rest'? Will this subcontinent, or rather Indic civilization as we know it, survive this violence or will it lead to further partitioning of the subcontinent and its Balkanization?

The Clash of Civilizations by Samuel Huntington (1996) popularized a contemporary reading of history that played to old prejudices of the West and nurtured fears of the Muslim world. Rather than the clash *between* civilizations, today, 'a clash is *within* virtually all modern nations—between people who are prepared to live with others who are different, on terms of equal respect, and those [who] seek the protection of homogeneity, achieved through the domination of a single religion and ethnic tradition.' (Nussbaum 2007: ix)

Twenty centuries ago, Emperor Ashoka's Edict XIII had set a high standard, and is worth quoting in full:

> Growth in essentials can be done in different ways, but all of them have as their root restraint in speech, that is, not praising one's own religion, or condemning the religion of others without good cause. And if there is cause for criticism, it should be done in a mild way. But it is better to honor other religions for this reason. By so doing, one's own religion benefits and so do other religions, while doing otherwise harms one's own religion and the religions of others. Whoever praises his own religion, due to excessive devotion, and condemns others with the thought 'Let me glorify my own religion', only harms his own religion…One should listen to and respect the doctrines professed by others.

The edict concludes with the admonition that an individual's religion grows through Dhamma and so all faiths are improved by tolerance and understanding. (tran Mark 2020: https://www.ancient.eu/Edicts_of_Ashoka/)

Ashoka's own empire may not have lasted very long. Like Gandhi he was too large a moral overdraft on his people. However, he remained the dominant religious force on the subcontinent for thousand years. His reign was the very opposite of Hindu Rashtra, as promoted today.

The uniqueness of Indic civilization was its capacity to accommodate difference with respect and tolerance. This is now in danger of being compromised or worse, brought down. For, once a civilization becomes self-referential and fails to reach out to and be enriched by the 'other' there will inevitably be a closing of the mind and hardening of hearts. Polarization of differences is the road to its decline and fall, and we seem to be on it; unless it is reversed before we cross the point of no return reconciling difference, there is strong potential for even more collective violence in India in the future.

CHAPTER THREE

RELIGIONIZING VIOLENCE

Revisioning Our Future – Demonic Deities, Violent Ideologies – Religionizing Terror – Charism and Institution – Faith and Ideology – Evolution of Hindu Traditions – From Hinduism to Hindutva – Tolerant Hinduism, Intolerant Hindus – *Dar al-Harb* and *Dar al-Islam* – Pan-Islamic Diversity – Indic Islam – Ganga-Yamuna Tehzeeb – Religious Buddhism – Ambedkar's Navayana – Buddhist Nationalism – Christian Origins – Colonial Distortions – Long Trajectory – Myth of Religious Violence

Revisioning Our Future

With the colonial policies of divide-and-rule, particularly after the Great Revolt of 1857, a slow but sure polarization began between the two major religious communities: Hindus and Muslims. This peaked with the two-nation theory propounded by ideologues like Savarkar and Jinnah. The Partition eventually divided India and created two independent states, which finally marked the point of no return. More than seventy years after the calamity neither side has come to terms with it. Faulting one side or the other or recriminations against some leaders rather than others serves little constructive purpose anymore. Rather we all must pick up the pieces, healing our wounded memories, and jettisoning the baggage of our simmering resentment and anger and move forward. What we now desperately need is a committed pluralism and tolerance for a reconciliation and healing.

In the Indian subcontinent, the national freedom struggle

could not bypass the religious question and its politicization. Gandhiji never countenanced the two-nation theory. He appealed to an inclusive Indian nationalism, and then he was careful to eschew any tilt to a nationalist chauvinism. He never appealed to religious or Hindu nationalism, though he publicly professed to be a devoutly religious and committed sanatani Hindu. For Savarkar, nationalism was ethnic rather than religious. His Hindu Rashtra would accept non-Hindu minorities as second-class citizens, subservient and submissive. Jinnah's appeal to Muslim nationalism was separatist, though he was not an observant Muslim himself. His Pakistan, the land of the pure, was to be a homeland for all subcontinental Muslims.

Today in India, communal polarization has rapidly escalated, mobilized by chauvinistic leaders who so far have reaped rich political dividends. In Pakistan an Islamist state has spawned violent religious extremists—'non-state actors'—beyond state control. In India we are still replaying the trauma of the Partition. The politicizing of religion and the religionizing of politics is a fated marriage whose children devour their parents. All through history, religious wars have been fought in the name of God and country, even internecine ones by believers belonging to the same religious tradition. Absolutizing one or the other becomes a pact with the devil. Externalizing the enemy as the 'other' makes for a convenient scapegoat, but eventually the violence will be internalized and turn on the original perpetrators.

What is perpetrated on the other eventually turns on the self, as one's *Intimate Enemy*. (Nandy 1983) In popular wisdom: 'What goes around comes around'. For in Ashis Nandy's words: 'the ancient wisdom implied in the New Testament and also perhaps in the Sauptik Parva of the Mahabharata: "Do not do unto others what you would that they do not unto you, lest you do into yourself what you do unto others"'. (Nandy, 1983: 31)

Meeting in the long dark shadow of the barbaric violence that followed in the wake of the Partition, the Constituent Assembly of India affirmed the secular understanding of the state in spite of some inevitable compromises that had to be made, as with colonial personal law. The Constitution it promulgated set an agenda for radical and lasting social transformation. The Preamble of the Constitution on 26 November 1949 articulated this compact, 'We the People' gave ourselves at the founding of our 'sovereign, socialist, secular, democratic Republic…to secure for all its citizens: justice, liberty, equality and to promote among them all, fraternity'.

The 42nd Constitutional amendment in 1976 added the words 'socialist' and 'secular' to the definition of the republic to make explicit what was implicit in the text, but neither was further defined. This is now part of the fundamental structure of the Constitution that cannot be abrogated, even by Parliament. We would need another Constituent Assembly to rewrite this. The intention of the amendment was to stymie the Hindu Right that had begun to mobilize ominously by then. When it did come to power in the late 1990s, it even called for a review of the Constitution, and still does so ever more stridently today, when it has a decisively overwhelming Parliamentary majority.

The same amendment listed the fundamental duties of citizens in Article 51A, Section IV A of the Directive Principles. As fundamental rights are the protection the state is bound to provide for its citizens, fundamental duties express the moral obligation of the citizen to their polity, their constitutional dharma. Fundamental rights are justiciable, fundamental duties are not, rather they describe an ideal citizen. However, in Indic civilization duties as dharma have a priority over rights as 'haq' or 'adhikar'.

In our Constitution the 'idea of India' as a unity-in-diversity is embedded in a sovereign, democratic, socialist, secular Republic. Thus, the cultural-religious dimension of pluralism and tolerance of Indic civilization is integrated into the political-economic one of rights and liberties in our Constitution. In rediscovering our history, then, it is imperative that we revision our future: for both, our Republic and our fellow citizens. This must be our constitutional dharma.

Demonic Deities, Violent Ideologies

Most post-Enlightenment secular rationalists perceive religion as contrary to reason and prone to extremes of irrationalism and violence, and the fatal cause of most wars. In their view, a radical secularization would bring a more peaceful and progressive world. Modern science and technology will show the way. In such secular wisdom, religion is oppressive and escapist; it is all about revenge, expiation and other forms of bloodletting and reason must debunk it. And more dangerously, it is religion's emotive appeal that lends itself to violence. Most violent conflicts and wars are blamed on religion. However, *The Encyclopedia of Wars* (Phillips and Axelrod 2004) lists 1,763 major conflicts in recorded history, and only 123 of them were fought over religious differences. The secular violence of divisive and totalitarian ideologies and institutions are rationalized away.

In *The Myth of Religious Violence: Secular Ideology and the Roots of Modern* Conflict, William Cavanaugh demonstrates how secular ideologies, particularly nationalist ones, 'can be just as absolutist, divisive, and irrationally fanatical as certain types of Jewish, Christian, Muslim, Hindu militancy....The real question is, what good is actually being worshipped.' (Cavanaugh 2009: 55) When a religious tradition is woven into the very fabric of a society as an integral part of its way of life, as in all premodern societies, then the religious may be distinguished from but not isolated from the secular. In fact, 'religion as separate from culture and politics, is an invention of the West'. (Cantwell Smith 1964: 18-19) Western modernity privileges the person over and above the community. And religion is conceptualized as a set of individualized beliefs and practices. Thus, making it a separate and separable activity of the individual.

However, 'the idea of religion as a personal and systematic pursuit was entirely absent from classical Greece, Japan, Egypt, Mesopotamia, Iran, China and India'. (Armstrong 2014: 2) In these societies, with a very few exceptions, religion, culture, politics and economics remain intertwined, mutually constitutive, inseparable in fact, if not in theory. The community was always primary not the person. 'Pre-modern faith had emphasised the sacredness of the community—the Sangha, the ummah, the Body of Christ.' (Armstrong 2014: 221) Religion was a way of life integrated into society, giving meaning and purpose to its people. If separated from society, secular ideologies substitute for it, and like all ideologies, these too are subject to the same dysfunctions. Both the sacred and the secular must be contextualized and historicized.

The grand narratives of Enlightenment were ideologically founded on a faith in science as the engine of progress on the way to the promised land of prosperity and peace, where reason not religion would rule. But along the way secular ideologies turned out to be as, if not more, violent than religious theologies. Religious wars were horrific. The war gods these honour are not serenely divine; they are cruel demonic deities, some even explicitly worshipped as fierce gods of war. These must be demythologized as the projection of our own repressed fears and anxieties of the 'other', perceived as different and threatening. But the secular ideological wars too have left *Fields of Blood* (Armstrong 2014) no less. Racism and eugenics, colonialism and imperialism, fascism and Nazism, Stalinism and Maoism have left a bloody brutal trail in their wake. Their horrors haunt us still. They must be demystified as the the illegitimate spawn of the Enlightenment and its failed promise of peace and prosperity. These were not religious but explicitly secular ideologies and even hostile to religion at that.

When religion and society are intimately entwined, then all collective violence in society is taken to be religious. Even today the very posing of the question—which is to blame, religion or the nation state?—misses the fundamental reality of our modern situation. Often religious extremism is a defensive reaction to an aggressive secularization. The brutal and repressive regime of the Shah of Iran was proactively secular but its violent suppression of any dissent provoked the extremist reaction that finally brought his downfall. The discontents of a failing modernization could lead to a blowback with religious nationalists seizing control, as is happening in contemporary India. Scapegoating religion and rationalizing the violence of authoritarianism and anomalies of secular states, only further compounds the situation and merely postpones the crisis.

But a careful deconstruction will uncover more than what meets the eye. If these demonic deities are not exorcised, they will surely devour their devotees. In secularized societies, violent ideologies must be contextualized and the root causes that give rise to and facilitate them must be addressed. Else the rot will fester and infect the whole body politic. The greatest danger is when religious extremism finds political expression or when political violence is given religious sanction. When a religious establishment supports the state, it will expect support from the state in return, and the limits to this will be set by the politics of the state not the ethics of the religious tradition. This is already happening with religious nationalism in its nation-building quest, as also with politicized religion and its politics of hate.

Underpinning both is an ethnocentrism, which privileges one's own and rejects the 'other'; which uses violence to polarize and mobilize people, and religion to legitimize and rationalize violence. It is crucial to realize that such exclusiveness and intolerance has religious as well as secular roots. The people of God are a chosen people from among the nations, yet there is a hierarchy among them. National boundaries are not open, migrants are not welcomed, and even within its borders citizens are unequal in status and dignity. Such self-prioritizing will necessarily cause conflict with those perceived as the 'other' and this will eventually spill over into violence unless coping mechanisms are found.

In *Old Societies and New States: The Quest for Modernity in Asia and Africa*, the author argues that the two continents are prone to collective violence and scapegoating the weak and vulnerable. This is exemplified in South Asia. The electoral democracies in South Asia have not met the rising expectations of their peoples, and the discontents rising from a skewed development have escalated. In modern Asia, a traditionally pacific religious tradition can provide the supporting inspiration for violent nationalism, which is rationalized as self-defence against hapless victims. A wounded history is constructed and imagined fears of the same in the future are activated. As Samuel John perceptively opined: 'Patriotism is the last refuge of the scoundrel.' (Boswell 1986: 182, 1st1787)

Communal conflict is an unconscionable instrument used to manipulate the electorate to partisan causes. Earlier it was employed pragmatically to gain easy advantage. Now it is programmatically pursued. Though this is officially denied the evidence is in stark contradiction. Nationalism is becoming a refuge of scoundrel politicians to distract from the failure of the governments to make good on their promises. For communalism, 'religion in danger' is the alarmist clarion call for nationalism, 'nation at risk' is the battle cry. An authoritarian government may contain but cannot resolve the popular unrest and resorts to charging its dissident citizens with sedition laws. The excess and arbitrary use of the sedition laws eventually undermines the very legitimacy of a government.

If the upstream causes of the people's antagonisms remain unresolved, and merely defused and displaced temporarily, the protagonists remain unreconciled. The contradictions and tensions are waiting to be used and exploited again. We tried it before in 1975–76, where the scapegoat was 'the foreign hand'. But now we are cascading into another undeclared emergency with the anti-nationals and minorities as scapegoats. Exploiting people's pain is fair game in populist politics. If 'everybody loves a good drought', (Sainath 1996) populist leaders find reasons for the same with communal violence.

Religionizing Terror

A spate of terrorist acts in our world today has left no one and no place safe and secure anymore. The popular assumption is that generally these acts are religiously motivated and peculiar to aggressive Abrahamic traditions, and not to pacifist Asian ones. But the data has not been critically scrutinized. The first complete data set of suicide attacks after 9/11 from the early 1980s to 2003, put together by Robert Pape showed this:

> Half the suicide attacks were secular,...95 percent of the suicide attacks were in response to a military occupation...most suicide groups, are driven by an ideal of nationalism; they want to control their destiny with a state...ISIS is composed of a leadership of about 25 people, which one-third is very heavily religious, for sure; one-third former Saddam [Hussein] military officers who are Baathists, who are secular; and one-third who are Sunni militia, Sunni tribal leaders. (Balch, 2015)

Marxist terrorists are surely not religious, and they were prominent in the 1960s. The Shining Path in Peru was one of the most enduring terror organizations. It was finally eliminated through ruthless state action. The Maoist movement still persists in India. Its use of violence is ideologically, not religiously, motivated.

In Sri Lanka, the violence was between Hindu Tamils and Buddhist Sinhala. But the Liberation Tigers of Tamil Elam (LTTE), one of the most committed and ruthless terrorist organizations, were motivated by their Tamil nationalism, not their religion. They made suicide bombings their visiting card before Jihadis did and got international attention for it. It took an unforgiving civil war over decades to bring a precarious and far from just peace.

Ashutosh Varshney perceptively notes:

> Sri Lanka was the first country outside Europe and North America to practice universal franchise democracy – as early as 1931, before India did so in 1947 and before Switzerland in the 1960s…
>
> …while suicide bombing as a form of normal politics was born in the Middle East, it was perfected in Sri Lanka by the Tigers. LTTE's suicide bombs have killed two heads of government in South Asia and a score of cabinet ministers since the 1980s. Moreover, Tamil Tigers are not a Muslim but a Hindu group. (Seminar Jan 2003, No 521)

The claims of Al Qaeda were more about Arab nationalism than Islam, though Islam was used to motivate the movement. The Islamic State of Iraq and Syria (ISIS), as the Islamic Republic of Iran before, used fanatical religion and brutal violence for their revolutionary state-building. Indeed, in pre-modern societies religion has always been used in nation-building: one God, one kingdom, one ruler. This is 'strikingly similar in many ways to the regimes that emerged during the French, Russian, Chinese' revolutions that used extremist ideologies that were purely secular, (Anderson, W 2015: 7) as also Italian Fascism and German Nazism.

The same must be said of the Khalistan and Sikh nationalism, or the United Liberation Front of Assam (ULFA), who were of the Assamese Vaishnavite, or the Naga Christians and their underground or the Kashmiri Muslim separatist movement. The readiness to name some as religious terrorists and not others reveals a prejudiced categorization, as does the obfuscation of some violent groups as non-state actors, freedom fighters, or exceptional individual operators. One's own terrorists are freedom fighters; the others are not. This is simply to negate the violence within one's own, individuals and groups, and blame it on others. This is a pre-emptive self-defensive strike.

Mark Juergensmeyer concludes: 'no one religious tradition has a monopoly on the justification and use of violence, and that the emergence of violent religious politics in recent years is a nearly global phenomenon.' (Juergensmeyer 2000: xi) No religious tradition is free from this equal opportunity employer. Yet all insist their ultimate mission is peace. While all struggle to domesticate violence, yet they use symbols of violence to propagate and/or defend themselves: the Christian cross, the sword of Islam, the Hindu trishul of Shiva, the Sikh kalwas and kripan.

Religion is a means for mobilizing people, though the goals of the violence may be far from religious. However, 'once a conflict becomes "holy", violence knows no bounds, compromise becomes impossible, because all combatants are convinced that God is on their side'. (Armstrong 2014: 226) In fact, 'these are not "holy wars" in the sense of crusades to win converts or control for a particular creed. Rather, in each case religion enters the picture obliquely—as an aspect of a contested social identity, a resource for political mobilization, or a justification for vengeful ideologies.' (Juergensmeyer 2000: xii)

The terrorists themselves are often only superficially or superstitiously religious. But they are people deeply hurt and angry at the perceived injustice done to them or those they identify with. Whether this perception is subjective or otherwise is not the point. They seek to restore their lost selves and lost worlds and find a sense of agency to redress their personal and collective humiliation. How this is motivated 'has much to do with the nature of the religious imagination, which always has had the propensity to absolutize and to project images of cosmic war. It also has much to do with the social tensions of this moment of history that cry out for absolute solutions.' (Juergensmeyer 2000: 242)

Terrorism then is a weapon of the weak, legitimized by religion. And vice versa, violence also becomes sacralized by religion-inspired absolute truth, blind obedience, and a literal interpretation of scriptural texts. (Allen Douglas 2006: 15)

However, when religious faith is tempered with sensible reason, it can also impact society positively to provide the spiritual and ethical basis of a just and decent social order. Politics then will be not so much about the hegemony of the dominant, but more concerned to empower the people, especially the weak and vulnerable. This precisely is the difference between Jinnah's Islamic Nationalism and Gandhi's Swaraj. Thus, 'in a curious way, then the cure for religious violence may ultimately lie in a renewed appreciation for religion itself'. (Juergensmeyer 2000: 242)

Charism and Institution

Every religious tradition is founded on 'experience', either the personal experience of an individual founder, as with the Buddha, or a collective experience of a group, as with the Exodus of the Israelites, or the cumulative experience of several persons, as with the Vedic rishis of old. Rudolf Otto's classic work of phenomenology, *The Idea of the Holy*, concludes that the mystical experience is always an encounter with a '*mysterium tremens et fascinosum*', a mystery awesome and fascinating. (Otto 1970) At times it is experienced as transcendent, eg., Brahman, Yahweh, Allah; at others as immanent, eg., Atman, the Holy Spirit, Dawa; at times as enlightenment with the Buddhism or in a kuan as in Zen, or as salvation as in Christianity, or as submission to the Almighty as in Islam. But always it is experienced paradoxically as a 'coincidence of opposites' that are reconciled mystically and mysteriously: awe-inspiring and enrapturing.

This original experience is the founding charism, and its font of inspiration and renewal. In articulating such an experience, all religious language limps, and especially when articulating a mystical experience. Yet, one cannot comprehend an experience without articulating it somehow at least to oneself, for we think in language. Further, religious experience can only be communicated in symbol and metaphor and recalled in myth and ritual. A religious tradition institutionalizes and ritualizes such expressions to preserve and communicate the original experience over later generations and in other geographic areas. This institutionalized tradition mediates the original experience for future generations.

However, as a tradition gets overlaid with new histories and different cultures, there can be a distancing from, rather than a mediating of that original inspiration—the core, the kerygma, the charisma of the founding experience. (O'Dea 1963) Authentic faith is founded on such experience but to continue inspiring people and vitalizing institutions to face the challenge of change, this experience needs to be continually renewed in each generation lest it lose its vigour; it must be reoriented to new situations and changing people lest it gets out of sync with the times and finally lost.

The dialectic tension between the 'institutional' and 'charismatic' is inherent in any society and pervades its social sub-systems, whether political, religious, educational or otherwise. Indeed, while all charismatic inspiration and authority needs institutionalization for continuity, yet at the same time it is alienated by these same institutional structures. This is what Max Weber called the routinization of charisma. (Weber 1947: 358–373) Both are necessary: the charisma brings dynamism to an enterprise and the bureaucracy institutionalizes and stabilizes it. Without a continuing inspiration, institutions tend to stagnate and ossify; without a functional routine, organizations tend to become instable and ineffective in their environment.

A dynamic, dialectic relationship between charisma and its institutionalization keeps institutions on the path of relevance and stability and preserves the original charisma through historical time and its spread through geographic space. This constitutes an inescapable dilemma, but the tension could be a source of creative growth and innovative adaptation, rather than of confusion and chaos or of rigidity and ossification, as would happen if only one or the other horn of the dilemma is overly stressed.

Now precisely because a religious experience is by its very nature 'extraordinary', it needs the ordinariness of institutionalization in a tradition. No founding religious experience has been preserved across centuries and continents without a strong and stable tradition. As Thomas O'Dea so insightfully points out: 'religious experience needs most yet suffers most from institutionalisation.' (O'Dea 1969: pp. 116-17) We must live this tension: between personal religious experience and institutional religious expressions. To privatize religious experience by limiting it to individual expression subverts its necessary social dimension; to absolutize a religious tradition by alienating it from genuine human experience perverts its essential liberating potential. For it is in the religious experience that we encounter this spiritual mystery.

Authentic religious experience is always inclusive and open-ended. Religious institutions articulate this in scriptures that express a religious tradition's doctrine and mythology, as well as in its evolving structures that help organize its ritual and practice. They set limits for the religion's followers. However, these limits can be flexible and porous or rigid and impervious. They can be limiting boundaries, always protecting and excluding; or open horizons, ever inviting, ever receding. Traditions based on doctrine and dogma emphasize the first, those premised on experience and spirituality, the second.

Yet there is space for a more open, less fundamentalist religion; for more inclusive, less fanatical commitments. We need a faith tempered by reason, not blind belief and uncritical commitment; we need a spirituality that is this-worldly and other-oriented. We must distinguish devotees from fanatics, religion from ideology. Ultimately, reconciling the magisterial claims of religion and state in a multi-cultural society is viable, not within a western secularism, but within a civil religion and a civil state. A civil religion demands a religious humanism, not as the least common denominator of various religious beliefs, but as premised on the core ethic found in all faith traditions.

Faith and Ideology

Without this continuous personal grounding in religious experience, 'religion' all too easily becomes an 'ideology', rather than a matter of faith. (Nandy 1993: 86) For religion as institutionalized beliefs and practices is meant to reconnect one with, and internalize the spiritual experience, which then results in religious 'faith'. When these get politicized, then religion operates as an ideology. Thus, faith is not so much what we believe in, that is belief focused on doctrinal content. It is more concerned with the act of self-surrender in trust.

To put this differently, there is difference between 'I believe *you*' and 'I believe *in* you'. The first refers to belief, the second to a personal encounter, which is focused on the spiritual experience one has had and continues to renew. In this sense Panikkar rightly insists on 'Faith as a Constitutive Human Dimension' (Panikkar 1983: 187–229) and the content of faith must fulfil, not negate this, i.e., belief must humanize the believers, not dehumanize them or demonize others. Good faith is focused on trust, bad faith is blind. Tolerance then becomes the sign of 'good faith'.

Ideology is 'the more or less coherent ensemble of ideas that make up critical awareness, i.e., the doctrinal system that enables you to locate yourself rationally…a spacio-temporal system constructed by the logos as a function of its concrete historical moment'. (Panikkar 1983: 21) A close-ended ideology is premised on an obdurate and obfuscating discourse, an open-ended one on an assimilative and clarifying one. A religious ideology, especially when politicized, is the opposite of and a betrayal of faith, insulating one from the foundational spiritual experience of that religious tradition. For religious faith expresses itself in unselfishness and commitment; a political ideology mobilizes for power and control.

Gramsci has shown how an ideology can become a hegemonic imposition by dominant classes on subaltern ones, co-opting social institutions and their agenda. Conversely, an ideology that is sacralized into a 'religion' becomes a basis on which to construct a collective destiny, with all the anomalies of an ethnocentric political chauvinism that divides and even fragments the very society it means to strengthen. Once religion becomes a critical identity marker, the entanglement of religious traditions in other social and political institutions becomes explosive, and often clerics and politicians in their pursuit of power have played a crucial role in this.

Here, religion is no longer just 'the opium of the people', but a weapon of the dominant, an agent of dehumanization and oppression, of demonization and disaster. In South Asia, religious riots easily lead to the 'demonizing of victims and their expulsion or annihilation in the idiom of exorcism', (Tambiah 1996: 20) making satanic beings of perceived foes. However tenuous the alleged reasons, political ideologies and vested interests provide the motivating compulsions, all in pursuit of a cause, rationalized in terms of a committed value, Weber's value-rationality (*wertrational*), rather than a calculated, objective, instrumental rationality (*zweckrational*). (Weber 1947)

This is an alienation from the founding inspirations. Whereas, if a religious tradition is true to its foundational faith, and the original spiritual experience, and seeks to witness and share, it could very well be tolerant and inclusive, an instrument of peace and liberation. The choice is a collective one, but it still is ours to make between a spiritual faith and a political ideology; a choice that doesn't exclude individual participation and responsibility. Too readily have aggressive ideologies sanctioned unethical and violent means as necessary to nobler ends of justice and peace. However, more often than not, violent revolutions have devoured their own children; a war to end all wars has never been the last. The quest for secular utopias has proved as illusionary as religious eschatologies and the never-ending search for the Holy Grail.

Too often the response to violence has been more violence, and even when such real politique is defensive, it too easily spirals out of control and sooner rather than later tips over into hostile aggression. This is a nihilistic paradigm from which a more constructive discourse must break free. Any viable alternative understanding cannot be based on the Hobbesian premise of *homo homini lupus* (man a wolf to man). We need a new discourse.

Religious fundamentalism has given rise to an identity politics which has promoted divisiveness and a politics of hate. The imperative is to find another model for *homo socialis* (social man), which must be internalized in civil society before it can survive let alone address the rough and tumble of power politics today. We need another model for '*homo religiosus*' that can be internalized in a 'civil religion' that will demythologize singular and exclusive identities and beliefs.

What is happening in our world today is a most shamefaced mobilization of religion as an ideology, not just a social and cultural affirmation of a group's identity and dignity, but an orchestrated political campaign to capture and manipulate collective power and pelf, even as claims of being humble servants of the people are repeatedly shouted from the rooftops. There are few innocents in this dangerous game, which only alienates religion from the wellsprings of a defining spiritual experience and empties it of all genuine religious faith, even as these political potentates claim to be defenders of the faith.

Religious traditions today, readily lend themselves to such political exploitation. Once they enter the domain of partisan politics, they are co-opted into the power game. Alternatively, it defensively retreats into institutional religion with its rites and rituals, sacred texts and magical taboos rather than a personalizing religious experience with its openness and spirituality. What eventually happens is a fossilization, or worse an absolutization of institutionalized structures and values, which are then are further corrupted by politicization, and mobilized for electoral politics. Ironically, modernization, which was expected to marginalize religion, secularize society and temper nationalism, has created discontents that have brought religion back into the mainstream of our disenchanted world, as extremist fundamentalisms. These fundamentalisms align themselves with chauvinist ethnocentrisms to become non-negotiable commitments.

Religious conflict is grounded in civic strife, but once secular battle lines are sharply drawn, then theological justification is readily invoked to legitimize violence and more. But this is not the monopoly of any single religious tradition. There are cultural faultlines too, between other traditions, which can be and have been activated for political gain, more so in recent times. Once such conflicts are religionized, religious traditions alienate themselves from their original charism.

The Buddhist aphorism attributed to the 9th-century Chinese monk, Linji Yixuan, expresses with incisive irony the necessity of going back to the original inspiration, which is always in tension with institutionalized tradition: if you see the Buddha on the road, kill him. You must destroy the notion of a physical Buddha outside oneself and instead search for your Buddha *within* in order to seek enlightenment and to attain Buddhahood. This search can be shared and supported in the Sangh, for even a monk is not an island unto himself.

Violence in religious traditions makes for many ambiguities and dilemmas. This leads to contradictions and conflicts between intended religious ideals and perceived social reality. In a pluri-religious society like ours, such situations become dangerously explosive. Moreover, they readily become politicized in the quest for dominance and hegemony. In such circumstances the spill over into collective violence is predictable. From religious wars and communal riots to genocides and ethnic cleansing, violence gets legitimized as an acceptable means to religious ends, often articulated in idealized and tantalizing metaphors such as Ram Rajya (the reign of Ram), Dar ul-Islam (Land of Peace), kingdom of God, the Zionist Jerusalem.

Evolution of Hindu Traditions

The term 'Hindu' was originally a geographic category used in the 7th century by the Arabs and earlier by the Persians and Greeks, for the region of the Indus valley and beyond. As a self-descriptive term, Romila Thapar traces 'Hindu' to the 15th century. (Thapar 1987) 'Hinduism' itself was first used in English around 1830. (Madan 1997: 177) The British census of 1871 first used it officially. The 1911 census made it an expansive grab-bag category and popularized it thereafter. Colonial debates and controversies sharpened religious self-definition and hardened religious identities.

Colonial historians constructed a history that was more a projection of their European imagination than a faithful reflection of the subcontinental reality. Relying on dominant Brahmanical textual sources, rather than neglected subalterns ones, oral traditions and archaeological findings, they constructed an idea of a homogenous Hindu community and reinforced it with their Census of India. It greatly simplified administration and the dispensation of personal law, but hardly reflected the reality on the ground. Rather, it reinforced religious identities as distinct and different. Once polarized and politicized, they soon became 'overwhelmingly significant' (Arnold and Turner *New York Times* 5 March 2018) all through postcolonial South Asia.

The term 'Hinduism' has now become a construction for a multiplicity of sundry religious beliefs, and cultural practices, distinct in their diverse orthodoxies, but with a 'family resemblance' (Wittgenstein 1958: 14) under an overarching Indic civilization. Only when these are deconstructed and critiqued can we realize how divergent subaltern versions and understandings are from dominant ones, and how different is their response from mainstream ones. (Omvedt 1995) The multiplicities of castes and their hierarchies exemplify this. D.D. Kosambi in *Myth and Reality: Studies in the Formation of Indian Culture* points to the dominance of Brahmanism as the original legitimating ideology. (Kosambi 1962)

But this has always been contested by a rich tradition of unorthodox non-Brahmanical alternatives. Ambedkar insisted that Buddhism was the authentic origin of Indic civilization, which was later corrupted and displaced by Brahminism/Hinduism. His incomplete manuscript on *Revolution and Counter-Revolution in Ancient India* (Moon ed. 1987a, Vol. 3) demystifies this early Aryan history as 'the worst kind of debauchery: social, religious and spiritual' (ibid. 151–52) and claims Buddha as 'the first Social Reformer and the greatest of them all'. (ibid: 164) Indic civilization was dominated by Buddhism, to the point that some scholars would insist that ancient India was Buddhist India. (Omvedt 2003: 118)

Vedic religion evolved into the Upanishads, whose abstract philosophical religion owes much to earlier shramana ones. Later the Puranic traditions followed with their exuberant expressions of popular religiosity, as was represented in epic poems such as the

Mahabharata and the Ramayana, which were eventually converted into religious texts by a Brahmin priesthood. Most famously with the interpolation of the *Bhagavad Gita* in the Mahabharata, we have the acknowledgement of the impersonal, nirguna Brahman fused with the devotion to a personal, saguna avatar of Vishnu in Krishna, as the high point of bhakti, premised on varnashrama dharma. *Gitabhashyas* (commentaries on the Gita) were common even from the time of Adi Sankara.

The *Bhagavad Gita* has now come to be the most influential religious text among Hindus. Bhakti or devotional cults are more persistent and pervasive among more popular folk religious traditions. However, the word 'Hindu' doesn't appear in the four Vedas, the Upanishads and the Buddhist scriptures. Even Adi Shankaracharya does not use the word 'Hindu'. The word does not appear in any ancient text. Historically, 'Vaisnavism and Saivism, today viewed as sects of "Hinduism", were actually independent religions with no less distinct an individuality than Buddhism and Jainism, or, for that matter, Judaism and Islam.' (Dalmia and Stietencron 1995: 22)

Bhakti or devotional religiosity are more persistent and pervasive among religious Hindus today than ascetic practice or mystical spiritualism. Indeed, the myth-making capacity among devotees is still very much alive as is evidenced in the spontaneous devotional cult of Santoshi Mata. Eventually, even they are subsumed into a sanatana dharma (an eternal dharma), by neo-Hinduism, they remain distinct sadhanas in the quest for moksha. What remains persistent across this multiplicity is the practice of caste and patriarchy, which affects all communities in the subcontinent.

There is no linear progression in this evolution, no recognized founder, no organized church, but rather a mosaic of cults and deities, of rituals and myths, which form a rich and distinctive pattern. They intersect and interact and draw on a common Indic civilization for their symbols and beliefs, which run the whole gamut from atheism to animism, from bhakti to tantra, from jnana to karma, truly this was a 'Parliament of Religions'. Radhakrishnan's *Hindu Way of Life* (1927) read as a spiritual quest, not a doctrinal creed, provides crucial insight into the underlying unity that grounds the diversity of the Hindu religious traditions. Indeed, it is difficult to reject or exclude someone who claims to be a Hindu. Already in 1910, the *Daily Hitavadi* in Bengal on 5 November concluded a discussion on this topic thus: 'Whoever Calls Himself a Hindu Is a Hindu'! (Sarkar 2002: 84)

Vedapramanya, the acceptance of the Vedas as revealed texts, is the only recognized criteria of orthodoxy for the sanatana dharma (eternal religion) of mainstream Hinduism. This puts a question mark on the numerous religious traditions, now assumed to be Hindu, that are not founded on this Vedapramanya. It becomes particularly pertinent for those communities that have not been completely Sanskritized, or rather Brahmanized, such as our tribals and Dalits as also others who want their own distinct identity.

After almost a century since their first demand for recognition, the Supreme Court finally ruled on 21 August 2006, that 'Jain Religion is indisputably not a part of the Hindu Religion'. Interestingly, the Ramakrishna Mission in West Bengal even filed a petition in the High Court in 1981 claiming minority status as a religion distinct from Hinduism, which the court upheld in 1985, but which was finally rejected by the Supreme Court in 1996. More recently the Lingayats in Karnataka have begun to contest their co-option into Hinduism with a new awareness of their own religious identity.

What we have, then, is a core of Brahmanical beliefs and practices expressing a minimal orthodoxy in terms of a personal/impersonal understanding of the cosmos, the practice of varnashrama dharma and the acceptance of caste hierarchy. But around this core there is a vast expanse of heterodox sects and cults that distance themselves either by default or with deliberation, to the point of being more in opposition than in continuity with this minimal orthodoxy. Belief was not relevant, though social customs were to be respected. It is a religion of orthodox practices, not of orthodox doctrine.

This has been the great strength of Hindu religious tradition down the ages, and its great weakness too. However, the perception as to which is greater varies with where one positions oneself in the heterogeneity versus homogeneity debate. Any attempt to homogenize such a rich and multi-faceted tradition under a hegemonic hierarchy will impoverish it religiously and devastate it culturally, even if it yields short-term political gains.

From Hinduism to Hindutva

There is a historical continuity between the Hindutva of the dominant caste-class coalition today and the nationalism of the Hindu renaissance of the late colonial period. Already by the early 20th century, Hindu revivalism privileged an aggressive Hinduism and otherized non-Hindus. With Hindutva this reached it apogee.

The ideologizing and politicizing of religious belief for partisan gain alienates it from authentic faith and undermines the religion's tradition itself. A religious tradition that compromises with violent extremism may begin by targeting outsiders, but sooner rather than later the violence will be internalized. It becomes less and less credible and acceptable as its human values are hollowed out. In the end a religious tradition itself will suffer the most from this fundamentalism and violence within.

The Crusades failed to win back the Holy Land from the Arabs, but legitimated aggressive religious war. This then was replayed in Europe with the Reformation and ended in the dividing of Christendom. The revolt of the Jewish zealots in Palestine eventually provoked the Romans into razing of the city and their Temple, scattering the Jews into the diaspora; Temple worship, the focus of the Jewish faith till then had to be replaced with the synagogue prayer services. After two millennia Zionism is now using violence to reverse this. As Wahhabism swept the oil-rich Arabian Peninsular, and the Islamic revolution overtook Iran, militant Jihadis have spread terror in the Middle East and beyond. This has brought enormous disruption to Islam and is largely responsible for globalizing Islamophobia, not to mention upping the ante on the Shia-Sunni hostilities within the Muslim communities.

Hindutva's co-optation of Hinduism is surely a presage of the same. This precisely is what Hindutva is doing to Hinduism. For, 'it's an attempt to standardise, essentialise, codify and systematise a vast universe of incommensurate beliefs, practices, rituals, theologies and narratives—to render Hinduism modern and modular'. (Vajpeyi 2014) Hindutva is premised on a caste-class collation that used an identity politics to co-opt lower castes to upper class concerns and interests.

This is consolidated by a politics of hate which finds convenient scapegoats in marginalized minorities and vulnerable communities: Muslims, Dalits and tribals are now the prime targets. However, human beings cannot live by hate indefinitely. Sooner or later the inherent caste and class contradictions in such coalitions must unravel. Then hate politics will turn inward on itself. Nor must we underestimate the potential of an opposition that can consolidate the majority of people marginalized and alienated by an upper caste-class dominant coalition.

The RSS establishes its hegemony through a multi-pronged multi-dimensional 'network of political institutions that will shape public policy as and for a proud Hindu nation'. (Lele 1995: xvi) Adjusting to new social compulsions, the Hindutva forces are attempting 'a national consensus based on a homogenized Hindu identity that must be flexible and must accommodate diversity'. (Lele 1995: xvii) Herein lies its own internal religious-cultural contradiction. Furthermore, this hegemony requires the cooption and subordination of other groups and local traditions into a pan-Indian hegemony. And here there is a caste-class contradiction.

Such hegemonization and homogenization is legitimized and sustained by a 'pedagogic violence' (Lele 1995: xvii) that selectively valorizes and condemns historical memories, cultural symbols and religious traditions. However, it will necessarily be unstable, if not unsustainable, if imposed with authoritarian means. It cannot be a democratizing and humanizing project which will have space for tolerance and diversity. How this affects traditional Hinduism and the sanatana dharma is already presaged in the escalating violence and hate—from communal riots to mob lynching, gang rape to murder—that brutalizes our people, both victims and perpetrators.

However, to conflate Hinduism with Hindutva is to obfuscate the difference between an ancient religious culture and a recent political ideology that seeks to gain popular religious legitimacy for partisan, chauvinist politics. Moreover, identifying India as Hindu turns a traditional Indic inclusivism into an excluding Hindu ideology; and treating Indian Muslims as aliens negates a millennium-old tradition of Indo-Islamic syncretic culture, besides the numerous other cultural streams that have flowed into and vitalized the rivers of Indic civilization that once made this subcontinent so culturally fertile and spiritually vibrant. To reduce Islam to the terrorism of some jihadis is to blacken a whole religion with the same broad brush and stereotype its followers with the fanaticism of a few. To liken all Christians to crusading proselytizers is to be grossly ignorant of the diversity within the Christian tradition and its continuing evolution and its tradition of charity and service.

Hindutva constructs a cultivated narcissism into an aggressive majoritarian politics of identity. Aggressively affirming, 'Garv se kho hum Hindu hain' (say proudly: we are Hindus), betrays more insecurity than self-confidence. And once religious belief becomes more a militant ideology than a humanizing faith, then conflict and violence readily follow. Hence, we must distinguish Hindutva as a political ideology from Hinduism as a religious faith. Cultural nationalism as an ideology fuses the cultural dimension of Hindu tradition with the political dimension of Hindutva in order to mobilize a Hindu religious nationalism, in its pursuit of a Hindu Rashtra, as yet ill-defined though its contours of caste, class and patriarchy are apparent.

This Hindu Rashtra is in contradiction with the constitutional understanding of India as 'a sovereign socialist, secular democratic' Republic. It will eventually change the very idea of India as envisioned in our freedom struggle. It is an explosive mix of religion and politics which puts a premium on religious homogeneity in its quest for national identity. It politicizes religion but cannot democratize it, religionizes politics but does not humanize it. This then becomes a dangerously brutal compulsion. Dominant groups exploit it to establish their hegemony over others in the name of national unity, which has unfortunately now become the refuge of scoundrels. Too often such ethno-nationalism brings with it horrific ethnic cleansing. Tolerance is given short shrift. It is perceived as weakness, if not a betrayal of national interests and religious concerns.

Tolerant Hinduism, Intolerant Hindus

Where can we situate Hindu tolerance in this trajectory of Hinduism up to this point? As a non-creedal, non-dogmatic religious tradition, Hinduism has a remarkable basis for tolerance, but then orthodox social practice contradicts it. This is the central paradox of Hindu tolerance. Historically, in the Hindu tradition, the intellectual acceptance of pluralism and tolerance has been all too often in contradiction to the existential practice of exclusion and hierarchy. 'Aryan priests, sages and mystics would frequently use the mythology and rhetoric of warfare to subvert the warrior ethos.' (Armstrong 2014: 40) The Mahabharata was precisely about such a tragedy that laid waste the country. Today the epic is being used for the opposite, to glorify aggressive warlike conflict. The Ramayana is a morality tale about a peerless man (maryada purush uttam). Today Ram saumya is being marginalized by Ram rudra and satvik Ram has been transformed into a rajasvik icon, and at times even a tamasik one. This Ram cannot be Valmiki's or Tulsi's hero.

The suppression of Jainism in the south was perhaps more violent than the absorption of Buddhism elsewhere. Brahaman orthodoxy was not tolerant to either of these heterodox shramana traditions. By the time of the Guptas the basic tolerance of the Upanishad period turned into paranoia and insecurity, and in the period of the *Puranas* was one of competition for royal patronage and popular support. In fact, 'much of what constitutes popular or devotional Hinduism since the classical period, the sheer ubiquity of violence in the great epics, the Puranas, and the general corpus of mythology belies any attempt to classify Hinduism as 'pacific' let alone 'Gandhian', notwithstanding the seeping into Hinduism of the Buddhist and, above all, Jain concept of *ahimsa*.' (Sharma 2016: 20)

However, although 'medieval and late pre-colonial Indian

society was violent… Nevertheless, there was relatively little harnessing of devices of collective memory or the recollection of historical grievances to orchestrate mass violence.' (Subrahmanyam 1996: 58)

The colonial regime popularized the idea of an India that lived in the 'little republics' of its self-governing villages. Untroubled by the invading armies that rolled by, they waited for them to settle and be absorbed in the culture of the land. But the Great Revolt of 1857 that very nearly brought their Empire down changed that perception. The divide-and-rule policy then followed—which opportunist leaders on all sides manipulated to their advantage.

Hindu tolerance has been projected as a popular perception, and thus highlights the paradox there. The leaders of our freedom movement too promoted the idea of a harmonious, inclusive India but this was an ideal to be attained, not history to get nostalgic over. 'Historically speaking, Hindus encountered universalist and proselytising religions at three different periods in their history, namely the rise of Buddhism and the arrival of Islam and colonial Christianity. Each provoked much resentment and, when Hindus had the power, considerable intolerance.' (Parekh: 2003)

Today, 'perhaps the most ominous social and political development in India in recent times is the rapid growth of aggressive Hindu chauvinism'. (Balachandra 1996: 125) Fuelled by electoral politics, it threatens to spiral out of control. It is not likely to be reversed as long as it yields political dividends. We seem to have reached a flashpoint in our continuing crisis, a whole tradition of Hindu assertiveness that now spills over into riots, pogroms and lynchings. This needs to be set in counterpoint to Hindu tolerance, that has all too easily and uncritically been proclaimed as characteristic of this tradition, while other religions are demonized as violent and intolerant.

In 1941 Savarkar's birthday wish was expressed in his slogan: 'Hinduize all politics and militarize all Hindudom.' (Mckean 1996: 71) On the other hand, Gandhi's declared agenda was to politicize spirituality and to spiritualize politics. Savarkar's Hindutva leads to a Hindu Rashtra, where the traditional tolerance of religious traditions morphs into an aggressive fascist ideology. The openness and tolerance of Gandhi is concerned with integral Hindu wholeness; the exclusiveness and aggression of Hindu fundamentalists and nationalists is obsessed with political dominance. Gandhi used the positive resources in the Hindu tradition to popularize his understanding of pluralism and tolerance that included more than just the religious. Hindutva uses the negative ones to construct and propagate an aggressive ideology. Gandhian tolerance reaches out in confidence and trust, not fear and insecurity. Hindutva is premised on resentment and violence. Such extremism is the challenge to Hindu tolerance today and to other religious traditions no less. Gandhian pluralism is our best guide in the struggle that has only just begun.

We need to creatively interrogate and constructively critique our religious traditions. There are positive possibilities in the paradoxes of our traditions that we must recover and draw on for a more proactive understanding of tolerance, not just a passive coexistence of separate and bounded communities, if this were possible any more in our world today. We have the long-established traditions of Jain non-violence and Buddhist compassion, Upanishadic universalism, Sufi-bhakti mysticism, Christian charity and Islamic egalitarianism, now we must build on them. But the most elementary resource we have is the basic goodwill and good sense of most of our people when they are not manipulated and panicked into unreasonable and antagonistic positions.

However, the rich possibilities in the Hindu theory of tolerance are overwritten by the realities of savarna hierarchy, punishing violations of the 'dharma of their caste on pain of social ostracism and, under traditional Hindu kingdoms, of legal sanctions'. (Parekh 2003) Moreover, once differences are hierarchically systematized within a community, the temptation is to do the same without. Outsiders are 'encapsulated', contained within a social space, and given their niche in the system. This has happened with most religious traditions and sects in their encounter with the bewildering complexity of Hindu traditions in the subcontinent.

However, the shameful underside of caste hierarchies cannot be dismissed: frequent atrocities against those at the bottom, especially the SCs and STs (Scheduled Castes and Scheduled

Tribes) in spite of very strict laws that in the end result is rare if any convictions. In spite of this, on 20 March 2018, the Supreme Court issued a slew of guidelines to dilute the provisions of the Scheduled Castes and Scheduled Tribes (Prevention of Atrocities) Act. The 'Bharat Bandh' (All India Strike) that followed prompted the government to seek a legal remedy against the order. Finally, in August 2018, the government of India enacted a bill to restore the act to its original form.

Gandhi credited all religions with the same fundamental values and similar resources to institutionalize them. Hence, Gandhi's ideas are relevant for any discourse on tolerance. More practically,

> to create a tolerant India, we need to do two things. We obviously need to mobilize the Hindu resources for tolerance. But we also need to acknowledge and face up to its deep-seated tendencies towards intolerance, and subject them to a systematic egalitarian and pluralist critique. This great cultural task was undertaken by a large body of thinkers from Ram Mohan Roy onwards, Gandhi being the last of them. We need both to build on and rethink it in the context of contemporary India. (Parekh 2003)

In our imploding world, we realize that tolerance must be at the centre of our religious belief and practice to avoid an eventual religious meltdown as the warring faithful fight each other into exhaustion or irrelevance. Precisely in the enduring encounter between living religious traditions which India so uniquely affords, we can all learn, not just to cope, but to mature into a society striving towards the common good of all in a modern, secular democracy. The risk of failure is great and it would be disastrous, but even a modest measure of success would be a challenging example to the world in overcoming the apparent tensions between religious traditions and secular modernity.

Dar al-Harb and *Dar al-Islam*

The prevailing perception of Muslim 'jihadis' as religiously inspired has generated a wave of xenophobia against Muslims in the West. 'All Muslims are not terrorists but why are so many terrorists

Muslims?' expresses a common prejudice, as though there was some kind of monopoly involved. Yet the Irish Republican Army (IRA) was not accused of 'Christian terrorism' in the West, nor is the United Liberation Front of Assam (ULFA) named 'Hindu terrorist' in India, nor are the Hindu nationalists, Hindu Rashtravadis, or the Abhinav Bharat, who indulge in similar acts of violence. Moreover, what is too readily dismissed is the role of the West in the present revival of jihad.

Today Islamophobia in the West, especially after the terrorist attacks there, is reinforcing the historical misrepresentation of Islam, which goes back many centuries to the Crusades and before, when Western Europe felt under threat by the Arabs. The war on terror today is perceived in the Muslim world as a replay of the Crusades. Its collateral damage is alienating even moderate Muslims. The wars the West initiated in the Middle East are still continuing, spilling over into civil wars and terrorism as in Syria and Afghanistan. It has left a refugee crisis that Europe must now cope with.

Earlier, immigrants were welcomed as workers, though never quite as equal citizens, now they are unwanted. Muslims are apprehensive about compromising their religion and culture in a secular environment. Their defensiveness leads them to withdraw into an uneasy conservatism, and they easily fall into a religious fundamentalism, which too many of their clerics encourage and promote. This only alienates them further in a modern secular society and reinforces the divide between Muslims and the rest.

This political conflict was precipitated by the West, beginning with its colonial aggression and now continuing into the present with its neo-colonial hegemony, which has been complicated hugely by war refugees and terror. The confrontation has coalesced along religious lines and it is convenient for the secular West to blame Islam as the villain and demonize Muslims, while they disown responsibility for the imbroglio their own aggression provoked, and the eventual violent defensive response. The action-reaction spiral still continues. Faced with overwhelming force, terror becomes the weapon of the weak and desperate. But this only further exacerbates an already bad scenario. This is a battle for the minds and hearts of people and it cannot be won by power and violence.

The challenge confronting the Muslim world today cuts deeper than even the crisis precipitated by the sack of Baghdad by pagan Mongols in 1258. Eventually, the Mongols were converted and Islamic civilization regenerated in other empires of even greater power and prestige. This is unlikely to happen today though some radical extremists may still dream of a similar resolution to the present questioning of the self-sufficiency of Islam.

Islamic theology divided the world into *Dar al-Harb* and *Dar al-Islam:* the land of peace where Islam (peace) was established, and the land of war. This was an Islamic version of 'the clash of civilisations': (Huntington 1996) Islam versus the rest. But as mentioned before, in the contemporary world the clash is within rather than between civilizations. (Nussbaum 2007) This is as true of Indic civilization today as it is of Brexit divided Britain or the protagonists in Trump's America. In the Arab world the clash is devastatingly fratricidal, peaking with the ISIS caliphate, which has now been destroyed but not the idea which inspired the battle. This only goes underground to re-emerge elsewhere. This was the horrible sequence to the pre-emptive Iraqi war waged by the West to destroy Saddam Hussein's non-existent weapons of mass destruction, but as we know it was the oil that the West eyed. It only brought more mass destruction to the Middle East Arabs, not the countries which started the war. The West does not seem to have registered what a massive betrayal of trust this must have been for Muslim world.

Islam in Andalusia demonstrated how the three monotheist Abrahamic religions could live in peace and harmony, and flourish. It was a culture that left a rich legacy in architecture and culture, learning and spirituality: the architectural wonder of the Alhambra palace in Cordoba, the Sufi mystic Ibn Arabi (1165–1240); the philosophers Abu Ali ibn Sina (980–1137), and Abu al-Wahid Ahmad ibn Rushd (1126–98), who brought Aristotle to the West where they were know known as Avicenna and Averroes respectively; and Rabbi Moses ben Maimonides (1135–1204) who did as much for Plotinus as well.

This was a time in Christian Europe when anti-Semitism corralled Jews into ghettos and terrorized them with periodic pogroms. Moslems refer to the Spanish Reconconquita as 'al-firdaws al-mafiud, (paradise lost). The introduction of the Grand Inquisition by the Church was the death knell of this example of inter-culturalism that has much to teach us today, when Jews and Arabs kill each other over possession of the Holy City of Jerusalem, and Moslem jihadis terrorize the West.

Pan-Islamic Diversity

The 'Muslim world' as a single religio-political construct was the creation of European imperialism. It was a defensive response to the rapid expansion of Muslim rule westward, the threat they felt from the Ottomans who were at the gates of Vienna in 1529 and again in 1683. When Jerusalem was eventually retaken in 1917 General Allenby made his historical remark that the Crusades were now finally completed. In 1920, Damascus was taken and the General went up to the tomb of Salaudin in the Great Mosque and cried: 'Nous revenons, Salaudin!' (We are back, Salaudin!)

With roles reversed, the essentializing of the 'Muslim World' now became a convenient device to stereotype and demonize the other, and thus mobilize their colonial expansion in the Middle East. They essentialized one and a half billion people across the globe from different nations and multiple cultures and treated them as a single entity, both inferior and dangerous for white people. Muslim leaders and elites bought into this single Muslim world. And in response Muslim reformers and revivalists began to project an ideal Ummah, the *Darb-ul-Islam*, for which good Muslims must wage a jihad.

Pan-Islamic fundamentalism thus was as much facilitated from within as from without, as an international phenomenon, and very much a political reaction to the aggression of the modern western world. A previously triumphant, confident Islam was far more open to other and newer influences. The great Islamic empires in Spain, India, the Middle East, Turkey and elsewhere exemplified this. Uniformity was not the inevitable end product of the Islamic principle of unity, tawhid.

However, pan-Islamic fundamentalism, as an international phenomenon is very much a political reaction to the aggression of the modern Western world. To imagine that the multiple ethnicities and languages, diverse cultures and subcultures, religious sects, and their popular religiosities can be forged into a single homogenous solidarity defies reality. The ideal Ummah remained eschatological, just as the Kingdom of God or Ram Rajya is always before us in the future, all ready now but not fully yet. As these are necessarily categories and concepts grounded in a theological understanding, they do not belong to a political ideology.

The original composition of the Ummah did not pretend to uniformity. Ethnic diversity of the Arabian tribal clans that prevailed even within the Islamic religious unity represented the Ummah. From its earliest beginnings, there is a plurality of religious belief and practice within the Ummah. The Shias and the Sunnis are one of the earliest and most enduring divisions in Islam, but there have been numerous other sects and denominations, interpretations and traditions, which have been accepted by mainstream Islam.

Culturally too, the process of Islamization has allowed for distinct diversities, even in the Middle East, the cradle of Islam. In other places, the process of Islamization has never been quite complete. Muslims in India and Indonesia are remarkably distinct from each other and even more so from Arab Muslims in the Middle East. Yet, they are extremely diverse within their own countries as well. The Arabization of Islam is more closely associated with the Wahhabism of the 18th century, now promoted and subsidised by the oil-rich states, like Saudi Arabia. It has little to do with the Quranic origins of the Ummah itself.

The failure of the United Arab Republic sounded the death knell on a unified Arab state across the Middle East. The imploding of the Islamic Republic of Pakistan illustrates the disaster extremist religious nationalism can visit on its own people. Unfortunately, in India rather than learning from this history we are condemning ourselves to repeat it.

Indic Islam

The Indian subcontinent with its enormous Muslim population and long history cannot be unaffected by this imbroglio in the near neighbourhood. The prevailing perception of Islam and Muslims in India, especially since the colonial period, and now in the post-colonial one has been much influenced by the West's, and then read into the events of the past. The resulting entanglements are difficult to sort out and disengage, even as they must not be ignored. But neither must the distinctiveness of Indian Islam be dismissed.

There are two opposite readings of the encounter of Muslims and Hindus in the subcontinent. The first, premised on religious nationalism, concludes to insurmountable antagonisms and unbridgeable chasms between them as with the 1927 perception of the post Andaman Savarkar's two-nation theory, which Jinnah espoused formally in 1941. The Partition did not bring peace but left the two hostile constituents at war with each other, between the two states and within them as well. Contrariwise, the second reading, premised on an understanding of an inclusive Indic civilization, perceives centuries of coexistence that created a composite subcontinental culture for an Indic civilization. Islamic Pakistan has rejected this, Bangladesh with its Bengali grounding is struggling to retain it; in India it is now under threat. Kashmiriyat was once an eloquent testimony to this subcontinental civilization. Today the still unresolved plight of Kashmiris is a symbol of the endemic communal violence in the subcontinent.

We reconstruct historical events depending on how we position ourselves in regard to this divide, but if we are to constructively engage each other across our divisions, we must learn from the mistakes stressed in the first religion-centric reading, and also be open to the possibilities uncovered by the second civilizational one. This will set the stage for better mutual understanding and a more meaningful exchange.

The Arab Muslims first came to India as traders who settled along the west coast. In 629 AD, in Kodungallur, Kerala, they built the first mosque in India. It was based on Hindu architecture and resembled a temple. Conquerors followed later. Muhammad bin Qasim, a young Arab general, occupied Sindh in 711. Marauding hordes from the north came as raiders, first Afghans and later Turks. Eventually they settled to found the Delhi Sultanate, which held power from the 12th to the 16th century. Babur (1483–1530) defeated Ibrahim Lodi at Panipat in 1526 and Muslim rule reached its zenith with the Mughals, cutting off further invasions from the north. The extent of their suzerainty was exceeded only by the British, who finally deposed Shah Bahadhur Zafar, the last Mughal emperor, in 1858, who was a mere figurehead by then but an enduring symbol of Hindu-Muslim unity under the more enlightened Mughals.

Regional-language texts use ethnic rather than religious terms for the conquerors, most commonly 'Turuska' or Turk. We can hardly pretend innocence to the destruction and brutality of the conquerors, whether Muslim or otherwise. Nevertheless, we also need to examine the present orgies of communal violence that have put Muslims so acutely on the defensive. To ascribe all this to religious differences between the protagonists and miss the real political exigencies involved is surely an exaggerated, one-sided perspective.

The eventual ascendancy of the British colonial power brought new challenges to both Muslims and Hindus. Political competition between Hindus and Muslims was encouraged by the British, who were determined to retain their power by playing one against the other. They established themselves as mediators and guarantors of the peace. Old antagonisms revived and intensified, and not even a Gandhi could contain them. Certainly, the encounter of Muslims and Hindus has been unfortunately skewed by colonial rule, but to put all the blame on the British, or any single party is escapist, to say the least. All were implicated in the fiasco. There is always much violence and many atrocities that conquerors wreak on the conquered, and history is written by the victors to enhance their own glory, until others in turn replace them and change the story.

In *Islam Today*, Akbar Ahmed (1999: 207) points to three types of Muslims in India: the critical, the defensive and the confused.

Too few Muslims are constructively critical, too many are defeatist and defensive, and most are confused and oppressed. Thus, the real issues affecting the community get lost in a passionate politics of identity from which only the political and religious elites are advantaged. Islam in India has distinctive features of its own. The assimilation processes have affected both Hindus and Muslims to form a composite indigenous, if not a completely integrated, new culture, which goes beyond mere separate coexistence.

Islam has not just adapted to, but even adopted, many of the particular characteristics of caste, notwithstanding the egalitarian ideals of Islam. Urdu, a new language, which originated in the Mughal camps and spoken by both communities, was born in the north but was also popular in the Nizam's Hyderabad, in the Deccan. Indeed, it is India's gift to Pakistan as its national language where it was not native. There are remarkable areas of cultural integration. Indo-Saracenic architecture has given us the Taj Mahal and more, as enduring symbols of this synthesis. Classical Hindustani music and Kathak dance are other remarkable aesthetic achievements.

Coming back then to the two readings of this history referred to earlier, we can identify Akbar and Aurangzeb as two 'ideal types' from this past. They represent two real possibilities for our future: a secular and civic tolerance or a religious and political fundamentalism. Revivalists and extremists see the Muslim community in decline and threatened by the non-Islamic world. The pan-Islamism they advocate as a response represents a shift from the folk Islam of the local masses to the high Islam of the Arabized elites.

Sufi movements, with their affinity to the bhakti traditions in India, have the potential to soften the polarities between Muslims and Hindus and among Muslims themselves in the subcontinent. Unfortunately, these are being sidelined by fundamentalist maulvis and mullahs, clerics and scholars, from within the community. They have their own vested interests, but if Islam in India abandons its quest for pluralism, both within and among the numerous religious traditions and sub-cultures of the land, there is a real danger of a pan-Islamist homogeneity overtaking the community.

Muslims in South Asia are in a unique position in the Islamic world, between Arabization and indigenization. Pan-Islamism today has become a politicization of religion that demands a closed option for the first. But there are other more authentic and viable interpretations that have favoured more open options for the second. Every religious tradition has a core that anchors its singular uniqueness. Yet, there are also specific particulars that contextualize and enrich it as well. If Islam is at the crossroads in the modern world, then Islam in India could well be at the cutting edges of a breakthrough to a creative and constructive response to the challenge. It would be a pity if it was lost.

Ganga-Yamuna Tehzeeb

The centuries-old Sufi tradition in the subcontinent is an expression of religious pluralism and cultural sensitivity. Religious fundamentalists are now dismissing it as syncretism or hybridity. Wahhabism of the 18th century, now promoted and subsidised from the Arabian Peninsular, is Arabizing Indic Islam with disastrous consequences. Pakistan has already been overtaken by it and now in India uncritical Muslim conservatives, on the defence from an aggressive Hindutva, are espousing it.

Demonizing a community is greatly facilitated by homogenizing it first. Diversity is a bulwark against this. However, at both the international and national levels, Muslims are being aggressively homogenized from outside the community and then demonized as the hostile 'other'. This traps them into mobilizing their communities in a defensive solidarity from within, and homogenizes them further in a spiralling hostility. Both sides then become locked into a self-fulfilling prophecy: a 'they are all like that only', 'I told you so' syndrome, from which neither party can easily escape. Such reciprocal hostility is simplified and self-justified. Acknowledging diversity allows for the complexity wherein to interrogate and critique this constructed homogeneity and challenge the ground for such antagonisms.

Muslims from the north of the subcontinent, e.g., the plains of the Punjab, have more in common linguistically and culturally with their neighbours of other faiths, than with Muslims from the south, say the state of Tamil Nadu. And vice versa for the Muslims in the south. The same holds for an east-west comparison—say between Bengal and Gujarat. Tamil Muslims have not been as Islamized as Muslims elsewhere in the north. (Bayley 1989) Gujarati Muslims are so eclectic and indigenized in their region, especially Shia sects, like the Bohras and the Khojas, that some conservative Sunnis even regard them as heretical.

The historically well-founded reality of Muslim diversity makes any facile assumption of Muslim homogeneity untenable. Yet, this has become more problematic today. They have been put on the defensive against a neo-colonial West and from Hindu nationalism in this country. Their own fundamentalists from within the tradition aggressively promote pan-Islamism, even as extremists of other traditions from without project a homogenized Islam onto them. This has often been the implicit ground for generalizing Muslim intolerance from some instances to the community as a whole.

In the Indian subcontinent the mass of local converts were from the intermediate and lower castes, not very many from the upper-caste elites. Certainly, uniformity was not the inevitable end product of principle of unity, religious or otherwise. The Sufi-bhakti traditions of the saints and poets became the underpinning for a Ganga-Yamuna tehzeeb, the culture of the Indo-Gangetic plains, which spread all over north India, and with Urdu even to Hyderabad. (Ahmad 2002: 2285)

This certainly happened at the zenith of Mughal rule with Akbar and was carried even further with Dara Shikoh (1615–59) the eldest and favourite son of Shahjahan (1628–58). However, expediency at times dictated less enlightened and more chauvinistic policies that were disastrous in the long-term. The accession of Aurangzeb to the Mughal throne and the execution of Dara Shikoh for heresy marked a turning point, precipitating subsequent divisions and antagonism that eventually came home to roost. If Akbar's is a positive, even a secular, response of a Muslim ruler in a Hindu society, Aurangzeb's epitomizes one of short-term opportunism that hollowed out the Empire as he confessed in a letter to his son on his deathbed in Ahmednagar in 1707. (Holden 1895: 304)

The sudden collapse of the great Mughal empire and its final abolition by the British in 1858 left a deep sense of loss in the Indo-Pakistan subcontinent. The 1878 elegy by Altaf Hussain Hali, 'Musaddas e-Madd o-Jazr e-Islam' or 'The Flow and Ebb of Islam' expresses this vividly: (Shackle and Mujeed 1997)

> When autumn has set in over the garden,
> Why speak of the springtime of flowers?
> When shadows of adversity hang over the present,
> Why harp on the pomp and glory of the past?
> Yes, these are things to forget; but how can you with
> The dawn forgets the scene of the night before?
> The assembly has just dispersed;
> The smoke is still rising from the burnt candle;
> The footprints on the sands of India still say;
> A graceful caravan has passed this way.

Religious Buddhism

Historically Buddhism is grounded in the experience of the Buddha and the enlightenment he attained. It was not a dogmatic religion and showed an open-minded inclusive capacity to adjust its beliefs and local cultures and traditions, to adapt its directions and orientations into new syncretic forms and innovative native expressions. Neither did it suffer from the 'graded hierarchy' of caste. (Moon, ed: V 3, p. 320) Hence, among the great religious traditions of the world, Buddhism is more easily enculturated and vernacularized. Its rejection of caste hierarchy and critique of Brahmin ritual, especially animal sacrifice as practised at the time, converted masses of people to its egalitarian and liberating gospel, and it spread from Afghanistan in the north to Sri Lanka in the south, all through Southeast Asia and into China, reaching Japan.

After Emperor Ashoka's (265–32 BCE) Kalinga victory, Buddhism received imperial sponsorship. There must have been some opposition from other religious traditions, which explains perhaps why he issued his 12th major rock edict which epitomized this universal tolerance.

The impressive monuments so widespread throughout the subcontinent are a testimony to the pervasive influence and popular support it had for nearly 1500 years. During the turmoil and disruptions of the Gupta period (BC 300–700), the quest for royal legitimacy, through Brahmin-controlled genealogies, ensured that 'the status of the Brahmin was firmly established'. (Thapar 1966: 166)

However, Buddhism could not displace the caste system. It was too deeply embedded in an interlocking division of labour, which Durkheim called 'forced'. (Durkheim 1933) Ambedkar more pointedly described this as a graded 'division of labourers', not just of labour. (Ambedkar 1995: 41)

Institutional Buddhism was centred in its monasteries. Taxila, in Afghanistan now, and Nalanda in Bihar are prominent monumental testimonies to its previous vibrancy. In the post-Mauryan period, it was vulnerable to hostile rulers who opposed Buddhism. Writing in the late 16th and early 17th century, Taranath, the Tibetan Buddhist chronicler, mentions three of them: Pushyamitra Shunga at the end of the Mauryan period; Mihirakula, who raided north India in the 6th century; and finally the Turks who invaded in the 12th century. With the arrival of Islam in north, Brahmanism adapted to the new rulers, better than the Buddhism, which like Islam was a universal and egalitarian, missionary and communitarian religion, whose peoples were engaged in international commerce and trade, and as such competitors. (Omvedt 2003: 175) Eventually, it was not a single decisive battle or a long-drawn-out war, but a continuing absorption and erasure that brought Buddhism's final demise in the subcontinent.

The absorption of Buddhism into Hindu religious traditions was not without its ambiguities. Vivekananda made a gallant attempt to overcome this by positing a reciprocity between the two: 'Let us join the wonderful intellect of the Brahmin with the heart, the noble soul, the wonderful humanising power of the Great Master.' (Vivekananda 1962: 366) But V.D. Savarkar had little empathy for Buddhist compassion. He bemoans how Hinduism was emaciated by Buddhist pacifism. For Savarkar, 'Buddhism had its centre of gravity nowhere'. (Savarkar 1964: 18)

For Gandhi, Buddha was a 'reformer of Hinduism', not the founder of a new religion. He wrote in *Young India*, (24-11-1927) that in his opinion: 'the essential part of the teachings of the Buddha now form an integrated part of Hinduism…for Gautama was himself a Hindu of Hindus…The Buddha never rejected Hinduism, but he broadened its base. He gave it a new life and a new interpretation.'

Sarvepalli Radhakrishnan's *The Hindu View of Life* (1972: 92) too considered Buddhism and Jainism to be 'protestant movements' within Hinduism.

Ironically, India takes pride in 'Bhagwan Buddha' as a son of India, while actually his birthplace, Kapilavastu, is in modern-day Nepal. Today India, still officially a democratic, secular state is moving towards a majoritarian Hindu Rashtra; and Nepal which was once a Hindu kingdom has been a Federal Democratic Republic since 2008.

The decline of Buddhism in India is testimony to the absorptive capacity of Hindu religious traditions which eventually assimilated and integrated Buddhism. With the *Puranas* of the Gupta period, the basic tolerance of the Upanishadic and the early Buddhist period turned into paranoia and insecurity. Buddhism was seen as a threat to Brahmin religious hegemony and a competitor for popular support and royal patronage. By the 9th century CE, the process of Hinduization was completed, and the Buddha became the ninth avatar of Vishnu. Contemporary Hinduism claims Buddhism as part of the Hindu tradition. But Buddhists outside the country do not accept this, neither do neo-Buddhists at home.

Ambedkar's Navayana

Nehru, the Kashmiri Pandit, and Ambedkar, the Maharashtrian Dalit, make very different conclusions on the Buddhist and Hindu periods of our history. Nehru's 'unity in diversity' is a nationalist reading of our history by an upper caste-class leader. His *Discovery of India* (Nehru 1947) finds a 'continuous growth and often conflict', (Nehru 1947: 89) a continuing dialectic of diversity and unity in 'a vivid and growing national life'. Eventually, he sees not so much a decline of Buddhism in India, as its absorption into 'a Brahmanism or (to use a later word) Hinduism, which became a symbol for nationalism'. (Nehru 1947: 105) The continuing thread in Nehru's *Discovery of India* is a plural, tolerant, inclusive Hinduism.

Ambedkar challenges this perception of subcontinental history from his conscientization at the bottom of these social strata from where his awareness of caste hierarchy and class stratification comes. He regards the Buddha as the first and greatest social reformer. (Gore 1993: 292) In recognizing the rights of shudras and women, Buddhism released an enormous vitality, suppressed till then, and engendered a vigorous religious and artistic revival. However, 'the triumph of Brahmanism' (Gore 1993: 229–30) heralds 'the Birth of Counter-Revolution'. (Gore 1993: 266–332)

Ambedkar's posthumously published, *Revolution and Counter-revolution* (1956) traces the conflict between Buddhism and Brahmanism (Moon ed. 1987a: Vol. 3) to 'serve an ideological purpose in his fight against the Hindu caste system and to strengthen the legitimacy of his resolve to convert to Buddhism'. (Gore 1993: 242) After pondering many religious alternatives he eventually led a large number of his followers into Buddhism on 14 October 1956 at Nagpur. This was meant to be 'a social rebirth, a gaining of a new identity, a way in which the Dalits were leading, not simply joining a movement for the recreation of India'. (Omvedt 1994: 248) However, the biggest constraint on Ambedkar's movement was the lack of a resource base with which to impose itself on 'the stronger and larger "nationalist" political leadership'. (Gore 1993: 215)

Ambedkar's *The Buddha and Karl Marx*, completed in 1956, brings out the socialist content of Buddhism, which for him, was more 'in consonance with Liberty, Equality and Fraternity, in short Democracy', (Moon, ed. 1979: Vol. 1: 77) than Hinduism or Marxism. *The Buddha and His Dhamma* (1957) reinterprets Buddhism more in terms of a political and liberation theology rather than as a religious spirituality. He rightly described his Buddhism as *Navayana*, a new vehicle, 'cleansed of the Brahminic interpolations of the doctrine of karma and rebirth'. (Gore 1993:

259) It offers a threefold challenge to Brahminism, Marxism and Buddhism too. (Omvedt 2003:1) This is the greatest potential of Ambedkar's movement.

Ambedkar's neo-Buddhists were mostly from his own Mahar caste, which dominates the Republican Party. Their biggest challenge is to forge an alliance beyond their Dalits. Here again it is caste, even sub-caste, jati, affiliations which trumps the class consciousness needed for a mass mobilization for all oppressed and marginalized in the country.

Yet Ambedkar's *Navayana* Buddhism was not just for an otherworldly nirvana. Rather it is a this-worldly ethic, which he explained in terms of 'liberty, equality and fraternity'. This becomes a critically relevant liberation theology for his life's pilgrimage, the liberation of his people. He was convinced of the emancipatory potential of religion with a this-worldly ethic for an engaged Buddhism, which is coming into its own today. Ambedkar was surely one of its earliest contemporary representatives. His Navayana has the potential to be the functional equivalent in South Asia of what Robert Bellah called 'civil religion' in North America, a religion for civil society, or as some would prefer, a post-religion religion. (Menon 2004: 1816)

Buddhist Nationalism

Buddhism as a non-violent religious tradition is based on a contemporary misconception that privileges Buddhist spirituality and philosophy and disregards Buddhist religious traditions and popular religiosity. The emphasis is on meditation, for peace and harmony. This amounts to a decontextualized and ahistorical understanding. It fails to recognize the critical role of Buddhism in the defence of the state and in promoting an aggressive nationalism today. For, 'the transformation of Buddhism is gravely distorted and deficient if there is no account of the political direction and transformation taken by Buddhism in this century'. (Tambiah 1992: 129) The prohibition of violence and the promotion of non-violence was never an absolute injunction, and there are many examples of violence in the history of Buddhist societies. This is not different from other religious traditions which are increasingly politicized today.

Indeed, it rationalized 'compassionate violence', which was likened to the amputation of a limb for the health of the whole body, 'amputation with kindness'. (Jenkins 2010) Moreover, 'Buddha himself did not preach non-violence to the Kings of his day due to the belief that it was a king's duty to strengthen and defend his kingdom'. (Jenkins 2010) For 'while radical pacifism evidently is found in the canon, so also the assumption that violence belongs to a separate sphere of activity, that of the warrior caste (kings)'. (Frydenlund 2013: 112) Military and punitive violence, which has 'historically been a consistent feature of its polities, often including monastic communities, appears to be radically and inexplicably inconsistent with the values expressed by its scriptures and inspirational figures'. (Jenkins)

A recent historical review of Buddhism by Michael K. Jerryson, *Buddhism, Politics, and Violence*, concludes that it is no different from other religious traditions, particularly with regard to state-sponsored violence. (Jerryson 2018)

In these old societies, violent nationalism played a greater rather than a lesser role. Like other major religious traditions, Buddhism has been politicized by nationalism in the quest for modernity. (Geertz 1963) How does a religious tradition like Buddhism that privileges non-violence and peace get co-opted to motivate and mobilize nationalist violence? 'Buddhist monks are rarely on the front lines of these campaigns—though they are targets of violence—but they are often essential supporting voices for nationalist agendas. Buddhism and nationalism are so closely aligned in Modern Asia.' (Marchman 2016) In fact they have become close partners in an aggressive nationalism in countries like Sri Lanka and Myanmar.

In Sri Lankan history there have been numerous wars between Sinhala Buddhists and Tamil Hindus over centuries, motivated and mobilized by an aggressive Sinhala Buddhist literature beginning in the 19th century, foregrounding Buddhism as the national religion of the Sinhala people and hence the inseparability of the two. (Tambiah 1992: 23) *Mahavamsa* chronicles the hero king of

Sri Lanka, Dutthagamini's slaughter of Damilas (Tamils) during his war to unify the island, and how it posed the conundrum on non-violence and was answered in a less charitable way. The king was comforted by eight arahants (enlightened saints) who justified violence against these 'unbelievers, men of evil life'. (Mahamavmsa Ch 25, vv 11-111) Dipavamsa celebrates the contribution of Buddhist monks to Sinhala civilization. (Tambiah 1992: 27) In 1946 the 'war monk', Bhikkhu Walpola Rahula's *Bhiksuvage Urimaya*, 'The Heritage of the Bhikkhu', (1974) preached Buddhism as the national religion of the Sinhala people, the Sri Lankan 'national culture'. The two cannot be separated: Buddhist religious extremism and Sinhala ethno-nationalism.

The British imposed a truce, but polarized the ethnic communities further. They categorized subjects by religion and governed them through personal law. This defined religious identities as distinct and separate. The identity politics of independent Ceylon fostered an increasing antagonism between Buddhist Sinhala and Tamil Hindus, beginning in the 1956 making Sinhala the only official language and later giving some recognition to Tamil in 1958. Thus began the marginalization of the Tamils. It finally precipitated a civil war, which ravaged the country for decades, from the 1970s to the brutal elimination of the LTTE in 2009.

Ven. Athuraliye Rathana, leader of the Jāthika Hela Urumaya (JHU) party that seeks to create a Buddhist religious state, aggressively asserts that to be a harmonious society: 'We have to kill the killer to save the innocent. We can bring happiness to people by destroying the LTTE.' (Liberation Tamil Tigers of Elam) (Deeglle: 2013: 17-18) Before the LTTE, the Marxist Janatha Vimukthi Peramuna (JVP), insurrection, 1969–99, led by Sinhala youth and supported by young Buddhist monks, swept the countryside in two waves. The first attempted a coup against the government in 1971, and was ruthlessly suppressed. 'Over 15,000 civilians were killed without proper judicial process by the combined Sri Lankan and Indian army operation. During the second JVP uprising, in 1987-1989, an estimated 60,000 civilians disappeared, most of them assumed killed by the Sri Lankan army and the state forces.' (Sahni and Tharu 2010: 198)

However, the traumas of violence and the burden of memory remained unhealed, open wounds. (Perera 2016) There is still little genuine reconciliation between the protagonists. The upstream causes, which drive the desperation of such violence, have not been addressed. An uneasy peace is being held together by an increasingly authoritarian government with a compromised record of human rights: 'one the most crucial features of recent Sri Lankan social and political history has been the rapid emergence of institutionalised forms of violence and terror throughout the country. In the context of which the country's traditions of civil liberties and democracy had been seriously dismantled.' (Perera 1998: 1–2)

Four years after the civil war ended, the Sinhalese Buddhist community still remains 'one of the most violent and militarized societies on the planet'. (Deeglle: 2013: 15) This is quite a retreat from the social democratic state that earlier was an example to the others in South Asia.

In Myanmar on the periphery of South Asia is another example of violent Buddhist nationalism. As mentioned before, the British colonial government categorized subjects by their religious identity and reinforced this with personal law, thus it became a significant identity marker. Once politicized, these ethnic identities inevitably become competitive and eventually hostile, and by 1961 the dominant Buddhist Bamar declared Myanmar to be a Buddhist state. The armed response of the Christian Kachin in the north marked the beginning of a series of ethnic wars. These peaked after the military coup in 1962. Since then the military junta has run the country and dictated terms. It still stymies any opposition, squashing even the peaceful protest of the monks in 2007.

The 1982 Citizenship Law did not recognize the largest Muslim population in Rakhine State. Islamophobic Buddhist monks agitated to drive the Rohingyas out from Myanmar. Young Rohingyas responded with defensive violence, which provoked a merciless backlash by the Myanmar army pushing them across of the border into Bangladesh, where they are now encamped as refugees. Myanmar's long history of exclusion and violence toward the Rohingya is still continuing.

Even with the partial success of the Burmese Democratic Movement in 2017 lead by Aung San Suu Kyi things have hardly improved. The top-down power-sharing still leaves the generals in charge with enormous authority in the present democratic structures their junta put in place. Myanmar is still officially a Buddhist state, while ethnic cleansing of the nationalist military dictatorship has now become programmatic.

Christian Origins

The origins of Christians from a Jewish sect who 'belonged to the Way' of Jesus of Nazareth (Acts: 2) to a world religion and now coping with a post-Christian secular age has been long meandering through many shifts and turns and highs and lows. Whereas in the Old Testament the priority was for justice and eventual peace, in the New Testament the emphasis is on love and especially forgiveness. The proverbial teaching on revenge, turning the other cheek (Mathew 5:38), is not to encourage evil but to oppose evil with good. The persecuted early Church was pacifist as Tertullian, Justin Martyr and St Cyril testify, for they saw violence and war as contradictory to their faith and conscience. (Bishop 1981: 12)

After centuries of persecution in the Roman Empire, Christianity became an officially accepted religion with Constantine the Great in 313 AD. Now the need to defend the Empire from barbarian attack and eventual invasion became critical. St Augustine (564–430) first proposed the just war theory in his City of God in the 5th century, to legitimate the defence of the state and in the cause of peace. This would then be God's war, *bellum deo autore*. (Windass 1964: 32) This was always understood as a defensive war.

However, the Christian Crusades from the 11th to the 14th centuries were launched with the blessing of the Church, because of European fears of being overwhelmed by Muslims. It made a war of aggression against infidels respectable. But later, wars between Christian princes, particularly the religious wars after the Reformation, needed a more robust and refined legitimation. This was provided first by the medieval scholastics led by St Thomas

Aquinas with his distinction of *jus ad bellum* (the right to go to war) and *jus in bello* (rights of combatants in fighting), and further elaborated and nuanced by the neo-scholastics of the Renaissance:

1. The cause has to be just.
2. The right intention must be maintained throughout hostilities.
3. The war is truly the last resort, all peaceful means having failed.
4. The means of waging war must be fair.
5. The good legitimately hoped for from war must be of greater benefit to mankind than the evils it involves.
6. Victory must be certain
7. The ensuing peace must be just and of such a nature as to avoid a further war.

(Regamey 1966: 252-253)

The expansion of Christianity in the West is popularly far better known than its early spread in the East, among the Arabs and Persians in the domains of the Zoroastrian rulers. It reached Central Asia by land and South Asia by sea in the early centuries of the Christian era, even before it had reached many parts of Europe. It was the official religion of Armenia much before it was in Rome. (Frykenberg 2003: 33) But much of this history was lost when first the Arabs overran the territories of the Byzantine and Persian empires, and later the Ottoman Turks too.

The conversion of Europe spread over a millennium was promoted not as a centralized movement but by the varied efforts of wandering monks and missionary bishops. By the late Middle Ages, numerous monasteries and much political patronage established and stabilized Christianity. By about the 14th century, Europe was called Christendom, the Kingdom of Christ. However, with the Protestant Reformation in 16th century and *The Dividing of Christendom*, (Dawson 1964) the separation of Church and State, and the consequent secularization in the West, religious authority no longer has the pre-eminence it once did.

The 'Age of Faith' gave over to the 'Age of Reason' with the rationalism of the Enlightenment, as modern West became progressively post-Christian. The rejection of any explicit mention of Christianity in the proposed Constitution of the European Union, in spite of pressure from the Vatican, is a rather unambiguous comment on how far Europe has come from the marriage of the Church and State in the Constantinian Empire all the way to the Germanic Holy Roman one, and its mediaeval identification with Christianity. This is now a distant cry from Hillaire Belloc's (1870-1953) 'the Church is Europe and Europe is the Church'.

Christianity came to India much as Islam did, first with traders from the Middle East and much later with colonial conquerors from the West. The Acts of St Thomas, though an apocryphal gospel attributed to one of the original twelve Apostles, may be a romantic tale, but rests on sound historical probability. The Syrian Christians in south India trace their origins to St Thomas. This is substantiated by the flourishing exchange between the Middle East and the west coast of India at that time.

All this flies in the face of the misconception that 'Christianity is essentially European and European religion has traditionally been Christian'. (Frykenberg 2003: 5) Yet in India, the identification of Christianity with the West, and particularly with Europe, lingers as a post-colonial hangover enormously difficult to shake off.

Colonial Distortions

The Portuguese arrived by the sea route with Vasco da Gama (1460–1524) at Cochin in 1498, looking for Christians and spices. Instead they were surprised to be greeted on the streets of Cochin in Spanish by a Jew expelled from Toledo. Indeed, later, they encountered local Christian communities well established and integrated into the local society even as they kept their own Christian identity and some minimal contact with the Chaldean patriarchate in Mesopotamia. They had their niche in the local caste ecology too.

Colonial imperialism with its wars of conquest that went in its wake—wars of racism, genocide, ethnocide, slavery—brought unimaginable horrors, in spite of whatever good it may have done to colonized peoples. Christianity could not escape being implicated in this colonial violence, which has not been forgotten or forgiven by the colonized, notwithstanding the yeoman service of Christian institutions and many heroic missionary figures who resisted the colonialists.

Yet the threat of Christianity that came with the challenge of Western colonialists was far more radical than that presented earlier by Islam and Muslim invaders. For not only was the colonial power politically and militarily dominant across the region for some two centuries, but it was also perceived as a more progressive culture and a more effective scientific civilization. Religious revivalists and social reformists did respond to this in a variety of ways and with varying measures of success. Some even speak of a Hindu 'Renaissance', with Ram Mohan Roy and others who challenged local traditions while criticizing colonial practice. There were also more fundamentalist reactions as with Maharshi Dayanand Saraswati's Arya Samaj (1875) and later by the RSS (1925), which is now in a dominant position with its Sangh Parivar and the BJP which it sponsors and mentors.

The colonial involvement in the missionary enterprise is too easily and uncritically taken for granted, by religious conservatives on the defensive. While it surely cannot be dismissed, it needs to be fine-tuned and contextualized. The compulsions of the colonial government were not always compatible with the goals of the missionaries. There was the inevitable conflict of interests between religious conversions by the missionaries and the political order and economic dividends of the colonial state. Even when the colonial governments were sympathetic to the missions, their priorities were not easily compromised, and often opposed by the missionaries but it was the dominant power and those aligned with it that prevailed.

The simplistic conflation of colonialism with Christianity leads to the crude assumption of an alien religion forced on hapless natives against their will. This is still used as a rhetorical device even against Islam. Once again, it is the voice of the dominant classes and castes, who speak for the subaltern ones, giving no real and effective agency to the oppressed as actors in their own history and proactive in the changes that affect them. This rather reflects an elitist mindset, one not too different from the racist colonials themselves.

Most missionaries were rooted in their own societies, and often had strong nationalist sentiments of their own. This became apparent when their colonial countries went to war against each other, fighting for God and country. This left the missionaries divided and the neophytes confused with this one God and his many waring countries. By and large the missionaries did not support the Indian freedom struggle. No doubt, there were notable exceptions, like the Gandhian C.F. Andrews (1871–1940) and the anthropologist Verrier Elwin (1902–64).

However, as the Indian Church matured, Indian Christians developed their own distinctive identity with its own peculiar characteristics: some carried over from its indigenous past, some derived from the colonial masters, both with variations across geographic regions and religious denominations.

There are many Christianities in India and many different mission theologies. Rowena Robinson has written on the Christians in Goa, (1998) and, with Sathianathan Clarke more generally, in India. (2003) In central India, the Chotanagpur tribal church, represents a well-established indigenous Christianity now, though in the Northeast, the indigenous churches are more westernized.

Today Christians are a very small minority of just 2.52 per cent, in the 2011 census with a fall in decadal growth rate of 7.0 per cent. However, the abusive arrogance of some of the early proselytizers cannot be justified. It belongs to the religious imperialism of a colonial history, which has left still unhealed memories with the traditional Hindu conservatives of a wounded past, which they seek to recover.

Long Trajectory

The rich encounter between Christianity and the religious traditions of India is best illustrated by the men who truly represented this dialogue. De Nobili had once envisioned a Sanskritized version of an Indian Church. Brahmabandhab Upadhyay started out as a nationalist terrorist, eventually converted and saw himself as a modern Hindu–Christian; reverend Narayan Vaman Tilak, a Marathi convert, was a Christian sant-kavi; Bede Griffiths, an English monk and Swami Abhishekananda, a French one, have both been emphatic about their debt to Hinduism and have blazed new trails at the cutting edges of their encounter with Indic civilization.

With the Second Vatican Council (1962–65), for the first time, other religions were described positively and appreciatively in an official document of an Ecumenical Council. In 1997, the World Council of Churches (WCC), in its statement from the Hindu-Christian Consultation held in Varanasi, condemned aggressive proselytizing in the pursuit of numbers that takes advantage of vulnerable people. Recently a multi-religious meeting hosted by the Vatican and the WCC at Lariano, Italy, made a far more elaborate statement. (Pontifical Council for Inter-Religious Dialogue, 1991) Hopefully now, such misled missionaries will be a thing of the past, at least for the mainstream churches as unwarranted prejudices defuse and dissolve over time.

In our own time, based on sober demography projections, Walbert Buhlmann sees 'the coming of the third church' (Buhlmann 1977) already on the horizon. This will certainly be a more international Church and more third world one than Western.

This transition from proselytization to dialogue is aptly summed up by Raimon Panikkar as he describes the historical evolution of Christianity through five sequential self-understandings. (Panikkar 1987, pp. 21–26) These are not discrete periods in time, but perspectives that follow on each other, even as they overlap with, and persist in each other.

Thus for the primitive Church, to be a Christian was to be a 'witness', a martyr, joyfully testifying to, and faithfully interpreting the founding events and experiences of their faith. Christians were a small and persecuted minority, but their faith was irrepressible and contagious. With the change in imperial policy of Constantine in the 4th century, Christians came into their own. They gradually became the dominant majority, and there was little room for martyrdom. The emphasis shifted to an internal 'conversion', a metanoia, a radical change of heart and turning to God, saying 'no' to the world and worldliness as best exemplified by the desert hermits in Egypt.

From the 8th century until the Renaissance, there was a very real danger of being overwhelmed by Islam. An aggressively militant Christianity gave rise to the 'crusade' to retake the Holy Land and failed. But with the advance of colonialism the balance of power changed and the crusading spirit was channelized into a 'mission' to colonize and rule as new worlds began to open up to the colonial powers. This was to be a Christianizing/civilizing mission, but its imperialism and racism inevitably brought exploitation and oppression as well. The experience of this period is still alive in the historical consciousness of the colonized and continues to influence their perceptions.

In the post-colonial period there is now a greater mutual respect and the approach to other religious traditions in and through 'dialogue', not as a strategy for the older 'mission', or a substitute for the earlier 'crusade'. Rather it must be as an authentic return to 'witnessing' to one's faith and a genuine 'conversion' of heart, learning from and enriching each other in an inter-religious encounter. There are still crusading evangelical sects focused on proselytizing, for whom there is no salvation outside their 'church'. These are still living with a colonial mission, albeit a religious one.

There are more extreme fundamentalists, who seem to crave the 'palm of martyrdom', like the early Christians, but end up caught in their own fanaticism. There are contemplative Christians who seek their own 'conversion' and withdraw from a this-worldly engagement to an otherworldly spirituality. But across the broad spectrum of the mainstream churches, the movement has been from proselytizing to dialogue with varying degrees of commitment and multiple levels of engagement. This engagement now is inspired by a vibrant liberation theology, contextualized and enculturated locally.

The post-Vatican Council colonial period has now brought a theology of liberation that was developed in Latin America and spread to Asia and Africa. It focuses on the structural violence in society, a residue of the colonial times in no small degree. It has now taken root in churches all over the world. (Heredia 2008)

The trajectory we have sketched here stretches from a closed, inward-looking soteriological religious tradition through an exclusive understanding of Christianity as discontinuous with other religious traditions, to a more open, inclusive one, in harmony and solidarity with others. Inclusiveness allows for a greater willingness to contextualize the older tradition in a composite culture, say an Indic-Christian one, and a greater readiness for secular fellowship in equality, like a civic association. Exclusiveness resists both.

Myth of Religious Violence

No mainstream religious tradition advocates violence as an end in itself. At most it legitimates violence as a means of last resort in a just cause and in self-defence. However, 'religion and violence have never been strangers'. (King 2007: 228) It has been used to motivate and 'amplify pre-existing possibilities for social tension into unprecedented paroxysms of religious violence'. (Gottschaulk 2007: 196) While non-violence is not equally privileged across religious traditions, even those that give it pre-eminence must come to terms with violence in the real world in which we live. It cannot be wished away. Hence they devise 'different strategies incorporating and normalising violence'. (Patton 2007: 32) Common to all tradition was the distinction between especially dedicated religious persons, priests, monks, nuns, who were expected to live the ideals of non-violence in their pursuit of salvation, and the laypersons in the worldly professions, who had to cope with the realities of a violent world.

For secular rationalists religion too easily becomes the scapegoat. They may reject religion but 'they cannot do without demonology'. (Gray 2007: 25) And 'once the idea of the diabolical foe is firmly planted, it is used to interpret every historical event—and it may even begin to shape history'. (Pantham 1986: 179; 1964: 51) In fact, the last century has been the most violent in history: the Great War and the World War, a Cold one and many hot ones, wars of liberation and wars of pre-emption, wars on terror and wars of non-state actors, state terror and terrorist organizations, besides random and targeted violence so endemic in our societies.

By and large these have been precipitated by protagonists, at least one of which has been secular: the Great War fought in the name of king and country, the World War between confrontational ideologies, and all of them 'in the national interest'.

No doubt, then, political ideologies have been no less incendiary, and if anything worse than religious traditions, in their history of violence, once again sanctioned as necessary means to nobler ends: justice, peace, revolution, a war to end all wars. Yet such secular utopias have proved as illusionary as religious eschatologies. Karen Armstrong found that 'of the many Lebanese bombings [in the 1980s], only seven of them were committed by Muslims, three by Christians. The rest, some 17 or so, were committed by secularists and socialists coming in from Syria.' She further argues that 'blaming religion allows Westerners to ignore the essential role that violence has played in the formation of our own societies—and the essential role that our societies have played in seeding violence abroad.' (Armstrong 2014)

With the separation of church and state, the churches have gotten more secular, and the states more militaristic: the nation has replaced the demon war god as a pseudo-deity, nationalism has become a pseudo-religion. The end point of this is a 'culture of violence', which must find a hate object, a real enemy, a suitable demon. This is surely overtaking our contemporary world, and South Asia is an apt example and with India now rather an exemplary one too. We so easily forget that 'once a conflict becomes "holy", violence knows no bounds, compromise becomes impossible, because all combatants are convinced that God is on their side'. (Armstrong 2014: 226)

Yet even all this cannot gainsay the history of religious violence and the contradictions between religious teaching and expedient practice that is so patent in the mainstream traditions. The unanswered question still stares at us: can the contradiction in using violent means to non-violent ends be resolved within the paradigm of contemporary political realism; how do calls to prayer become calls to war; can a people who worship a warrior god be a people of peace? We are meaning-seeking animals and when we fail to find it we are alienated from ourselves, from others and from our world, and we fall into anomic despair. Extreme reactions, then, become an ever-present possibility, rather a dangerous probability, whether this be to religionize all politics or to militarize all religion, to paraphrase V.D. Savarkar.

Religion and politics are so intimately intertwined it is difficult, if at all possible, to separate them in a religious society. Conventional wisdom has created 'the myth of religious violence', and neglected the issue of 'secular ideologies and the roots of modern conflict'. (Cavanaugh 2009) In Savarkar's Hindutva, politics must rule supreme; with Nehru's dharma-nirapekshata the state was to distance itself from all religion; Gandhi's sarvadharma-samabhava (inclusive tolerant religion) and a dharmik rajniti (ethical politics) were both to be lived together. His life was this message.

CHAPTER FOUR

COMPREHENDING VIOLENCE

Polarizing Communities – Banality of Evil – Clarifying Concepts – Causes and Motivations – Terrorizing Violence – Cosmic War – Defusing Terror – Collective Conscience – Levels of Analysis – Socio-psychological Level – Eco-political Level – Socio-cultural Level – Socio-religious Level – Historical Context – Anatomy of a Lynching – Nuanced Response

Polarizing Communities

Most of us are familiar with a Gujarat that once was 'an open multi-ethnic society based on a long history of in- and out-migration. Tolerance and pragmatism have for long constituted the core of civic culture in Gujarat. It is the birthplace of Mahatma Gandhi who not only advocated ahimsa (non-violence), but also mobilized the masses for passive resistance against the foreign rule,' and yet, 'since the 1980s and 1990s, this region has been the scene of frequent, grisly communal holocausts. Domestic violence against women and atrocities against the Dalits continue unabated in various parts of Gujarat'. (Shah 2003: 10)

The pogrom of 2002 in Gujarat was the tipping point to a new nadir in the politics of polarization and hate, leaving its mark on the rest of the country. The mass hysteria that followed represents the co-optation of people into an authoritarian, patriarchal, upper caste-class movement that has not and cannot address the underlying contradictions of the burgeoning capitalist development in the state. But for how long can such tensions be contained? Can these tensions be resolved within the 'Gujarat model' when they are not being credibly addressed, there or elsewhere? How long will it be before the situation unravels? The writing on the wall must alert us to this real possibility.

The BJP's performance in the Gujarat Assembly elections in 2017 for its 182 seats is revealing: from 127 seats in 2002 to just ninety-nine in 2017, just seven more than the halfway mark of ninety-two. In spite of the vigorous and personalized campaigning by the prime minister and some help from the staggered dates, the party won sixteen seats by margins between 200 and 2000 while fifteen seats were lost to the Congress by margins of less than 3000. The total tally of the Congress was seventy-seven seats and with its allies eighty. This is not a convincing win but rather a clear indication of disillusionment among voters, especially rural ones. In urban areas fear and hatred towards the Muslim minority from Hindus, who feel the need for a strong man who will protect them, seems to have prevailed.

But the rate of unemployment among youth is a simmering issue in the state ready to boil over. The massive support to Hardik Patel over reservations for this community is evidence of this. Hardik was neutralized with multiple charges, which seem rather dubious while the PM's election campaign used fear of Muslims and Pakistan to trump this real issue, confronting the state.

Gujarat 2017 elections opened new possibilities for the coming elections beyond the state. The assembly elections in 2018 were a clear rejection of this BJP neoliberal saffron model since its dominating victory in the state elections in 2013, especially where the BJP and the Congress were the main contenders. In Rajasthan the BJP was convincingly defeated, with just seventy-three seats, down eighty-nine, while the Congress won with 112, up ninety-one in a house of 199. In Madhya Pradesh, the BJP with 109 seats, down fifty-six, while the Congress gain as many to win with 114 in a house of 230. Chhattisgarh was a wipe out for the BJP, with just fifteen seats, down thirty-four, and the Congress with sixty-eight, up twenty-nine, in a house of ninety. In Telangana, the regional Telangana Rashtra Samithi swept the polls with eighty-eight seats in a house of 119, while in the Mizoram National Front with twenty-six seats in a house of forty left just six to the Congress and only one to the BJP. How does this augur for future elections, especially parliamentary ones?

Unfortunately, the opposition parties are still fragmented and divided. They may well lose elections without the BJP actually winning them. When there has been an alliance of the opposition parties, a mahagathbandan, the BJP has been trounced. However, the failure of a government to deliver on its earlier promises is no guarantee its replacement will do any better. This would leave the voters with one set of rascals being replaced by another. Even a credible and effective replacement will need a convincing alternative narrative to reverse this slide and the saffronization of civil society. Only a critical citizenry will be able to undo the politics of hate and polarization, and unpack the majoritarianism and authoritarianism that has been allowed to overtake them. But we need first to unlearn the violence we are visiting on ourselves before our constitutional compact breaks down into a Hobbesian war of all against all. We must find a healing compassion before a further desertification deadens our hearts.

The contradiction between Gandhi's committed ahimsa and new 'Gujarati asmita' needs a historical and contextual perspective, if we are to understand and respond effectively to the 'Hindu Rashtra' project that has now taken root in Gujarat and spread beyond to the national scene. How could a pluralist society be co-opted so rapidly by a chauvinist cultural nationalism? Gujarat has now grown beyond a hegemonic 'Hindutva' into a far more dangerous new monster with its two faces: the Gujarat model of development of neoliberal free-marketeers to win over middle-class moderates and more crucially engage the corporates as well; and when development falters, to shore it up with a fall-back to the Gujarat model of polarization, used chauvinistically to win elections, engineering communal conflict and consolidating vote banks.

In this age of post-truth and alternative facts (alt-facts), the neoliberal saffron narrative has many takers among the faithful, and even among moderate Hindus, and of course among the rising urban middle class, whose aspirations outrun realistic possibilities and are so prone to believe in the wild promises of strong populist leaders. Large corporations and big capital that have the most to gain from the neoliberalism of this model so willingly turn a blind eye to stresses and strains endemic to it. These are now surfacing with rural distress of farmers and the unemployment of urban youth. The Saffron Parivar sees this as the way to power themselves to a Hindu Rashtra even as they ignore the human cost involved. The saffron brigade and the corporates play on the insecurities of people to further this Janus-faced model and generalize it to the whole country.

Indic society is endemically plural, the result of an evolution over centuries. This is Nehru's 'palimpsest' (Nehru 1985, 1st 1946: 58), a given that cannot be wished away. Tolerance has to be at least a pragmatic minimum survival option. We are now being corralled into a homogenizing cultural nationalism, promoted by a hegemonic 'Hindutva', which is morphing into an intolerant and divisive big brother Sarkar which targets all dissent and difference.

The massive co-optation of people into an authoritarian, patriarchal, upper caste-class movement has not, and cannot, address the underlying contradictions of the burgeoning capitalist development in the state. This is privileging economic growth with little concern for social equity. A cultivated politics of hate is engineered with communal riots and fake news. It precipitates lynchings and atrocities on the vulnerable and polarizes the electorate to help win elections. In a functioning democracy this cannot be sustained indefinitely. But if the contradictions are not resolved within our democratic Constitution, then they will only be contained by authoritarianism careering over into fascism, and/or tackled extra-constitutionally.

Banality of Evil

In our increasingly violent globalized world, brought together and pulled apart by capital accumulation and mass consumption, by genocides and wars, and much else, what role do religion or caste, language or race, patriarchy or politics, and other divides play in legitimizing such violence? There is a surfeit of free-floating violence in our societies. Can we then speak of a 'culture of violence' or are we experiencing a failure of culture and a retreat into a new barbarism? These are hard questions that will not go away. Unfortunately, 'the media is a fundamental element in this process, not only because of what the media show, but also because of what they silence, turn aside or hide'. (Ferrándiz and Robben 2007: 67) No wonder violence now seems banal.

Like a treacherous half-truth, a partial understanding of violence more often than not amounts to a dangerous misunderstanding. Violence is rarely if ever an end in itself; as a means it is an ambiguous, if not a dangerous, aberration. However perverse, however misconceived the relationship between the ends and means, means are always justified in terms of the ends they are meant to achieve. Sadly though, violent means far too easily displace the goals they were intended for, if they do not subvert or betray them. It sets off a spiral of violence that ends with the exhaustion of the protagonists or the defeat of one of them, only to fight another day, if not in the present generation then the next. Revenge becomes loyalty to the dead! Wars to end all wars have merely displaced them to limited but continuing wars, like bush wars, guerrilla violence and terror. The present-day Middle East is ample evidence enough of this.

'A recent estimate of the [20th] century's "megadeaths" is 187 million', (Brzezinski, 1993: 12) including 62 million civilian victims. (Steger, 2003, p. xiii) It would seem that the human proclivity for collective violence has not decreased, though policing in some countries may have improved, giving citizens some sense of security. Yet violence of all kinds finds ample expression in internal conflicts: civil strife and minority bashing, communal riots and pogroms, ethnic cleansing and genocides. The root causes of such violence are first within ourselves, rather than without in the 'other', in our hearts and minds, the culture and structure of our communities, our societies, our countries. Yet we easily cathect our negativities on the 'other' to create a 'them' versus 'us' divide at the service of our own inner demons. Comprehending violence, then, is more complex than it may seem.

Most ordinary citizens are socialized by the culture of the

system to accept its structure, especially when challenging it might have uncomfortable consequences. A few will be conscience-driven enough to dare to question their legitimacy and act on their convictions. But unless the legitimacy of the system, which underpins the violence, is deconstructed and demythologized, challenged and dismantled, the violence will not only not be resolved, but will merely be displaced elsewhere. Even if suppressed, it will simmer below the surface only to re-emerge again in the same or another form, because its wellsprings have not been plugged.

The everyday ordinariness of such social legitimacy normalizes the destructive consequences of violence. Hannah Arendt attributes this to 'the fearsome, word-and-thought-defying banality of evil'. (Arendt 1977: 252) This was true not just of the racist Nazi holocaust, but of all those who perpetrate mass murder, and communal riots and various kinds of systemic violence, that is culturally rationalized.

On 24 March 2016, the International Criminal Court at Hague, sentenced the Bosnia Serb Radovan Karadzic to imprisonment for forty-nine years on ten counts for crimes against humanity, including genocide. But for the accused 'the verdicts stirred barely a flicker of the eyelids', and similar observations were reported in the 1970s with John Vorster, prime minister of apartheid South Africa, or Zhou Enlai in China. (Burns, *New York Times*, 26 March 2016) Such persons are capable of putting on a façade of civility and turning on the charm, say all the right things and, like Hamlet's mother, 'smile, smile, smile and still be a villain'. (Act I, Sc 5, v 108)

Like Adolf Eichmann, these would be certified as normal by psychologists. But the delusions they suffer from are astounding. Eichmann, the architect of Hitler's holocaust, was convinced he was justified in obeying his Fuhrer's orders. Karadzic felt he was misunderstood. His ethnic cleansing was only so that Muslims would return to their homeland, where, he said, they would one day build statutes to him out of love. He even claimed to believe that 'hatred really damages the one who hates, not the one who is hated'. (Burns, *New York Times*, 26 Mar 2016)

South Asia is not new to such mass violence: the Partition

in 1947, Bangladesh's secession in 1971, the long civil war in Sri Lanka, the unrest in Baluchistan, ethnic cleansing in nearby Myanmar. In India we have state violence against its restless people in Kashmir and the Northeast, continuing violence by Maoists in central India and the violent reprisals by the state, the deliberately instigated on-going communal violence and wolf-pack mob-lynchings. What is even more alarming is not so much the support this gets from extremists but also the passive acceptance from those who were once moderates. Increasingly, we see a corrosive politics of hate that demonizes the other and legitimizes violence against them.

The pogrom against Muslims in Gujarat in 2002 was a murderous demonstration of this. Ashok Singhal, as president of the VHP, claimed, that 'the recent communal violence in Gujarat symbolised the first positive response of Hindus to Muslim fundamentalism in 1,000 years.' (*The Hindu*, 23 January 2002) Babu Bajrangi, the Bajrang Dal activist, after tearing out the unborn foetus from a Muslim woman's womb, smashing it and killing the woman, boasted on camera: 'After killing them I felt like Maharana Pratap,' (Siddhartha K, *Tehelka* 29 August 2012) the Rajput king who fought Akbar in the 16th century. Those who instigate mob-lynchings of Muslim cattle traders think they are cleansing this Hindu Rashtra of beef-eaters, as police encounter specialists do with criminals.

Politicians use communal violence to mobilize their vote-banks, while emphatically claiming innocence of any such intention. Some vociferously condemn the vote-bank politics of others, while polarizing the electorate to create their own one. However, human mobs can be rented by political bosses, or instigated by social media. This is now part of the scenario in many countries. The leaders of the ethnic cleansing in Bosnia, the Sri Lankan and Myanmar genocides, the communal conflagrations and mob-lynchings in India are stark instances of horrific collective violence and apparent normalcy.

How is such delusory denial of responsibility for mass violence possible by individuals and communities? How can such people live with it without any sign of remorse, seemingly unaffected, unrepentant, living what seem to be normal lives? Like the mafia boss with his 'happy family' life at home, while his henchmen are out murderously at work elsewhere under his orders. To unravel this conundrum requires careful critical reflection, not available on instant order. Unlearning violence is a long and arduous process.

Clarifying Concepts

Etymologically 'violence' is derived from the Latin 'violentia', vehemence, passionate, uncontrolled force. The verb 'violare' means to violate, infringe. (Honderich 2003: 15) Here we understand 'violence' as violation. Dewey elaborated this as when 'force gone wrong, is harmful, destructive'. (Dewey 1980: 211–15, 244–51) Unlike nature's forces, when humans are responsible for such force it will have an ethical significance, negatively as violation of a human good as when used aggressively, or positively as affirmation of the same, as when used defensively. The Sanskrit himsa goes further. It is more than the act of doing harm, violation. Grammatically speaking, it is a desiderative; this means the desire to harm, the antecedent to the act of harming. This is more radical, but it does not include unintended consequences, though these ought to be subsumed in the act that follows on the desire. The Arabic word 'enuf' is used for violence as vehemence or force, while 'ijbar' is more indirect, referring to coercion, restraint.

John Galtung is most expansive in his understanding of violence. He distinguishes between direct violence against persons, which can be directly opposed and prevented as a law-and-order matter; and structural violence, which is built into the structure and requires restructuring, a more difficult and radical remedy. According to him, 'Violence is present when human beings are being influenced so that their actual somatic and mental realizations are below their potential realizations.' (Galtung 1969: 168) This is not the utilitarian greatest good of the greatest number as conceived by Jeremy Bentham (1748–1832), but a deeper ethical understanding of a society where every person has the possibility to realize their full potential, where the good of each is the good of all and vice versa. This is the 'common good', understood as the social conditions, both structural and cultural, that make possible the human fulfilment of each member of the community.

It may seem too broad an understanding of violence, but there is so much violation of human persons and groups from the social structures they live under: structures of class, caste, religion, gender, and the culture socializes them into acceptance. Only those who are privileged and comfortable within their society can afford to ignore such violence: the wealthy, savarnas, hierarchs and patriarchs; those in the very topmost percentiles, who suffer from affluenza. For these groups violence is but single events that need better law enforcement, not a change in the social status quo. This is a disengaged view of violence from those at the top of the social structure. For the poor, Dalits, tribals, minorities, women, the violations and indignities they suffer, the restrictions of their life-chances and life-choices…this is an institutionalized violation of their rights and dignity, a marginalization of their identity.

Violence is endemic in our society. It is embedded in our social structures and internalized in our culture; it can be contained but not exorcised and eliminated. It has infected our politics where the name of the game is the quest for power as also our economic systems which pursue profit and vested interests as their primary motivation. It has no care for the common good, nor concern for the last and the least.

In this study our concern is collective violence in a broad, inclusive, multilevel discourse. Such violence can be between communities defined by ethnic identities, such as caste, religion, race, even language and region; or by interest groups, such as class, ideology, or special interest. In South Asia the communal violence is mostly premised on ethnic identities, tipping over into ethnic cleansing and genocide. This is the prime arena of such collective violence, whether the identities are polarized based on religion or caste, language or race, or some other divisive marker. The struggle is mostly covert rather than overt.

Causes and Motivations

An ethnic riot is patterned and not entirely unplanned. (Horowitz 1985: 1) In fact, 'to kill in a crowd is, in effect, to kill with impunity. Staging crowd action as an expression of authentic public emotion and outrage is one of the oldest and most sophisticated political technologies among political activists across the Indian subcontinent.' (Hansen 2008: 30)

It can be triggered by some immediate event, but its deeper upstream causes lie in the culture, structure and history of the protagonists. It all adds up to a breakdown of a sense of moral community between the adversaries. This forms the context to the violence, as happens when a society is polarized into hostile opponents. Circumstances of 'uncertainty, impunity and justification', especially, facilitate the violence. (Horowitz 1985: 326) Here's where community leaders and opinion makers contribute to the deep background upstream causes of inter-community violence or to stymie them. Thus, the concatenation of four underlying variables best explains the deadly ethnic riot:

1. A hostile relationship between two ethnic groups;
2. A response to events that engages the emotions of one of these collectivities, a response usually denominated as anger but perhaps more accurately rendered as arousal, rage, outrage, or wrath;
3. A keenly felt sense of justification for killing; and
4. An assessment of the reduced risks of violence that facilitates disinhibition.' (Horowitz 2001: 525)

The cadre on the ground and the ringleaders there are held responsible: the organizations that sponsor the violence, the ideologues in the background that legitimize it, the media that spread biased and fake news, are all implicated. But they seldom, if ever, are held accountable and penalized. And these people never will be if such events are dealt with merely as a breakdown of law and order and not issues of structural injustice. The root causes need to be included in the broader discourse.

Regarding the motivations of the actors, case studies have been quite revealing. Chitralekha summarizes the findings of her ethnographic study, *Ordinary People, Extraordinary Violence*, (2012) of the Maoists in central India and the saffron rioters in Gujarat, thus:

> Most people who killed in the name of the cause did not doubt its veracity… (Chitralekha 2012: 7)
>
> This kind of conviction is not gathered in a hurry. It is well into place in early childhood, often initiated at home but 'completed' in organized forums… (ibid. 8)
>
> To be really convinced it is important that at this stage there are not too many conflicting voices around to confuse… (ibid. 9)
>
> Significantly, however, belief was rarely the reason people killed. (ibid. 10)

The motivations were as banal as, 'to fulfil psycho-social needs as ordinary and as universal as recognition, sense of achievement, social status, *izzat* (honour) in one's peer group and *samaj* (in one's own community not the hated other)…' (ibid. 6)

What seemed to be involved was 'a real and deeply poignant politics of recognition'. (ibid. 224) She elaborated differential motivational profiles for the Naxalites, and the RSS shakha cadre. For the Naxalites, she finds, about a fifth are 'committed' (ibid. 82)…These are generally better educated and their commitment to the cause more ideological. About a fourth are 'opportunists', mostly from the upper and middle castes (ibid. 90)…The rest were 'drifters', who had made an occupational choice for lack of more attractive work-life options (ibid. 94).

Among the RSS cadre she distinguishes three types of active participants: 'First are the mob leaders who instigate. They lead the killing and generally are "political climbers". (ibid. 136) Second are the "killers and killer rapists". These are young and have no role in strategy. Protected from risk, their participation brings "social visibility, potency and power". (ibid. 153) Violence is justified as self-defence and rape is a twisted response to the perceived Muslim "threat to Hindu male sexuality"'. (ibid. 164).

The third category are rioters, who indulge in looting and arson but do not kill. These are dropouts, jobless or just poor. These categories are highly porous with 'more of a circumstantial and logistical boundary than definitive ethical choices'. (ibid. 176) Both categories have 'key-players' (ibid. 177): the 'local supporters' and 'ideological instigators', who 'may not dirty their hand in violence at a local level'. In Ahmedabad, RSS shakhas were active for over a decade creating a 'sharply rising resentment and "anger" against Muslims'. (ibid. 218)

In the areas they now control, the Naxalites have been active for decades, using violence to fight against the injustices and indignities inflicted on the locals. Such initiatives have a long gestation period, they are investments for the long haul: creating the sense of Hindu hurt and entitlement, for the RSS; ideologies that justify violence as apolitical means to social ends with the Naxalites. These are the upstream springs of the downstream violence and unless they are tackled, no law-and-order effort can be effective as a lasting resolution of the underlying antagonism.

Terrorizing Violence

The mass deaths in the Twin Towers attack in New York on 9/11 in 2001, compelled the world's attention and opened a new era of anxiety for the West. But terrorism is far older than this century. There are prototypes: the Israelite Zealots at the time of the Roman occupation of Palestine to the Irgun at the founding of the state of Israel; the Nizārī Ismāʿīliyyah, commonly called Assassins, a breakaway group from Shīʿite Islam, who occupied a string of castles in the mountains of Syria, from the 11th to the 13th centuries, to the present-day jihadis and other terrorist groups. Given the interdependence of fine-tuned societies in a globalized world, contemporary terrorism is far more terrifying and complex. In the context of mass collective violence it acquires new urgency.

To sooner and better deal with such terror, here is a working definition of terrorism: 'violence, perpetrated by individuals, groups, or state-sponsored agents, intended to instill feelings of terror and helplessness in a population in order to influence decision making and to change behavior.' (Moghaddam 2013)

Terrorists intend to disrupt normal civic life by creating extreme fear in people. They do so by provoking a panic reaction in the form of either greater retaliatory violence by the state or from the affected groups of people against the groups the terrorists represent. Deep-seated alienations and resentments are left unaddressed and unresolved in society; and they finally coalesce into anger and rage, and eventually spill over into overt violence, even savage brutalities. Reprisals bring retaliation, which is often even more barbaric and merciless, setting off a spiral of violence and distorted communications. It leads to endemic mistrust and deeper misgivings, upping the ante with each turn of the spiral. This represents a failure of rational communication. (Habermas 2003)

Acts of terror must be read as 'public performances, symbolic statements, aimed at providing a sense of empowerment to desperate communities.' (Juergensmeyer 2000: xii) A psychoanalytical explanation would see in such performative violence, a cannibalistic desire to devour the feared and powerful other, and become feared and powerful thereafter. It is a demand to be noticed, recognized, to be taken seriously, even to the desperation of suicide. People who feel totally disempowered with no effective voice are readily socialized by leaders into terrorist organizations. The most extreme ones among these divide the world into 'them and us', 'good and evil'. (Moghaddam 2013)

George W. Bush, the then American President, did this with 'axis of evil' in 2002. But then it is always they who are the bad guys (Iraq, Iran and North Korea) out to get us, the good guys (Americans) who must now fight back. There can be no grey area between such good and evil. After 9/11, in an address to the joint session of the US Congress on 20 September 2001, President George Bush was unambiguous: 'Either you are with us, or you are with the terrorists.' (*New York Times*, 21 September 2001)

Dzhokhar Tsarnaev and his younger brother, who bombed the Boston marathon in 2013 killing two, were classified as terrorists. And because the boys were Muslims, this was perceived as another example Islamic extremism. President Obama explained: 'Any time bombs are used to target innocent civilians, it is an act of terror.' But on the other hand, Dylan Roof, who gunned down nine Black worshippers 'during a prayer service at the Emanuel African Methodist Episcopal Church in downtown Charleston, South

Carolina in 2015, is 'widely portrayed as a hater and not a terrorist because, based on the available evidence, he is a white supremacist and not a Muslim extremist...a deranged lone wolf rather than a terrorist'. (Chong 2015)

It would seem that *your* crowd bombings are terrorizing people; *our* mass shootings (legally defined in the USA as the death of five or more persons due to gun violence) are merely the act of a 'deranged lone wolf'. The same happens closer home: when members of a minority religious persuasion kill people, they are terrorists acting for the collective, for which the community is liable; while the killers from the majority religious community, gaurakshaks and other lynchers, are exceptions to the rule in a tolerant, peaceful community. This anomaly is becoming the elephant in the room: the *other* is the bad terrorist; *we* are promoting a worthy cause or responding in self-defence.

Cosmic War

Gods of war and extremist ideologies divide the world into warring sides. Religious fundamentalism and ideological conviction lend themselves to sharply defined social identities that are totalizing and impervious to other worldviews. This is a binary universe where those who are not for you are against you. The consequent tension inevitably leads to conflict and confrontation, in a win-lose game. This gets locked into a zero sum understanding of power in the struggle for dominance. The options for survival are flight or fight. Some groups may prefer to withdraw and found counter-cultural communities away from the mainstream. Others perceive this as unviable because the whole cosmos is involved in the conflict, and the victorious utopia will be theirs: as religious fundamentalists would believe if not here, then in the hereafter; or as the ideologically committed would hold, if not now, then in the inexorable march of history.

For these extremists, the present struggle will necessarily build up to an Armageddon. Mark Juergensmeyer aptly calls this 'cosmic war' and elaborates its script as so 'central to virtually all of the incidents of performance violence'. (Juergensmeyer 2000: 146)

As with all intensely participatory drama, warfare needs rituals and myths, symbols and images, as also heroes and exemplars. Secular ideologies have to invent and socialize them into people; religious traditions have a vast repertoire to drawn on. This is why cosmic war seems driven by religious belief when, in actuality, it turns religion into a galvanizing and violent ideology, not a spiritually inspiring faith. In the same way, secular ideologies become functional equivalents of religion, even though they may be overtly anti- or a-religious.

Cosmic warriors are obsessed with the compelling need to bring some kind of order and harmony into a world of injustice and oppression, of rapid and radical change, when the old is lost and new still unborn. Religion and ideology in their different domains foreground the promise to contain the chaos and restore the lost paradise so yearned for. They offer some sense of purpose, of meaning, something to live for and to die for, in an estranged and disenchanted world.

This is where these warriors find value and their extreme commitment must be read in the light of Weber's value rationality. Those who do not share this value or cannot even understand it are beyond the pale. For instance, suicide bombers obviously do not value human life, their own or others'. To threaten them with capital punishment is a gross misjudgement. The use of torture on alleged terrorists has been rationalized by hyper-legality with terms like 'enhanced interrogation'—an obvious and not too subtle obfuscation. For the victim, it becomes a confirming, self-fulfilling prophecy.

Several conditions can be associated with this war: 'The cosmic struggle is understood to be occurring in this world rather than in a mythical setting…Believers identify personally with the struggle… The struggle is at a point of crisis in which individual action can make all the difference…' (Juergensmeyer 2000: 161)

These are some of the characteristics of a cosmic struggle: 'The struggle is perceived as a defence of basic identity and dignity. Losing the struggle would be unthinkable. The struggle is blocked and cannot be won in real time or in real terms.' (Juergensmeyer 2000: 161) Together these give cosmic war an aura of the sacred.

Defeat must not be entertained; loss can only be no more than transitory, merely a prelude to the final victory of a predetermined destiny, either beyond our horizons now, or even beyond our cosmos later.

Religious violence, rooted in its binary of good versus evil, often seeks to establish its own religious state in place of the prevailing regime. This has been a recurring quest of violent religious extremists, beginning with the zealots of Roman Palestine and the medieval crusaders of Europe and Assassins of medieval Syria, ISIS in the Middle East, the Taliban in Afghanistan and Pakistan, and the Khalistani, Bajrang Dal and the Vishwa Hindu Parishad in India. The counter-violence of the state also has its own motivating nationalist ideology with its binary divisions of good and bad along the axis of evil: either you are for us or against us, a nationalist or an anti-nationalist, a secular liberal or a religious fundamentalist. Though each has its own take on and justification for their cosmic war, paradoxically now, 'these differences are getting smudged; in its new incarnation religious violence too is acquiring many of the features of state violence' (Nandy 2013: 103) and vice versa.

Defusing Terror

Trying to repress or contain terror with violence is counter-productive. At most, it can be a temporary, transitory measure to reassure the people who are targeted and then panic. Since 'terrorists have a vested interest in provoking violence', (Varshaney 2003) brutal retaliation only confirms them in their convictions and commitments. Fearful bystanders may feel somewhat secure that action has been taken, terrorists have been dealt with and punished; but this is merely a temporary break before the next violent terror attack. The root causes of the terror remain in place.

The use of torture may break a person or force a confession. But such confessions are of little value, and there are more intelligent ways than 'enhanced interrogation' of getting relevant information. Ali Soufan, FBI agent till 2005, winner of the Kennedy award of 2018, and author of books on Bin Laden (2017) and Al Qaeda

(2011), rubbishes the claims of the effectiveness of torture, and blames the lack of coordination between the CIA and the FBI for security failures like 9/11. (*New York Times*, 22 April 2009) In the end it only succeeds in brutalizing the torturers themselves.

Such cruel brutality fatally compromises the crucial link between law and justice and leaves us with a system of enforced order without credible law. More effective would be to address the upstream roots of such violence: choking off finances, cutting off communication links, better intelligence gathering, and most crucially addressing the deep-rooted causes in the communities that spawn such violent persons. If you try to eliminate terrorists when the community from which they recruit feels violence is justified, you end up with genocide. This is hardly a civilized response.

To bring these people back into the mainstream, the upstream causes of their alienation must be addressed. To understand them better we need first 'to reconstruct the immediate, and the more significant longer term context that makes participation in such violence possible'. (Chitralekha, 2012: 25) They must be given effective voice and choice, a sense of being treated with fairness and decency, given effective participation in decision-making structures, so that the past may heal, the present may be shared and a project for the future envisaged. (Moghaddam 2013)

Such a democracy cannot just be procedural, it must be substantive as well, committed to liberty, equality, fraternity, premised on constitutional values and law, not populist or chauvinist policies and practice. In other words, we need a broad social justice of restoration and healing for the common good, not a narrow legalistic one of retribution and revenge for partisan interests. This requires an ethical and sensitive expression in our culture, its values and norms, as also our legal structures, our political and legal systems. The Afzal Guru case is a pertinent example of our collective failure in this regard.

Afzal Guru was awarded the death sentence by a Delhi court on 18 December 2002 after being convicted of conspiracy to attack Parliament on 13 December 2001 under the notorious Prevention of Terrorism Act, 2002 (POTA), under which confession in police custody is deemed acceptable in court. The death sentence was upheld by Delhi High Court on 29 October 2003, and finally two years later on 4 August 2005, his appeal was rejected by the Supreme Court as well. Following the rejection of a mercy petition by the President of India, he was executed on 9 February 2013 and his body was buried within the precincts of Delhi's Tihar Jail.

Even while acknowledging that 'there is and could be no evidence amounting to criminal conspiracy', the judgement nevertheless went on to confirm the sentence because 'the incident, which resulted in heavy casualties, had shaken the entire nation, and the collective conscience of society will only be satisfied if capital punishment is awarded to the offender'. This 'is a stain on India's democracy' and leaves a pertinent question unanswered. As Arundhati Roy has asked: 'Who crafted our collective conscience on the parliament attack? Could it have been the facts we gleaned from the papers? Or the films we watched on TV?' (*The Guardian*, 2 Feb 2013)

Collective Conscience

The origins of the concept of 'collective conscience' can be traced to the sociology of Emile Durkheim in his influential text, *Division of Labour in Society* (1893), where he concludes: 'The totality of beliefs and sentiments common to the average members of a society forms a determinate system with a life of its own. It can be termed the collective or common consciousness.' (Durkheim 1997: 38–39)

Crime offends against this consciousness and so must be punished so that society can be safeguarded. The punishment of crime and deviance defines and reaffirms this consciousness. This becomes the unintended functional necessity of crime. This is what courts do when they sentence convicted criminals to exemplary punishment and this too is how the death penalty is being used in India.

In 1980, the majority of four Supreme Court judges restricted the death penalty to 'the rarest of rare case'. (Bachan Singh 2 SCC 684) In 1983 Justice M.P. Thakkur in the Supreme Court first articulated the 'shock to the collective conscience' as grounds for the death penalty. (Machhi. 3 SCC 470) However, in 2009, Justice J. Ganguly has cautioned the court not 'to prioritise the sentiments of outrage' insightfully adding: 'The expression "rarest of rare cases" is not to be read as a mere play on words or a tautologous expression…This is a very loaded expression and is not to [be] trifled with. It is pregnant with respect for the inviolability of human life. That is why the word "rare" has been used twice and once in a superlative sense. Therefore, the significance of this expression cannot be watered down on a perceived notion of a "cry for justice".' (Rameshwarbhai 5 SCC 740)

Moreover, later that year, Justice S.B. Sinha was especially critical of factoring in collective conscience into a death sentence meant only for the rarest of the rare: 'Public opinion is difficult to fit in the rarest of rare matrix. People's perception of crime is neither an objective circumstance relating to the crime nor to the criminal. Perception is extraneous to conviction as also sentencing, at least in capital sentencing according to the mandate of the Bachan Singh.' (Santosh 6 SCC 498).

There are obvious difficulties with the judicial use of collective conscience. Already in 1970, Justice Douglas Black of the United States Supreme Court opined: 'Judges are as human as anyone, and as likely as others to see the world through their own eyes and find the "collective conscience" remarkably similar to their own.' (397 US 254)

Judges are not equipped to assess public opinion, which in any case is volatile and extremely difficult to judge in a divided and diverse population of more than a billion in India. Today public opinion is largely formed by the media, which has as notorious a memory and attention span as a mass population. What happens if the collective conscience goes counter to the law and the Constitution? Are the courts to be ruled by majoritarian aspirations and perceptions? Will political populism decide the dispensation of justice? Are the courts to be subjected to the tyranny of the majority as politicians are? Should personal conscience cease to be true to itself?

After serious evaluation, a hundred and forty countries have abolished the death penalty de jure or de facto. It has not been found to be an effective deterrent. India was on this path with its 'rarest of the rare' criterion. Now violence and terror and the ill-advised blowback has created mass hysteria, fear and rage. If we do not find another way of coping with this real danger, we will end up internalizing the violence we visit on others. As Gandhiji warned, an eye for an eye will make the whole world blind.

Levels of Analysis

Though the focus of this study is collective violence, we must distinguish several levels at which we need to respond. For, collective violence is not a matter of interaction between individuals, nor is it concerned merely with an aggregate of individuals, the sum of all its parts. This would be an unfortunate reductionism. Rather, collective violence concerns groups and communities, embedded in a social structure and held together by common identities, which colour and orient their social behaviour. There are then several levels of discourse which correspond to this structure, which must be considered for a more comprehensive understanding of these phenomena and a more effective response. Here we flag four such levels and the historical context of collective violence.

Socio-psychological level

The first level is socio-psychological. At this level, collective violence must be understood in terms of inter-personal relationships and interactions and even though it cannot be understood solely in such terms, we must address it. What are the individual's psychopathologies involved in collective action that allow individuals to be aggregated into such violent groups? How are violators and victims involved in this entanglement?

Here we can explore in the violators the 'narcissism of grandiosity', which seeks to fulfil a perceived 'rightful' and 'manifest destiny', to correct historical wrongs and avenge hurtful memories. Complementary to this, in the violated, there is the 'narcissism of victimhood'. This sense of victimhood can also be found in the violator too, but as an inverted image, used to rationalize their aggression.

Here violator and victim often reverse roles, because both come from unresolved feelings in regard to some violation, real or imagined, whether this precipitates the active involvement of as perpetrator or the passive aggression of the sufferer. In both, violence is seen as legitimated by a perverted sense of 'justice' that expresses itself in sadistic or masochistic exaggerations.

A negative self-image and deep insecurities are the root causes of such pathologies. Thus Sudhir Kakar in his *Colours of Violence* (Kakar, 1995) explains how the loss of self-esteem for the masses, and a consciousness of defeat for the elites leads to apathy, chronic discontent, or rebellious rage at those held responsible for the loss of old social forms and ideals. (1995: 190) As Ernest Wolf points out, 'a social identity can support a crumbling self the way a scaffolding can support a crumbling building'. (Wolf 1988: 48) In such a situation of humiliation and helplessness, mobilization and support are readily provided by group fanaticism and extremism. Ashis Nandy (1983: 38, 68–69) too has explained how an inadequate and insecure male ego, at times under the apparent challenge of the machismo of the 'other', is inclined to overcome its insecurity through violence. Franz Fanon would even privilege violence against oppressors by victims in order to recover their subjectivity, as he explains in *The Wretched of the Earth*. (Fanon 1961) But this has only made our world even more prone to violent aggression.

Ashis Nandy writing on *The Loss and Recovery of Self*, shows how it takes a Gandhi to demonstrate how 'activism and courage could be liberated from aggressiveness' (Nandy 1983: 54) Examining such pathologies may help to understand why there is so little remorse or memory in the aftermath of collective violence. These are moments of collective madness that all those who are implicated in it seem eager to forget, whether they are the perpetrators or the sufferers, those otherwise implicated or mere bystanders. However, such amnesia can only be very partial and selective. Unhealed wounds of the victims and the unresolved fears of the violators, the suppressed memories of the passive witnesses can only fester and become the breeding grounds for even more violence and terror. Unaddressed psychopathologies of the violators only become more dangerous and violent if they are allowed to go scot free; those of the victims become more oppressive and unpredictable if not dealt with in time; and apathetic witnesses become more indifferent.

Moreover, just as at times a superiority complex can be a mask for an unacknowledged but subconscious sense of inferiority, and vice versa, an inferiority complex projected as a superiority one, the narcissism of grandiosity can be the inversion of narcissism of victimhood. When such inversions reach psychopathological proportions, it calls for analysis by professionally competent social psychologists.

In the socio-psychological perspective then, collective violence is understood in terms of group relationships that precipitate inter-group conflict and tension. Thus, when narcissism as a self-referent preoccupation is aggregated to the group level, it becomes a powerful jingoistic chauvinism. This is often perceived as altruism since the individual is sacrificing for the sake of the group and is pursuing the group's goals and purposes and not one's own. It may well be one more reason for the lack of remorse that accompanies such chauvinistic collective violence, which is then justified and legitimated in the eyes of the individual, who is now quite completely absorbed into the collective.

Thus escape from personal responsibility is near total, when this narcissism expresses itself in a sense of collective victimhood, a sense that the world has been unfair and unjust to one's community and/or social group. This festering wound may then precipitate vengeance in the name of 'justice' for 'our' group, at times even to the point of suicidal revenge.

Eco-political level

The second level, eco-political, is premised on a structural analysis of society and based on interest groups. In the Marxist perspective, communal violence is nothing but an aspect of the contradiction in the political economy, which in the given circumstances rather than grounding itself in the social reality of class contradictions and interest politics, gets trapped into the 'false consciousness' of communal conflict and expresses itself in identity politics. For Marxists then, such conflict is but the clash of class interests that are communally manipulated and used to distract from the real issues and thus protect vested interests of the dominant classes. A resolution of the underlying class contradictions and tension is therefore a *sine qua non* in addressing collective violence. For the communist this can only be done by class struggle and if necessary, by class war.

On the other hand, liberals would give more importance to the political, not just to the economic. Thus Sandra Freitag (1990) sees communal violence as an attempt to appropriate public space for essentially communal group purposes; Paul Brass (2003) sees the communal riot as one more systematic manipulation of electoral politics within a procedural democracy. This, of course, distances the polity from any effective substantive democracy; just as appropriating public space for private purposes contracts rather than expands the rights of citizenship and subverts rather than enhances the role of civil society.

Within a national society, the role of the state becomes crucial in any conflict mediation. This is not to deny the importance of other actors, community leaders citizens' associations, NGOs in civil society. Their role becomes correspondingly more crucial as the state fails in its role as a just and fair mediator. But here again there must be more than 'narcissistic compassion'. There must be not merely affective 'consciousness of kind', but rather an effective empathy that does not restrict fellow-feeling to one's own or similar people, but extends to the larger community of citizens and beyond.

Only a genuine pluralism in society can adequately address this challenge without alienating or assimilating the 'other'. This will eventually further internalize in society the very violence that the dominant group perpetrates on the subservient one. Exorcising this 'demon' later is always a difficult and painful process. Thus in the colonial era, occupying regimes were rarely if ever non-violent, even when they intended to be paternal. The violence they perpetrated on their colonial subjects today finds its expression in the terrible wars between the colonial powers that engulf the whole world. Not that these wars resolved the conflict between these warring nations. It ended in a cold war, in which two nuclear armed powers faced off, restrained only by the threat of Mutually Assured Destruction (MAD).

In the community of nations today even a sole superpower has not assured peace. Today it is actually subverting peace and foregrounding a chauvinist nationalism, very much as fascist states did earlier. We are left with a world of military misadventures and continuing terrorism in an escalating spiral of violence. There seems to be no effective solution to the intractable problems this has precipitated: the mounting human tragedy we are faced with on a global scale, displaced populations, war refugees and economic migrants, environmental degradation.

The Hobbesian 'war of all against all', so deeply embedded in the DNA of our world, has become a self-fulfilling prophecy. It is the matsyanyaya wherein the big fish feed on the smaller ones. Free-market neoliberalism undermines economic equality, as cultural nationalism does communal harmony. And there are no prophets left to turn us to the paths of peace.

Socio-cultural Level

At the socio-cultural level, the perspective is premised on a cultural analysis of diverse ethnic groups. For often, the social divisions—whether they are founded on class interests, cultural divides, such as caste, language or other kinds of group identities—follow cultural faultlines that underscore earlier divides. This further reinforces vested interests on either side and in fact provides a whole symbolic and ritual repertoire that can be used to facilitate the mobilization and manipulation of violence through the use of powerful popular images and myths. Unfortunately, the parties to such collective conflicts have been more adept at using these more for violence than reconciliation, unlike Gandhiji and those inspired by him—Martin Luther King, Nelson Mandela and the Dalai Lama—did. In such situations the need for third-party mediation becomes imperative.

To understand how a riot becomes a routinely enacted public ritual to reinforce this agenda of fanaticism and extremism, Stanley Tambiah's concepts of routinization and more importantly, ritualization of collective violence may help us to perceive some of the organized and anticipated programmed and recurring features and phases of seemingly spontaneous chaotic and orgiastic actions of the mob as aggressor and victimizer. (Tambiah 1996: 230)

Certainly, 'public performances' are important, especially in situations of collective behaviour. However, there can as well be public events geared towards reconciliatory and integrative social purposes, they need not necessarily be directed to violent and disruptive ones. What is chosen will depend very much on our worldview: whether this privileges a desire for conflict or inspires a need for reconciliation.

In the *Clash of Civilizations* (1996), Huntington speaks of cultural faultlines that are irreducible and can only be frozen into a fragile equilibrium of competing and ultimately irreconcilable civilizational contradictions. The difficulty with Huntington is that he seems to be carried away by the geological metaphor of the faultline, which only changes or shifts within geological timeframes. But cultures are not written in the inner crust of the earth, they are not hard-wired in our heads; rather they are constructed by human beings and hence can be deconstructed and reconstructed on varying and alternative bases by these very human beings, though this is a generational endeavour.

This is not to say that cultural faultlines are not important, but rather that they are never inevitable or permanent. There are certainly alternative readings of history that are clearly in contradiction to Huntington. In fact, rather than stress the clash of civilization what we need today is to emphasize the dialogue of cultures. Unfortunately, whether within the national or the international community, the dominant and the powerful seem to have little time for this mutual exchange.

But before such a reorientation or reconstruction, we must first understand the identity crisis that underlines these cultural divides. In a situation of alienation and anomie which is brought about by the rapid social changes precipitated by modernization, especially when interest politics have failed to address the real needs of people—concerns of equity and equality, of social justice and human rights—identity politics takes over, and this often becomes the politics of passion. For while claiming to affirm positive identities, it often plays on real or imagined grievances. And while it is easy to mobilize groups on this basis of opposition to an out-group and affirm the unity of the in-group, it is much more difficult to gear such mobilization towards the genuine interests and real concerns of the members of the in-group. For, the politics of passion inevitably involves its own compulsions and irrationalities that, time and again, have benefited leaders more than the people.

It is, indeed, critical for social identities not to become exclusive and 'solidary' or monolithic. Rather in a pluralist society we need inclusive and positive, secure and multiple identities. In India the identities we hold in common as citizens, as members and participants in an overarching Indic civilizational and cultural unity need to be privileged, if the unresolved contradictions and conflicts in our subcontinental society are to be contained and negotiated peacefully and respectfully, before they spill over into the collective violence that is now reaching proportions that could engulf us all.

Regrettably, the 'cultural nationalism' being promoted in our country today is a movement to protect the vested interests of various upper caste-class elites. It draws on the popular religiosity of Hindu masses to promote a Hindu nationalism that is supposedly cultural but in reality is aggressively political, obfuscates economic class inequalities, while exploiting cultural, religious and other ethnic divides. Hindutva is precisely the ideology that promotes such a nationalism premised on upper caste/class interests. It is at best Sanskritic and at worst Brahminical, both of which are quite alien to the subaltern classes of this country, whatever their religious affiliation may be.

One can see parallels here with pan-Islamism that seeks a theocratic state today; as also with Western Christianity and its imperialism that fought for God and country, and in its day legitimized colonialism as part of the white man's burden; or more ominously, as with National Socialism and its racist inspiration that produced the genocide of the holocaust. The 'blut und boden' (blood and land) cry of the Third Reich ominously echoed by the pitribhu, punyabhu, (Fatherland, holyland) shibboleth of Savarkar and the Sangh Parivar. Culture and race have served to legitimate collective aggression and exclusion. It easily spills over into religious violence, which is the next level we discuss.

Socio-religious Level

At the religious level, collective violence often develops its own theology of suffering or of aggression. Within a given religious worldview, it is always possible that certain religious texts and doctrines, myths and beliefs allow for this. The theologies of suffering have always appealed to the victims, just as the religious justification of aggression has ruled the conscience of the victors. Thus suffering can be justified as the will of God or Allah or as karma carried over from an earlier birth, and therefore not entirely the responsibility of the violators but something to be laid at the door of the victims themselves or their gods.

The Christian crusade it in its day was legitimized by an aggressive religious understanding of a holy war, supposedly willed by their God, not a defensive war but a war of aggression. Today, the Christian right, claiming to be a 'moral majority', has launched a new crusade against the religious fanaticism of others. They vigorously back the neo-conservatives in their 'war on terror', which uses massive state aggression and terror all in the name of democracy and freedom. The religious jihad is also being misused in pan-Islamic ideologies to legitimate violence and establish a theocratic state, while the Bajrang Dal and the Vishwa Hindu Parishad are now doing no less for a Hindu Rashtra. Thus we have 'new crusaders' fighting the 'axis of evil', self-selected shaheeds avenging Allah, and the religious warriors on their rath yatras proclaiming Ram Rajya, just as Christian Crusaders once did in the Holy Land.

However, such 'a ruthless, clinical theology of violence must inevitably lead to loss of self and of signification.' (Nandy 1994:

26) For too long, we in India have flattered ourselves as being a tolerant people with a liberal religious philosophy from above, even as we use this to compromise and protect political and communal interests from below. But without an acknowledgement of our own failure and guilt there can be no meaningful and healing forgiveness, either sincerely asked for or gratefully received.

What we need is a theology of forgiving that does not amount to forgetting. In South Africa, an Anglican pastor, Father Michael Lapsley, whose hands were blown off by a letter-bomb during the apartheid struggle, has talked of a bicycle theology that must be eschewed. It reasons thus: You steal my bicycle, and I forgive you when you ask for forgiveness; you get forgiveness and to keep the bicycle as well. I get the merit for forgiving but I have to walk. Keeping the gains of the violence and injustice one has been responsible for is like benefiting from stolen goods. Indeed, benefiting from them cannot be justified even when these have been stolen by others, previous generations, for instance. Surely, fairness demands that some reparation be made to those who might have more legitimately inherited the benefit.

In other words, both victim and violator must experience a genuine sense of closure, where the past does not cast a dark shadow of regret and resentment on new beginnings; or else grievances and anger of the victims, guilty consciences and bad faith of the violators will fester and come back to haunt us. Forgetting without healing only allows the sense of hurt and injustice to remain unresolved. Forgiveness by the violated is indeed important, but so is the violators' confession of guilt and their asking forgiveness from the violated. The violators must be named and shamed. Confession and forgiveness are essential for both, to redeem the violator as also to exorcise their violence, for the recognition of the violated and the healing of their hurt.

However, it is surely the victims that must claim our compassion. Their healing requires recognition of their hurt, the injustice and humiliation inflicted on them. Most importantly, they need help to put together their broken lives. To promise the victims redress in another world does little to help them reconstruct their lives in this one. They need healing in this one too. Moreover, the psychological trauma of being violated and then neglected and forgotten is surely one of the worst and most inhuman sufferings inflicted on the victims of such violence. More than just blaming the victims it amounts to damning them as well.

And for violators, admitting their violation to their victims testifies to the authenticity of their repentance and change; it is a first step in the reconciliation process. Denial and suppression leave the way open to a recurrence, perhaps in more disastrous ways and even self-destructive, self-hating ones.

Historical Context

An explanation at one level cannot stand alone. It must be read in the context of the others for a holistic comprehension and an integrated response. Moreover, the four levels of collective violence indicated must be considered in the appropriate historical background to contextualize our present: where we came from and how we got here, and how we can begin our trek to where we want to be. This would help us recover the 'religious tolerance from everyday Hinduism, Islam, Buddhism, and Sikhism, rather than wish that ordinary Hindus, Muslims, Buddhists and Sikhs will learn tolerance from the various fashionable secular theories of statecraft.' (Nandy 1992: 86).

The Sufi-bhakti traditions, so embedded in the living popular religious traditions of our people, have been the basis of the traditional inter-community tolerance in Indic society down the ages. This is evidenced by the peoples of India, at times in spite of their elites and leaders, who today have manipulated people to adopt a false consciousness of communal conflict and violence, making religion a political ideology to suit their own partisan interests.

The need for a genuine religious pluralism, grounded in these popular traditions, and a celebration of our multi-culturalism is where we must found an active civil society, premised on constitutional values and norms. Here we will find practical strategies for effectively dealing with the upstream causes of the collective violence that infect our society today. What we really need is our own Truth and Justice Commission that will heal the wounds of the past, sublimate historical memories that have simmered in our collective unconscious, and inspire hope for our future together.

Any attempt at lasting reconciliation must address the multiple levels at which collective violence affects a society; and this requires a neutral space for mediation. However, the parties to the conflict may be too entangled to do this for themselves on their own. At times, the victor can impose a resolution but if this does not address the real needs of the victims and is not accepted by them as fair, it cannot be lasting or stable. The experience of the Truth and Reconciliation Commission of South Africa demonstrates the effectiveness of third-party mediation. The special importance of the state as the protector of vulnerable people, of the human rights of all its citizens is paramount in situations of communal violence.

Anatomy of a Lynching

On the 17 July 2018, in response to a writ petition in *Tehseen S. Poonawalla vs Union of India*, the Supreme Court, alarmed at the recent increase of public lynchings, directed the Government of India to enact a law in regard to mob lynchings and it set out guidelines as well. (Reportable in the Supreme Court of India civil original jurisdiction writ petition (civil) (NO.330 OF 2018, pp 9-10, https://www.sci.gov.in/supremecourt/2018/3158/3158_2018_Judgement_01-Oct-2018.pdf)

However, as mentioned before, treating such horrific collective violence as a law-and-order problem, as the Court implied, simply fails to address the upstream causes of collective violence. Repeat performances, then, are inevitable and the new level of violence eventually becomes the new normal. Judicial commissions, investigating riots and pogroms, even ethnic cleansing, often do the same: dealing with lawbreakers and attempting to restore order, rather than with the societal reasons, not merely the occasion, for the breakdown of public order. This must be done in the context of the multiple dimensions involved and a response made accordingly.

Lynchings are not acts by individuals, they are collectively engaged and murderously violent acts. Whether by commission or omission, by fault or default, actively engaged or passively approving, we are all involved, we cannot be neutral bystanders. Race or language, caste or class, political or religious communities may be the faultlines along which antagonism grow and spill over into overt violence. As with all collective violence, here too, for an incisive understanding and an appropriate response, the multiple levels involved must be distinguished though they cannot be separated. Thus lynchings involve several levels as well. At the socio-psychological level, personal psychopathologies, insecurities, suppressed anger, emotional imbalance are the source of the conflicts. At the eco-political level, it is competition for scarce resources and ideological differences that coalesce and activate vested interests, which then become aggressively self-protective. At the socio-cultural level closed and totalizing community identities can murderously clash when on the defensive and provoked. At the socio-religious level, religious traditions and practices may feel threatened evoking the 'religion in danger' syndrome.

The historical context for these mobs must be traced back to colonial India. In the official perception, the crowd was perceived as faceless, aggressive and irrational. It was driven by religious passion and beyond the ken of colonial sociology. (Pandey 1990) Because 'the effects were dangerous and destructive', crowds 'had to be dealt with through overwhelming and resolute force.' (Hansen 2008: 4) Such a stance refuses to entertain a sociological explanation for the social fact of such a crowd, contra Durkheim who convincingly argued the opposite.

In postcolonial India, Thomas Hansen distinguishes 'two categories of public violence': against the state and the communal crowd, 'both of which mark a breaking of a norm and the creation of an exceptional situation, both of which are widely endorsed and perfectly legitimate elements of political life in the wider population'. (Hansen 2008: 9) He suggests three plausible reasons for such crowd violence: as 'a legacy of the anti-colonial struggle…a form of collective catharsis…the imperative of visibility'. (Hansen 2008: 11–18) Collective expressions of anger are 'always a risky if not dangerous game for movements and individuals, a game where one risks forfeiting goodwill and legitimacy'. (Hansen 2008: 20) Of the two, the communal crowd is the 'more dangerous, and more ambiguous'. (Hansen 2008: 21) The crowd protest against the state is largely within the domain of interest politics, and generally open to rational articulation and negotiations. Hence common ground can be found for social compacts and political alliances, in other words, a practical civil life for citizens and a pragmatic politics for the state.

The communal crowd is squarely in the area of identity politics, and identities are not readily amenable to rational calculation, they are embedded in our way of life, giving us a sense of how we are and where we belong. It is threatened by change and resists negotiation and compromise. When under threat, real or imagined, the crowds mobilize and polarize their world into a 'them' and 'us' dichotomy, and the more the threat is felt, the more passionate, the more unreasonable and uncompromising they can become. When the passions are negative, this readily tips over into the politics of hate, nurtured on a sense of self-righteous grievance and irrational insecurity.

The two types of politics are not binary dichotomies, one can slip into the other or both can be implicated in a particular instance of such 'performance violence'. (Juergensmeyer 2000: 146) Thus ethnic and religious divides lend themselves to be mobilized into a politics of passion and hate by slogans such as, 'our honour has been violated', 'religion in danger'. Affirmative action and minority rights divide interest groups that lend themselves to politicization. But surely there is an overlap between the two, though one or the other may be more foregrounded in particular instances.

Thus caste atrocities and communal killings—perpetrated by lynch-mobs or by individuals—riots and pogroms are obvious instances of identity politics motivated by passion and hate. But vested interests of caste hierarchy are also involved, for they are threatened by reservation quotas and affirmative action. And so they need to protect themselves, draw the line, 'show them their place', 'teach them a lesson'. Minority rights, even when they are protective and not promotive, are seen as discriminatory, and as compromising the majority community's interests. Political leaders use this 'appeasement' to whip up a politics of passion against minority communities.

In India, linguistic conflict has been largely defused and contained with linguistic states. The Partition was supposed to be the answer to Hindu-Muslim orgies of violence. However, post-Independence political leaders on both sides have mobilized religious identities and upped the ante, driving a politics of passion into a hate politics. This consolidates support in their own communities and becomes a convenient alibi for their own failure to break the prevalent hegemony and deliver on the revolution of rising expectation of the country's masses, or their own community's expectations.

Extremist organizations thrive on such negative passions. Their members are indoctrinated into a single worldview, which provides 'a thick ideological buffer against guilt'. (Chitralekha 2012: 149) Alternative views are not permitted nor any exposure to them allowed, lest their 'faith' be questioned. This is a walled-in consciousness with singular and totalizing identities. Ideologically derived slogans and sound-bites are repeated over and over till they become part of accepted 'common sense', 'stock wisdom'. Demonization of the other dehumanizes them and rationalizes brutal scapegoating on them, without guilt or remorse.

How do we explain this 'transformation of human character of good people…led into the temptation to do the unthinkable to others?' (Zimbardo 2007: xiii) When situational forces are sufficiently powerful to overwhelm otherwise ordinary people, they set aside temporarily, personal attributes of morality, compassion, or sense of justice and fair play and indulge in such horrible brutalities, of rape and murder, even mutilation and desecration. In Philip Zinbardo's *The Lucifer Effect: Understanding How Good People Turn Evil* (2007), he describes his Stanford prison experiments in which normal people were grouped as 'prisoners' or 'guards'. The experiment demonstrated how easily power relations degenerate into brutal torture. The experiment had to be abandoned. In his TED talk (https://blog.ted.com/ted2008_will_ev/) he identifies seven steps on the slippery slope to dehumanization:

1. mindlessly taking the first small step
2. dehumanization of others
3. de-individualization of self (anonymity)
4. diffusion of personal responsibility
5. blind obedience to authority
6. uncritical conformity to group norms
7. passive tolerance of evil through inaction or indifference

William Golding's *Lord of the Flies* (1954) illustrates how even with children the descent into barbarism is slippery and cruel.

Marco Olson's *The Logic of Collective Action* (1965) shows how there is a tipping point at which increasing numbers rush to join in the collective activity. This genie once let out of the bottle cannot be put back at will.

Nuanced Response

Violence has become ubiquitous in our world. The media reportage serves it up to us in commodified, consumable packages of news and features, with little concern for analysis and response. It even becomes a perverse voyeurism. Eventually, its everyday familiarity makes it easier to accept, till we reach the point of information overload and filter it out to acceptable levels then rationalize away our own implication in it. However, we are all involved actively or passively, by commission or omission, directly or indirectly. The banality of such violence has so overtaken us that we are quite blasé until it suddenly crashes into our comfort zone, and directly impacts our lives as it did on 9/11 in New York and 26/11 in Mumbai. Till then it is none of our business.

Moreover, we seem to be unwilling, unable and unready to address the upstream causes where the roots of such violence lie. Such neglect cannot be benign. Our hasty response to violence with rationalized counter-violence, even if it is defensive, or worse pre-emptive in anticipation of an attack, only accelerates the action-reaction syndrome, thus further compounding and complicating the violence itself. The evil only gets more deeply embedded in society, internalized in the members, ready to surface again. For even when it is apparently eliminated, others take to similar violence on cue, sometimes in another theatre. The war on terror has not ended terror; rather it has globalized it.

Violence in society is a pervasive and complex phenomenon. It hollows out our cultural values and brutalizes our social relationships. We must address collective violence in a nuanced and complex manner at all these levels in which it is embedded into society. If it is to have any effective traction at the many levels of its upstream causes, we must deconstruct the deep background from which these arise. For, the sources of this collective violence are complex: at the socio-psychological level the issue is anxiety and fear; at the cultural one, it is identity and dignity; at the political one it is participation and agency; at the economic one the issue is equality and equity; and finally at the religious one it is secularism and freedom of conscience.

The *Loss and Recovery of Self* (Nandy 1983) discusses how the eventual recovery of self inevitably brings insecurity and anxiety that easily morphs into anger. This can be further manipulated by vested interests into violent rage. Containing and reversing this trajectory requires deconstructing the narrative of old lost selves in their old lost worlds and recovering them again with a new narrative, the birthing of new selves in new worlds. Rather than using a scaffolding to shore up a crumbling self and compounding the problem, this demands reconstructing a new self around the original core identity into one with multiple identities, flexible and fluid, not a singular totalizing self-identity.

At the socio-psychological level, we need such multiple identities, both personal and community, which will eschew violence and embrace non-violence. Rationalizing homogenization in a society destroys the multiple identities of plural society, undermining any tolerance and setting the stage for conflict between individuals and communities. The discourse here must confront the imperative of pluralism for a peaceful society. It must accept and celebrate the diversity of persons and groups as mutually enriching, not merely cope with differences. It must not seek an assimilation of identities into a dominant one, or the integration of communities into the prevailing hegemony, but premise itself on a 'politics of recognition' (Taylor 1992: 25) wherein each person and community will have its human dignity and unique identity, the first being universal for all, the second peculiar to each community.

At the eco-political level, we are faced with the dilemma of economic growth and equity. Liberal democracies privilege free enterprise and profit-driven growth; socialist states pursue a planned economy for social equality. But both have lost their way and betrayed what promise they might have had. Liberal democracies mutated into neoliberal free market capitalism of different hues, whether white or saffron, black or yellow; socialist states privileged state capitalism and bureaucratized civic life. We need the dynamism of free enterprise, not for profit but for the common good. But most of all we need fraternity/solidarity to hold together freedom and equality This is imperative for a just and decent society.

At the socio-political level, we need to bring a compatibility and complementarity between procedural and substantive democracy. In liberal democracies, 'nationalism', never without its ambiguities, has been used as a fig leaf to manage the fallout of growth without equity, using distracting slogans: 'America first', 'I want my country back', 'Vande Mataram'. Authoritarian leaders who compromise citizens' rights are elected even in democracies, which are no longer so 'liberal'; the once socialist states have opened their economies to the market in a globalizing world but still have not effectively integrated democratic freedoms and civil rights. In India, the accelerating inequalities of jobless growth are being contained by authoritarian suppression, and collective violence becomes a means of scapegoating the vulnerable. This calls for a critical discussion of both nationalism and neoliberalism and the structural violence these embed in the social system, leaving it prone to the overt collective violence overtaking us.

At the socio-cultural level, the issue is the contradiction between the pluralism of Hinduism and Hindutva, its contemporary politicization into an exclusive aggressive ideology. As a religious tradition Hinduism has coped with cultural differences not by exclusion, but rather by inclusion into its complex social structure. Its own internal diversity was the basis for this. The Ganga–

Yamuna culture (Ahmad 2002) expressed this composite culture in Urdu, in Indo-Saracenic architecture and in Hindustani music. However, Hindu-Muslim unity in the First War of Independence in 1857 unravelled in the freedom struggle and culminated in the Partition of 1947, thanks to a colonial policy of divide and rule and chauvinist political leaders.

In Independent India, these cultural faultlines continue to be politicized. This distracts from the divisive hierarchies of caste, to the advantage of the upper castes, the savarnas, and of the inequalities of class, to the advantage of the upper classes and their vested interests and corporations. The multiple identities of persons can only be formed and nurtured in communities which are pluralist and open. This must start with a socialization process in the family and be confirmed in the school. However, it will not be sustainable if it is not carried further into the public domain and privileged, so that the mutual hostility of groups becomes an on-going dialogue of communities. An exclusive culture with impervious community boundaries is isolating and impoverishing. In our multicultural society, to contain violence and facilitate peace, the urgent need is for an inter-cultural community dialogue that is open and transparent, and premised on an equally open and honest self-critical intra-cultural community one. This can tap our rich cultural resources for understanding and tolerance across cultural traditions.

At the socio-religious level, the issue is one of religion as a source of hatred, conflict and violence or a resource for reconciliation, peace and harmony. In no religious tradition have its devotees been innocent of violence, and at times even the grossest brutalities. Popular religiosity has been politicized and exploited to serve purposes alien to genuine religious ones. Given the depth and pervasiveness of popular religion in this subcontinent, it becomes urgent to demythologize religious traditions, so that dehumanizing and superstitious beliefs do not distort a humanizing and spiritual faith. Blind faith is always 'bad faith'. Here lies the real contribution of a religious faith tradition. Gandhi understood and foregrounded it. Political ideologues and religious extremists do not. Neither for that matter do secular rationalists.

These four levels are so implicated in each other, that though they can be distinguished, they cannot be separated. The discussion must focus on dialogue as the precondition for peace; and forgiveness for reconciliation. The power of religious faith is its appeal beyond human reason to the human heart. But faith must be meaningful and reason humanizing, for an inter-religious dialogue to work towards peace and reconciliation. And as with culture, religious faith too must be premised on an equally open and honest self-critical dialogue.

In conclusion, putting together these discourses at multiple levels must finally add up to an alternative narrative, which can engage the stakeholders in refining their response lest we end up on the slippery slope to becoming a failed state. Though this can be a gradual process and a failing state may go unnoticed and unaddressed for too long before the final denouement, the human cost is frightening, and the rebuilding may well take generations. There are enough and more examples of such states to serve as a warning for others. In South Asia too there are states trembling on the brink, decimated by internal conflicts, even civil war. India has coped with such exigencies before: at its very founding in 1947 and later with the Emergency of 1975–77. The present situation is turning precariously into an undeclared emergency and well might tip over into a full-fledged one.

If this is not reversed and soon, it will hollow out our democratic institutions, and subvert a culture of inclusion and tolerance for one of exclusion and aggression. We need a second freedom movement to recapture the vision and mission of the first, and recreate another India.

The following chapters will take up the several discourses indicated here, but first we must discuss the place of non-violence in our world vision of a harmonious society, so much part of our Asian vision of utopia.

CHAPTER FIVE
INTERLOCUTING GANDHI

Gujarat Model – Peace Initiatives – Historicizing Ahimsa – Contextualizing Gandhi – Conversing with Gandhi – Gandhi's Critique – Colonial Imperialism – Industrial Capitalism – Rationalist Materialism – Gandhi's Relevance – Neo-colonialism – Post-industrialism – Post-modernism – New Hermeneutic – Gandhi's Counter-Culture – Swaraj – Swadeshi – Satya – Reinterpreting Hinduism – Our World Today – Post-socialism – Globalization – Violence – Gandhi's Synthesis – Counter-cultural Transformation – Constructive Alternatives

Gujarat Model

The socially engineered experiment in the laboratory of Gujarat is now being extended to the whole country, no longer as an experiment, but as the new normal after the last two general elections in May 2014 and 2019. However, the 2017 state assembly elections shook the government's confidence, exposed the widening cracks of the Gujarat model of development built on the Gujarat model of communal polarization. Additionally, the October 2018 attacks on migrant workers from Uttar Pradesh, which began in north Gujarat and spread across the state resulted in a mass exodus of thousands of the Hindi-speaking workers, disrupting local industries. (*Financial Times* 9 Oct 2018)

Moreover, the extension of this model to the rest of the country has left a trail of promises broken and hopes betrayed as indicated by the results of the by-elections after the landslide victory of 2014. The few successes have been hyped to obfuscate the skulduggery and opportunism. There is evidence in the legislative assembly elections in four states in the Hindi heartland that presage the slow unravelling of the Gujarat model of communal polarization and neoliberal capitalism. No amount of fear and violence, or free-market enterprise, can deliver on the slogans and promises of the good times coming, 'achche din aanewale hain', nor can the Gujarat model of development obfuscate the realities affecting people's everyday lives. This might have built into an anti-incumbent crescendo but the saffron brigade fought a desperate campaign for the general elections of 2019, using the emotive plank of Hindu nationalism and playing on Hindu insecurity and fears from which a strongman prime minister was projected as their only protector and promoter.

This drew attention away from the government's non-performance on all it promises in 2014. With a sympathetic chief election commissioner, some would say even partial, the BJP won an incredible landslide victory. The Parliamentary figures for the 545 elected MPs seats say it all: the BJP won 303 seats, and with its alliance partners in the NDA, a total of 358 seats; the INC got just 52 seats, and 91 with its alliance partners in the UPA. This represents an enormous Hindu nationalist revival, and given the record of such majoritarian nationalism, minorities, especially Muslims, are fearful and insecure.

The pogrom against Muslims in Gujarat in 2002 needs no retelling. It opens old wounds of the victims while the violators sink deeper into denial. The state-sponsored Sadbhavana Yatra, conducted on 30 November 2012, was more a political performance, a PR exercise for the consumption of a public of faithful believers and followers. The state chief minister's public refusal to wear or receive a Muslim prayer cap was telling it like it is. For the protagonists, victims especially, and violators too, there is no healing yet, but rather distrust and fear of each other. Majority of the violators have no regrets. They flaunt their dominance and flout their privileges, subvert established statutory institutions and procedures. The victims retreat into ghettos for the security of their lives and livelihood. And yet in spite of this, non-state initiatives for peace have been discouraged and stymied.

Non-violence is fundamentally intended to give peace a chance, and imagine another world is possible. Building non-violent initiatives to impact a situation of violence, particularly in the wake of traumatic violence, like the pogrom in Gujarat or any number of communal and caste riots in our land, requires courage and discretion, prudence and discernment. What is often lacking is the imagination to think out of the box.

Peace Initiatives

When you have a narrow and authoritarian base for decision making—a trusted lieutenant, a few confidants in the cabinet, the support of an unelected prime minister's office—you end up with a structure too centralized for democratic and participatory governance. The inevitable result is crony capitalism. (Chancel and Piketty, 2017) When a government stalls and compromises on fundamentals, civil society, the voluntary and NGO sector must step in.

The experience of the mohalla (neighbourhood) committees in Mumbai, formed in 1994 after the devastating post-Babri Masjid demolition riots across the city, is still an exemplary initiative in confidence building among the protagonists in the aftermath of the violence. Initiated by Julio Rebiero, former director general of Punjab police and former Indian ambassador to Romania, Sushobha Barve, a social worker, and Satish Sahney, the police commissioner at the time, it was essentially premised on the agency of local civil society. (Barve, 2003) Various groups were organized by mohalla committees to create a space for airing and resolving local issues between the minority community and the police, and between Muslims and Hindus.

In the first instance, the participants included aggrieved Muslims and local police and in the second local, Muslims and Hindus, with facilitators in both instances. This was a much-needed confidence-building measure. Local civic functionaries were included later to address common issues that needed community solutions. Deliberately excluded were political parties and government officials so as to eschew extraneous influences.

These mohalla committees were not without their difficulties and limitations, but they have been among the most successful initiatives and they certainly bear replication. However, in spite of some threat from vested interests, including political opposition from those engineering communal polarization, they are thriving. There are today forty-five such mohalla committees in Mumbai and recently they celebrated their twenty-fifth anniversary.

However, in Gujarat, except for perfunctory 'peace committees' convened to satisfy government directives, there was no effective peace initiative by the Government after 2002, in spite of the fear and distrust between the minority and majority communities, and between Muslims and the police. Even the initiatives taken by the civil society were stymied. It would seem that the peace might soften the polarization of communities and affect the positive political payoff from the violence.

In Halol a small town near Varodara in south Gujarat, local cricket matches had helped ease the growing tension between communities. (Nampoothiri and Sethi 2012: 109–115) A Cricket for Peace Tournament was organized in 1996 by the local mohalla committees with the police. They were revived in 2001 by Janvikas, an NGO active among the victims of communal violence. Thirty-two mixed neighbourhood teams and local police stations took part. The tournament became an annual event with the police commissioner's rotating trophy. With time, even the girls wanted to play and five teams were made. And although the Muslim girls began in purdah, soon all restrictions were ignored.

'Cricket for Peace' was a success beyond expectations. National sport celebrities, like the three-time billiards world champion Geet Sethi and the legendary test cricketer Kapil Dev were invited to give away the prizes. Huge crowds were attracted, foregrounding the potential and possibilities of sport for communal harmony.

However, Hindu extremists panicked at the success and tried to scuttle the tournament by sowing discord and suspicion. Undeterred, in 2006 an even bigger tournament was proposed but then the district collector refused permission on the spurious grounds that it was disturbing communal peace and refused to entertain any appeal or meet the organizers. After the violence of 2002, just when such initiatives were most needed, they were discouraged on by the party in power and the local administration. 'Cricket for Peace' had grown into a threat to a government that thrived on polarization and so it had to be stopped.

It is difficult to avoid the implication that the government seems to have a vested interest in the continuance of the polarization of Hindus and Muslims that results in rich returns at the hustings. This is the back up to the precarious Gujarat model of development just in case it fails. And the closer it comes to that the more we can expect the promoters of the model to rely increasingly on communal polarization to consolidate the Hindu majority vote bank. Unfortunately, a collective political opposition, both viable and credible, has yet to be cobbled together.

Nor is a peace process with non-violent initiatives gaining any momentum in Gujarat or elsewhere. Significant exceptions have jogged people's consciences. Anhad's Karwan-e-Mohabbat (literally, 'the Caravan of Love'), a peace initiative, deserves special mention. They visited the sites of the lynchings, reached out to the families of victims, and brought their stories into the public domain. (Mander 2018) But there has been little mainstream support for this. On the contrary, fear still prevails in the deep recesses of people's minds. In 2002 the 'other' was the Muslim. Today it is also the Dalit, the supposedly migrant Muslim from Bangladesh, even Hindu interstate migrants, from the Northeast—in other words, anyone who is different can be constructed as 'the other'. On 2 October 2018, a mob attacked Hindi-speaking migrant workers in a factory near Vadnagar, Gujarat. On 3 October, there was an attack in Chandlodia, Ahmedabad. By 7 October, the six districts were affected chiefly in industrial estates and industrial belts. On 8 October, there were attacks in villages near Vadodara as well. The attacks triggered an exodus of thousands of migrant labourers from Gujarat to their native states. The Uttar Bharatiya Vikas Parishad claimed around 20,000 people had left Gujarat. A total of fifty-six FIRs were lodged and 431 people were arrested, ten of whom were arrested for spreading rumours and hate on social media. The government of Gujarat provided security to hundreds of factories, with seventeen companies of State Reserve Police—making it clear that this was not a case of state-engineered violence. And suddenly repentant politicians and reconciliatory ministers began appealing for the return of the migrants. (https://en.wikipedia.org/wiki/2018_attacks_on_Hindi-speaking_migrants_in_Gujarat)

All this only goes to show how rapidly a targeted scapegoat can be changed depending on the mob's sense of grievance or justice. Is the rampaging against Hindi-speaking migrant workers a presage of more to come? Are some Hindu nationalists with their heightened sense of grievance, transmuting into a narrower linguistic ethnocentrism? Has the Gujarati asmita (identity), which was evoked in the election rhetoric after 2003, turned against non-Gujaratis in the state in the same way it once targeted Muslims? Is this similar to the reversal of the trajectory of the Shiv Sena in Maharashtra: from Marathi linguistic chauvinism to Hindutva, and now to marginalization by Hindu nationalism of the BJP? The Maharashtra Navnirman Sena, a breakaway group from the Shiv Sena, has also attacked migrants from Uttar Pradesh and Bihar in 2008 and 2013.

This narcissism of victimhood disguised as a narcissism of grandiosity once let out of the bottle, is difficult to put back. Hate and revenge, opportunism and ethno-centralism set a new normal for the level of acceptable violence in society which we can already perceive in our country and our world as well. This is not the tryst with destiny we once made. Now we must mine our history, particularly our freedom struggle, to find another path.

Historicizing Ahimsa

The term ahimsa has a long and complex history. Monier-Williams' *A Sanskrit-English Dictionary* merely transliterates ahimsa. (Monier-Williams 1899: 125) In the Vedas the debates were over the correct form of sacrifice. For the Buddhist and Jains, ahimsa meant 'innocuous, harmless behaviour'. (Bouillier 2003: 27–28) It is 'in the *Upanishads* that non-violence began to be projected as a universal virtue, along with other ethical principles such as truthfulness, non-stealing, celibacy, kindness, straightforwardness, forbearance, temperance and cleanliness.'

(Hardiman 2007: 11) All forms of animal sacrifice were eschewed and this led to vegetarianism, especially among the Brahmins. However, ahimsa was considered a mental and practical quality that only those belonging to the higher castes and status groups were expected to practice—so, the Brahman could refuse to eat meat or sacrifice animals; the Kshatriya warrior could wage war as duty that was detached from any desire for glory or revenge; or the ruler could award corporal punishment as a supposed moral necessity to maintain the correct social order. People from the lower caste were not expected to practice 'non-violence' of this sort…The boundaries between what was considered himsa and ahimsa were always a matter of debate, and they shifted constantly over time. (Hardiman 2007: 31)

In the *Bhagavad Gita*, one's personal dharma sets the context for ahimsa. As a Kshatriya warrior, Arjun was doing his duty waging war. His dharma was to fight with nish-kama-karma, (detachment), without any desire for glory or revenge. For the sant-kavis, ahimsa was a personal quality of the bhakts (devotees), whose devotion would bring them the final victory of moksha. Gandhi brought ahimsa out from the private into the public domain. The Gujarati saint Narsinh Mehta (1414–81) expressed this most movingly in his hymn, '*Vaishnava jan to tene kahiye*', which later became Gandhi's favourite.

In the West, civil or passive resistance emerged out of the emancipatory movements in 19th century. Though these protests might have begun non-violently they could tip over into violence from any side. (Randle, 1994: 8, 10, 21–22) Gandhi's campaigns in South Africa for the civil rights of Indians there were categorized as non-violent passive resistance: 'I believe that nonviolence is infinitely superior to violence, forgiveness is more manly than punishment.' (*Young India*, 11 Aug 1920) Furthermore, in Gandhi's reckoning, this is foregrounded as a major philosophic principle in ancient India. Ahimsa is usually translated as non-violence or non-killing. Gandhi did use these terms but found them to be inadequate translations. For Gandhi, ahimsa was synonymous with love. He thought the Christian understanding of love best captured the multi-valiancy of 'ahimsa'. (Gandhi 1935: 7–130)

Contextualizing Gandhi

Indic civilization's experience with Islam was very different from that of the West. In coastal areas, especially in the south, Muslim Arabs came as traders, and the exchange was largely peaceful. In the north, the Muslims came as conquerors: the Mughal Empire, which flowered into a composite culture, but was finally overtaken by the British.

The Great Uprising of 1857 almost succeeded in ending the East India Company rule, and the Hindu-Muslim unity it demonstrated was praised even by Savarkar who wrote *The First Indian War of Independence, 1857*. (1970, 1st 1908) The divide-and-rule policy employed by the British thereafter finally ended with the Partition. However, the trauma of colonial rule by an alien and distant civilization precipitated an existential crisis in the self-understanding of the Indian peoples.

In the 18th and 19th centuries when one in three British men were married to Indian women, (Dalrymple 2002) the exchange was far more equal, appreciative and adaptive, and there might have been the possibility of fusion and hybridity contrary to Kipling's idea that 'East is East and West is West and never the twain shall meet'. Dalrymple argues that *The White Mughals* (Dalrymple 2007) might have changed that. However, the barbarities committed by both sides during the Great Rebellion of 1857 caused too much distance and mistrust between them. The freedom movement picked up the pieces and struggled not just for swatantrata, independence from British rule, but rather for swaraj, self-rule, beginning with ruling the personal 'self' as the basis for ruling the collective 'self'.

Gandhi was its architect and dominant force. His was a new vision in a new conceptual language that drew from the rich heritage of Indic tradition that challenged the very basis of the founding assumptions of Imperial rule, not from within but from without. Little wonder that the white sahibs did not understand, nor know how to cope with him. But neither have the brown sahibs to date. Many of the leaders of the freedom movement did not quite comprehend Gandhi's 'swaraj' that was to be founded on ahimsa, satya and satyagraha, (non-violence, truth and truth force) much less its implications for personal and social living.

In South Africa, Gandhi's fight for the rights of Indians there espoused non-violent passive resistance, better categorized as civil disobedience. His approach was twofold: selected demonstrations of collective non-violent civil disobedience against unjust laws; and the Tolstoy Farm for his followers to live, learn and internalize their commitment to non-violence and its implications. Here his perspectives on a non-violent mass movement against an intransigent opposition matured into what he would call 'ahimsa' in the freedom struggle in India.

When Gandhi returned from South Africa in 1915, he redirected the efforts of the Indian National Congress, which was by then the most prominent movement for Independence, towards a mass struggle for swaraj, committed to ahimsa and satyagraha. Indeed, for Gandhi, the personal was the political. He began with peaceful 'civil disobedience' in South Africa inspired by the counter-culture from the West: the ideas of Leo Tolstoy, John Ruskin and Henry David Thoreau. However, he considered 'civil disobedience' an inadequate term. Gandhi first used 'ahimsa' in India in 1916, and called his method of resistance, satyagraha. (CWMG, Hindi version, Vol. 13, 293)

Gandhi's ahimsa was launched as a mass movement into a violent world which was between world wars, when violent extremist ideologies and dictatorial leaders from the far right and far left dominated the stage. He was determined not to let the same happen in India. Already, the liberal Indian National Congress was more interested in elite debates than mass action. The constitutional path preferred by its leaders like Gopal Krishna Gokhale seemed too slow and compromised. Violence seemed to be the more effective alternative to remove the colonial government, and extremist groups were also on the rise. Gandhi had met extremist Hindu nationalists in 1906 in London. Three years later, on 24 October 1909, he shared stage with Savarkar for the Dussehra celebrations. Here Gandhi spoke of Rama the pacifist, Savarkar of Maa Durga the Mahishasura mardini (demon killer). It was an ominous presage to the fateful encounter with Nathuram Godse, Savarkar's ardent follower, on 30 January 1948.

Gandhi made ahimsa the authenticating characteristic of our Indic heritage, though it was not associated with political activism until Gandhi's satyagraha. In the past ahimsa was a personal ethic that hardly ever inspired public protest or political mass movements. At the time, however, 'It was seen as a doctrine that inculcated political passivity. Radical nationalists in India often condemned it for its contribution to the political enslavement of the Indian people under British imperial rule.' (Hardiman 2007: 23) Assertive nationalist extremists, like Lala Lajpat Rai and others, blamed the passivity of Indians for their submission to foreign imperial rule.

On the contrary, in 1916 Gandhi argued that ahimsa protest campaigns demand a special courage and that it was its neglect and perversion that had emasculated our people. (CWMG 1916, Vol. 15, pp. 251–54) He asserted that the practice of ahimsa in protest campaigns required 'the most soldierly of a soldier's virtues'. On 25 February 1919 he had warned against extremist nationalism, in a letter to Sir Dinshaw Wacha that 'Satyagraha is the only way, it seems to me, to stop terrorism'. (CWMG, Vol. 15, 107) At the opposite of the political spectrum from these extremists on the right were those on the left. Marxist historians like Rajani Palme Dutt found that the 'seemingly innocent humanitarian or expedient term [that] contained concealed within it, not only the refusal of the final struggle, but the thwarting also of the immediate struggle by the attempt to conciliate the interests of the masses with the big bourgeoisie and landlord interests which were inevitably opposed to any decisive mass struggle.' (Dutt 1940: 307–08)

With Gandhi's dominant influence on the freedom struggle, neither of these two extremes played much of a significant role. If anything they had a negative impact. The Hindu right nationalists became the mirror image of the Muslim League, with both Jinnah and Savarkar espousing the two-nation theory of religious nationalism: one demanding political separatism, the other aggressively promoting exclusive cultural nationalism. The Quit India Movement demanded a boycott of the war effort; the Marxists and their fellow travellers joined the war effort because of their extra-territorial commitment to the then Soviet Union, by now one of the Allies.

With the progressive marginalization of Gandhi in post-Independent India, the violent religious nationalism of Pakistan is now finding a mirror image in the majoritarianism of Hindutva and its violent pursuit of Hindu Rashtra. Now more than ever we need to turn to Gandhi to realize the futility and dubious morality of violence and to show us the more courageous way of ahimsa, and satyagraha: 'to imagine our opponent as a human being, and to understand the significance of his or her action'. (Spivak 2004: 93)

However, idealizing Gandhi uncritically too easily misses the crucial urgency of contextualizing him for our situation today. It is not so much just the Gandhi of the then and there, as the Gandhi of the here and now that we must engage with and allow him to engage with us. If we need to recall what he did then, it must be to understand what we must do now, in other words we need a critique to contextualize Gandhi for our time.

Hero-worshipping Gandhi fails to interrogate him; ignoring Gandhi fails to allow him to interrogate us. Rejecting Gandhi will not make him go away. We need a two-way critique of Gandhi, a two-way interrogation, not just interrogating Gandhi, but allowing Gandhi to interrogate us. Only in interlocuting him, will we find a Gandhi relevant to us and the issues of our day. For even his failures—and there were many—are as much a comment on ourselves as on him. Did we fail Gandhi or did he fail us?

Conversing with Gandhi

Gandhi's 'ahimsa' and its implications can only be comprehended when it is read in the larger context of the other major themes of his life and message: swaraj, satya, satyagraha, seva and moksha. He explained their intimate entwining: ahimsa cannot be pursued except with satya, and satya cannot contradict ahimsa. The way to one is through the other, and the integration, the synthesis of the two is expressed in seva (service) which is the way to moksha. The ultimate goal that unifies his entire this-worldly agenda is to seek this God and Truth wherever this led him. 'Ahimsa is my God and Truth is my God. When I look for Ahimsa, Truth says, "Find it through me." When I look for Truth, Ahimsa says, "Find it through me."' (*Young India* 4-6-1925) Realizing this Truth through ahimsa was his moksha.

Gandhi's life endeavour was to integrate a comprehensive perspective and a compelling praxis of his concerns. These are perhaps the more imperative in our day than they were in his: a politics beyond pragmatism, a patriotism beyond nationalism, an ethics beyond utilitarianism, a spirituality beyond religion, and an uncompromising commitment to just means for just ends.

Gandhi is an uncomfortable interlocutor who still intrudes into our everyday lives, only to be trivialized and dismissed from our contemporary living. Yet today more than ever, when his dream of *Hind Swaraj* (Gandhi 1909) is being dismissed by Hindu Rashtra, we need a critical appreciation and re-interpretation, not so much to interrogate Gandhi, which easily becomes an escapist exercise, but rather to allow Gandhi to interrogate us: our understanding of unity and diversity, our commitment to tolerance and dialogue, our practice of assimilation and pluralism, his challenge to live simply, to eschew consumerism, to walk lightly on our earth, to embrace an ethic of ahimsa, satya and seva, especially to serve the last and least as the authentic marga (path) to moksha.

In other words, we must enter into his context and comprehend his worldview from within as it were, while being fully aware of our own situation in our world. We need to be aware of the concerns and aspirations, fears and hopes that make up his world and ours, and as we question him from where we are, we must allow his fundamental options and commitments, his values and the mindset to challenge us in our life and calling.

Gandhi is a critical traditionalist whose ideas do speak to critical modernity today, as in the sustainable development debate and sundry ecological movements There is much in 'modern civilization' Gandhi rejects, but not the liberative contribution of modernity: civil liberties, religious tolerance, equality, poverty alleviation. Rather his attempt is to integrate these positive elements with a liberating re-interpretation of tradition. In his unique way he sets up a creative encounter for this integration, even as some see him as radical and others as reactionary. With his critique from within the tradition, Gandhi becomes the great synthesizer of contraries if not of contradictions, within and across traditions.

Gandhi's Critique

Three recurrent themes sum up Gandhi's critique and rejection of the modern West: colonial imperialism, industrial capitalism, and rationalist materialism. We seem to have learnt little from India's experience with the shadow side of what these have done to our peoples in our on-going scramble to catch up with the West.

Colonial Imperialism

Gandhi was one of the first to realize that colonialism was something to be overcome in our own consciousness first. British colonialism was first justified as a supposedly Christianizing mission, but very soon this was articulated in terms of a civilizing one. In rejecting this Christianizing/civilizing mission, Gandhi was subverting the legitimacy of the colonial enterprise at its core. As Nandy (1983) explains, unless this *'Intimate Enemy'* was exorcised and exiled, unless we addressed this 'loss and recovery of self under colonialism', we would always be a people enslaved by one power or another, whether foreign or native. (Nandy 1983:63) Gandhi was unambiguous in rejecting any exchange of an external colonialism for an internal one, a white sahib for a brown one, or to replace a colonial 'Hindustan' with an independent 'Englishtan'! (*Hind Swaraj* Ch.4) His understanding of swaraj would be founded on the recovery of the personal self, before extending it to the collective self. This freedom, a freedom from fear of the unjust ruler, was grounded in the self-confidence that Gandhi's non-violent struggle brought to his people.

Industrial Capitalism

Gandhi sees capitalism as the dynamic behind colonial imperialism. Lenin too had said as much, and like Marx, Gandhi's rejection of capitalism is based on a profound repugnance to a system where profit is allowed to degrade labour, where machines are valued more than humans, where automation is preferred to humanism: 'Machinery has begun to desolate Europe. Ruination is now knocking at the English gates. Machinery is the chief symbol of modern civilization; it represents a great sin.' (*Hind Swaraj* 1909 Ch.19) He was acutely sensitive as to how machinery can dehumanize and technology alienate. He extended the critique to the professions of medicine and law: the poor hardly benefit from these professional services, though they are often their victims.

However, this rather Luddite perception of machinery in 1909 began to change by 1919 right up to 1947, as he gradually conceded to some positive aspects such as it is time and labour saving, even as he warned against the concentration of wealth and the displacement of workers that it caused. (Parel 1997:164–70, 'Gandhi on Machinery, 1919–47') Quite rightly, according to Gandhi, what gives such a system its reach and capacity is the technology on which it is founded. Gandhi was very concerned with the shadow side of such technology, which is the very basis of industrial capitalism.

Rationalist Materialism

Gandhi finds the uncompromising rationalism of Western civilization a dangerously truncated humanism. His incisive remark is much to the point: 'Experience has humbled me enough to let me realise the specific limitations of reason. Just as dirt is matter misplaced, reason misplaced is lunacy! I plead not for the suppression of Reason, but for a due recognition of that in us which sanctifies reason itself.' (CWMG, 6:106)

Certainly Gandhi is right in insisting on the unreasonableness of not setting any limits to reason. More recently a post-modern world has emphasized the aggressive and destructive march of this 'age of reason' with its grand narratives. But Gandhi was not one to throw out the baby with the bathwater. He would test his faith with his reason, but he would not allow his reason to destroy his faith. What makes such technological rationalism even more destructive in Gandhi's view is its flawed materialism. That is, the negation of the spiritual, the transcendent, or in other words, the denial of a religious worldview. Thinking of him as just another ascetic upset with a hedonistic society would be a trivialization of Gandhi's critique. His critique cuts much deeper. He sees India as the Kurukshetra, the great battle ground of these two antagonistic worldviews.

For Gandhi, satya was much more than what could be grasped by science or reason. For him, there was a reality beyond that perceived by the senses. It is this transcendent reality that gave meaning and value to our present one. In this, Gandhi is very much in the mainstream of Hindu tradition, whether in its philosophical or popular expression. Indeed, most religious traditions would be similarly sensitive to such a transcendent world, even when it is not perceived as wholly otherworldly.

Today we may not be sympathetic to such a worldview. And yet a materialism that is over deterministic leaves no scope for human freedom and hope. It is here that we must find the relevance of this transcendent dimension to human life, that Gandhi so emphasizes. It is this reaching out to a beyond, to a something more rather than a nothing else, which gives this human freedom and hope its dynamism and a reach beyond its grasp.

Gandhi's Relevance

However, it is the failure to adequately address this downside of the very success of modernization that has precipitated its present crisis: its relentless pursuit of profit and consumerism, its unbridled individualism and permissiveness, its pragmatic pursuit of short-term goals at the cost of long-term fallout. But while conceding the shadow side of modern civilization which Gandhi stresses, we must not overlook its positive contribution to human welfare, i.e. its scientific and critical spirit of inquiry, its extending human control over the natural world and its organizational capacity. Such achievement would imply a certain 'spiritual dimension' that Gandhi seems to have missed. (Parekh 1995:209)

In fairness to him, it must also be conceded that the focus of his criticism is modern civilization of a specific period; his condemnation of colonialism focuses on its imperialistic inspiration; his rejection of industrialism derives mostly from its capitalist context; his apprehensions about excessive rationality is in regard to its truncation by materialism and positivism.

However, once the real limitations of Gandhi's critique are acknowledged, we can contextualize and interpret his relevance for us today. His insistence on greed and want as the decisive dynamic of modern civilization emphasizes how our active moral being is transmuted into passive consuming—whether this be with regard to politics in our neo-colonial world, or technologies in our post-industrial times, or culture in our post-modern age. These will now be some of the issues on which we must allow Gandhi to interrogate us.

For 'the kinds of questions Gandhi asked nearly eight decades ago are the ones which now face both the underdeveloped and the post-industrial societies caught up in a deep upsurge of confusion and disillusionment.' (Sethi 1979:3)

Gandhi's critique anticipated these. It was decidedly prescient and more relevant now than earlier.

Neo-colonialism

Gandhi's rejection of the supposedly civilizing mission of colonialism brings into question the whole legitimacy of colonial rule at a fundamental, ethical level. He would have India unlearn much that she has from the modern West. Rather he suggests that it was this dehumanizing civilization that needed to be 'civilized'. If anything there ought to be a reversal of roles here! For if Indians 'would but revert to their own glorious civilisation, either the English would adopt the latter and become Indianized or find their occupation in India gone'. (HS, Preface to English Ed.)

Thus, he opens up a host of ethical issues between the colonizer and the colonized, the dominant and the dominated, the oppressor and oppressed. The post-colonial era brought such issues into sharper focus across the world. Now with globalization in a unipolar world, such concerns with empowerment and disempowerment, dependence and inter-dependence, growth and equity, alienation and anomie have gained, not lost their urgency. Moreover, closer home this widening divide bears down on us more decisively than ever before. Our new economic policy increasingly represents a whole new vision of society, that takes for granted the internal colonialism we are experiencing today, as for instance between Bharat and India, the bahujan and the twice-born jatis, the savarna and the avarna castes, the toiling masses and the privileged classes, the oppressed people and the oppressor groups, the minority communities and the majority one.

In a post-colonial world, with independence already seventy years old one would have thought that we, as a society, would have found our own distinctive place among the nations, and all our people their place in the sun. Yet, the world in which we live in today can only be described as a neo-colonial one, internationally divided into developed and developing nations, intra-nationally between privileged and underprivileged citizens, and more recently between citizens and non-citizens, i.e., migrants, refugees and at times even legitimate minorities relegated to second-class citizenship. Moreover, these divisions are mutually reinforced, not just economically and politically but culturally and socially as well.

The victory of the West over our minds still prevails. It is still the centre of our world for we have not the self-respect, the self-reliance, the self-sufficiency to centre our 'self' and so we condemn ourselves to remain on the periphery of someone else's centre. If there is a global system emerging, it is more strongly a western than an eastern one. No matter how much we urge that it is modern rather than traditional and no matter how hard we try to be modern, we are not allowed to catch up with and beat the West at its own game, though we seem willing to lose our souls in this vain attempt. Gandhi, of course, would want us to walk to the beat of other drummers, on our quest to self-realization.

The colonial masters had stripped our collective identity of any intrinsic dignity by denigrating us as a cowardly and passive people. Gandhi sought to reverse the damage to our collective psyche by his 'redefinition of courage and effective resistance in terms of, or non-violence'. (Roy 1986:185)

The issue then of our identity as a nation and a people still remains to be resolved. Such identities are only viable in a genuinely multi-cultural world. Gandhi's urgings in this regard are certainly relevant today even as we struggle to maintain a certain cultural pluralism in our own society where the propagation of a cultural nationalism is growing every day. Gandhi was a deeply rooted yet very open person: 'I do not want my house to be walled in on all sides and my windows to be stuffed. I want cultures of all lands to blow about my house as freely as possible. But I refuse to be blown of my feet by any.' (*Harijan* 9 May 1936, 100)

In urging us to be open to the future, he would not want us to lose our sheet anchor in the past. Today we seem to be in danger of losing both: openness and rootedness. Yet 'nothing could be more anti-Indian than attempts to make an ideology of Indianness and to fight, instead of incorporating or bypassing non-Indianness.' (Nandy 1980:112)

Post-industrialism

With the new information-intensive technologies moving away from the energy-intensive ones, there was surely much hope for a new freedom from degrading and monotonous work. However, what seems to have come in to replace this demeaning monotony is not a new dignity of labour but rather a compulsive consumerist society, which is dehumanizing in newer ways. Moreover, the new information technology we have evolved has led to an info-overload that now finds its expression in 'infotainment'. Platforms on the internet have been perversely misused which has caused great harm to many.

This should hardly surprise us since the ethic underlying post-industrialism is the same as that which underpinned industrial capitalism, namely, the profit motive and the market mechanism. Gandhi's critique was precisely a condemnation of these. If we find his ideas of trusteeship a little naive and impractical, we still have no alternative answer to humanizing a system that seems to have betrayed what possibilities it might have had of bringing freedom and dignity to the toiling masses. While absolute poverty is declining, relative poverty is rising in a grossly unequal world.

Moreover, technology, be it energy- or information-intensive, in the public or the private domain, has its own intrinsic dynamism, that instrumentalizes our world and inevitably leads to a disenchantment and loss of innocence that can only bring us to the 'iron cage', as Weber warned long ago. Our environmental crises and ecological breakdowns are surely a manifestation of this loss of innocence, even to the point when we want newer technologies to repair the damage already done by the older ones.

The faith of one such recent technological ideologue runs thus: 'the deterioration of the environment produced by technology is a technological problem for which technology has found, is finding and will continue to find solutions'. (Medawar 1973:135) Hence extra-technological solutions to such problems are dismissed. Gandhi was precisely rejecting such a naive 'nineteenth century optimism which sought for the positive sciences the liberation of humanity'. (Nandy 1986:102) But such anti-modernism then was ahead of its time!

Post-modernism

The excessive and aggressive rationalism of this age of reason, now seems to have turned on itself with the post-modern revolt. But this revolt has thrown up its own irrationalities. It seems to have lost the liberating project that was implicit in modernity, and by devaluing reason, it seems to have fallen into another kind of romance of power: might becomes right with the relativizing of ethics, since in a relativist world there may be no accepted reference point for arbitration between subjective differences. Paradoxically, what started in our post-modern venture as the affirmation of marginal peoples and groups, now has been co-opted in support of the status quo.

For the kind of subjectivization of ethics that this post-modernism has led to, undermines the appeal and the claims of any justice. For without an objective basis for rights and values, there can hardly be any mutually accepted legitimacy to arbitrate conflicting claims, when consensus irrevocably breaks down—a situation not uncommon among our deconstructionists. Even 'consensual universals' are of little use in *The Quest for Meaning* (Ramadan 2010) when the consensus breaks down. So then might becomes right, and the power its own legitimation, its own truth.

Gandhi's trenchant critique of modernity was focused on

modernist rationalism, but was equally opposed to a post-modern rejection of rationality. What Gandhi was pleading for is a richer concept of rationality and a meta-theory of rationalism. (Parekh 1995:165-6) Certainly, he would want one that would buttress and not undermine an objective basis for ethics and justice. He wanted to contain excessive rationality within reasonable bounds without an irrational revolt against reason itself, but he would emphatically reject any forced choice between totalizing rationalism and relativizing subjectivism.

A New Hermeneutic

This is but the beginning of a dialogue with Gandhi on the three basic themes sketched in this section: freedom from the colonizer, the intimate enemy lodged in our consciousness, the one from whom we must have swaraj in its deepest and most authentic sense; an alternative to the capitalist ethic in a world where the known socialist states have collapsed, and where the crisis of capitalism itself seems to go unnoticed; the relevance of a reasonable rationality, particularly for a society that is still as tradition- and caste-bound as ours.

Such were the concerns Gandhi had during 1909 and they remained the same throughout his life. If he refused to change anything that he had written in *Hind Swaraj*, it was nonetheless fine-tuned, by his own personal growth and search for moksha, and contextualized by his later political commitments and agenda. Certainly these represent themes that are not alien to us, and even as we contextualize Gandhi's basic concerns in the pilgrimage of his own life, we need to reinterpret and recontextualize them in our own, so that they can be more relevant, and our dialogue with Gandhi richer. We need a new hermeneutic for this.

Gandhi's Counter-Culture

Hind Swaraj presents us with an idealized version of Indian culture that is a counterpoint to the 'modern West' Gandhi so harshly criticized. He distances himself from the bourgeois democracy of the British parliament, (HS Ch.5) as well as from the political pragmatism of Garibaldi's unification of Italy. (HS Ch.15) Neither was Japan's blind imitation of the West an acceptable model for India, even after its 1905 victory over Russia. (HS Ch.4) For with regard to 'true civilization', India 'has nothing to learn from anybody else'. (HS. Ch.13) This was an obvious but deliberate hyperbole.

Thus Indian culture is emphatically affirmed as the very opposite of the West: centripetal, adaptive, contemplative. But Gandhi was not blind to the very real defects and deficiencies of our ancient civilization, and he wanted to 'utilise the new spirit that is born in us for purging ourselves of these evils'. (HS Ch.13) Hence, Gandhi was really re-interpreting Indian culture even as he idealized our ancient traditions. Already in *Hind Swaraj* we can see the beginning of such a re-interpretation, open yet rooted, which finds fuller expression in Gandhi's later life. Here we pick out three seminal themes: swaraj, swadeshi and satya.

Swaraj

It was at the Calcutta Congress in 1906 that 'swaraj' was first used by Dadabhai Naoroji to mean national independence, that is, freedom from colonial rule. But Gandhi radically re-interprets the word and gives it a dual meaning. The original Gujarati text uses 'swaraj' in both senses. Gandhi's English translation makes the duality explicit: swaraj as 'self-rule' and as 'self- government'. The first as rule over oneself was the foundation for the second, self-government, a community governing itself. In this second sense local self-government was what Gandhi really had in mind. Gandhi very decidedly gave priority to self-rule over self-government, and to both over political independence, swatantrata.

To an anguished soul wondering what a mere individual could do after reading *Hind Swaraj* he wrote: 'Emancipate your own self. Even that burden is very great. Apply everything to yourself. Nobility of soul consists in realising that you are yourself India. In your emancipation is the emancipation of India. All else is make belief.' (CW 10:206-7) Indeed, he believed 'if there were only one such Indian', as he was to prove in his own life, 'the English will have to listen to him'. (HS Ch.20)

Essential to both meanings of swaraj was a sense of self-respect that is precisely Gandhi's answer to colonial rule. For Gandhi, freedom in its most fundamental sense had to mean freedom for self-realization. But it had to be a freedom for all, for the toiling masses, and the privileged classes. Gandhi's sarvodaya expressed this. But most importantly for the least and last Indian, Vinoba Bhave termed this antyodaya. In this sense sarvodaya was precisely the patriotism that Gandhi espoused. It focused on people's welfare not on national pride: 'By patriotism I mean the welfare of the whole people, and, if I could secure it at the hands of the English, I should bow down my head to them.' (HS Ch.15) And so he could write: 'My patriotism is for me a stage on my journey to the land of freedom and peace.' (*Young India*, 13 April 1924, p 112) And yet swaraj was not something given by the leaders, Indian or British, it was something that had to be taken by the people for themselves.

Clearly then, the foundation of swaraj in both its senses had to be threefold: self-respect, self-realization and self-reliance. This is what Gandhi tried to symbolize with the chakra and khadi, both much misunderstood symbols today. Even before he wrote *Hind Swaraj*, in London in 1909 with some earnest Indians, he had 'many long conversations about the condition of India and I saw in a flash that without the spinning-wheel there was no swaraj. I knew at once everyone had to spin.' (CW 37:288) Later in his 'Constructive Programme' (CW 75:146-66) he advocates khadi with all its implications for 'a revolutionary change in the mentality and the taste of many'. For Gandhi, khadi 'is the symbol of the unity of Indian humanity, of its economic freedom and equality and therefore, ultimately, in the poetic expression of Jawaharlal Nehru, the livery of India's freedom.' (CW 75:146-66, 'Constructive Programme', no. iv)

Today the chakra and khadi have not retained this powerful multivalent symbolism. Yet the ethic that Gandhi was trying to introduce and inscribe into Indian political life was that swaraj must never mean 'capturing power by a few', but rather generating power for the many to resist domination of any kind. He was acutely aware that 'real swaraj will not be the acquisition of authority by a few but the acquisition of the capacity of all to resist authority when it is abused'. (Prabhu 1961: 4–5)

For Gandhi 'civilisation is that mode of conduct which points out to man the path duty'. (HS Ch.13) Hence the basis of his swaraj could not be just rights, it had to be duties as well. In fact, Gandhi privileged duties over rights, but it is neither true nor fair to say that Gandhi did not envisage a regime of rights. He did affirm the rights of the individual, but these were never without duties to the community. For Gandhi real rights are legitimated by duties they flow from, for both are founded on satya and dharma. The modern theory of rights reverses this priority and founds rights on the dignity and freedom of the individual. However, comprehensive morality can never be adequately articulated or correctly grasped in terms of rights alone.

Swadeshi

Swadeshi is the means for Gandhi's quest for swaraj. Fundamentally it meant 'localism'. This was not an isolated localism of the 'deserted village', which Goldsmith romanticized, or the degradation of caste oppression that Ambedkar revolted against, but rather the local neighbourhood community, the village as the node in a network of oceanic circles that overlapped and spread out in its ever-widening embrace. It is this commitment of the individual to one's 'desh'—the more immediate village neighbourhood, rather than country or nation—that was Gandhi's Indian alternative to Western nationalism. (Parekh 1995: 56–7)

He does seem to idealize ruralism, and to privilege this 'Gospel of rural-mindedness', as he called it, (*Harijan* 16 May 1939) against urbanism as a way of life. His basic insight is surely sound, for he perceived that power in India was inevitably monopolized by the urban elite, at the expense of village folk. Gandhi was trying to reverse this dependency and make the state serve the weaker sections. His was an egalitarianism, not just a romantic inspiration. Mao attempted as much in China.

But the village Gandhi idealized was not just a geographic place, or a statistic, or a social class. It was an event, a dream, a happening, a culture. His use of 'the term village implied not an entity, but a set of values'. (Sethi 1979:23) It brought together his three basic themes of swaraj: self-respect, self-realization and self-reliance.

In privileging the rural over the urban, Gandhi was arguing for a minimal state. Any exercise of state power made Gandhi suspicious, since he saw the state essentially as an instrument of violence. He would have preferred an 'ordered' or 'enlightened' anarchy of self-ruled, self-controlled individuals, not as isolated atoms but as persons in a community of communities. Perhaps he was too influenced by the colonial state in generalizing his negative perceptions. It was only in the communal cauldron at the time of Partition, that he began to see the need of state power to contain and end the violence. And yet our experience of the post-colonial state in this country would bear out his apprehensions even as we seem to be careening into anarchy.

Gandhi perhaps did not fully appreciate the role of the state as an agency for regeneration and redistribution, in planning and coordination. But he was acutely sensitive to the centralized state appropriating what belonged to the local community and the individual. He was deeply suspicious of power being used in the cause of freedom or even to contain violence. His swadeshi was an attempt to address this complex dialectic on an ethical rather than a political foundation.

Satya

Truth was not a matter of theory but of practice in Gandhi's work. His autobiography, *The Story of My Experiments with Truth*, is surely an indication of this. But Gandhi's truth has little to do with experimental science and the method first indicated by Aristotle and later elaborated by Francis Bacon. Rather his truth, satya, was an experiential one, a reflexive understanding of oneself very much in the tradition of the Buddha and the ancient rishis of this land.

The experimental method of course is the foundation of the

predictive sciences, the experiential one can only leave us with an interpretive discipline. But Gandhi's life's journey was not to predict the outcome of his life's struggle, but rather to interpret and direct his own and the struggles of the masses for what could be legitimately claimed.

For him satya, truth, was an absolute reality that we could only partially grasp. Thus the many-sidedness of truth that we experienced was nothing but a consequence of such relative knowledge. Overcoming these limitations of our 'relative knowledge' for a more comprehensive grasp of this 'absolute truth' could never be forced by violence. Only ahimsa, non-violence, could make the quest for such truth viable. Gandhi operationalized this quest in his strategy of satyagraha, or truth-force. Moreover, he makes no ethical separation between means and an end. Both must be morally good. For him, 'the goal did not exist at the end of a series of actions designed to achieve it, it shadowed them from the very beginning.' (Parekh 1995: 142)

Thus, satyagraha was not just a political strategy, for Gandhi, it was both a means and an end. It was basically a method of dialogue that would bring two disagreeing parties not just into mutual agreement, but into the realization of a deeper truth together. Thus the dichotomy between the oppressor and the oppressed is transcended in this 'heightened mutuality', but even beyond this 'satyagraha ruptures the trichotomy among the oppressor, oppressed and emancipator', (Pantham 1986: 179) for it seeks to involve all three in this quest for greater self-realization of the truth. From the satyagrahi as the initiator, this required a demanding discipline: 'those who want to become passive resisters for the service of the country have to observe prefect chastity, adopt poverty, follow truth and cultivate fearlessness'. (HS Ch.17)

In *Hind Swaraj* Gandhi defines 'passive resistance', as he called it then, 'a method of securing rights by personal suffering'. (HS Ch.17) Clearly there is a non-political dimension involved in this strategy as well, but that does not make it any less effective politically. 'Gandhi's satyagraha then was an ingenious combination of reason, morality and politics; it appealed to the opponent's head, heart and interests'. (Parekh 1995: 156)

This was a 'vernacular model of action' (Parekh 1995: 211) that his people understood. But it was Gandhi who first used it so effectively to mobilize them and to appeal to their oppressors. In fact, he was the first leader to bring non-violence at the centre stage in the struggle for freedom from the British. He was well aware that adopting 'methods of violence to drive out the English' would be a 'suicidal policy', (HS Ch.15) and his *Hind Swaraj* was precisely intended to stymie such a soul-destroying venture.

Reinterpreting Hinduism

Gandhi locates himself as an insider to mainstream Hinduism, the sanatan dharma that he claimed to follow. The radicalism of his re-interpretation goes unnoticed precisely because of this. Gandhi does not reject, he simply affirms what he considers to be authentic, and allows the inauthentic to be sloughed off. 'Gandhi's Hinduism was ultimately reduced to a few fundamental beliefs: the supreme reality of God, the ultimate unity of all life and the value of love (ahimsa) as a means of realising God'. (Nanda 1985:6) His profound redefinition of Hinduism gave it a radically novel orientation. In sum: 'Gandhi's Hinduism was an ingenious intellectual construct...For him religion culminated but was not exhausted in social service and it had a spiritual meaning and significance only when inspired by the search for moksha. Gandhi's Hinduism had a secularised content but a spiritual form and was at once both secular and non-secular.' (Parekh 1995: 109)

Thus, for example, one of the most remarkable and yet unremarked re-interpretations of Hinduism that Gandhi effected was that of the *Bhagavad Gita*. Here was a text intended to persuade a reluctant warrior on the legitimacy and even the necessity of joining the battle. Gandhi re-works its nish-kama-karma to become the basis of his ahimsa and satyagraha.

We have only to contrast Gandhi's Hinduism with V.D. Savarkar's Hindutva to see how starkly contrary they are. Savarkar's 'Hinduize politics and militarize Hinduism' is the very opposite of Gandhi's sarva-dharma-samabhav. Gandhi did not believe in a separation of religion and politics. But he brought a religious ethic to politics rather than political militancy into religious communities. Savarkar's ideology was narrow and exclusivist in its conflation of janma bhoomi and puniya bhoomi. Moreover, it played on the insecurities of the traditional upper-caste elite, now trying desperately to make the transition to a modern upper-class. Hence in spite of its pretensions of being nationalist and modern, its militant chauvinism and authoritarian fundamentalism make Hindutva the very antithesis of Gandhi's Hinduism. It is in fact but a contemporary synthesis of Brahmanism.

This is why in the end he is vehemently opposed by the traditional Hindu elite, who finally recognized and felt threatened by the challenge he posed. As a protégé of Savarkar, 'Godse not only represented the traditional Indian stratarchy, which Gandhi was trying to break,' (Nandy 1980:86) in a sense his 'hand was forced by the real killers of Gandhi: the anxiety-ridden, insecure traditional elite concentrated in the urbanised, educated, partly westernised, tertiary sector whose meaning of life Gandhian politics was taking away'. (ibid.: 87)

But then again precisely because he presents himself as a Hindu in his interpretation of Indian culture, he was seen as too inclusive by traditional Hindus, and at the same time as not ecumenical enough by contemporary non-Hindus. Hence his appeals for Hindu-Muslim unity were rejected, by the Muslims as being too Hindu, and questioned by the Hindus for not being Hindu enough.

Gandhi's failure to bridge the religious divide between Hindu and Muslim was matched in many ways by his failure to bridge the caste divide between Dalits and others. He never quite understood Jinnah, or his appeal to Muslim nationalism. One could say the same in regard to Ambedkar and his Dalits, who have never forgotten or forgiven Gandhi for the imposition of the Pune Pact. We can only wonder now whether separate electorates for Dalits then would have made reservations for Scheduled Castes unnecessary now. What we do know is that the caste divide has only deepened with increasing conflict and indeed the same can be said about the religious divide and religious conflict in this country.

Yet for Gandhi, the unity of humankind was premised on the oneness of the cosmos, which was a philosophical principle that was ontologically prior to diversity. This is precisely what an advaitin would hold. Hence for him unity in diversity was the integrating axis not just of Hindu but of Indian culture as well, and indeed of the cosmos.

Thus the legitimacy of religious diversity was rooted in the fundamental Jain principle of anekantavada, the many sidedness of truth. Once this was conceded as a foundational truth, then religious tolerance was a necessary consequence. But this was not to be a negative tolerance of distance and coexistence, but rather one of communication and enrichment. (Heredia 1996) Indeed, Gandhi would ground the dialogue between East and West in their religious traditions, since for him religious rootedness was precisely the basis for mutual learning.

In cultural matters, however, he was an assimilationist, not in the sense that he wanted other cultures to be assimilated to his own, but rather all cultures to be enriched by each other without losing their identity. This is now called interculturalism. Gandhi's cultural assimilation, then, was opposed to political revivalists and religious nationalists, to Tilak and M.M. Malaviya as also to Dayanand Saraswati and of course Savarkar. In Gandhi's understanding, an open and understanding dialogue must precede not follow a free and adaptive assimilation. The basis for such a dialogic encounter would have to be a 'pluralist epistemology'. But Gandhi was convinced that it would only bear fruit when it was 'sunk in a religious soil'. (HS Ch.20) Thus an enriched diversity would then contribute to a more invigorated pluralism and an enhanced unity. This was precisely Gandhi's understanding of Indian culture and civilization, and indeed, he had grasped its fundamental strength and the secret of its survival.

Our World Today

Against Gandhi's critique of the western civilization and his affirmation of Indian culture, we must now locate ourselves with regard to the critical issues of our world today to dialogue with him. By now it should be apparent that the real contradiction is not so much between an English West and an Indian East, as between ancient culture, whether East or West and modern civilization. Here we have chosen three such issues as being the most fruitful for this encounter: the collapse of socialism and the crisis of capitalism, globalization in an interdependent world and the unresolved violence of our atomic age.

Post-socialism

In our present world, the socialist ideal is being discredited as a god that failed, when the once socialist states collapsed. It would seem that the sky had fallen for those with political commitments on the left. Now we have to come to terms with 'self-interest' and the 'profit motive'. Yet we can hardly accept the kind of exploitation that our labourers are still subjected to in a system that benefits a few at the expense of the many. Moreover, today the crisis of capitalism is everyday more apparent with the taming of the much acclaimed Asian tigers as the new model for the cornucopia of development and progress; and the growing unemployment in the West cannot but presage further crises there as well. In China and India growth is slowing down—or rather has already slowed down—with unanticipated consequences. Indeed, there is a growing interest in a democratic socialism, which is privileged in our Constitution.

However, with liberalization and privatization as accepted policy today, the Bharat verses India divide, that Gandhi had intuited long ago, is, if anything, rapidly and disastrously growing. Only now, the elite of Bharat seems to have been co-opted by the privileged of India, even as the refugees of India have been forced into an urbanized Bharat.

Much noise has been made about the disagreements between Gandhi and Nehru, and their diverging models of development. Nehru did not share Gandhi's predilection for the 'village' or his suspicion of technology. (Nehru 1958: 507–10) Nehru is right in affirming that Congress had never completely accepted, nor had Gandhi himself imposed his understanding of *Hind Swaraj*. (ibid.) But in the exchange of letters in 1945, (Parel 1997: 149–56) it is quite clear that the axis of their reconciliation was precisely around this quest for equality. Their paths may have been different but Nehru's socialism and Gandhi's swaraj were both oriented to this quest for equity and equality across all the divides of caste, class, region, etc. This is how Gandhi put together their understanding in 1945:

> the real question…is how to bring about the highest intellectual economic, political and moral development… In this there should be equal right and opportunity for all…equality between town-dwellers and villagers in the standard of food, drink, all other living conditions… In order to achieve this equality today people should be able to produce for themselves the necessaries of life… If we try to work out the conditions for such a life: we are forced to the conclusion that the unit of society should be a village, or call it a small and manageable group…self sufficient (in the matter of their vital requirements)…in bonds of mutual cooperation and inter-dependence.' (Nehru 1958: 511–12)

Gandhi was quite radical in urging equality, even more so than the Communists. He would have equal wages and bread labour for all, following Ruskin in his *Unto this Last* (1921, 1st 1862), who wanted a more humane economy based on 'social affection' not on the self-interest and competitiveness of 'economic man'. A section on 'economic equality' in Gandhi's 'Constructive Programme', (CW 75: 146–66) affirms it as 'the master key to non-violent independence', for it means 'abolishing the eternal conflict between capital and labour…levelling down of the few rich…and levelling up of the semi-starved millions'. (ibid.) Hence Gandhi's concept of equality is not grounded in impersonal and competitive individualism, as it seems to be in the West, but in cooperative and compassionate non-violence, on 'fraternity' not just 'liberty'.

At first, he saw no contradiction between such fraternal equality and the idealized hierarchy of the varna system. But in his later years he reversed himself to urge that a 'classless society is the ideal, not merely to be at aimed at but to be worked for'. (Harijan Feb. 17, 1946, p.9) By now he was promoting inter-caste marriages and hoping 'there would be only one caste known by the beautiful name Bhangi, that is to say the reformer or remover of all dirt'. (*Harijan* July 7, 1946, p.212)

But if Gandhi's quest for equality is something that our complex world cannot accommodate, we seem to have given up not just this ideal of equality, but even the quest for equity in the distribution of the rewards and burdens of our society. Today Gandhi's proletarian 'levelling down' certainly seems to be much more viable than Tagore's elitist 'levelling up'. If Tagore would have all Indians to be brahmans, Gandhi would want all of us to be shudras, workers or rather bhangis, reformers. This 'responsible, respectful, non-violent, non-contractual, non-competitive, non-hegemonising, symbolic equality had a place in Gandhi's life and in his theory of life'. (Nandy 1986: 111)

In such a scenario the relevance of Gandhi's idea of sarvodaya as the goal of swaraj is something we need to re-examine. Certainly, state capitalism masquerading as socialism was hardly Gandhi's idea of the India of his dream. But a decentralized participative democratic and humane society is certainly more attractive, and one may dare say, a more viable ideal today, than the kind of consumerism and inequitable divisions that the new economic policies in our country seems to welcome.

We are now coming back to the panchayati raj and local self-government that Gandhi urged long ago. Indeed, the principle of subsidiarity, that is, the devolution of authority downwards together with the delegation of coordination upwards, seems to be the only viable solution to national governments that are too large to address local problems, though not national ones, while being too small to cope with global ones.

Today the 73rd and 74th amendment to the Constitution once again affirm panchayati raj and Tribal self-rule. We are coming back to a devolution of powers that Gandhi had urged in his ideal of swaraj and had tried to have written into our Constitution. Hopefully this will be a presage of more to come.

Globalization

Globalization and the alienating homogeneity that it must inevitably promote is the very opposite of the localism and the celebration of diversity Gandhi's 'swadeshi' was meant to encourage. Today we are rushing headlong into this globalizing world, and hoping to find our place in the sun in the community of rich and powerful nations by at least joining their game, though we cannot beat them at it.

However, Gandhi's principle of swadeshi, 'simply means that the most effective organization of social, economic and political functions must follow the natural contours of the neighbourhood,' thus affirming 'the primacy of the immediate community'. (Roy 1985: 114) Gandhi's 'goodness politics', as it has been called, (Saran 1980: 691) could only really operate on such a scale.

For Gandhi, 'decentralization means the creation of parallel politics in which the people's power is institutionalised to counter the centralising and alienating forces of the modern state...Thus the Gandhian decentralised polity has a built-in process of the withering away of the state.' (Sethi 1986: 229)

But before this is dismissed as too naive or impractical for our sophisticated and complicated world, we might pause to think of the kind of politics our centralized states have in fact spawned. The very hegemonic homogeneity it promotes succeeds less at obliterating difference of interests than at alienating minorities and enkindling their resentment. On the contrary, to take a lesson from ecology, micro-variability is needed for macro-stability in political and economic systems as well.

Gandhi's swadeshi could never mean ethnocentrism. He was no jingoist nationalist or cultural chauvinist, who would negate the global dimensions of our common humanity, even as he firmly stood his local ground. His concept of 'oceanic circles' was precisely an attempt at articulating inter-related levels of human social organization. Unlike some Hindu and Muslim 'nationalists' Gandhi never used 'nationalism' for narrow sectarian purposes. He mobilized his people as 'Indians' not as Hindus or Muslims. His nationalism was anti-imperialistic not chauvinistic, a struggle for political justice and cultural dignity. (Nandy 1994: 3) He was a patriot who wanted 'Indian nationalism to be non-violent, anti-militaristic and therefore a variant of universalism'. (Nandy 1995: 14) He was only too aware of the number of 'nationalities' that could be mobilised in India.

Indeed, an ecological understanding is now propelling us to a new and deep realization of our interdependence. We have only one earth, and we must learn to share and care. Gandhi refused to see our relationship to nature in dominating imperialistic terms. We are not so much God's vice-regent over the universe as a contingent part of the cosmos, debtors born, whose proper response to life must be the 'yagna', service-offering of our lives for others. (Parekh 1995: 88)

Thus, with regard to the economy and the polity, Gandhi would have the village as his world; but with regard to culture and religion, it was the world that was his village. Surely here we have a viable example of thinking globally and acting locally. Indeed, today the global ecological crisis has begun to press on us anew the relevance of Gandhi's paradoxical ideas. The institutional individualism that seemed to be the very foundation of the democratic quest in the West seems quite inadequate to battle the ecological crises of today. For it privileges individual rights over the common good. But even enlightened self-interest has no answer to the 'tragedy of the commons' except an external coercion. (Hardin, 1986)

However, for Gandhi, 'individuality' must be 'oriented to self-realization through self-knowledge…in a network of interdependence and harmony informed by ahimsa'. (Roy 1986: 84) Nor was this to be an interdependence of dominant-subservient relationships so prevalent in our local communities and global societies. His swadeshi envisaged a more personalized and communitarian society on a human scale, yet extending to include both the biotic and even the cosmic community. This was the logical extension of the Jain doctrine of 'syadvada', that everything is related to everything in the universe in 'a great chain of being'.

However, the Gandhian ideal was a community modelled on the joint family and on varna as a non-competitive division of labour. Later in his life his own promotion of inter-caste marriages testifies to a change in his views. Yet even as we critique such Gandhian ideas, we must discover in dialogue what value and relevance they have for us today. For ultimately, Gandhi insists on both: that the community is not a mere means for the self-interest of the individual and that the individual is not a mere resource for the concerns of the community. And this would go for the community of communities, that our global community must be.

Violence

There can be no negating the liberation that modernity has brought in our post-modern world to vast masses of people. But for all its much-vaunted 'rationality', some would rather say because of it, modernity has failed to cope with the endemic irrationality of violence. Now after two world wars, and a global cold war, not to mention the many smaller hot ones that have been a continuing presence on this earth, we cannot help but realize that modernity has not effectively or ethically addressed the problem of violence, either at the individual or group level, and certainly not at the national or international one.

If Gandhi's ahimsa seems impractical, what are the alternatives to the violence we have trapped ourselves in? How would Gandhi, the apostle of ahimsa, respond to our claim to be a nuclear weapons state? What all this has to do with the quality of life of our impoverished masses remains a question that must haunt us. If Gandhi was right in claiming that 'to arm India on a large scale is to Europeanise it', (HS Ch. 15) then what would nuclear arms do? Do they Americanize us? And this is an initiative being pushed by our cultural nationalists. But then in a globalized world it is surely only the elite that will get to strut and fret upon this global stage, while the masses of our people are a passive and manipulated audience to this theatre of the macabre.

The whole effort of the modern world in dealing with violence has been to control the other. Yet mastery over others has not meant less violence for ourselves. Only now we become the perpetrators, not the sufferers of violence. Gandhi's attempt begins with controlling oneself, as it is the first source of violence one must master in order to fearlessly and non-violently win over the violent others.

Thus, while the modern world gave primacy to rights and

privileged freedom, Gandhi privileged duty and gave the primacy to conscience. His concern was with 'socialising the individual conscience rather than internalising the social conscience'. (Iyer 1973: 123) Certainly Gandhi has much relevance to our present need to once again bridge this dichotomy between rights and duties, and integrate both in a more comprehensive freedom of choice and the obligation of conscience, in a humanist worldview and a more genuinely humane world-community. This is our only real chance for peace in our now globally inter-dependent world.

Gandhi's Synthesis

Gandhi's effort can be interpreted as an attempt to integrate the positive elements of modernity with a liberating re-interpretation of tradition. In his unique way, he sets up a creative encounter for this integration, even as some see him as radical and others as reactionary. With his critique from within the tradition, Gandhi becomes the great synthesizer of contraries if not of contradictions, within and across traditions. His purna (comprehensive) swaraj would harmonize rights and duties, head and heart, individual and community, faith and reason, economic development and spiritual progress, religious commitment and religious pluralism, self-realization and political action. He brings together philosophical discourse and popular culture in enlightened renewal and social reform. Not since the time of the Buddha, some have argued, has such a synergy between the philosophic and the popular in our traditions been experienced. Thus Gandhi integrates the Upanishad and the Tulsi Ramayana in his religious synthesis. When it comes to bridges across traditions, Gandhi brings the *Bhagavad Gita* together with the 'Sermon on the Mount' and reads one into the other. In fact, if he has Christianized Hinduism he has certainly also presented us with a Hinduized Christian spirituality.

Precisely as a re-interpretation from within, Gandhi can so much more effectively and authentically integrate into his synthesis elements from without. Because as Ashis Nandy writes, 'Gandhi was neither a conservative nor a progressive. And though he had internal contradictions, he was not a fragmented self-alienated man driven by the need to compulsively conserve the past or protect the new.' (Nandy 1980: 71)

Thus 'effortlessly transcending the dichotomy of orthodoxy and iconoclasm', (Nandy 1980: 71) he reconciles meaningful faith and reasonable modernity. In the best traditions of this land he combines both faith and reason. For faith and reason are implicated in each other. The blind faith of a fundamentalist, revivalist version of religion was totally unacceptable to Gandhi. He would constantly critique faith to ascertain whether it was meaningful and reasonable in terms of basic human value commitments. And so too he would demand of reason the same fidelity to these values as well.

However, the ascetic dimension of Gandhi's integration at times loses the aesthetic one. A criticism of Gandhi's ashrams was that it grew only vegetables not flowers. (Parekh 1995: 209) Growing vegetables represented more than the Gandhian pre-occupation with vegetarianism and bread-labour. But that his ashram did not grow any flowers would indicate a certain distancing from the aesthetic. Indeed, Gandhi surprised and shocked Tagore when he claimed he could hardly enjoy the glory and the beauty of a sunset when so many of his brothers and sisters could not but be ground down by very burden of their lives.

But in rightly emphasizing the need for renunciation, certainly a message that our consumerist and self-indulgent world needs more than ever today, the Gandhian ashram seemed to miss out on the need for celebration, which our tired, alienated, dis-spirited and pessimistic world needs almost as much. We do need the self-renunciation Gandhi espoused, as well as his affirmation of selflessness. But we also need to celebrate the other, and the enrichment that comes from this encounter.

A re-interpretation of Gandhi would precisely allow such a celebration if only we can realize that for him the ultimate other is the 'utterly Other' who is the final quest of our self-realization in moksha, and yet realized only in our encounters with each other. For while Gandhi's understanding of moksha as service is a seminal breakthrough, even this can be enriched by affirming not negating the other dimensions of life. It is only thus that we will be able to bring some wholeness to, in Iris Murdoch's unforgettable phrase, the 'broken totality', of our modern world.

Counter-Cultural Transformation

It is certainly not our intention to idealize Gandhi into a new 'ism', neither post- nor neo-Gandhianism. In urging a re-thinking and a re-interpretation, we want to be sensitive to the special contribution Gandhi has made, but in a critical way. In trying to see his relevance for our times we want to enter into a meaningful dialogue with him. Idealizing him by being blind to his limitations or being insensitive to the context in which he lived can hardly be helpful to anything constructive or creative. We need an open-ended critique of Gandhi, not a close-ended 'ism', as seems to have happened with some of the official Gandhians. Gandhi is, indeed, greater than their 'Gandhianisms' and he will be more relevant than those of any others as well. Ernest Renan, with Gallic irony, is supposed to have once said, that when fate could not destroy a great man it sent him disciples in revenge. Perhaps we may need to save Gandhi from such a fate.

Gandhi is certainly a counter-cultural inspiration that cannot but be relevant for our times, though all too often he is made into a counterfeit idol. In these times of a dangerous Hindu cultural nationalism, and the marginalization of the old 'Congress culture' as we see in these and others on the national scene, not to mention the increasing irrelevance of the official Gandhians, we need to rethink and revive the counter-cultural inspiration of Gandhi's oppression-centred, victim-oriented, spiritually grounded and uniquely Indian political philosophy. (Parekh 1995: 6)

His life was a continuing series of controversies and contestations with those in power on behalf of the powerless. He never lacked opponents—among the British and even the Indian elites. He did not want India's freedom fighters to settle into the status quo and often found himself isolated and alone particularly at the end of his life, which was far from being one long triumphant procession. Even his followers in the Congress did not really grasp the full impact of his life and message. In his last days he would often sing to himself Tagore's inspiring and moving song in 1905, '*Ekla chalo re Ekla chalo*' (Walk alone):

> If they answer not to thy call, walk alone,
> If they are afraid and cower mutely facing the wall,
> O thou of evil luck,
> open thy mind and speak out alone.
>
> If they turn away, and desert you when crossing the wilderness,
> O thou of evil luck,
> trample the thorns under thy tread,
> and along the blood-lined track, travel alone.
>
> If they do not hold up the light when the night is troubled with storm,
> O thou of evil luck,
> with the thunder flame of pain ignite thy own heart
> and let it burn alone.
>
> (from Som 2009: 254)

Yet one of the great contributions of Gandhi was precisely his centring of the periphery: in politics with sarvodaya and later antyodaya; in religion by de-brahaminizing Hinduism, de-institutionalizing practice and personalizing belief; in education by his proposal for 'nai talim' or basic education as it came to be called, insisting on the integration of education and life; in the economy by symbolically urging khadi as a unifying and levelling symbol. Not all his efforts were successful or perhaps even practical, but they did make a contribution which is still valid today, and challenge us too. And all Gandhi's original ideas can be found seeded in his *Hind Swaraj*.

There can be no doubt that Gandhi was an authentic 'organic intellectual', articulating and symbolically expressing the people's aspirations. But he was no less a uniquely transformative leader, who changed persons and structures, and transformed a people and their culture, made leaders out of ordinary people, and inspired his people with noble ideals, albeit for a while. Here was a yugapurush if ever there was one. If we are looking for a new synthesis for a counter-culture, we must take Gandhi as a dialogue partner in this project but first we must redefine and re-interpret him. We do believe that such an encounter will help us to re-examine and reconstruct ourselves as well.

In a globalizing world, we all seem to be impelled to a kind of a global culture, that uniform least common denomination, a kind of common minimum programme. However, this is ultimately based on Western civilization which is in fact the dominant strand in such a culture. When Gandhi was once asked what he thought of western civilization, it is said that he remarked rather impishly, that it would be 'a good idea'. The challenge today for us in our globalizing world is to find another, a better, a more integral, a more human ideal for our society, for our world today. There can be multiple modernities, which integrate the modern by drawing critically on others, as also our own cultural heritage and make a symbiosis of the best in each. This is more than a generational process even in our new cyber world. But we must have the imagination to begin now.

Gandhi has been severely criticized as impractical, as someone who took out an impossible overdraft on human moral resources. But this is to claim that human beings are not capable of a metanoia, a radical change of heart that can open up new perspectives, not just for individuals and groups, but for entire societies and whole cultures as well. What we need are organic intellectuals and transformative activists who can articulate and precipitate such a social movement. The cascading crises that our society and our world is experiencing only underline more emphatically the need to find new ways of redefining ourselves and understanding our problems, before we can begin to respond to the situation. This can only be a collective effort, and it can learn from the experimental and dialogic methods of Gandhi.

Constructive Alternatives

Gandhi's satyagraha struggles stamped India's freedom movement with a distinctive national identity. However, what is not given due importance was the constructive programme, which he insisted must accompany non-violent resistance to transform structures of oppression and injustice. 'For Gandhi the success could be achieved only through intense constructive work at the heart of every campaign'. (Hardiamn 2007: 58) Non-violent action campaigns depended as much on constructive work as on civil resistance.

They are the 'twin dimensions of Gandhi's approach to conflict transformation—constructive work and active satyagraha'. (Rigby 2007: 180) Talking to his co-workers in 1944 Gandhi emphasized that through the constructive programme 'you can make the villages feel self-reliant, self-sufficient and free so that they can stand up for their own rights. If you make a real success of the constructive programme, you will win Swaraj for India without civil disobedience.' (cited Ostergaard and Currell 1971: 3) Furthermore, Gandhi perceived such programmes as providing a creative alternative to the current systems and practices that supported and promoted the status quo, building swaraj bottom-up.

Gandhi's ashrams were the experimental venues for these creative alternatives, where satyagrahis were trained, and where ashram life provided the satyagrahis the discipline for the practice and internalization of ahimsa. They were also a 'dialogical space', where 'community living and experimenting together was made possible by an abiding faith in the dialogue that they shared with each other and with Gandhi, both individually and as a community'; here 'the larger quest for self-realization and swaraj gave meaning and context to the ashram'. (Suhrud 2005) Gandhi's constructive work programmes were centred on local ashrams, where ashramvasis lived and worked among the people, especially the poor and marginalized, thus linking the middle-class leaders with the people.

This established links between leaders, who were often middle-class savarnas and people who were not. Gandhi presciently intuited that it would be the basis for the credibility of the leaders and the trust people posed in them. They were not seen as outsiders from somewhere else, but their own people from their own neighbourhood. The beginnings of this constructive work in the villages would necessarily be small and rather symbolic, but as they won credibility among people they would gain momentum and hopefully build up into a larger national movement.

The success of Gandhi's satyagraha depended on such a trained cadre, credible and committed, who led the people. These ashrams were a critical training ground for his satyagrahis, and meant to be a long-term investment accompanying the struggle for swaraj from the bottom-up, rather than top-down, as a reformist political process. Unfortunately, it has been relatively ignored in the literature on non-violent resistance. To the people, however, such constructive programmes made satyagrahis credible and acceptable and their resistance just even if formally not legitimate Those who denied its validity would see this as mere tokenism, and even those who acknowledged the efficacy, subtlety and adaptability of Gandhi's methods, 'have failed to contextualise the strategies that Gandhi adopted in their time and place in Indian history'. (Hardiman 2007: 58). They have thus failed to see the vital intertwining of these two dimensions of his approach: his constructive work programmes and non-violent resistance.

However, Bob Overy (1982) is a significant exception. Overy argues that they 'failed to see that non-violent action depended for Gandhi as much on constructive work as on campaigns of civil resistance. For Gandhi, success could be achieved only through intense constructive work at the heart of every campaign.' (Hardiman 2003: 58) Thus while Richard Gregg's *The Power of Non-violence* (1959) does not relate the manual and social work of the satyagrahis to his analysis of non-violent resistance, Joan Bondurant, in *Conquest of Violence* (1958) treats constructive work as expendable once the contentious issues have been resolved and/or the struggle suspended. (1988: 118) It is not seen, as Gandhi did, as a necessary element of his satyagraha in its own right. In Gene Sharp's major work on *The Politics of Non-violent Action,* (1973), the role of constructive work was almost entirely missing. (1973: 856–7) Though in his *Gandhi as a Political Strategist* (1979: 77-86, 219–212) he does mention it as being important to Gandhi's whole approach.

Peace activists tend to focus on the subtlety and adaptability of Gandhi's non-violent methods for social transformation. They miss the critical importance Gandhi gave to combining this active non-violent resistance with constructive work campaigns to ground its credibility and foreground creative alternatives in replicable spaces. In conclusion: 'the significance of combining what we might term "resistance" and "reconstruction" as twin dimensions of any movement to challenge and transform situations of injustice remain as relevant today as they ever were'. (Rigby 2017: 181)

Gandhi's challenge for us is combining these twin dimensions of social transformation, and non-violent resistance in creative alternatives, bringing them into the public area and contextualizing them in our time as he did in his. Furthermore, 'while his non-violence was rooted in his deep religious faith, Gandhi was also a sophisticated political strategist who greatly advanced non-violence as a successful method of struggle even by those who did not share his entire moral framework'. (Zunes et al. 1999) It was a coincidence of opposites, the mahatma and the politician, the renouncer and the activist, that contextualized Gandhi's appeal for the Indian masses.

Today we must combine these dimensions in a holistic integration of the spiritual and the secular, of resistance and creativity for the peaceful social transformation of our people, so that we can be midwives to the non-violence which 'is yet in the womb of the future'. (Kripalani 1938: 23)

CHAPTER SIX

SPIRALLING VIOLENCE

Contextualizing Violence – Karwan-e-Mohabbat – Atrocities and Hate Crimes – Avatars of Ethnocentrism – Patriotism and Nationalism – Critical Choice – Politics of Hate – Hindutva Project – Counter-narrative – Hindu Victimhood – Unhealed Traumas – Constitutionalism and Populism – Celebrating Diversity – Minorities and Majority – Dignifying Difference – Social Democracy – Saffron Neoliberalism – Inequality Fallout – Indian Scenario – Inclusive Growth – Growth and Equity

Contextualizing Violence

The continuing collective violence in contemporary India today can be traced back to the divide-and-rule policy of the colonial regime which ended with the trauma of Partition. Both sides have neither forgiven nor forgotten, and the blame game continues. With the active aggressor it becomes an ethic of hate. Over time, this gets embedded in an active politics of hate, a culture of divisive polarization, both sustained and supported by an ethnocentrism in its many avatars, that divides the world into a hostile them and us, along cultural faultlines, and the discontents of the inequities of neoliberal economics. The passive approver, too, becomes part of this scenario, more by default and compromise.

Leaders like President Trump, divisive issues like Brexit and chauvinist nationalisms are not strangers to that world anymore. In spite of inspiring other movements with its non-violent freedom struggle, India in its South Asian context is no longer an exception.

Populism has foregrounded violence to which populist welfarism is hardly an adequate answer. The recent Parliamentary elections have lessons to teach us in this regard.

Reversing this cycle of aggression and revenge between victim and violator becomes extremely urgent; for once violence becomes endemic in a society, its upstream causes get structurally embedded and any restructuring implies deep commitment to change for long-term solutions. At times these may well be generational ones. The alternative to a total solution may well imply a complete submission, or even elimination, of one or the other party to the violence. But 'might is right' can hardly be acceptable in any society that aspires to be just and decent, which even extremists pretend to. Whether on the right or the left, extremists have now turned away from Gandhiji's inspiration and legitimized the powerful as rightful leaders and rulers in society. However, as with socialism and democracy, non-violence is making a comeback in heroic, though exceptional, ways. The new interest in peace studies is evidence of this.

Karwan-e-Mohabbat

Anhad, an NGO working for peace and reconciliation, launched Karwan-e-Mohabbat (caravan of love) that foregrounded the possibilities and difficulties of such peace and reconciliation ventures. This Caravan of Love consisted of a group of exceptional volunteers—writers, journalists, social workers, teachers, lawyers—all entirely crowdfunded.

It set out on 4 September 2017 from Nagaon in Assam with an aim to end by reaching Porbunder in Gujarat, the birth place of Gandhiji, on his 148th birth anniversary. It passed through eight states. The volunteers visited the families of the victims of mob violence and traumatized survivors, where there were any. The purpose was twofold: 'to respond with solidarity to the everyday fear that has settled in the hearts of Muslims, Dalits and Christians, and to challenge and break the worrying silence of the majority with a call to conscience.' (Mander 2018: ix)

Their record of their experiences and reflections mark a trail of tragedy and trauma for the victims, but so far mostly unregretted and even justified by the violators. Dominant groups target easy scapegoats among the weak and vulnerable, the marginalized and minorities, especially Muslims. Suspicions and false charges of cow slaughter and beef eating are trumpeted by state-supported gaurakshaks, who then are emboldened to attack and lynch suspects on flimsy grounds, often based on fake news and rumours. The government is implicated with its silence and even covert sponsorship that immunizes the attackers from the law. The police too are complicit; mostly the victims get charged and arrested, while the perpetrators are unidentified or let off on bail.

In Alwar, Rajasthan, in spite of having all the required documents to transport the cattle he had bought, Pehlu Khan was beaten to death by a mob on 1 April 2017. The police chose to take the cattle to the shelter before taking the victims to hospital, where one person arrived dead. (NDTV 23 Jul 2018, https://www.ndtv.com/india-news/taking-alwar-mob-victim-to-hospital-cops-stopped-for-tea-cow-transport-1887678) Due to a botched police investigation, in spite of eyewitnesses and video evidence, all six men charged were let off on 14 August the same year. The state plans to appeal, but such injustices go deeper than state agencies of law and order. Such injustices have inflected large swathes of our society, with violent prejudices. The *Rajasthan Protection from Lynching Bill*, 2019, passed on 5 August 2019, was tellingly opposed by the BJP in the State Assembly. Alarmed at the rising mob violence, the Supreme Court had even urged the central government to pass an anti-lynch-law bill, but besides Rajasthan, only Manipur has passed one.

Everywhere, the Karwan found minorities and the marginalized, especially Muslims, 'living in endemic and lingering fear, and with hate and state violence, resigned to these as normalised elements of everyday living'. (Mander 2018: x) Karwan did attempt to hold Aman Sabhas, peace and reconciliation meetings, with local assistance. This was to affirm solidarity with the victims' families and publicly acknowledge the injustice they had suffered. In some places they were welcomed, as at the local gurudwara in Ramgarh district headquarters in Jharkhand, in others they were denied entry.

The story of Mohammad Akhlaq, who worked as an iron smith, is a typical example of what ominously seems like planned strategy. A resident of Dadri, which is just 60 kms from Delhi, he was falsely suspected of eating and storing beef at home in September 2015. He was dragged out of his house and beaten to death. The police first filed a case against Akhlaq for violation of the beef ban laws, which prohibited the storage and consumption of beef. Later a forensic investigation found that the meat in Akhlaq's refrigerator was not beef. But it made little difference. Only after a public outcry were some BJP officials who were involved arrested. When one of them died a natural death in prison, thousands attended his funeral where his body was draped in the national flag. The then union minister of tourism Mahesh Sharma was there, too, to express solidarity with these mobsters. The main accused, out on bail, planned to stand for the 2019 Parliamentary elections. He did and lost. (https://clarionindia.net/five-years-after-akhlaq-lynching-situation-remains-grim/)

With silence of the prime minister, who is otherwise quick to tweet his condemnation of other matters, and the blessings of a Union minister, what message does it send out? Surely a deliberate encouragement to more of the same. Less than a month after Akhlaq's murder, in Jammu and Kashmir a Muslim cattle transporter, Zahid Rasool Bhat, was burnt to death allegedly for transporting cows for slaughter. (*Alliance for Justice & Accountability Minority rights violations in India*, http://www.latimes.com/world/asia/la-fg-indian-trucker-beef-20151019-story.html) Similar lynchings have happened earlier elsewhere.

It would seem that in states like UP, Haryana and Rajasthan majoritarian parties have outsourced lynching to gau rakshak mobs, and the partisan police are deeply implicated as well. The threat of a public lynching now seems to be a way to keep the unwanted in their place. Major disturbances are not needed now; they are avoided as well because they may invite backlash and bad publicity. This has had a devastating effect on the social psyche of the minority community. Any reconciliation is on the terms of 'forget and forget', leaving the victims to cope on their own.

Karwan's attempted reconciliation in Giridih, Jharkhand,

where Usman Ansari and his family had a miraculous escape from a violent mob. Ansari supported his family with a small dairy of eight cows. Falsely charged with killing his sick cow, he was dragged out of his house beaten within an inch of his life and his body set on fire—the most dreadful dishonour to the dead for a Muslim. Miraculously he escaped from the mob, as did his daughters, thanks to the timely intervention of a police officer. But now the family is reduced to beggary.

Ansari so feared another attack that he went into hiding. For the village, all that was required was for Ansari to tell the police that the men who had been arrested were innocent and that he did not recognize those who had tried to kill him, and they would leave it at that, sweep it under the carpet till the next time.

Lynching has become the weapon of choice to intimidate and suppress the minorities and marginalized. According to a Reuters report, '28 Indians—24 of them Muslims—were killed and 124 injured' between 2010 and 2017. (https://datajournalismawards.org/projects/hate-crime-watch/) To people it made satyagrahis credible and acceptable and their resistance just, even if formally not legitimate. Mob violence is videotaped and widely circulated; it becomes a public ritual performance, expressing dominance and polarization in the community. (Tambiah 1996)

Shockingly, there is a complete lack of empathy for victims. 'One consistent finding was that families hit by hate violence were bereft of protection and justice from the state'. (Mander 2019: xi) Rather they are demonized to the point of not being human anymore. The obverse of this is the dehumanization of the perpetrators as well. They claim their suffering is real and undeserved, the others deserved what they get; they are the victims, and others are in the way of their future progress. The lack of compassion and ability to do a 'reciprocity of perspectives' locks the perpetrators into a narcissism of victimhood and a narcissism of grandiosity. (Nandy 2013) This has been expanded to the national level as is so evident in the majoritarian discourse on nationalism. These lynchings are but a microcosm of the creeping stain of the terrible collective violence in our society.

But the government is in complete denial. There is at present no centralized data available on lynchings, which have been reported in cases of theft, witchcraft, and recently over child theft and cow-protection. The Ministry of Home Affairs (MHA) did furnish some data on mob lynchings recorded by the states: between 2014 and March 2018, 45 persons were killed in 40 cases of mob lynching across nine states, and at least 217 persons had been arrested. Fourteen states did not participate in the study. (https://indianexpress.com/article/india/ncrb-plans-to-create-database-on-lynchings-indin-mob-killings-4742279/)

National Crime Records Bureau (NCRB), which tabulates and analyzes crime data from across the country every year, had planned to collect detailed data under the new sub-heads of death due to mob lynching, murder by influential people, killing ordered by khap panchayat and murder committed for religious reasons and lynchings as well. But the government refused to publish the data separately. The data collected was to be merged into the main category. This resulted in partial delay of the agency's report for 2017, and more importantly obfuscated the true picture of violent crime. The only conclusion that can be drawn is that the government found the data rather embarrassing and was covering up its failure to tackle these violet crimes.

Atrocities and Hate Crimes

In situations of pervasive collective violence in a society, neglecting the root cause of violence can only bring more of the same; or worse, a cycle of revenge waiting for the next turn of the screw. This does not end with the death of the perpetrators, because revenge is often seen as loyalty to the dead, fuelled by hatred for the living. Collective violence thus takes on the intense personalized characteristics of a family feud, and even though the individual protagonists are strangers to each other, they represent groups that are violently opposed. In India, religion and caste are the dividing faultlines. These are not rational antagonisms and hence no longer are simple issues of law and order. For the law itself and those who enforce it may be part of the problem, perhaps not so for the dominant violators who have the advantage, but certainly for the violated.

It is against this background that the Supreme Court's dilution of The Scheduled Castes and Tribes (Prevention of Atrocities) Act, 1989, amended and strengthened in 2014, seems an anomaly and is been reviewed and legislatively corrected. Yet all this violence is just the tip of the iceberg.

The Hate Crime Watch (HCW, https://datajournalismawards.org/projects/hate-crime-watch/) arrives at a figure of 254 hate crimes based on religious identity between 1 January 2009 and 29 October 2018, involving some 91 persons killed and 579 injured. Ninety per cent of these were reported after May 2014, when the present government came to power. (Muralidharan 2019: 34) The over-representation of minorities is also telling: the 14 per cent Muslims in the country account for 62 per cent of the victims; 2 per cent Christians account for 10 per cent victims; and the 80 per cent Hindus account for just 10 per cent victims.

When collective violence is seen in historical perspective, the upstream causes are not essentially different, though the context may well be. It may take generations to reverse the spiral of violence for it needs a positive engagement from all concerned. No final solution lasts forever. Negativity and hatred are alien to the human spirit. Forced submission is always under threat whether from the victims who may rise in revolt or the violators who change for a multiplicity of reasons, not excluding social conscience.

This is particularly true in situations of social change, like the transition from tradition to modernity in our contemporary times, where once dominant ideologies have played themselves out, as we have seen with colonialism and racism, for instance. Alarmingly though, they seem now to be making a comeback in another avatar to find another scapegoat. In India, as with many new states in 'ancient societies', (Geertz 1963) nationalism becomes the motivating mobilizer in their quest for modernity.

In sum, then, containing and then reversing the cycle of collective violence, in which we are now trapped, demands that we come to terms with our wounded history and unhealed memories of Partition. Our freedom struggle was foregrounded not on an exclusive nationalism, but an inclusive one; not on a politics of violence and hate but a politics of non-violence and compassion;

not a culture of polarizing and politicizing difference, but a culture of diversity and unity, protecting the minorities and marginalized; on an economics of development premised on equality and equity. All three are foundational for real reconciliation and lasting peace.

Avatars of Ethnocentrism

In 1959 Barbara Ward listed 'five ideas that changed the world' in her book of the same name. They are: nationalism, industrialism, colonialism, communism, internationalism. Three of the two have long begun an afterlife of sorts: industrialism in a post-industrial society of the new electronic revolution; and colonialism in a post-colonial third world, morphing into a neo-colonial one still dependent on the old colonial powers; communism evolved into a post-socialism with market characteristics, a state-sponsored authoritarian capitalism. The first and the last in the list are the two that still have traction: nationalism, now increasingly authoritarian and intolerant; and internationalism as reflected in neoliberal capitalism in its many hues and skewed inequalities. The consequent social tensions are only heightened by multinational corporations (MNCs) and their charters.

There are many avatars of nationalism premised on very different understandings of 'the idea of India'. But not all can comprehend and embrace the tryst we made long years ago with destiny in our struggle for freedom. In a once-secular India, today the politicization of religion by ethnocentric Hindu nationalism has marginalized religious minorities, accepting them on sufferance as lesser citizens. Scheduled castes and tribes are absorbed into the bottom of the social hierarchy. This is quite contrary to the freedom movement, which strove to remain secular and inclusive, especially of Gandhiji's last and least Indian. Today Hindu nationalism has become a powerful and populist mobilizer for the government in power. Obfuscating itself as cultural nationalism does little to delink it from its religious roots. Savarkar's Hindutva (1989, 1923) has an alarming acceptance even among moderate Hindus. Such an exclusivist aggressive religious nationalism aimed at uniting Hindus against the rest is surely one of the deep background causes of collective violence, and Muslims are the preferred targets though Christians are not excluded, nor are Dalits or tribals. This has polarized our peoples and traumatized minority and marginalized communities with a politics of hate. This cannot augur well for the commonweal.

Rather we need a nationalism as a patriotism premised on an inclusive love of all our peoples. Though the two words are often used interchangeably there is a critically nuanced difference. Nationalism has become a political ideology that prioritizes the nation, an abstract construct which can have many avatars. A true patriot's loyalty to the people of his country is not exclusive and denigrates no one. Genuine patriots would be able to make their own the epitaph Nehru chose for himself: 'This was a man who with all his mind and heart loved India and the Indian people…' This patriotism has been expressed in a commitment to people's integral welfare, and faith in an idea of India with its multicultural, pluri-religious society as less a nation-state, than a multi-nation-state-in the making. Constitutionally, India is a union of states, it is a federation, not a unitary state. Hence there are many Indias in the one India, diversity in unity, or vice versa.

The Directive Principles of State Policy contextualize our fundamental and civil rights. This was the basic agenda: governmental devolution, federalism, local self-government, economic socialism for an egalitarian society, minority rights and affirmative action for the vulnerable. There have been many twists and turns in this epic saga, and the jury is still out on whether this will be a failed experiment or a prophetic sign of the future for a world still struggling to cope with difference and diversity.

Indeed, 'the accommodation of differences is the essence of true equality'. (Kymlicka 1995: 108) Moreover, 'societal diversity enhances the quality of life, by enriching our experience, expanding cultural resources'. Hence protecting minority cultures 'is increasingly recognized to be an expression of overall enlightened self-interest'. (Falk 1988: 23) Furthermore, 'polyethnic rights for ethnic groups can be justified in terms of promoting equality and cultural diversity within the mainstream culture'. (Kymlicka 1995: 127)

Tagore rejected a narrow aggressive nationalism for a broad inclusive patriotism. Gandhi's swaraj was rooted and open; his patriotism meant the welfare of all people, swaraj and sarvodaya, and authenticated by antyodaya. Nehru discovered that unity in diversity are the heart of the Indic civilization. Ambedkar's republican India was constitutionally founded on the values of justice expressed in liberty, equality, fraternity. Contrariwise, religious nationalism on the subcontinent betrayed this 'idea of India' in 1947 and it still has to be effectively recovered even today.

In the freedom movement, nationalism as a mobilizing ideology was to be at the service of the people, and not vice versa: the people must not be sacrificed on the altar of nationalism. Rather religion and politics must embrace the seva-marg and not sacrifice people to false gods. A nationalist ideologue would want India to be a great power. But this does little to make for a happy and prosperous people, a just and decent society, as our Constitution projects. This is precisely what a patriot would want.

Surely we can do with a surgical strike into the prejudice and hatred in our hearts and minds, and instead make room there for a tolerant, committed patriotic love. If this 'idea of India' falters it may well prejudice the rest of the world community of nations against the viability of a multicultural, pluri-religious society in a nation-state. The challenge we face today is to shine a light in a darkening world and not yield to a populist ethno-nationalism where identity politics becomes a politics of chauvinist passion, not sensitive reason. We need a politics of enlightened interest, to deal with the real issues and concerns of people.

Here I am using 'ethno-nationalism' as one premised on a distinct and shared ascribed identity, as opposed to a 'political' nationalism based on more pragmatic common interests. Nationalism has the nation as an identity marker, such as Indian, Pakistani, etc. Ethno-nationalism is identified by the ethnic group: Hindu, Muslim, Tamil, Marathi, etc. Both types are inclined to chauvinism and exclusivism.

What democratic political parties opt for is finally a function of what they anticipate from the electoral returns. Collective violence is used, programmatically by rightist religious political parties, and pragmatically by other secular ones, as a strategy as long as it yields positive electoral returns. Electoral competition and building winning coalitions dictate the parties' options. If the returns anticipated are negative, riots and collective disturbances are curbed. (Wilkinson 2004) This is a betrayal of the democratic republic 'We the People of India' founded. For here electoral democracy trumps substantive democracy.

Our freedom movement marked the awakening of Indian nationalism as it evolved the idea of India expressed in our Constitution and summed it up in its Preamble: 'We the people of India.' It served as an overarching consensus all through the Nehruvian years. With the breakdown of that consensus after Nehru, came the rise of an alternative quest for a Hindu Rashtra. This is an articulation of Savarkar's ideology in his *Hindutva* (1989, 1st 1923), which is the very counterpoint of the inclusive nationalism our freedom fought for. It is essentially an exclusive nationalism that Hannah Arendt describes as 'tribal': 'Politically speaking, tribal nationalism always insists that its own people is surrounded by "a world of enemies", "one against all", that a fundamental difference exists between this people and all others. It claims its people to be unique, individual, incompatible with all others, and denies theoretically the very possibility of a common mankind long before it is used to destroy the humanity of man.' (Ardent 1951: 227)

This is the root cause of so much collective violence in the subcontinent. (Nussbaum 2007) Given the contradictions between Constitutional India and Hindu Rashtra the clash is inherent and inevitable. For, identifying India with the Hindu majority is a thin disguise for a savarna-led majoritarianism that is becoming increasingly hostile to other minorities and marginalized peoples of the country.

Here we need to pose some hard questions. Can there be nationalism without a Nation in India? (Aloysius 1997) Can there be a real nation without empowered citizens, but only passive subjects? Can there be empowered citizens without 'liberty, equality, fraternity', (especially fraternity) for all? Can a majority rule a nation without an effective regime of rights for all citizens?

And what of minorities—religious and linguistic? After one Partition of the subcontinent in 1947 and another secession in 1971 that formalized the linguist divide of Pakistan, what have we learnt about alienated minorities who have no stake in the future project of the state? Surely we can anticipate that uniformizing the subcontinent would Balkanize it? How can we distinguish an inclusive patriotism from an exclusive nationalism? (Nandy 2012) In our response to such questions lies the upstream causes of downstream violence.

Patriotism and Nationalism

Churchill once sarcastically remarked: 'India is no more a political personality than Europe. India is a geographical term. It is no more a united nation than the Equator.' (Langworth 2012: 163). However, the survival of the Indian Union after the sunset of the British Empire has proved Churchill wrong, in spite of Britain's hasty exit from the subcontinent and the Partition chaos that followed. The European Union (EU), too, is proving him wrong. Clearly, perspective colours perception: an Imperialist, like Churchill, would differ drastically with the Indian Nationalist movement, which he opposed and plotted against. He could not envisage an overarching national identity for the subcontinent except as a colony of the Empire. He misses the reality of a national identity construction contesting the imperial one, though Great Britain itself is a construction of three small states.

Nations are constructed on the basis of a shared sense of collective identity and destiny of a people; a 'nation' seeks political expression in a political 'state'. They are 'imagined communities', (Anderson B 1983) premised on 'invented traditions' (Hobsbawm and Ranger 1983) and a selective history. Nationalism is the ideology that drives this process of nation-building: 'Nationalism is not the awakening of nations to self-consciousness; it invents nations where they do not exist'. (Gellner 1964: 169) As people constructed a common socio-cultural-historical identity, they sought to give it a political and economic expression to it as a unified nation-state. However, 'once a national identity is forged and established, it becomes immensely difficult, if not impossible (short of total genocide) to eradicate'. (Smith 1993: 131)

Today nationalism has become the legitimizing creed of the modern state's claims to authority, the political projection of a people's right to self-rule. 'Old societies and new states', in 'the quest for modernity', (Geertz 1963) often begin with pretensions to a rational secular inspiration. But unsurprisingly some ethnic identity from the past proves the more effective mobilizer. In these societies, rational interest politics and passionate identity politics implicate each other (Taylor 2008) and evolve into an ethno-nationalism, premised on a distinct and shared ascribed identity, as opposed to one based more pragmatically on common interests and commitments. This is surely more likely with an exclusive nationalism than an inclusive one.

Nationalism as devotion to one's country easily becomes exclusive: my country, right or wrong. When national interests clash, countries inevitably becomes antagonistic and hostile to towards each other, which results in violence and war on the world stage, rather than dialogue and tolerance, leading to a compromise for the greater common good and peace. Such a chauvinist nationalism thrives on finding or creating national enemies, whether within or without.

However, as Nussbaum writes in *Political Emotions*, 'Patriotism is a strong emotion taking the nation as its object. It is a form of love, and thus distinct from simple approval, or commitment, or embrace of principles. This love involves the feeling that the nation is one's own, and its rituals usually make reference to that idea… patriotism as a non-exclusive love of one's country is premised on a self-confidence and openness to other countries without fears and suspicions.' (Nussbaum 2015: 208)

Political leaders often find it convenient, even profitable to confuse nationalism and patriotism so as to mobilize their followers on the basis of a chauvinistic politics, masquerading as nationalism, rather than painstakingly cultivating a patriotism as a love for one's people that reaches out to other peoples as well. Thus 'patriotism' is rooted yet open, while nationalism can be aggressive and chauvinist. To paraphrase Mother Teresa from a different context: I love all nations but I'm in love with my own! Such patriotism is a far more viable basis for a national community in pursuit of the common good, rather than the self-interest that the social contract of Thomas Hobbes (1651) which grounds our politics today, both national and international, whether this self-interest be individual or group, national or international. This plagues communities in our country and nations at the UN, despite so much pious rhetoric.

An exclusive nationalism is premised on some privileged identity, usually ethnic or at times regional, it privileges the state, and de facto reduces other ethnic citizens to subjects. Such an ethno-nationalism will subsume local languages and dialects, ethnicities and subcultures in a uniformized national identity. These are sacrificed to the uniformity of the nation-state. Surely such uniformization compromises the real freedom and autonomy of people who might want to preserve their own culture and language in the larger national context, for unity need not imply uniformity. Ethnic identities are very deeply embedded in a peoples' consciousness. Yet an exclusive nationalism as a political ideology is a powerful mobilizer but not the wisest policy adviser.

This is not Gandhiji's idea of swaraj, and furthermore not compatible with the constitutional idea of India. On the other hand, an inclusive nationalism is pluralist and more accommodating, because it sees diversity as an enrichment and a strength and is therefore willing to adjust to the 'different other'. It is committed to people's real issues and concerns.

The contrast between these two perspectives is startling. An exclusive nationalism governs with authoritarian dictates and sanctions, dissent is treated as subversive and punished in an attempt to silence any opposition. Only some electoral form of nominal democracy may remain, but its substantive content is hollowed out. Such procedural democracy can lead to a democratically elected dictatorship that can be difficult to dislodge. The potential violence of a government against its own people, especially the minorities with a view to polarize civil society and consolidate their vote bank, cannot be gainsaid.

An inclusive nationalism prioritizes its citizens and protects them with a regime of rights derived from the Constitution. It seeks consensus through discussion and comprise. This participatory involvement of people gives them a stake in the outcome. Thus it defuses the potential for violence among contesting protagonists, and buffers the negative impact of state interventions. Gradualism is implied in attaining its goals. The danger is that there can be a displacement of goals over time with the rising expectations of an impatient people. This happens with populism, too, a disillusionment with the great leader who does not fulfil his promises.

Critical Choice

A critical choice has to be made between these two perspectives: an ethnocentric nationalism for a religious state, a Hindu Rashtra, for India, and a more pluralist understanding of our nation premised on our Constitution. Over the last five years, Hindu nationalism has been the ideology of the elected government. But it has never spelt out what this Hindu Rashtra might imply, thus giving ample space for obfuscation. However, whatever the structures and policies turn out to be, it is not difficult to surmise what the Hindu Rashtra with its neoliberal leanings is likely to do once empowered. It will privilege Hindus to the same extent it disenfranchises other religious minorities. Muslims, in particular, would be especially hard hit. They are a convenient scapegoat. Upper castes would be foregrounded, Dalits and tribals, and the poor would be marginalized. Large corporations would be advantaged while the smaller ones are absorbed by them. Essentially it would be a majoritarian state with a free-market economy. The social democracy of the Constitution with its commitment to bring liberty, equality and fraternity to all citizens, its concern for the under privileged, and minorities would be off the radar with the RSS-BJP's saffron neo-liberalism.

Much of this is already happening. Moreover, neo-liberal capitalism promotes a uniform culture by prioritizing economic consumerism over cultural diversity, when it comes to returns on investment; it favours the uniformity of the market that provides economies of scale over the diversity of peoples that must be engaged and negotiated with. However, 'A country that is made of consumers instead of citizens is not only economically fragile, but also politically unstable and ethically weak. Corruption (another unifying characteristic, unfortunately) is not only debilitating from a political and economic point of view, but also escalates the potential for social conflict and even violence…The degree of socioeconomic inequality and the scourge of corruption are much more inimical to the acceptance of diversity and the avoidance of conflict than communal tensions or local separatisms.' (Toscano 2013)

This double-whammy must now be seriously contested and democratic elections offer the occasion to reset the terms of engagement. For, though each incident of violence has its immediate causes, the collective understanding of the political state is one of the most crucial root causes of them all. The mindset of the perpetrators causes violence to escalate, and it is further nourished by political ideologies of aggression and hate. In response this needs a new narrative that will heal our wounded history which is now being seeded with hate, and initiate a new politics of compassion. (Nussbaum 2015) For a nation founded on a non-violent inspiration that overcame an Empire this should be a relevant and pertinent challenge.

In India today 'nationalism' is a contested term that opposing constituencies with their contrary ideologies seek to co-opt for their partisan purposes. It has become the shibboleth for distinguishing good citizens from bad ones, the loyal from the seditious. To make a critical analysis of this contemporary crisis and come up with a committed response we must search for the origins of our nationalism. Many players are implicated in the complex dilemmas and anomalies in this historical drama of nation-building. Our freedom struggle unambiguously opted for an inclusive nationalism, premised on a patriotic love of India and her peoples that neither denigrated or excluded the different other. It was unity in diversity not uniformity. However, already, then, Hindu nationalism prioritized Hindus and eventually evolved into Hindutva.

The violence of an exclusive nationalism, especially a religious one, has been chauvinistically used to precipitate a violent politics of hate and polarization. This perpetuates and even accelerates a spiral of violence that threatens the foundational premises of our Republic. An exclusive politics will eventually use overt or covert violence on the excluded. This can reach alarming levels, setting a new normal for violence with each turn of the spiral.

Breaking free from such a scene will demand another kind of politics, a politics of non-violent inclusion and tolerance, which can only be founded on empathy and compassion, the much neglected 'fraternity' so crucial to our Constitution. This was once foregrounded in the freedom movement, but even then it could not prevent Partition.

Politics of Hate

Since the time of its birth in the freedom struggle, Indian nationalism has been contested by opposing constituencies with their antagonistic ideologies, seeking to co-opt it for their own partisan purposes. Many strands were interwoven into its texture, even in the Indian National Congress itself. The Gandhian one prevailed, till the Nehruvian consensus became dominant after Gandhi in Republican India. Different trends came to political prominence at different times in the ideology and culture of national freedom struggle and after.

But whether it was the genteel liberalism of Gokhale, or the aggressive revivalism of Tilak, the radical reformism of Gandhi, or the democratic socialism of Nehru, the uncompromising 'annihilation of caste' by Ambedkar, or the surreptitious privileging of the revivalists, down to the pragmatic politics of the national opposition and regional parties, all through these phases the level of discourse never descended to the crudity and callousness of political debates and disagreements today. Satyagraha was the privileged means for opposing the colonialists. Dissenters within the movement, and there were many, were not considered subversives. Opponents were to be respected even if they had to be opposed. To make his first cabinet more representative, Nehru even had in his cabinet, members like Syama Prasad Mukherjee who later quit to found the Jan Sangh in 1951, the political arm of RSS.

However, the horrific violence of the Partition has never been exorcised, its contagion only contained and controlled within limits, though it breaks out every once in a while, with drastic consequences for its victims. Moreover, the underlying contradictions in our society, of caste hierarchy and class inequality, of regional disparities, communal loyalties and gender bias have not been resolved. Nehruvian gradualism over the decades was stymied by what Adlai Stevenson in 1953 called the 'revolution of rising expectation' the world over. (Look, 22 Sept 1953, 46) Expectations of the now free and independent people in their headlong rush to catch up with the modern world that seemed to have left them behind. But the discontents of modernity, more especially a failed or faltering modernity, left in its wake an anomic and alienated people, insecure in this changing world, anxious and fearful at their old world dying even as the new one was yet to be born. A complacent politics and endemic corruption disillusioned people as over time multiple crises accumulated.

This is a situation ripe for populist leaders to project themselves as saviours to a gullible people, longing for a quick fix, facile solutions to complex problems. Taking advantage of people's vulnerability these leaders polarize them into an 'us and them' in a zero-sum game. The scene is then set for collective violence between the protagonists and a spark can ignite a conflagration, with an unpredictable loss of life and property. Public discourse shifts from resolving issues through discussion and compromise, to consolidating the 'us and them' polarization around constructed identities. This is the crucial shift from a politics of interests, which favours rational responses to resolve an issue, to a politics of identity, which is fuelled by passions not readily amenable to reason.

Once such polarization gets embedded in social structures, it becomes institutionalized and self-sustaining. Thus institutionalized prejudice rationalizes institutional violence and morphs into multiple expressions of a politics of hate. This has reached alarming levels already and it tends to peak at election time. Such negative passions subvert democracy. However, if we accept 'the definition of democracy as "government by discussion" it implies that individual values can and do change in the process of decision-making', (Buchanan 1954:120) but always within a regime of citizen rights.

A law and order approach to such issues deals only with the downstream symptoms of such a politics. This is necessary in any fair and decent society but never sufficient. Nor will a purely rational argument carry the day or sound convincing to people prejudiced emotionally and intellectually by their negativity. Addressing the structural causes of this negative politics would demand a deeper commitment to another politics based on an alternative narrative, an alternative vision, but one with an equal and opposite emotional and intellectual component to reverse or at least neutralize hate.

For this our commitment to liberty, equality, fraternity must be principled and rational. But even this will cut little ice when emotions are strong and negative. And thus Ambedkar insisted that there must be a strong emotional component of constitutional patriotism and morality, something so obviously wanting in today's political scenario. The realpolitik of Machiavelli and Chanakya rule the day, while the examples of Ashoka and Akbar are marginalized as impractical. Political ambitions are pursued with little regard for the propriety of means. Winning power at any cost is the name of the game.

The political dimension of this hyper-nationalism by self-serving politicians so easily exploits the anxious and insecure with promises of a utopian future—'good days are coming'. Gullible people are taken in, only to wake up and find out they are no longer free and equal citizens but subjects of the state, in which they have lost their political agency. Such populist leaders mobilize majoritarian support and visit the people's frustrations on helpless scapegoats, who must learn their subordinate place in this society.

The other dimension is religious fundamentalism. Religion in its popular expressions is emotional, and at times volatile and unpredictable. When politicized by extremist nationalism, religious tradition is displaced by a political ideology of religious nationalism. The Partition surely originated here, with the Muslim League's Islamic nationalism and Congress's uncompromising intransigence. Since then religious communal riots in India have reaffirmed and deepened this religious divide.

However, religious nationalism is no guarantor even for internal peace and stability. Religious nation-states are neither truly democratic nor tolerant of difference. Disputes are settled by intimidation and violence. This does not make for a stable state and certainly not a rights driven one. Pakistan's warring religious factions within Islam are precipitating a failed state there. At the bottom of all this is the politics of hate overtly expressed or covertly exercised. It politicizes religion while religionizing politics, an explosive mix that precipitates horrific collective violence. This is a deep background cause of collective religious violence.

In a different context, caste atrocities have a similar dynamic: putting the out-group in their place, lest it become a threat to the status quo of the caste hierarchy. Not that religious differences, even within a tradition, are new to India, nor are the rigid hierarchies of caste. Our Constitution has dealt with minority rights to preserve our diversity, and affirmative action for disadvantaged and the discriminated. Populism attempts to address them directly, and thrives on a politics of 'them versus us', which is then driven into a politics of hate, by populist leaders demonizing the other.

A politics of hate breeds a 'culture of suspicion', especially in times of crisis. This easily morphs into a 'culture of terror', which is unleashed on the minorities and the marginalized, the suspect 'other' who is different. Obviously, we must stop feeding this monster, with the hate and violence that have become embedded in our hearts and minds. For this we need an alternative narrative to challenge and displace this neoliberal saffron one.

What is alarming about hate politics is it feeds on itself, readily finding new hate objects and new narratives as older ones pass their shelf-life. It becomes a self-fulfilling prophecy that fuels its own suspicions. This undermines trust and confidence between groups and communities that are different, religiously or otherwise. We are on this carousel and are not able to get off as it turns faster and faster, driven by communal tensions which spill over into collective violence.

Hindutva Project

Contemporary hate politics needs to be set in historical context. Hindu nationalism, especially in its Hindutva articulation, allows the projection of a politics of hate into the national discourse. We need to imagine another kind of community and foreground, another set of traditions to counter the aggressive exclusivist mindsets of the Hindutvawadis. We are more likely to find these in the Sufi-bhakti traditions and their popular expressions of religiosity. We are not claiming that subaltern alternatives have all the answers for such an enterprise, but they do represent a challenging horizon of revolt and revolution. This can fuse with others to construct the identities and the ideologies we need, rather than using an ethno-religious nationalism to uniformize our rich cultural and religious traditions and legitimize the construction of a majoritarianism with little regard for minority sensitivities, or for that matter any respect for a critical and factual history.

In its Hindutva articulation, the project of Hindu nationalism from its very origins is to mobilize Hindus into a politicized ethnic group and to construct this into a dominant majority. Little wonder then that the RSS did not take part in the freedom movement except as a kind of tokenism. They perceived its secular character and inclusiveness as a threat to their religious identity and no help to their partisan course.

Rather they used the colonial government as a shield for their own agenda. 'Right from its inception in 1925, the RSS was not in any way active during the national movement.' (Yoginder Yadav, *Hindu* 26 Sept 2018) Its quest for a Hindu Rashtra was the very contradiction of the expansive patriotism of Tagore, the inclusive nationalism of Gandhi, the secular democracy of Nehru and the constitutional republicanism of Ambedkar.

In their Hindu Rashtra, non-Hindus would become subordinate minorities and/or sub-nationals, provided they knew their place as second-class citizens, and presented no threat to the Hindu majority. Moreover, the way it exclusively equates 'Hindu' and 'India' severely undermines our multicultural, pluri-religious Indic civilization. Today the BJP is seizing the high ground and projecting a hyper-nationalism, and pillorying dissenters as anti-national. These very ethno-nationalists had stayed away from the national freedom struggle for their partisan reasons. The irony cannot be missed and the anomaly must be exposed.

Counter-Narrative

Revisiting our freedom movement, we do find the inspiration for a counter-narrative there. But this requires that we break out of the prison of our present consciousness and transcend the categories that constrain us. Our freedom struggle was a mass movement of millions, a loose collective coalition with a bewildering ethnic diversity, of religious traditions and caste hierarchies, regional cultures and languages, of racial descent and shared histories all held together by the quest for freedom from the coercive political power of the colonizers. It was not just the collective pursuit of independence, swatantrata, but to be free to be our authentic selves, swaraj. Its substantive content and action strategies evolved within this movement in which Indian nationalism gestated into maturity. Is it not surprising, then, that those who did not participate in the freedom struggle have their priorities elsewhere and are not always compatible with the freedom movement ideals, or the Constitution of our republic? Their real priority was Hindu Rashtra, not swaraj, certainly not purna swaraj.

As the freedom struggle evolved into a democratic and secular movement, the traditional elites of upper caste Hindu and Ashraf Muslims felt threatened by these new developments. The Muslim community felt threatened in a democracy with a Hindu majority, which would end in a majoritarian rule, where they as a minority would be marginalized. Traditional Hindus, especially from upper castes felt disoriented by secular and political changes that might disadvantage them, disrupting the traditional hierarchies of caste. Partition attempted an impossible territorial separation of these two major communities that lived together for almost a millennium and evolved a composite Ganga–Jumna tehezib that stood the country well in 1857. But then that was a revolt of the elites trying to shake off the foreign yoke for their own independence rather than for people's freedoms and rights. It has been seen by some as a feudal revolt rather than a people's movement.

The national freedom struggle was a mass movement for self-rule, for Swaraj, in its multivalent complexity, individual and collective self-rule, and its extension to purna swaraj and antyodya. Independence, swatantrata, from colonial rule, was to get it out of the way so we could be agents of our own transformation, from subjects of a foreign ruler to citizens in their own land with justice spelt out as liberty, equality, fraternity. If Gandhiji did not celebrate our Independence Day it was because he felt we had short-changed ourselves; we had accepted swatantrata when we should have been aiming for swaraj.

Hindu Victimhood

We need a reality check on the sense of Hindu victimhood, which is a constant theme with Hindu nationalists. Even from their dominant position today, they still play on historical Hindu hurt, nurturing hostile suspicions against minorities. Rather than building the self-confidence of the community, communal leaders find more traction in exploiting their people's anxieties and fears and posing as protectors and saviours. This is true of minority communities as well. This narcissism of victimhood is used to rationalize an aggressive response to the threatening other, which then evolves into a narcissism of grandiosity. Pankaj Mishra describes the conflation of victimhood and grandiosity: 'An acute consciousness of the defeat and humiliation of ancestors, an awakening to historical pain, and a resolve to rectify the wrongs of the past with superhuman efforts at power and glory in the present and future'. (Mishra *Times of India*, 22 Jan 2017)

But first those who inflicted this humiliation and pain, must also be put in their place. For Hindu nationalism, the enemy-other is the Muslim. Where Muslims are in a majority they exercise similar majoritarian dominance. The ethnic cleansing of the Pandits from Kashmir is a stark instance of this, and worse has happened in Pakistan. Yet an emphatic denial of the millennium of Islamic rule, which surely has its golden age with the Great Mughals, is quite unrealistic. This heritage belongs to all Indians, who can be justly proud of it, like the Taj Mahal in Agra. But it hurts Hindu pride when the Muslim is perceived as the dominant 'other'. Too many Hindus now find it hard to accept that Muslim ruled then. Hence the attempts to erase all trace of it, if that were at all feasible. Yet, as Romila Thapar writes: 'Far from being victimized, Hindu culture flourished along with other cultures in these centuries. This is demonstrated in texts such as Madhava's *Sarvadarshanasangraha* on the prevailing schools of philosophy and Samayasundara's *Artharatnavali* on linguistic explorations and belief systems. Sayana wrote his renowned exposition of the Rigveda in the fourteenth century.' (*Outlook* 11 Jul 2016)

It was the time of Sufi-bhakti movements of religious renewal, and intense devotional poetry. The Mughal court patronized the translations of many Sanskrit religious texts into Persian. It was a time of intercultural exchange between the two communities.

Unhealed Traumas

But the trauma of Partition left unhealed wounded memories, which polarized a false consciousness in both communities, and each began to see the other as a threat. The colonial predilection to advantage themselves with their policy of divide and rule began after the trauma of 1857, and gained momentum over the century. (Chandra 1984: 21) Vulnerable minorities, representing the different other, are too weak to resist and are subjected to a subtle and at times a violent ethnic-cleansing. They finally retreat into ghettoes, which only further polarizes our society. However, the way a nation treats their different minorities is a sure indication of the health of that society as just and decent. This does not enter into the Hindutva discourse.

Our counter-discourse must revisit our history and not accept blindly John Mills' convenient periodization that puts the British as the latest and most advanced civilization over those of medieval Islamic and ancient Indic civilization. In medieval India, religious differences were not polarized and embedded in historical memories of hurt and resentment. (Subrahmanyam: 1996) Loyalty to your feudal overlord was more important than to your religious community. Certainly, there was not the sense of woundedness carried over generations fuelling continued bitter conflict. How else can we explain the Hindu-Muslim unity of 1857 which came so close to ending the rule of the East India Company?

However, in the freedom struggle the insecurity of the Muslim community vis-à-vis the Hindu majority evolved into religious nationalism demanding a separate homeland for subcontinental Muslims. The response of Hindu nationalism only confirmed their fears and consolidated the divide. With colonial collaboration and an uncompromising leadership on both sides, this resulted in the Partition and the chaos it inflicted on the subcontinent. And after the Partition whatever remained of a composite Hindu-Muslim culture began to unravel. One of its first indications was the marginalization of Urdu in India as Hindi was pushed into prominence. Pakistan became an Islamic State, while in sharp contrast India chose to become a secular republic and carry forward the legacy of our freedom movement. A secular state in a religious society represented a huge leap of faith.

Secularism represented an inclusive nationalism, but it never quite defused the subterranean ethno-religious nationalisms that fed and drew on people's search for their lost selves and their lost world. Bipin Chandra recognizes the emergence of 'new ideologies, new organizing principles of politics', but argues that secular nationalism 'provided a real solution to a real problem—national liberation as against colonial domination…' (Chandra 1984: 20-23) The secular state was understood either as religious neutrality as dharma nirapekshta; or as equal respect for all religions, sarva dharma sama bhava—the first more Nerhuvian and Western, the second more Gandhian and indigenous. Religious neutrality was privileged but it was not emotive enough to counter religious nationalism; respect for all religious traditions was evocative and had its echo in popular religiosity. But Westernized secular rationalists eschewed religion generally; they preferred a straightforward separation of religion and state.

In a multicultural, pluri-religious society like India, a union of multi-nations states, our nationalism had to be different. An enforced uniformity, religious, cultural, or linguistic, as the prelude to national unity could only bring the hegemony of dominant groups, as is happening today. Ours has to be a unity that allows for diversity without inequity, thus enhancing the capabilities of the disadvantaged community to find its place in the larger society. The idea of a unilinear social evolution within a single national tradition, religious or otherwise, in which all communities are co-opted and merged is more likely to stimulate resistance. Sub-nationalisms could Balkanize the subcontinent further. In the melee of the blame game following the first Partition, we have failed to learn this lesson and are in danger of repeating it. It happened in 1971 with Bangladesh.

We have not learnt that people's collective identities matter enormously. When threatened, this leaves them prey to extremist leaders. These leaders politicize collective identities into a potent brew that reinforces their own prominence. Like ethnocentrism, religious nationalism too has its roots in the perceived threat, real or imagined, to a personal and collective identity. A counter-narrative must defuse the threat. Ignoring or worse rubbishing the other's insecurity can be dangerously counter-productive with unforeseen consequences, when the hostile communities reach an impasse. Today the real threat is of extremist Hindu nationalism leaving in its wake a large mass of minorities and dissenters as second-class citizens, whose rights are ignored or abridged. This cannot make for a stable state, or a just and decent society. What kind of nationalism can a divided nation pretend to? What will be the overarching unity that will keep people under the Indic umbrella when they are oppressed and unwanted? Will the diversity of Hindiusm be uniformized by a religious nationalism, like Hindutva? Extremists do not ask such questions but this should worry moderates at least.

Today there are dangerous authoritarian and even fascistic proclivities in our subcontinental politics that go uninterrogated. We need to counter this homogenizing authoritarianism with diverse identities and varied ideologies, which can challenge and displace the dominant hegemony of caste-class relations and reorder the social relations in society. Ram Mohan Lohia's socialist movement attempted this with Other Backward Castes (OBCs). Today most states of the Indian Union are evolving distinct regional identities which may eventually subvert the uniformity demanded by Hindu nationalism.

A viable and effective subaltern alternative can counter this homogenization and challenge and displace the dominant caste-class hegemony and reorder social relations. However, the quest for equality and justice of subalterns and minorities must not sacrifice their social identity or human dignity, by getting co-opted and subverted at the regional level, as ethno-nationalism attempts they do at the national level. Uniformity and homogeneity are precisely what the dominant groups attempt in order to retain their hegemony, at the national and state level.

However, we first need to imagine another kind of community and evolve and invent a newer set of traditions. We are not claiming that subaltern alternatives have all the answers for such an enterprise, but they do represent a challenging horizon of revolt and revolution, which can fuse with others to construct the identities and the ideologies we need for this brave new world, rather than using an ethnocentric nationalism to the legitimize the construction of a majoritarianism with little regard for minority sensitivities.

Constitutionalism and Populism

Our counter-narrative must then be contextualized in our national freedom struggle as its first source of inspiration. For it is here that Indian nationalism was born and its contours articulated in our Republic's Constitution. This served reasonably well for decades after Independence, but it faltered in fulfilling the promise of rapid development, of peace and prosperity, though it did lay the foundations for this.

However, as crises multiplied and governments became less effective, populist leaders mobilized people beyond the constraints of a constitutionally governed state. Such populism is used by authoritarian leaders who promote themselves as saviours of the people. Here we have the beginnings of the fascist state, which uses hate politics and finds easy scapegoats. This has an obvious affinity to exclusive nationalism of whatever kind, religious or racist. We can find the counter-narrative to this in the constitutional state as the opposite of the populist one.

Hence our narrative must be grounded in the Constitution we gave ourselves. It was an inclusive India premised on fundamental rights, and a celebration of diversity, a compact hammered out in the Constituent Assembly over two years, bringing together the broad consensus on what our people had fought for. Our democratic Republic was founded on it. Inevitably, there is an implicit tension between, on the one hand, the organs of the state, in particular the compulsions of government in responding to new political demands and needs, and a consequent expansion of rights of people; and on the other hand, the propriety of the courts in interpreting the Constitution authentically and creatively. This has increasingly become a tug-of-war between the state administration and the judiciary.

At times the temptation is to fall back on extrajudicial activism when matters become critical and urgent. In his last speech at the closure of the Constituent Assembly, 25 November 1949, Ambedkar warned: if the people of India 'adopt revolutionary methods however good the Constitution may be, it requires no prophet to say that it will fail'. (CAD 25 XI: 330) This surely was an early warning against the extra-constitutional methods of populist politics which has little in common with the due process of constitutional governance. Rather populist mass mobilization for collective self-interest, as competitive politics often dictates, undermines this by mobilizing extra-constitutional means.

However, elected governments faltered in protecting and promoting the constitutional rights of all citizens, so eloquently expressed in the Preamble to our Constitution. They failed to implement the constitutional agenda on the integral development of society and progress for all its citizens, as pointedly outlined in the Directive Principles of State Policy. It is not the Constitution that has failed us but we, the citizens, who have failed the Constitution. Inevitably this has precipitated a cascade of crises and opened the door for populism.

Regrettably over the years mainstream political parties and their successive governments have failed to effectively address the real long-term challenges which have and still confront India. In their pursuit of lesser short-term partisan goals, vested interests and poor governance have prevailed. Hindutva's pursuit of a Hindu Rashtra, with its cultural nationalism and 'majoritarianism', is really a chauvinist populist endeavour. However, forcing a democratic republic into a sectarian, communal polity would be a violation of its basic structure.

The consequent displacement of a politics premised on people's real interest by a politics of constructed identities based on selected similarities, has polarized our society into multiple oppositions: regional and linguist, ethnic and religious communities, class strata and caste hierarchies. The consequent disruptions leave us with an unresolvable contradiction between the constitutional idea of a republican India as a liberal democracy, premised on liberty, equality and fraternity and the reality of our broken civil society and fractured political institutions. Today religion and caste are the main faultlines and increasingly disruptive and dangerous. Patriarchy and the gender divide too, but these as explained earlier, are outside the scope of this book.

Constitutional propriety imposes some compelling responsibilities on all citizens, especially the leaders and opinion-makers. Fundamental rights must be correlative to fundamental duties. In 1976, these were written into the Directive Principles of State Policy, (Pt IV A) as the 42nd amendment. The Constitution calls us to pursue justice, liberty, equality, fraternity, for all our citizens, with due process within the constitutional framework. Overstepping the limits of constitutional propriety from political compulsion or benign neglect, from judicial overreach or weakness, compromises the Constitution itself and invites a crisis, and eventually a constitutional breakdown and a collapse of the State. We need a constitutional ethic of fidelity to pursue constitutional ideals and values, and to forge a political and civic culture in the public discourse not the rabble-rousing rhetoric of populist leaders.

Our concern is not just electoral democracy but substantive democracy, i.e., a regime of rights that is egalitarian, participative and inclusive. Or as Ambedkar put it: not just 'one man, one vote', but 'one man, one value'; (Ambedkar 1978: 47) not just political democracy but social and economic democracy as well. What we can be proud of is the resilience of our electoral democracy, which legitimizes the elected government. Constitutional democracy pursues constitutionally defined political goals and ideals within a regime of rights and with due process and constitutional propriety. In other words, it is a procedural democracy as well. However, democratic states are not immune to populism, with tyranny of the majority and even elected dictators.

Only a critical and alert citizenry can best protect 'constitutional democracy' from falling into 'populist democracy'. (Béteille 1999) This is an enormous challenge. The Directive Principles of State Policy mandate the pursuit of social and economic democracy. This meant countering the entrenched institutions of caste and community, of patriarchy and landlordism and to do this within the democratic framework of the Constitution.

This is the real challenge for our democracy: to follow through and complete the social revolution begun with the freedom struggle, promulgated in the Constitution and contextualized in the Directive Principles of State Policy as: democratic rights, civil liberties; governmental devolution: federalism, local self-government; economic socialism for an egalitarian society; and minority rights and affirmative action for the vulnerable.

In contrast to a constitutional democracy, a populist one has little patience with constitutional restraints of checks and balances or due process. For 'populist politics is often constructed from a blend of nativism, bigotry, grandiosity, and coarse speech'. (Coll 2017) It depends on a charismatic leader mobilizing a mass movement for populist interests. When such a movement comes to power in a state it tends to be authoritarian and majoritarian and is not restrained by a regime of rights; might becomes right, and the ends justifies the means. The shibboleth is: the people are supreme, I am accountable only to them. Béteille understands such populist democracies as pursuing 'the interests of the people, viewed as a more or less homogeneous body, above considerations of constitutional procedure, or, as some would put it, above "mere legality". The proponents of populism do not in principle deny the value of rules and procedures, only they are prepared to override them when that can be justified by an appeal to the interests of the people.' (Béteille 2008: 37)

Such populist democracies project themselves as the rule of the people, not the rule of law. Dubious government action is thus justified. These leaders mobilize people to get themselves elected to power but once in office they easily forget the promises they made and do not feel constrained by the democratic rights and civil liberties they took advantage of to get elected. Electoral democracies, if not committed to constitutional propriety and morality, do produce such 'democratic dictatorships'.

Constitutional morality and propriety become tokenism and easily dispensable as mere means to legitimate popular ends. An authoritarian government dismisses due process, and convenient legislation is easily passed to rationalize this, while the judiciary is corralled into mere tokenism. All this is done in the name of 'the people', an abstraction that becomes a proxy for authoritarian rule, by leaders who sometimes 'break the constitutions they inherit, or bend the functioning of those charters until they become, gradually unrecognizable'. (Coll 2017)

The majority is privileged, while minorities are marginalized. Dissenters become non-people, and the poor and underprivileged are deprived of voice and choice; they become invisible. This is a prescription for disaster and eventually, after much drift and obfuscation, leads to the strong leader syndrome. Today we see 'in the world's swelling ranks of populist-nationalist leaders, a gallery of strongmen in countries rich and poor, some more democratic and some less so, who govern partly through intimidation and a certain curated arbitrariness, a methodology of deliberate surprise'. (Coll 2017)

Such leaders undermine democratic institutions. Ultimately, constitutionalism is the only patriotism for a democracy, while populism by transferring agency to the leader, infantilizes people. (Borradori 2003) Moreover, 'coalitions and collegiality are more effective than the strongman's rule', for 'populists are often instruments of elite groups: They mesmerise the people with words during their election campaigns and betray them once in power.' (Jaffrelot 2018)

Today caste and gender, ethnicity and region have become faultlines. But most acutely it is the religious divide of the majority-minority that is being aggressively exploited to consolidate vote-banks for electoral gains, while communal polarization consolidates extremist leadership. Despite all pious talk to the contrary from all sides, collective violence still periodically rips apart the fabric of our society, leaving wounded people in fractured communities, crying out for relief and justice that is delayed if not denied.

Yet we can be proud of our democracy which has shown enduring resilience in spite of the hiccups, like the Emergency of 1975–77. But this is as yet electoral democracy. A substantive democracy has still a long way to go to bring Gandhi's swaraj to his least and last Indian, or the justice liberty, equality, fraternity of our Constitution. This was the talisman he gave Nehru for the India of his dreams: 'Whenever in doubt recall the face of the poorest and the weakest man whom you may have seen, and ask yourself if the step you contemplate is going to be of any use to him'. (Collected Works, V. 89: 125)

Prioritizing Gandhi's 'poorest and weakest' will require a very different kind of politics.

Celebrating Diversity

If the Constitution of our Republic represents a political roadblock to religious nationalism, the multicultural and pluri-religious tradition of this land constitute another huge obstacle, complicated further by caste and class divides. As a multi-nation state there are many collective identities waiting for recognition and acceptance. To subsume them all into a single national identity, as Hindu nationalism proposes, would be grossly inadequate and alienate such communities more than integrate them. Enforced uniformization would not be possible in a multicultural, pluri-religious country such as India without eventually Balkanizing the subcontinent.

Religious nationalisms thrive on a religious homogeneity: one creed, one code, one cult. They then attempt to translate this into a political hegemony: one ideology, one party, one nation. However, the inherent diversity among Hindus, of caste and tribe, of language and region, of gods and sages, has proven extremely resilient to any externally imposed uniformity. Nevertheless, addressing the endemic hierarchies of caste and insoluble inequalities of class need serious commitment to affirmative action for the last and the least.

When there are many imagined communities in a single polity, we have a multi-nation state. A pluri-religious, multi-cultural society demands a correspondingly adequate ideological construct, not the nationalism of the unitary nation-state, and certainly not the exclusive ethno-nationalism such as Hindu Rashtra would demand, but rather a pluralism for a multicultural, pluri-religious multi-nation federal state, a union of states.

Our national movement integrated the county by legitimizing cultural diversity within an overarching civilizational unity. Indeed, the idea of India is only viable as a multinational state. However, while historically we succeeded in accommodating an astonishing diversity, we have failed to bridge the religious divide between Hindus and Muslims. It has been politicized and exploited by both the majority and minority communities. Moreover, the transition from old hierarchies and persistent hegemonies to egalitarian and celebratory pluralism does not go uncontested and is still incomplete. A just resolution of such dangerous social tensions must be in terms of human rights for all persons and collective rights for each community.

The Supreme Court judgements have affirmed that minority rights are part of the basic structure of the Constitution, the most authoritative being the eleven-judge bench in 2002. This is a baseline for a pluralism that will protect and preserve our diversity. The Constitution guarantees protection of minorities by the state, so that as vulnerable communities they are not absorbed or co-opted into the larger majority. But it does not mandate state promotion for them, so that the state must position itself as equidistant from all communities. In a democracy, minority rights are a protection against the 'tyranny of the majority' (Tocqueville 1882) but they are abused when community identities become hostile and antagonistic.

Linguistic nationalism is no longer a threat to the state as it once was, when the Justice Party first made its demand for a separate Tamil state in October 1938. However, linguistic nationalism was defused with the linguistic reorganization of states in 1960. This was a recognition and affirmation of regional language identities within the larger national one. Sadly, this has not happened with religious identities.

Minorities and Majority

When identities are constructed around ascribed differences, the basis of an opposition is set up between 'them' and 'us'. Whether the difference is perceived as antagonistic or complementary sets the scene for hostile conflict or constructive collaboration. By and large we have managed to contain linguistic antagonisms by devolving governmental authority to regional linguistic states and giving these communities an inclusive and larger identity, with a real stake in the country. We need to do this now with other local and marginalized communities, with tribals, and Dalits, and especially religious minorities: forge an over-arching inclusive identity and give them a stake in the future of the country.

If we renege on this through political short-sightedness and opportunism we risk deepening contradictions rather than celebrating complementarities, which our Constitution enshrined in the linguistic and religious minority rights as the statutory expression of a minimum protection for these vulnerable communities. The Supreme Court judgements have affirmed that minority rights are part of the basic structure of the Constitution, the most authoritative being the decision made by the eleven-judge bench in 2002: 'The essence of secularism in India is the recognition and preservation of the different types of peoples. With diverse languages and different beliefs, and placing them together so as to form a whole united India. Articles 29 and 30 do not do more than to seek to preserve the differences that exist, and at the same time, unite the people to form one strong nation.' (2002 8 SCC 481, para160)

This is a baseline for a pluralism that will protect and preserve our diversity. White light includes the wavelengths of all the seven colours, yet the rainbow has its own special beauty. So do the polyphonic voices in dialogue make the symphony. 'Moreover, our Constitutional protection of minority rights must be compatible with Constitutional fundamental rights. This requires a negotiation for a sustainable social compact on the basis of both human and cultural rights. However, the inequalities and tensions precipitated by saffron neoliberal capitalism has left us with "a xenophobic nationalism that handily identifies fresh scapegoats for large-scale socio-economic failure and frustration".' (Mishra *Times of India*, 22 Jan, 2017)

To be able to address this effectively depends on the understanding of 'human rights in popular consciousness', (Anderson M 1998: 5) as also a sensitivity to minority cultures and their vulnerabilities. Continuing violence 'establishes collective fear…When fear becomes a way of life…a culture of terror has emerged'. (Sluka 2000: 22–23) This is a defensive reaction that constructs the other as dangerous and threatening, and the self as victim. However, unless we can address the upstream causes of these downstream effects we well might compound this aggressive militancy, not contain it. Politicizing the nation on the basis of majority and minorities, easily lead to a majoritarianism, which infringes and even overrides democratic rights and civil liberties of minorities and other dissenters. This is the very antithesis of an inclusive, participatory democracy. Such a politicization around negative ideologies and exclusive identities might in the end polarize society to the tipping point, and precipitate the solution of a formal division for a compromised peace to avoid ethnic cleansing and eventual genocide.

However, majoritarian paranoia of the minority, believing they are the victims, merely defending themselves against minority aggression and usurpation of their legitimate rights, is not peculiar to India. Whatever hurt and injustice they felt, its real source is more likely the multiple social failures elsewhere. Scapegoats are readily found or constructed on whom they can vent their frustration at the supposed injustice and hurt they claim to have suffered. But the real causes of failure and consequent resentment is not addressed. Blaming the victim is the name of the game. Community leaders and opinion makers use this in order to protect their position and advantage themselves.

Today our polity is hurtling into an authoritarian free-market economy. Electoral waves have seen a swing from left to right and back again. This may achieve Pareto's 'circulation of elites' but it does not result in sustained social transformation. Moreover, there has been a continuing advance of an aggressive, majoritarian religious extremism, as also of a defensive, minority religious fundamentalism. They become but mirror images of each other, locked in an escalating spiral of covert antagonism, which inevitably spills over into overt violence. In such a scenario, it is always the weakest the most vulnerable who pays the price, whether the Muslim in Ahmedabad, the Christian in Kandhamal, the pandit in Kashmir, not to mention the SCs and STs.

The multidimensional pluralism of our society once stood as a bulwark against the tyranny of the majority. (Tocqueville 1882) Hindu nationalism and its quest for Hindu Rashtra would impoverish our society by undoing the rich diversity of our Indic civilization, its inclusiveness and tolerance. With the multiple pluralities of this subcontinent, imposing a uniformity is a formula for unending contestation and conflict, because beyond a point of desperation, victims will find ways of fighting back. Contemporary terrorism must be seen in this context, as it is increasingly becoming the weapon of the weak against those perceived as their unresponsive victimisers.

Dignifying Difference

The idea of India that the freedom struggle fought for was a unity-in-diversity; two poles of a continuum, which must be held together. For without some unity, by itself diversity could fragment a community into smaller and smaller ones with little in common and minimal or antagonistic interaction. In such a segmented society there can be little, if any, mutual enrichment. Societies with rigid hierarchies and impervious socio-economic stratification experience this. On the other hand, unity without diversity flattens a society into a uniformity which is not enriching either. However, the limits of tolerance will differ with each society.

Indic civilization had an astounding capacity to absorb different others, without assimilating or integrating them. They encapsulated them in their hierarchical niche and allowed them to find their place in the sun within the social boundaries set. This was then a multicultural society with many strands woven into its overarching civilization. It was surely one of the great civilizations of our world but not without its shadow side: the curse of caste, the burden of tradition, the oppression were all par for the course. The 19th-century India renaissance and the freedom movement addressed these anomalies. However, as we have seen, the response had two perspectives: the first, as social transformative one, inspired by the 'idea of India' in the freedom movement and looks to the future, as expressed in our Republic's Constitution; the second, a traditional revivalist one, inspired by the concept of 'Hindu Rashtra' as expressed by Hindutva ideologues and looks back to the past. The independence movement is located in the first, and was dominant for a half century after Independence; Hindu nationalism, which is located in the second, has been in ascendance for last couple of decades. Today the liberal idea of India emphasizing pluralism is in retreat and Hindu nationalism emphasizing uniformity is the dominant ideology.

The difference between the two perspectives is now polarized along religion, which now has become an identity marker for individuals and communities. This generates strong passions on both sides. This can only up the ante on collective violence. We need a pluralism to affirm and foster both the individual and the community rights. Before celebrating a mutually enriching diversity of India, the challenge is 'to contain and defuse such collective passions, we must recognize and guarantee both equal dignity and unique identity for every individual person and each human community. The first is founded on human rights and is committed to enforcing equitable rights for all individuals, e.g., the right to life and liberty of conscience. The second is premised on collective rights and is responsible for ensuring the cultural identity of each group, e.g., the right to language and religion.' (Heredia 2007: 122)

This is the foundation of the unity underlying diversity in a society that anchors the viability of a multicultural, pluri-religious society in a nation-state.

Unfortunately, people on the defensive often define their identities negatively—by what they are not, rather than positively by what they are. The first tends to be exclusive, and the more definitive it is the more rigid, singular and totalizing. This makes for hostile antagonisms, at both the individual and collective levels. Positively defined identities are the very opposite: more inclusive, flexible and open. It is apparent that hate politics and passionate populism is premised on negatively defined identities, while a counter-narrative and reasoned constitutionalism is found on positively defined lines.

Respecting the other's difference does not compromise oneself, one's own identity and convictions, just as leaning another language does not estrange you from your own. But with an openness to all cultures that may freely blow about one's house, we must be rooted in our own culture and not be blown off our feet. Acknowledging '*The Dignity of Difference*' is a necessary condition for 'pluralist harmony', a multicultural, pluri-religious society; like 'a musical lesson for the cultures of the world: to exist in counterpoint with one another…a counterpoint that exemplifies the musical cosmopolitanism of our time'. (Sacks 2002)

If we are both rooted and open in identity, as Gandhi was, we would be able to say with Muhammad Ibn 'Arabi, the mystic, philosopher, poet, sage of Spain (1165–1240):

> My heart is open to all winds:
> It is a pasture for gazelles
> And a home for Christian monks,
> A temple for idols
> The Black Stone of the Mecca pilgrim,
> The table of the Torah
> And the book of the Koran.
> Wherever God's caravans turn,
> The religion of love shall be my religion
> And my faith.
>
> (Cited Hsu-Ming Teo, *Desert Passions*, 2012: 17)

Social Democracy

The Republic we proclaimed on 26 January 1950 was constituted as a democratic union of states, inspired by the gradualism of Fabian socialism to build a social democratic polity. This which was the only realistic option for a multicultural, pluri-religious multi-party India. We are a nation in the making, or rather a multination state venture. It has been a functioning electoral democracy for the last seven decades, over which period it has moved on from Nehru's democratic socialism to a neoliberalism, which now has saffron hues. However, the Indian Republic has yet to become a truly substantive democracy and fulfil the promise of its tryst with destiny.

India embraced the democratic path to a socialist economy. Civil liberties and democratic rights were guaranteed and society would be as far as possible egalitarian and equitable. We adopted a planned mixed economy, where the heights of the economy would be owned and controlled by the state, while private enterprises would function within set limits. Conscious of the millions in dire poverty, all the thirteen Five Year Plans, prioritized 'growth with social justice and equity'. The idea was to build a more prosperous and egalitarian society. But the burden of the consequent regulations, which came to be called the 'license permit raj', empowered officials to extort huge rents; it was a prescription for corruption and non-performance.

People were disillusioned with the 'post office socialism' (Galbraith 1963: 4) that failed to uplift them for a variety of reasons, including corruption, overreach and political interference, but principally for lack of accountability. A financial crisis of diminishing reserves overtook the Reserve Bank in the 1990s. In response the economy was liberalized, but the bureaucratic maze remains in place.

Saffron Neoliberalism

Earlier theories of 'growth first, equality will follow', and 'the trickle-down effect' have been discredited. Today the underprivileged are not waiting for a trickle, they want their rightful share of the full flow of benefits. But the government's neoliberalism is hardly sensitive to issues of equity, equality and redistribution. For 'neo-liberalism is a political economic theory of the state committed to the laissez-faire market fundamentalism ideology that goes back to Adam Smith and David Ricardo' (Schultz 2018) more recently articulated by Friedrich Hayek (1899–1992), winner of the Sveriges Riksbank Prize in Economic Sciences in Memory of Alfred Nobel. It is committed to free-market and free trade, privatization and limited government, not to the underprivileged.

The BJP government adds a saffron hue to this neoliberalism, in keeping with its quest for a Hindu Rashtra. Moving away from its origins of small shopkeepers and traders, the saffron brigade has accepted the warm embrace of international corporates and big businesses, and distanced itself from minorities and the poor. This saffronization will favour the savarna upper castes and adversely affect others. Moreover, in a pluri-religious society, any espousal by the state of one religious tradition, whether Christian, Islamic, Buddhist or Hindu, will inevitably disadvantage the others. This has happened all over South Asia.

The Hindu Rashtra is the polar opposite of an egalitarian and inclusive India our Republic was constituted to be. It has never been defined, only vague references and preferences are available. Depending on how much traction the sound byte gets in terms of appealing to people it is changed accordingly. Once it was 'cultural nationalism' in the 1990s then 'India Shining' in the early 2000s till 2004. Later it was 'Rising India' and more recently 'New India'. Such vague indicators obfuscate rather than explicate the term. However, the actions of the Hindu Rashtravadis (enthusiasts for Hindu Rashtra) speak louder and more truly than their words. For finally, Hindu Rashtra is not an inclusive endeavour, certainly not for the non-Hindus. And given their rich diversity, it is doubtful, whether all Hindus, moderate and secular ones particularly, would approve it either.

Capitalism and neoliberalism in particular readily take on religious or racist colours, as long as the returns are profitable. For capitalists generally, and neoliberals especially, labour-saving, capital-intensive technology is more profitable and less burdensome, regardless of the unemployment crisis jobless growth creates. GDP figures fudge the issues. For if the benefits of growth accumulate with the rich and are not shared with the poor, who must wait for a trickle down, or they accrue to one community and not others, the gap between the haves and have-nots widens and deepens. The whole democratic system becomes unstable and vulnerable to demagogues and populist leaders.

Inequality Fallout

In 2019, in the first comprehensive survey of unemployment in the country, unemployment rates stood at 6.1 per cent. Even as the GDP rose, unemployment figures did too, and in 2019 reached their highest level in forty-five years. (Reuters 31 Jan 2019) The government's response was neither to confirm nor deny; it just refused to release the report until after it was reworked to a more favourable conclusion.

Unfortunately, inequality and equity have not been given the attentive study they warrant. It is considered by some as the natural consequence of growth and would even out over time. Moreover, in a hierarchical society such disparities are taken for granted. In the meanwhile, relative poverty, i.e., the difference between those who have and those who do not, skyrockets. Since the 1990s, inequality has been creeping up on us. Unemployment compounds this further. Much of the unrest eventually boils over into civil disobedience and violence, and finds convenient scapegoats elsewhere. Politicizing the identity of the other provides weak and vulnerable victims on whom to vent their frustrations. But the systemic inequality remains unaddressed at its roots, neither in the economic dynamics of neoliberalism nor in the hierarchical culture of our society.

Yet, without equal citizenship for all our people, there can be no substantive democracy. It will be hollowed out, leaving behind only the skeleton of the election process. A democracy without equal citizens is a contradiction. It is unviable, if it could ever be stable. Electoral democracy is a necessary means to more substantive democracy. It gives people a sense of participating in the democratic process, but if politicians do not deliver on what they were elected to do, it becomes an illusion of inclusion. 'Democracy has thus become "the new opiate of the masses" which numbs the poor to their poverty'. (Gooptu 2014: 22) But social inclusion is not an add-on extra; it is essential to any democratic citizenship.

The focused pursuit of profit is the raison d'être and the first priority of all capitalist systems. Many economists now think that contemporary capitalism is a failing system. (Streeck 2017) But this system has proved capable of reinventing itself repeatedly after each crisis. It changes along the way, submits to regulations and then often subverts them. Tax avoidance by the rich, and multinational corporations is a case in point. In India there is a real tussle between those using the market to promote growth and others insisting on regulating it for greater equity.

The statistics are telling. *The Economist* (25 Oct, 2018) reports: 'In last year's Credit Suisse report, the richest 1% seemed to claim more than half of the world's wealth. But new and improved estimates suggest the share of the one-percenters may have peaked or levelled off. Between 2016 and 2018, it fell in Brazil, Britain, France, Germany, India and Russia and flattened off in America, Canada, China, Italy and Japan.'

In an interview with *The Economist*, (19 Sept 2018) Christine Largarde, the MD of the International Monetary Fund, admitted that 'inequality has been reduced between countries. But not within countries'. Moreover, 'since 1980 the top 1% globally has seen twice as much of the gains from growth as the bottom 50%'.

But besides bad news there is mixed news too. 'Over 1bn people have been lifted out of extreme poverty since 1990, amid global integration…This is a remarkable achievement, unprecedented across the entire span of human history…Yet almost 800m people remain mired in extreme poverty today.'(ibid.)

Indian Scenario

In India too, over seven years of high growth many million have been lifted over the poverty line of one dollar a day. In the 1990s, the percentages below the poverty line were in the forties. They came down to around 21 per cent in 2018 according to official figures. (GOI Ministry of Statistics) But 21 per cent adds up to more than 200 million still left behind.

The Oxfam India Inequality Report, 2018, is more precise and incisive in its data. (Oxfam India 2018) The super-rich billionaires now own 15 per cent of India's GDP, up from 10 per cent five years ago. Are we now moving 'From British Raj to Billionaire Raj?' (Chancel and Piketty 2017) India's richest 1 per cent now hold a huge 55 per cent of the country's total wealth.

Moreover, the 'levels of inequality are not only high, but also rising over the last three decades', especially since the economy began to liberalize in the 1990s. It has only gotten worse since then as the free-market overtook the economy. Adequate measures to counter inequality are still wanting. Unsurprisingly, we are among the most unequal societies in the world. On the inequality index, India ranks 131 out of 152 countries.

Furthermore, when inequality is structural, as ours is, it has further implications. The most unequal countries have the poorest public services. This amounts not just to a denial of some minimal surety against unanticipated need, like a health crisis or a death of the wage-earner in the family, but a denial of access to basic services like health and education, housing, etc., essential human capital for sustained growth. The poorest and discriminated, Scheduled Castes and Tribes, minorities and marginalized suffer the most. This condemns them to their ascribed status and role, and so the system reproduces itself.

Of the sixty-nine billionaires in 2010, four out of ten had inherited wealth. Today India has 104 billionaires collectively worth some 347 US billion dollars. On the other hand, Oxfam reports: 'The bottom 50% of the population held 9% of the total assets in the country in 1991 but has seen the share decline by one-third to only 5.3% by 2012. As against this, the share of wealth held by the top 1% has increased from 17% in 1991 to 28% by 2012.'

The kinds of active tensions and even hostility gross inequality can breed should not be underestimated, even when accepted with passive resignation. Neither of these is compatible with a functioning democracy, for both amount to a structural exclusion of citizens and their rightful claims on the state. Furthermore, exclusion makes it so much more difficult to maintain trust and co-operation across groups and communities. Reducing inequality must be a central concern for a stable democratic society. But in practice Oxfam reports, 'inequality is no longer only a moral and philosophical concern' in public discourse.

While growth is essential to lift people out of poverty for a better life, unlike neoliberal capitalism it must be within a framework that facilitates distribution of the benefits and an inclusion of all involved. The state has a critical role here. Sometimes democratic pressures can force concessions and subsidies from the state, though ideally the state itself should be more proactive. But reducing poverty does not necessarily mean reducing inequality. Rather it may well increase relative poverty and create other divides as capital-intensive, hi-tech growth does between the highly skilled, the specialists, the professionals and low-skilled, non-specialists, lay persons. This is rationalized as meritocracy but does not consider those who had no access to the means to gaining such merit. It is happening in India and it betrays our idea of social democracy. Ever since the economy was liberalized, the GDP has gone up and equality down on the inequality index. It would seem 'India is regressing into being in fact if not in name, a republic of privilege, where large numbers are denied the most basic of rights'. (Muralidharan 2019: 39)

Inclusive Growth

Inclusive growth institutions must build human capital. The Inclusive Growth and Development Report 2017 of the World Economic Forum makes some pointed suggestions towards this building human capital:

1. Active labour-market policies
2. Equity of access to quality basic education
3. Gender parity

4. Non-standard work benefits and protections
5. Effective school-to-work transition

However, how well growth benefits society as a whole depends on the quality and equity of human capital formation to reshape the assumptions and priorities of the way modern market works. This can only be realized with the engagement of all stakeholders (WEF Inclusive Growth and Development Report 2017): 'Policies and institutions supporting social inclusion are not solely a luxury of high-income countries…It is possible, indeed essential, to be pro-labor and pro-business, to advocate a strengthening of both social inclusion and efficiency of markets through a stronger focus on institutions.'

However, economic divides of class are not the only dimensions of exclusion and inequality in India; there is caste, religion and gender as well. Caste is certainly the more intransigent, but religious extremism is the more violent, gender inequalities are very one-sided cutting across other divides. Upper castes and classes do reinforce each other and then the division is strengthened by caste identity and class interest. The same happens with the poorer religious communities: religious identity motivates and mobilizes them. But in both instances, their identity becomes bound to the community they belong to. This often degenerates into an exclusive partisanship that is community centered. Its concern is community advantage, not growth or equity. Moreover, as we have seen, identity politics can trump interest politics.

In such divided and unequal societies, it is difficult to find common ground on which to resolve collective differences and co-operate on common goals. The lack of trust breathes a corrosive culture of suspicion. This eventually erodes human social capital. Social frustrations on all sides build up and eventually boil over into covert civil disturbances and collective violence. Populist leaders advantage themselves in the confusion, building on mistrust, rather than building up trust. This is where the politics of hate and of populism is sourced, in unequal and divided societies. Ultimately growth without equity is a formula for disaster.

Growth and Equity

Growth is essential to expand income and welfare and lift people out of poverty, but it cannot be prioritized over inequality, which is the shadow side of the uncritical pursuit of rapid growth. The stark data we have presented on our unequal country and our world is but a pinhole view of the problem of inequality in our world, and it is not limited to India. But it has not had the urgency it should in the policy discourse as a national or global issue in the public domain.

Increasing inequality adds up to an instability that cries out for redress. Moreover, the aspirations of urban middle classes for upward mobility are increasingly frustrated by unemployment and income stagnation, while the poor have no project in the future. This makes for an explosive tinderbox. Blaming earlier governments and their parties is becoming a hollow alibi, particularly while at the same time promoting the neoliberal free market, which surely is the cause of this disparity. 'Wealth inequality has increased since 1991, and the value of assets follow the hierarchy of the caste structure and occupational groups.' (Oxfam 2018)

Inequality began to rise in the 1990s, with the introduction of economic reforms in 1991, and continued with the high growth rates in the 2000s. Compounding this was unemployment, rising dangerously to unprecedented levels. Indeed, unemployment is the Achilles heel of growth in many countries worldwide, precisely when its benefits are not equitably spread and shared with all. Crony capitalism and patronage politics prevail.

To distract people from such real issues, pragmatic and programmatic violence is unashamedly used to polarize the communities and manipulate people's anger, projecting it onto convenient scapegoats, like minorities, especially Muslims, and on Dalits and tribals. When vikas (development) fails to deliver on the rhetorical promises lavishly made for elections, then the fall back is on Hindutva. The evocative slogan: 'sab ka saath, sab ka visvas' (development for all and with all) becomes a cruel joke on those on the wrong side of the rich-poor economic divide. This has been the strategy in winning elections: when uncertain, start a riot. This was the strategy for the 2014 general elections. For the 2019 elections, 'sab ke saat sab ka viswas' was added. An even more cruel joke on the insecure minorities, especially the Muslims.

Whether on the national or international scene, collective violence creates insecurities that give the government an opportunity to project itself as a strong protector of people's safety. But such strategies do not defuse the underlying crises simmering below the surface and boiling over into frustration and anger. They do not address unemployment or the agricultural crisis. These are not resolved by this polarizing and scapegoating on the vulnerable. Such a cynical strategy may win at the elections, but it does not generate creative or constructive jobs for unemployed youth, or help the desperate lot of farmers. The root cause is that growth is not inclusive. For, capital-intensive growth is labour-saving. It is more profitable but unless labour has the human resources to keep pace with this accelerating change, it will be socially disruptive.

To prioritize a more equitable equality, investment must be made in human resource development. Here, the state has a critical role to play. For in developing countries, especially, private enterprise is unlikely to do so, certainly not on the scale required. In many countries their success story was built on this: selected state intervention at strategic points in the economy to invest in human capital with basic services, like health, education, employment, housing for all in critical areas where investment is beyond the income of the workers and the returns are too long-term for private capital, and more social than individual. This means distributing the benefits of growth so that people are included as active agents in it and not passive recipients, of state welfare.

This is precisely the unresolved contradiction of neoliberalism and its markets: developing oases of prosperity in the desert sands of poverty. For Indian society, this is an *Uncertain Glory.* (Dreuze and Sen 2002) Besides the human costs involved there is a real danger of violent sandstorms burying the oases. Already collective violence, diverted onto the different other, the religious minority and subaltern communities has reached new normalized highs. It shows no sign of abating as long as it yields electoral dividends.

Anthony Giddens criticizes market socialism and constructs a six-point framework for a reconstituted radical politics:

1. Repair damaged solidarities.
2. Recognize the centrality of life politics.
3. Accept that active trust implies generative politics.
4. Embrace dialogic democracy.
5. Rethink the welfare state.
6. Confront violence.

(Bryant, and David, 2003: 247–73)

Reversing the cycle of violence demands a new politics of empathy and compassion, premised on tolerance and dialogue. This can only be effective when we can do a reciprocity of perspectives with the different other. To counter the ethnocentrism, exclusiveness, hate and authoritarianism that has overtaken our public and political life we must put in place a politics of non-violent inclusion and fraternity, which supports liberty and equality and is the third and perhaps most crucial dimension of our constitutional justice.

CHAPTER SEVEN

BRIDGING THE FAULTLINES

Fractured World – Political Passions – Truth and Reconciliation – Ubuntu for Restoration – Contextual Responses – Divide to Rule – Agency for Civil Society – Reconciliation as Process – Sacralising the State

Fractured World

We have seen contemporary collective violence in India being used to polarize people—to exploit their differences ethnic and otherwise, portray minorities as alien to the Hindu cultural nationalism as understood by the Sangh parivar, while marginalizing the SCs and STs as outside the savarna castes' fold. It feeds on their own insecurities and fears and, with an explosion of expectations, turns this into a politics of hate, excluding other ethnic communities. This narrative of divide and polarize to consolidate is not new. The differences and antagonisms between communities have always been there; the colonial divide-and-rule imperial policy culminated in monstrous excesses as was witnessed during the Partition. Moreover, the discontents of an uneven and skewed modernity eventually added to the alienation and anomie of people, while dominant groups looked for scapegoats among the vulnerable. Someone had to be made responsible for their plight.

Today we have reached a point of polarization and hostility, especially against the Muslim community, which corrupts community relationships and erupts into overt collective violence ever so frequently, not to mention the prejudice minorities and marginalized people face in society at large in their struggle to live decent lives and in their dealings with government agencies. This cultural nationalism of upper caste/class derives from an ideological understanding of Hindu Rashtra to which the OBCs, SCs and STs are co-opted. It is the denial of the inclusive India we struggled for in the freedom movement and enshrined in the Constitution of our Republic.

The main communal divides among the protagonists considered here are: Hindu nationalists versus others considered as anti-national. This political rhetoric swept the last general election in 2019. In spite of the government's performance falling far short of its promises, there was no anti-incumbency. The counter narrative of another different India, diverse, tolerant, concerned for Gandhi's last and least Indian, must be premised and accompanied by a process of reconciliation for peace and harmony for any real traction with people in order to touch and change their hearts and minds. Obviously this is generational change that must be grounded in the contemporary reality but must also draw on our ample Indic traditions from where we can learn to cope with such situations.

A chauvinist ethno-religious nationalism, of hate, insecurity and fear, has overtaken our Republic. We did find an alternative narrative to this during the freedom movement. More than ever we need the same politics of compassion to address the deep cultural and political roots of these antagonisms, both personal and social, though here our focus is on the political not the personal. For once again, the faultlines of religious nationalism, which partitioned the country in 1947 are being revisited, the chaos that followed is being revived and the violence and genocide being re-enacted. This is surely going to take post-Independent India to a very different destiny from the tryst we made at Independence. Pankaj Mishra has called it: 'Our New Culture of Cruelty'. (*New York Review of Books*, 22 May 2018)

There is no single and assured path to peace, but it is important to learn from the past and reorient social norms and traditions to accommodate new measures adapted to our present circumstances for peace and harmony, which are such treasured values of our

Indic heritage. Today the victims of violence and their perpetrators are locked in a deadly embrace. *The Economist* referred to the spiral of violence in our world as 'a cycle of savagery'. (*The Economist* 8 Mar 2015) Indeed, national extremism is becoming a global phenomenon. But for agents of reconciliation and peace this is precisely what needs to be transcended, in order to begin to heal the warring protagonists of our world. And it is always easier for the stronger player in the conflicts to be more generous in making the first move while pursuing a reconciliatory process. Can we set an example of such reconciliation and peace in our polarized, fractured world? This will be the unique witness of our people and an example to the world.

We need to recall the incredible story of *Ghaffar Khan: Non-violent Badshah of the Pakhtuns*, (Gandhi 2004) the 'Frontier Gandhi', as he came to be called. The Taliban of today are recruited from the same Pashtu tribesmen whom he mobilized into a non-violent movement for Independence in Peshawar, then the North West Frontier Province (now in Pakistan). For this, he recruited an army of Khudai Khidmatgar (Pashto for 'servants of God'). 'Honour' was of very high value for his Pashtun tribesmen and it would not be easily compromised. Traditionally it was shown in physical courage and often by avenging the deaths of their clansmen, on the principle of a life for a life. Ghaffar Khan was a natural leader, a transparent and devout man, who won over the hearts of his people with his honesty, simplicity and power of example. He persuaded his people that the greater bravery was in non-violence, ahimsa.

Inspired by Gandhi, he joined the Indian National Congress, and faced arrest, prison and exile, but the resistance displayed by him and his clansmen was courageous, persevering and without retaliation. Ghaffar Khan and his Khudai Khidmatgars strongly opposed the proposal for the partition of India, and felt betrayed, 'thrown to the wolves' when the plan for the Partition was hurriedly finalized without consulting him. After Independence and before his assassination, Gandhi was planning a trip across Pakistan to meet him.

Rajmohan Gandhi concludes his biography of this non-violent Badshah of the Pakhtuns thus:

> The naturalness of his Islam, his directness, his rejection of violence and revenge, and his readiness to cooperate with non-Muslims add up to a valuable legacy for our angry times. This legacy may be of help to Muslims and non-Muslims today in the task of overcoming divides between Islam and the West (and modernity), between Afghanistan and the subcontinent, between Islam and the subcontinent's Hindus, Sikhs and other non-Muslims. His bridge-building life is a refutation of the clash-of-civilizations theory. (Gandhi 2004: 276)

Ghaffar Khan was surely a true follower of ahimsa. We need to foster more such bridge-builders across our divided communities today.

Political Passions

Passion as a heightened emotion is notorious, ambiguous and not easily trusted, particularly when it becomes extremist and obsessive. This is especially so when it is political and in the public domain. Violence, even when it is not premeditated, whether personal or collective, is driven by negative emotions such as fear, anger and hatred. Rabble rousers, fear mongers and demagogues find it easy to exploit people's insecurities and fears to their advantage, not necessarily to the benefit of the people they claim to speak for. However, positive emotions such as empathy, compassion and love can be mobilized for just the opposite: to contain and restrain violence, bring reconciliation and healing.

In her book *Political Emotions*, Martha Nussbaum makes a convincing case for the concept, (2015: 6) 'not just as impulses' but as having 'an evaluative content' as well, which can be intuitively grasped. It is imperative to rationally analyze them, and not to follow them uncritically. There is the 'challenge to make sure that the content of the endorsed emotions is not that of one particular comprehensive doctrine, as opposed to others.' (Nussbaum 2015: 6) Positive political emotions are needed to reinforce a public culture of commitment to positive norms for peace and reconciliation, and inhibit negative ones that foster negativity and disgust towards other groups of citizens.

Public emotions that feed fantasies of invulnerability are dangerous and encourage extremism and prejudices, and reinforce stereotyping the other, rather than contributing to render political principles and institutions stable and peaceable. Such a public culture demands an active and critical citizenship. For we must not forget that 'political emotions are the real emotions of real people'. (Nussbaum 2015: 283)

A zero-sum understanding of social interactions easily tips over into negative politics. A counter-narrative must not just address the premises of this politics but add a counter-emotion to neutralize and reverse its emotional appeal. This is precisely what the politics of passion attempts. There is ample evidence of this in Gandhi's politics all through his life, a man one could describe as incapable of hate. It was present in his methods of satyagraha, premised on ahimsa, which was more than just non-violence but 'love'—as he himself translated ahimsa. None were excluded, not even the enemy, who was not to be hated. This demanded empathy and compassion from his satyagrahis.

Martha Nussbaum insists that such love matters. It means generosity and concern, compassion and even forgiveness. It is the best antidote to egoism and self-centredness. It is both personal and public. For instance, love of one's nation is not just an ideological construct, but more so an emotional, even passionate attachment to the people of the national community, inclusive of all its diverse citizens who share the same history and geography. The nation-state is premised on a regime of rights and duties, supported by the rule of law and order. It becomes a national community when citizens are bonded together by positive emotional attachments, such as love, compassion, shared loyalties and common commitments. There should be little room here for hostility and violence between communities. This is an inclusive nationalism and it is not extremist. An exclusive nationalism is exactly the opposite, where fear and hate divide and polarize citizens, favouring some and excluding others, precipitating conflict and violence both within and without the nation. The same hold for love of one's own community, ethnic and especially religious. It can be positive and open or negative and hostile to the other.

In sum then, the interrelationship between passion and politics, especially for a democratic society, is critical because human emotions set the limits on possibilities and transformations of a people. (James 2003: 224) Michael Ure's *The Politics of Compassion* underscores the 'role that the passions can and ought to play in the political arena for democratic politics, global civil society and cosmopolitanism and political reconciliation and repair'. (Ure 2014: 2)

The reality of collective violence is staring us in the face. The fractures between hostile communities could get even wider and deeper. Coming to terms with the past must be a healing and reconciling process. It must help the protagonists to move forward. Soon after the 2019 general election results were announced, in his acceptance speech on being chosen to lead his party, the prime minister told his winning National Democratic Alliance (NDA) MPs in the central hall of parliament that his goal was 'Sabka saath, sabka vikas, sabka vishwaas' (With everyone, for the development of all, with the trust of all). Realizing that the 'minorities have been made to live in fear' he insisted, 'we have to win their trust'.

Building a new future for the next generation demands some minimal level of trust to begin building bridges across divides, and not walls of separation. Seeing the opponent as human helps develop mutual empathy and respect. This may well be a long and difficult journey but the alternative of not working towards mutual acceptance and tolerance becomes an invitation to further violence and deeper divides. Coming to terms with the past must be with a desire to promote better relations between communities, or else wounded memories and unhealed traumas will become the ground for further conflict to avenge past wrongs.

Imposing a solution by the victors, or a mediator, is not likely to produce a stable and lasting resolution. The victors can afford to be more generous and the victims need to be less vengeful. For it is not so much the similarities among people that makes them equal but mutual respect that enriches them, even when they hold different truths.

An ethical legal approach would address this on the grounds of truth and justice. Even where this is able to contain and restrain the violence and perhaps provide some protection in the future, there still remains much to be done if there is to be any remedy in terms of an effective therapy to heal wounded memories and redeem troubled consciences. A statutory adversarial legal procedure, or worse any positioning for political advantage will only perpetuate the cycle of violence and, as happens at times, victims and violators change places. In Gandhi's words, an eye for an eye would only make the whole world blind.

Truth and Reconciliation

To effectively heal wounded memories and redeem troubled consciences, a statutory adversarial legal procedure does not help, since the adversaries all too often are unreconciled and can contest the outcome in higher courts. With collective violence on a mass scale, no legal system would be able to sustain the burden of so many legal prosecutions. Inquiry commissions take unduly long and then their conclusions are more often than not unacceptable to one or both the parties, and their recommendations unimplemented. Our legal system is grounded on evidence, due process and fairness. Healing hurt and changing hearts is not part of this adversarial process, for it is based on retributive justice, not on a restorative one.

We can learn from 'The Truth and Reconciliation Commission' of South Africa, and how it came to terms with the horrors of Apartheid and the systematic use of state violence against non-whites. Desmond Tutu explains this approach as 'amnesty for truth'. (Tutu: 2004: 13) This is based on 'Ubuntu', the African emphasis on community, and restorative justice. In this approach, healing began with the perpetrators confessing their wrongs in public, while those present were free to question them. When done honestly and hopefully with some measure of repentance and regret, and victims too are no longer fearful or vengeful, and when both sides would rather seek closure and move on, it becomes a relief on the conscience of the perpetrators and a reassuring public acknowledgement of the sufferings of the victims.

The real legitimation for such an 'amnesty' for this comes

from a culture of rights in a humane society that is respectful of individuals and groups; a culture of peace between its diverse communities that is sustained by consensus not force; a sense of community that gives persons a sense of individuality, acceptance and belonging, participation and agency in the human community. In societies where fear and hatred rule, Ubuntu would not work. There can be no sense of an integral community where it is broken by negative emotions that divide and polarize it. However, the retributive justice of the courts and their due processes is not a very effective way to reconciliation. Moreover, with collective violence the number of litigants and lawyers, investigators and witnesses required, would make it impractical, if not impossible to deal with all the cases reported. The resources for this are simply not available.

The South African experience of the Truth and Reconciliation Commission offers us a viable mechanism for dealing with collective violence at multiple levels. The emphasis here is not to negate the violence that has been perpetrated. This would be untruthful, an 'a-sathya', a non-reality and can only further the injustice. Rather the accountability of the amnesty seekers must be stressed with a frank admission of their violations, bringing these out into the open with a public confession by the violators themselves. Only then can the truth be addressed not in terms of a retributive or punitive justice, but with a restorative or a remedial one; a justice that seeks not revenge but reconciliation sustained by a confession of guilt by the violators and forgiveness from the violated. This would depend on a willing and truthful admission by the violator, and the equally willing acceptance by the violated. Only thus can the truth of forgiveness and the justice of reconciliation come to light.

What is essential to succeed at any meaningful reconciliation in such a difficult and arduous quest for truth and justice is third-party mediation. This, of course, must be done from some neutral ground and in any crisis of law and order it must, of necessity, be the state. For it is the state in the public sphere that must guarantee security and equity, justice and fairness, reverse social injustices, redress economic inequalities and address political exclusions. However, even as a third-party mediator the state will need the support of civic society, and hopefully the two can work in tandem.

But if the state itself is compromised and partisan, what we have will be an enforced cessation of overt violence, which might be acceptable to the dominant parties, but leave the victims to their fate with no acknowledgement of what they have suffered, no real justice, no reparation, but gestures expressing antipathy rather than empathy. This is not reconciliatory politics but divisive and oppressive governance.

For restorative justice to be truly remedial and reconciliatory it must also operate beyond the statutory adversarial procedure of a court or even an ethical legal perspective of the legislature; it must be comprehensive enough to embrace the multiple levels of difference and various kinds of protagonists. Hence, engaging civil society in this process and creating an alert and critical citizenry is crucial.

Reconciliation is a political virtue, necessary for victims to recover their dignity and for the perpetrators to redeem their conscience. It is 'a move beyond old wounds': 'The acid test of reconciliation is the willingness of those who were harmed to live as neighbours with those who once harmed them. It does not mean that they have to forgive, only that they are able to coexist without recrimination.' (Cantacuzino *The Tablet* 5 May 2015). Reconciliation must include the active participation of those involved in the conflict, including third-party mediators.

Ubuntu for Restoration

In South Africa, the general expectation was that once Apartheid was overthrown and the majority black population took power, their pent-up rage would explode into violence and precipitate a veritable bloodbath of ethnic cleansing and perhaps even genocide. In a country of some 40.2 million, with just 8.9 per cent whites, a genocidal backlash was an ever-present possibility. This had happened before in Haiti with the massacre of the French in 1804 by the blacks.

However, in South Africa as the violence between white minority and the oppressed black majority escalated, both sides realized something had to done before the country raced over the precipice to its self-destruction: no winners, all losers. In India, too, we do not want to repeat such horrors from the past, but find a common ground for communicating with and between the parties to the conflict and thus begin a process of healing and reconciliation.

This is the story of many failed states, which collapse from within unless the situation is reversed and some measure of civility re-established. Retrieving the situation after this implies a strategy of building a national community bottom-up. This is a task for the long haul. However, at times like these, charismatic leaders have emerged and drawn on the deep resources of their heritage to recreate positive possibilities for oppressed peoples, thus defusing the tensions and conflicts, and opening the future to new possibilities. Authoritarian dictators and tyrants use their charism for the exact opposite.

Gandhi turned the potential for violence in our struggle against British imperialism with ahimsa, non-violence, and used satyagraha, truth-force. He drew on the traditional Indic ideals of tolerance and truthfulness, peacefulness and harmony, transforming these to support the movement for swaraj (self-rule). His Ram was the maryada purush: Saumya Ram, Ram the gentle, not Ram Raudra, Ram the angry. He inspired Ghaffar Khan in Pakhtoonistan, who changed the ideal of honour and heroism among his warring tribals to Gandhian non-violent resistance; Martin Luther King to adopt non-violence in the civil rights movement in America; and Nelson Mandela's magnanimity towards his white oppressors. All these were essentially Gandhian.

In South Africa, Nelson Mandela with the support of Archbishop Desmond Tutu and the judiciary, as also the cooperation of white leaders transformed the hatred and fear of the black majority and the white minority with The Truth and Reconciliation Commission. The foundation for this was 'Ubuntu', a typical African concept, though equivalents are found elsewhere as well, especially in tribal and more egalitarian societies:

'Where the world has not been broken up into fragments by narrow domestic walls', (Tagore 1913 *Gitanjali* No. 35) as Tagore wrote. Here is a sense of belonging to a larger community, of being more a part of the whole than apart from it. Descartes's 'I think therefore I am' set a new foundation for rationalist thinking for independent individuals. The African starts with 'I am because we are', the person-in-community.

As Michael Onyebuchi Eze explains in his book, *Intellectual History in Contemporary South Africa*:

> 'A person is a person through other people', strikes an affirmation of one's humanity through recognition of an 'other' in his or her uniqueness and difference. It is a demand for a creative intersubjective formation in which the 'other' becomes a mirror (but only a mirror) for my subjectivity. This idealism suggests to us that humanity is not embedded in my person solely as an individual; my humanity is co-substantively bestowed upon the other and me. Humanity is a quality we owe to each other. We create each other and need to sustain this otherness creation. And if we belong to each other, we participate in our creations: we are because you are, and since you are, definitely I am. (Eze 2010: 190–91)

Thus Ubuntu interiorizes in people a culture that becomes the foundation for the legitimacy of mutually acceptable remedies for the parties in cases of massive collective violence. As described by Eze, Ubuntu favours mediation over confrontation, restorative over retributive justice, reconciliation over estrangement, mutual understanding over punishment. In other words, sensitizing the parties to the negative impact the dispute is having on the parties themselves and striving to change conduct rather than to punish.

Ubuntu then is a resource for restoring broken relationships, between individuals in the personal domain, and more so between communities in the public sphere by opening up mutually acceptable remedies. However, any reconciliation process must start with a minimum level of mutual respect expressed in effective tolerance and genuine dialogue. Its focus is on restoration of the wounded community, not the punishment of individual or collective wrongdoing. Such reconciliation is a far surer and better path to healing wounded communities, and restoring their compromised dignity and negated identity. Even the perpetrators will find more fulfilment in the resulting communal peace and harmony.

Contextual Responses

At Nuremberg, the trial of war criminals was pursued in wartime tribunals by the victorious allies. They were treated as demanding retributive justice from the criminals. Executions and imprisonments followed. But the political issues of racism and colonialism were not dealt with in an effective manner. For the Convention for a Democratic South Africa (CODESA), launched in 1917, the political issue was a transformation to a democratic system. But first violence had to be stopped, traumas healed, with restorative, not retributive, justice. The dismantling of Apartheid began with universal franchise for all South Africans, minority rights and property rights were to be protected. Their vision was of a multi-coloured Rainbow Nation in one big bow across the South African sky.

Ugandian academic and author, Mahmood Mamdani, explains how CODESA went beyond Nuremberg's individual criminal justice:

> CODESA presents us with a radically new way of thinking about justice. To begin with, CODESA distinguished between different forms of justice—criminal, political and social. It then prioritized political justice, the reform of the political system, over the other two. A shift of logic from the criminal to the political led to decriminalizing both sides to the conflict. By turning enemies into political adversaries, CODESA also changed the goal post. The goal was no longer the internment and punishment of individuals charged with so many crimes, but a change of rules that would include them and their constituencies into a reformed political community...

By focusing on the link between creating an inclusive political order and an inclusive rule of law, it calls for a deep reflection on the relation between politics and law. The point was not to avenge the dead, but to give the living a second chance. (Mamdani 2015: 5, 12)

CODESA stabilized reconciliation between political opponents. Both sides realized the way forward would have to be through reconciliation and healing, for this the Truth and Justice Commission was constituted. Once communication channels were opened, with some workable transparency, the reconciliatory process picked up momentum. Non-communicative enemies now became interactive political adversaries, victims of violence now saw themselves as survivors with a new life to make, even the naming and shaming of the perpetrators had the salutary effect of disabusing them of their supposed racial superiority. However, none of this would have happened without the people's culture of Ubuntu, and the charismatic leadership to draw on it to affect this. On the contrary, there might have been another genocide as in Rwanda. (Mamdani Mahood, 2001)

The Peace and Reconciliation Commission in South Africa is an exemplary achievement of reconciliation in our times. Though it could not claim complete success, it did succeed in defusing a situation that might have exploded into ethnic cleansing or even genocides. Charismatic leaders like Nelson Mandela of the African Nationalist Party (ANC), and F.W. de Klerk of the white supremacist national party realized that they were getting trapped in a maelstrom of spiralling violence drawing them all into its depths. Their only option was to sink or swim together.

Drawing on their African Ubuntu cultural recourses, they designed a procedure to bring restorative justice to bear on what seemed too large a problem for the courts. This was truth-telling for amnesty. An official from the judiciary presided over and mediated the proceedings. The perpetrators were given an assurance of non-prosecution in court, provided they would confess their criminal atrocities in a public forum to their victims, who could question the confessant. At times, the mere narration of the cruelties would bring the listeners to tears, so barbaric were some of the stories told. But the victims felt that the suffering inflicted on them was recognized by society. Too often this is denied or trivialized or simply ignored. For the perpetrators, the confession itself was an admission of guilt and a plea for forgiveness. They were thus named and shamed, a punishment that opens the door to transformation. This is what restorative justice is about.

However, it was Ubuntu culture that made the Truth and Reconciliation Commission viable and largely successful. Its impact was clearly on the political transformation of a nation divided by the racism of Apartheid to pursue the ideal of a rainbow people, of diversity and light. Residual issues of reparation and rehabilitation of the victims, and the acceptance and reintegration of the perpetrators were beyond the scope of the Commission. What it did was to begin a process of genuine reconciliation and set the stage for further tolerance, peace and harmony. It was left for others to work this through.

Others have tried to replicate this model elsewhere: Peru, Rwanda and Cambodia had set up commissions for this purpose. However, the contextual situation in each case was different and the cultural resources required to deal with them varied. Accordingly, each path would be different to suit the social terrain, and situate itself in the prevailing context. The deeper the negativities of hatred, fear, demonizing the other, the more difficult the reconciliation. Yet doing nothing to heal the wounds on the victims' personhood, and not disturbing the conscience of the violators, compounds the situation and makes any rapprochement so much the more difficult.

A process of reconciliation can only begin when the mindset of the protagonist is ready for it, or else it most likely be rejected. Reconciliation is hardly possible in a pervasive culture of suspicion that feeds into a backlash. As a minimum, to begin with there must be a rapprochement of sorts: an end to the violence and some assured protection and security for the victims and the more vulnerable; ending the corrosive rhetoric that feeds suspicion and fuels fear with a minimum level of trust. This is basic for an honest reciprocity of perspectives, on which we can found a larger inclusive process of reconciliation. Otherwise the process can flounder on its own self-fulling prophecy, confirming the worst in the other, a pause in the continuing cycle of violence.

In the contemporary Indian scenario, reconciliation of the

protagonists seems like a distant dream. And yet peace is something to be desired by all concerned. Continued collective violence in any society, inevitably becomes a lose-lose game for all, protagonists and bystanders. Yet, the experience of the Karwan-e-Mohabbat was that not all parties to the conflict want reconciliation, especially those who had been advantaged by conflict and can rely on immunity from the law. The state is responsible for enforcing the law of the land, and when it fails to protect the victims, it is already compromised on the side of the violators. This further encourages the violators to up the ante on their level of aggression or turn it down, according to their advantage.

Obviously, there is a politics that takes advantage from collective violence, especially inter-communal violence, and as long as this yields positive returns at the hustings it will continue till the point of diminishing returns. In such situations, the point of entry for reconciliation may not be the domain of the political where the powerful may block it. But other spaces can be found in civil society, where people, especially the victims of violence, and those with a civic conscience, would want a reconciliation of the parties involved as the alternative may make all of us the worse off.

We cannot fight hate with hate and violence with more violence. Rather, understanding of the underlying causes that maintain the system and the illusions that sustain it can be dissolved, so that the system is delegitimized, and its executors can be deprived of power. 'It is compassion, and the understanding of the causes of suffering it brings, that is the greatest gift we can offer those suffering innocents.' (Edward 2001: 168)

Divide to Rule

In India, the antagonism between the majority and minorities goes back to the colonial times implicitly, which explicitly fostered a politics of divisiveness so that the colonized peoples would not be a united front against their rule. The mainstream freedom struggle was to overcome and contain these differences of cultures and interests in an overarching canopy where all would be welcome and each given a respected place of dignity, and protection of their unique identities. There were other movements, less interested in ending colonial rule than in positioning themselves to advantage in the postcolonial landscape.

Finally, the Muslim League, with some help from the British and the inflexibility of the Indian National Congress, carved out a Muslim homeland. But religion proved to be a very inadequate unifying factor. Bengali East Pakistan seceded, and ethnic rivalry in West Pakistan is overtaking the country. Trying to contain a failing nation on religious identity which scapegoats on religious minorities only ends with turning to seek 'heretics' and unbelievers among your own.

Relying on the military to hold the country together drains the resources for development and people's welfare. The military need an enemy to justify itself and blow up its budget, and the obvious one is its Indian neighbour, with Kashmir providing a readymade occasion for a low-level proxy war using extremists to create terror and disruption.

Religious states of whatever denomination have not done very well by all their citizens. They marginalize other religious minorities, then turn against the non-believers among their own. Religious political power corrupts religion into a political ideology, even as the religionists get more extreme, feeding on their own religious fervour. Yet even among religious fundamentalists and nationalist extremists once their struggle starts running into a dead-end, where there is little difference between winners and losers, moderation becomes necessary.

Such breakthroughs come after some cataclysmic collective catharsis: the protagonists are shocked by their own brutality, and realize the necessity of changing course or a third-party intervention by persuasion or force to bring an end to the violence and facilitate a rapprochement. The great rebellion of 1857 could have resulted in a change of form and substance of governance as happened in other dominion territories, like Canada and Australia and New Zealand. In South Africa, Gandhi was hoping for such a solution for all colonial territories but was disillusioned and charted a new course in his *Hind Swaraj* of 1908.

The pogroms and genocides which preceded and followed

the Partition were contained for a while by Gandhi and the shock of his assassination, which forced a pause. Both sides were more preoccupied with national honour, as the stories of the repatriation of abducted women in *The Other Side of Silence: Voices from the Partition of India* by Urvashi Butalia (2000) demonstrate so movingly. However, no healing process followed. Strong post-Independence leaders kept the communal demons at bay but as later leaders fell into a pragmatic politics, at times not very principled, and began losing its popularity, other regional players seized the day.

Among these contenders, the RSS-sponsored BJP grew to be the main alternative, and in the last two general elections the Indian National Congress (INC) has been cut to seize while the dominance of the BJP has grown. The latent antagonisms have been pragmatically and programmatically exploited by communal forces and the prejudiced stereotype of the Mussulman widely internalized. The Muslim community's response was assertive and even aggressive at times. The increasing fundamentalism and extremism of the community did them no good but rather provoked similar reaction from the Hindus. Each blames the other whenever communal violence irrupts. When self-defence is called for, the Muslims find the numbers are against them: 14.2 per cent or 172 million as per the 2011 census. Neither community has benefitted from this violent imbroglio, especially the vulnerable and marginalized, the poor, women and children, who are always the most negatively impacted by such collective violence and social insecurity.

The communal polarization has consolidated the leaders' position in their communities on both sides. Though they are ones responsible for the upstream poisoning of communal relationships, with their rhetoric of hate, violence and revenge, they are rarely if ever booked for it. Rather the little fellow on the street, the activist for justice and peace, the defenders of human rights, the ones the government perceives as dissenters and therefore anti-national subversives, are the ones booked and prosecuted, for 'inciting disaffection between communities', or even 'making war against the state'.

The Citizenship (Amendment) Act (CAA) passed by the parliament in December 2019 is a case in point. This must be read in the context of the National Population Register of Citizens (NPRC) already mandated by the Citizenship Act of 1955, which lays down rules for the acquisition and determination of Indian citizenship. These have been amended five times, but the latest amendment passed by Lok Sabha, proved to be highly controversial. It mandates a National Register of Citizens (NRC) to be made from the NPR, which requires detailed documented proof of citizenship. It puts a question mark on every citizen, and especially the minorities and marginalized, on whom the impact will be particularly detrimental. Many of the poor, especially the rural poor, will not be able to provide the documentation required, and many millions would become non-citizens even though they have lived here all their life.

The Act also facilitates citizenship for non-Muslims from neighbouring countries but excludes Muslims. This division of non-citizens violates the Constitution because equality before the law is fundamental. Further, it is in contradiction of constitutional values. For making distinctions on religious lines undermines our secularism, as well our unity that the Preamble pledges us to: 'Fraternity assuring the dignity of the individual and the unity and integrity of the nation'.

In Assam, where the implementation of the NCR was mandated by the Supreme Court, two million have been rendered stateless. How many millions would be rendered 'stateless', if it is implemented across nation? Some state governments are already planning detention camps. Will these become concentration camps? Appeals to Supreme Court to strike down the Act have failed. The court refused to put a stay order on it. Yet experts from here and abroad have emphasized the unconstitutionality of the Act. Even the UN High Commissioner's intervention was not entertained on the grounds of national sovereignty as this was an internal matter. The spin the prime minister puts on the CAA might spin us all to our doom.

In Delhi and many parts of the country, Muslims and others, who care for a secular India, opposed and protested peacefully, against the Act, as is their constitutional right. But the response of the state was brutal. Inflammatory speeches by BJP leaders led to communal violence in northeast Delhi, leaving many dead. This is only a presage of worse to come.

More often than not, dissenters pay a heavy and disproportionate price for something quite trivial. It as though the right to feel insulted and hurt is now a cognizable offence. Those who challenge the prevailing hegemony must be shown their place, lest they get out of hand. The situation of the marginalized Dalits and tribals runs parallel to that of the minorities. Caste prejudice and antagonism and religious prejudice and pride have similar roots: the inability to accept the different other as a challenging enrichment but rather see them as a threat to the status quo and their narcissistic egos.

Agency for Civil Society

There are numerous NGOs working for peace and reconciliation. Relevant examples are the local community-based Mohalla Committees discussed in Chapter 5. Started after the Mumbai riots of 1992–93, they managed to address local issues together with the police and civic officials participating in the process. They were triggered by people realizing the need to tackle neighbourhood problems as neighbours, and approach the local administration as a collective body. The police too realized that a force of 60,000 cannot maintain law and order, and sustain peace without active public support and collaboration.

People from the communities themselves must take responsibility for maintaining harmony, with civic and political support and facilitation. This opens up a channel of communication between the two hostile sides with third-party mediators. They could become an apt site for reconciliation at this local neighbour level. The approach has proved viable and successful and is now spreading across the country. These Mohallas become little circles of light, which can multiply and light up communal harmony across the land.

More recently, in July 2019, the Maharashtra government issued a notice for a district- and commissionerate-level peace committee, expanding the membership and including civic and elected local officials. However, such government-level initiatives though good by themselves, must not take away from people's participation and agency in the process, and must not infect the committees with partisan politics. Mohalla committees are important sites for civil society and state interaction; as 'Mohalla Committees of Mumbai' have proven to be 'Candles in Ominous Darkness'. (Thakkar 2004)

The core activities positioned them with credibility for a larger, more positive role in defusing tensions. Basically the committees take up complaints concerning the police along with civic issues of health, sanitation, water, waste disposal, etc. More critically, they promote communal harmony in the neighbourhood by celebrating the festivals of different communities, and organizing integrative activities like sports. A very successful Cricket for Peace tournament organized by the committees with the police participation has been an annual feature since 1996. Sadly after the 2002 pogrom, it was discouraged by the local government.

In defusing communal tensions before they boil over into violence, Mohalla Committees become a listening space, which can provide psychological support and space for opening new channels of communication and better understanding on all sides. Such sites need to be multiplied and co-ordinated, up-scaled into a movement that compels the government to pay attention to their needs, as Jockin Arputham did in Mumbai by founding the National Slum Dwellers Federation in1976.

However, there are difficulties and obstacles mainly from the system and people's mindset and prejudices. The police are not accustomed to being queried and easily resent it. Breaking into strong communal networks is a difficult and slow process, facing prejudice and negative feeling for the 'other' becomes a risky and delicate task. Yet these committees have made a difference, besides peaceful coexistence as a minimum, local leadership has grown, respect for law and other religions increased. But more importantly, 'The experience of the mohalla committees in Mumbai draw our attention to the basic and vital fact that common problems call for common action, and the ability of local life to cope with critical situations has to be constantly discovered and rediscovered...

but the constructive work taken up for the common good, based on compassion and not on passion, can be the cornerstone of a healthy relationship between the civil society and the state.' (Thakkar 2004: 586)

In the aftermath of collective violence, there is an urgent need for a transitional justice that will help restoration and reparation. The immediate issue is working out a practical reconciliation, while the larger issues of structural injustice are left to be dealt with in more peaceable circumstances. This will demand a new justice paradigm, and a shift from a retributive to restorative model of justice.

Among other civil society agencies that restore some measure of justice reconciliation in the wake of collective violence are peace committees that are very similar to mohalla committees in their composition. However, they are not merely localized but function at the level involved in the instance of collective violence being addressed: local, national or international. They do not deal with local civic issues but work for peace and harmony among people in the aftermath of the violence. They are third-party mediators trying to bring the conflicting parties to the negotiating table. The credibility and acceptance of such peace committees will depend on the credibility and acceptance of its members. Their approach is very much like second-tack diplomacy, mostly in the background and coming into the light when necessary

The People's Tribune, or the court of the people, approach is closer to an alternative juridical procedure. They were inspired by Bertrand Russell's International War Crimes Tribunal, an alternative to the normal tribunals where usually the victor's justice prevails, as at Nuremberg. (The same strict standards used for the Nazis were never applied to the Allies.) Many similar though less prominent tribunals have been set up and some made permanent.

The Indian People's Tribunal on Environmental and Human Rights is an independent body set up by the Human Rights Law Network (HRLN) on 5 June 1993. It has been active in investigating human rights and environmental abuses. It provides an alternative outlet for the victims denied justice because of official obstruction that delays and then denies justice. These tribunals hold public hearings where the victims can tell their stories. This cannot give them retributive justice, but it legitimizes their grievances and brings some positive affirmation, restoring the victims violated dignity. In other words, they are afforded some measure of restorative justice. The tribunals become a people's court as an alternative to the formal juridical system

These tribunals are an effective means to affirm the unrepresented and give voice to the voiceless, to recognize those unjustly treated by the system where the formalities of procedure override the substance of justice. Generally, a people's tribune consists of a jury headed by a retired judge with members of the legal fraternity and representatives of civil society. The purpose is to 'encourage victim communities to fight for their rights…highlight the imperatives of equity and human dignity in the search for true development…and highlight the environmental and human rights abuses being perpetuated on communities and individuals by the ruling elite in pursuit of unsustainable "development" objectives.' (Lewis 2003: 10)

Where there is large scale violation of human rights, as with instances of collective violence, even with a large scale of civil society participation and agency, we may not be able to undo the injustice. The least we can hope is to name and shame the perpetrators and offer them amnesty for reform and truth-telling. Though public tribunals have no juridical power, they are an effective means of helping to keep alive in the public conscience the ethical issues involved, which are often left hanging, because of inadequate laws and the formalized legal processes, and faulty and wrongheaded policies. These tribunals are focused on the moral questions not legalities and policies. Ideally there should be no contradiction between law and ethics, or public policy and the common good. But in practice, compromise and vested interests intervene.

Reconciliation as Process

The only lasting diffusion and reversal of this subcontinental collective violence lies in the reconciliation and healing of the warring factions between and within the subcontinental countries, and more specifically the communal divides that obtain there.

However, Indo-Pak relations are beyond the scope of this book. Our focus here is on the warring factions within India. Contemporary majoritarianism in India has alienated the minorities and the marginalized. Tensions have repeatedly boiled over into overt collective violence. The most dangerous polarization in India now is between Hindus and Muslims. A rapprochement between the activists at the local level of the mohalla and the peace committees have made some progress. The prime minister urging his party men to help make minorities less insecure, in his acceptance speech after the 2019 elections, might provide a breakthrough to begin a reconciliation process.

We can learn from the Truth and Justice Commission of South Africa as also from the peace initiatives in this country to help the reconciliation process. But first we must be grounded in the local situation. Desmond Tutu insists: 'There is no handy roadmap for reconciliation. There is no short cut or simple prescription for healing the wounds and divisions of a society in the aftermath of sustained violence.' (Bloomfield 2003 Foreword)

Creating trust between violent enemies requires that they reach out to each other. It is difficult for either party to make the first move. It is easier for the strong, though it is more needed by the weak. Neither is it easy to find a third-party mediator acceptable to all the protagonists, worse still if the antagonisms remain alive and active. Meaningful reconciliation has little chance, if any, in such a situation of on-going violence.

If such trust is to bring a lasting reconciliation it must come to terms with the past, accepting, understanding and most importantly, discerning what to forget and leave behind and what to remember and carry forward. Failure to resolve the past will almost certainly mean failure for any enduring reconciliation. For reconciliation can be mediated between the protagonists, but not imposed from without or within the groups. Usually it is the state and its administration of justice that have the responsibility of being the mediator. But if they are compromised and corrupt there is nowhere else to turn.

The partisan implication of the state itself in such collective violence makes any resolution or reconciliation extremely problematic. Vested interests lobby against change that may adversely affect them, regardless of the consequences, the contradictions and violence that has been precipitated. When the state fails in its function as a just and fair mediator, other actors in civil society must assume a critical role of impartial mediator and hold the state accountable for keeping the peace. It can always raise the issue of justice in a larger forum, even if does not have the power to enforce it. However, the moral authority of credible agents of reconciliation should not be underestimated. For ultimately the polity reflects society and vice versa. Civil society then becomes the locus for a people's movements that have in the past even effected a non-violent regime change by undermining its legitimacy.

Any attempt at a lasting reconciliation must be a participative process involving the parties to the conflict at some minimum level of consensus, beginning with the cessation of violence, basic mutual respect, and a minimum common agenda in neutral space. These may not obtain at first but they can be built along the way. Though hostile entanglements between the parties to the conflict often require third-party mediation.

A third party can enforce a precarious peace, as happens in wars between nations, or the protagonists realizing that they are all being trapped in a lose-lose situation from which only a negotiated compromise can redeem them. This is how Apartheid in South Africa was dismantled, and how in Ireland the 'Good Friday' agreement ended 'the Troubles'.

To bring the discussion to a conclusion, the *Handbook* for *Reconciliation After Violent Conflict* (Bloomfield 2003) lists the following characteristics for the process of reconciliation:

- finding a way to live that permits a vision of the future;
- the (re)building of relationships;
- coming to terms with past acts and enemies;
- a society-wide, long-term process of deep change;
- a process of acknowledging, remembering, and learning from the past; and
- voluntary and cannot be imposed.

In other words: 'Reconciliation is an over-arching process which includes the search for truth, justice, forgiveness, healing and so on. At its simplest, it means finding a way to live alongside former enemies—not necessarily to love them, or forgive them, or forget the past in any way, but to coexist with them, to develop the degree of cooperation necessary to share our society with them, so that we all have better lives together than we have had separately.' (Bloomfield 2003: 2.2.1)

This is the minimum common ground to begin a reconciliatory process. However, any effective reconciliation must be premised on a minimum level of mutual tolerance and dialogue to overcome the difficulties and dangers that accompany reconciliatory attempts. There is always a risk in trying but then the risk of not trying maybe far greater, leaving the situation to a continuing conflict.

In South Africa, in 1991–94, the Convention for a Democratic South Africa (CODESA) focused on the crucial political issue: a transformation to a democratic system without further violence. In 1996, the Truth and Justice Commission followed and dealt with victims of Apartheid with a restorative justice. The commission continued as an Institute for Justice and Reconciliation after 2003. What made this process workable and largely successful, too, was the tradition of Ubuntu on which the leaders drew, which carried the process through its seven years.

In India, we have our Constitution as the political framework for 'liberty, equality, fraternity'. Our Constitution attempted 'to foster this revolution by establishing the conditions necessary for its achievement'. (Austin 1966: 50) But we still have not internalized the constitutional ethic it implies, as the framework within which 'to foster this revolution'. Consequently populist mass politics dictate our agenda, while constitutional propriety is given short shrift, while majoritarian Hindu nationalism has polarized our people with a politics of hate.

To defuse this situation we must draw on traditional Indic resources, which encourage neither extremism nor intolerance. Exorcising our demons of unacknowledged insecurities and fears is essential to address the causes of our communal hostilities. Today this demands long-term efforts at change in our public civil culture;

we must go from being passive subjects to alert citizens. The social transformation our Constitution calls for desperately needs a cultural revolution to support and sustain it. Social conservatism, like the prevalence of caste, religious fundamentalism, political opportunism, hate speech and communal prejudice are keeping communal hatred alive to the advantage of some politicians, but to the bane of the ordinary people, who are propagandized and co-opted to causes alien to their genuine interests and real needs.

All this only ups the ante on the alienation of our people from our constitutional 'revolution', and contributes hugely to the upstream, deep background causes of the collective violence overtaking us today. To begin this process of reconciliation among the hostile protagonists, and bring a healing touch to our battered, bruised world, more than ever we desperately need a renewed culture of tolerance and peace.

The need for a genuine pluralism and an active civil society cannot be overestimated, as also the urgency of practical strategies for effectively dealing with the fundamental causes of such violence. What we really need is our own Truth and Justice Commission that will heal the wounds of the past, sublimate historical memories that have simmered in our collective unconscious, and inspire hope for our future together. And if this seems too utopian a dream to strive after then the alternative is a collective hell from which there will be no escape. But we must first heal the past, if we are to recover our future.

Sacralizing the State

All claims to individual and collective rights are demands by the claimants to have their identity recognized and their dignity affirmed. Pluralism thrives on its diversity. The constitutional affirmation of minority rights as part of its basic structure is a guarantor of the multicultural, pluri-religious richness of our peoples, which acknowledges 'the principle of equality between groups qua group' before the law. (Sheth 1989: 8) This was Gandhi's interpretation of secularism, once implied now explicit in our constitution: sarva dharma sama bhava (equal respect for all religions), rather than the Nehruvian dharma nirpekshata (equidistance from all religions).

However, many Hindus now argue that as the majority community, they must be given pride of place in the nation. For such people, true nationalists can only be Hindus, culturally if not religiously as well; and vice versa, all Hindus must be nationalists. Hence the outrage at any suggestion of 'Hindu terrorists', notwithstanding the violence of organizations like the United Liberation Front of Assam (ULFA) from 1979 till the truce of 2011. These Ahom people are Vaishnavite Hindus. And there are other extremist organizations committed to violence too, e.g., the many 'senas' known for their violence. In actuality, all communities have their shadow of violence. The difference is how they cope with it.

A majoritarian religious nationalism would sacralize the state into a theocracy, where the survival of religious and other minorities would depend on the goodwill of the dominant ethnic majority. This is the Savarkrite Hindu Rashtra. Many developing nations have taken this route of religious ethno-nationalism to development, but it has meant strife not just between but even within communities. The Islamic state of Pakistan is closer to a failing state than the darul al Islam (land of peace) once envisioned. Buddhist nationalism in Sri Lanka brought the nation into almost three decades of civil war, after which it has not quite recovered its liberal democratic traditions. Now Islamic militancy has dramatically announced its presence in the island. Bangladesh was founded as a secular state in 1971, became an Islamic one in 1988, and secular again in 2010, yet it still struggles with religious extremism. India was an exception but now 'perhaps the most ominous social and political development in India in recent times is the rapid growth of aggressive Hindu chauvinism'. (Balachandra 1996: 125)

A majoritarian religious nationalism, with its extremist and violent proclivities, does not speak to the real issues of people. It distracts them with pie in the sky promises, good days are a-coming ('acche din aanewale hain'). However, the Hinduism of our people is a multiplicity of religious traditions held together by a broad civilizational worldview, transcending national borders and geographic boundaries, to create a civilizational unity in diversity, inclusive of minorities. Whereas Hindutva is a narrow communal ideology of Hindu religious nationalists that seeks to polarize in order to consolidate its political base.

It is a closed ideology that seeks unity in uniformity; it is suspicious of diversity; it is intolerant of pluralism, which it would want to flatten into uniformity. Polarization for political again takes reconciliation off the agenda. Little wonder that when left to the chauvinistic politicians, the spiral of violence escalates and once again the minorities and marginalized bear the brunt of the conflict. Religious nationalism and fundamentalism are not a constructive response to our present predicament. It is more a misreading of the situation than a legitimate interpretation. It is essentially a defence response from a threat-perception coming from without.

What is needed is the openness and tolerance of a Gandhi, who is concerned with integral Hindu wholeness; not the exclusiveness and aggression of Hindu fundamentalists and nationalists preoccupied with political dominance. For him 'unity in diversity' was the integrating axis not just of Hindu, but of Indian culture, and of all humanity as well. Once conceded, this becomes a foundational truth, and tolerance a necessary consequence. This is not a negative tolerance of distance and coexistence, but rather one of communication and enrichment. Gandhi himself is a remarkable example of such an open yet rooted person. In religious matters, his sarva dharma sama bhava implies not just a radical faith in the validity of all religions, but further a fundamental faith in the adequacy of each religion for all those born into it: 'I do not expect the India of my dream to develop one religion, i.e., to be wholly Hindu, or wholly Christian, or wholly Mussalman, but I want it to be wholly tolerant, with its religions working side by side with one another.' (*Young India*, 22-12-1927)

However, Gandhi's own understanding of religion transcends religiosity. It is essentially a spiritual quest for moksha, but one rooted in the reality of service to the last and least in this world. This was Gandhi's understanding of Indian civilization, its culture and religion. I believe he had grasped the fundamental strength and profound secret of its survival over mill.

CHAPTER EIGHT

A HEALING TOUCH

Indic Pluralism – Plural Societies – New Scenario – Levels of Tolerance – Ideology and Myth – Pluralism and Tolerance – Pedagogy for Pluralism – Culture of Tolerance – Hermeneutics of Dialogue – Domains of Dialogue – Dialogue for Reconciliation – Multiple Belongings – Culture of Violence – Peace and Power – Bridging the Divides – Points of Engagement – Cultural Disarmament – Beyond the Horizon – Taking Back Democracy

Indic Pluralism

In the bewildering diversity of the Indian subcontinent, reconciliation in the aftermath of collective violence will take on contextual specificities: religious pogroms are different from caste atrocities. Pogroms ghettoize the Muslim minority further while performing the equivalent of an ethnic cleansing of other neighbourhoods; caste atrocities against Dalits reinforce caste hierarchy with its social barriers and boundaries. Hence reconciliation must be contextually nuanced. However, in all such collective violence there are common background issues which need to be addressed. Basically this concerns the tolerance of difference of diverse kinds in a plural society.

In English, 'tolerance denotes not merely the absence of intolerance but a more positive attitude'. (Doniger 2014) In general, however, the focus is on passive tolerance, endurance: in Sanskrit 'samadarshana' (looking upon all things as the same), and in Buddhism 'upeksha' (indifference, forbearing). (Doniger

2010) When society is hierarchical and patriarchal, hegemonic and unequal, any threat to the status quo will be resisted by the dominant communities and classes. But the critical question remains: how does a multicultural, pluri-religious society cope with difference?

The European model of the nation-state chose homogenization: one language, one people, one religion where possible, and at times even one leader. More commonly in the West's model for coping with differences, especially when the other was the different outsider, it meant assimilate or eliminate. The colonial comprador class and the genocides of the indigenous people testify to this. These nation-states made a bloody path through modern history, against their own minorities within and precipitating numerous wars without, including two that engulfed most of the world. The inner demons of the Christian West were projected into an anti-Semitism, which was genocidal.

The Indic model of dealing with the other was distinctly different: tolerate and encapsulate, accept the outsiders and give them a niche in the social hierarchy and contain them there. Most migrations and invasions across the mountains in our earliest history were handled thus. The inevitable interactions across traditions and a sharing of each other's cultural heritage yielded a rich composite culture that is best called 'Indic'. A comprehensive hierarchy based on ascribed status faithfully reproduced the system over generations, but still left room for generational change. However, this was made possible by the active engagement with and finally positive acceptance of the other, not mere passive acceptance of and resignation to fate.

This unique pluralism was something to be proud of. Early Indological studies in the West left scholars quite amazed. However, today the dominant Hindus claim to be the true indigenous people of this land, while all others—Muslims, Christians, Parsis, Jews—are foreigners. This is an intolerant rejection of our pluralist heritage in favour of Hindu fundamentalism and political extremism.

But once the economic political system begins to change and new culture is no longer as supportive as earlier, the system begins to weaken and groups jockey to position themselves to their advantage. The contestation is not likely to be peaceful and the outcome not acceptable to all. The conflict can then become violent and prolonged. Inevitably, the process gets politicized and long dead faultlines are emphasized and exploited. This only polarizes the minority-majority divide further. It cannot reconcile them or heal the alienation from each other; coercive imposition or sanctions from third parties can at best contain them until the next eruption.

In the aftermath of violent conflict, reaching across to the other side may well be a non-starter, and in a prevailing 'culture of suspicion', it could become counter-productive. Continuing violence can only polarize the combatants further and set off a spiral of violence that engulfs us all, even the bystanders. In such circumstances, without some measure of reconciliation and healing, we already have a repeat performance waiting for a trigger to set it off.

We need to bring in an understanding of pluralism as a given in societies of differentiated structures and diverse cultures. We need a tolerance that will pick up the threads of the tangled mess we have tied ourselves in and undo the knots of our negativities—prejudice, stereotypes, dogmatisms—to the mutual advantage of all the protagonists. Hopefully, engaging with the other in non-threatening ways will help to perceive the other as human too and begin to neutralize and defuse tensions.

However, politicizing difference can lead to exactly the opposite result. History witnesses such instances even into our own era. Vested interests are being sorted out through ethnic cleansing regardless of the human cost; communal violence is used as strategy to mobilize support and redraw the political map in blood. Today in a globalizing world, conflicting economic interests are being interpreted as a 'clash of civilizations' with irreconcilable religious worldviews.

Plural Societies

Most modern societies are inevitably plural because of their complexity and scale. Structural plurality implies 'a social structure compartmentalised into analogous, parallel, complementary but distinguishable sets of institutions'. (Van den Berge 1969: 67) Cultural plurality implies different cultures or sub-cultures with their distinctive individual and collective identities within an over-arching civilizational unity, where distinctive identities are contained in a larger, layered one.

The complexity and scale of our modern world cannot be contained in any single worldview (weltanschauung) (Rahner 1969: 26), nor can a dominant one be imposed in a free and open society. In traditional societies, the plurality of groups was accepted and integrated in a social hierarchy, where each had its protected niche. Caste hierarchy was the epitome of this. However, this pluralism was not premised on either individual freedom or social equality. Rather it was based on a bonding of individuals in the group, and of groups in society.

In 'mature Western democracies' plurality is more structural, whereas in post-colonial societies, especially in South Asia, plurality is quite decidedly more cultural. And more often than not it is the cultural dimension that is more resilient in the segmentation and compartmentalization of a plural society. Social differentiation must also mean social integration. However, there is an obvious interaction between the two. Moreover, this larger unifying social order will also have a structural and cultural aspect. Structurally it is often the market and the polity that integrates diverse groups in common social order. Culturally a common religion, language or older tradition can become the basis for a more inclusive civilizational unity. We need to further explore how far such structural and cultural plurality pertains to Indian society.

Often the tension between these two polarities of unity and diversity has been dealt with by emphasizing one and abandoning the 'other'. Pluralism, however, seeks to resolve this tension differently: holding on to both to construct a higher-level unity that allows for diversity at lower levels. Just as human beings are different, human communities are also different. Recognizing and respecting difference does not take from unity nor does it make for uniformity. While 'Unity in Diversity' was once official policy in India, today pluralism is under a menacing threat. National extremists are trying to impose a national uniformity, which is really the culture of the Hindu heartland. Such a Hindi/north Indian hegemony will not be acceptable or viable in many states of the Union, especially in the south and the northeast. It will be resisted as before, even violently.

Pluralism then is a way of coping with a plural society, and attempts to reconcile the polarity between universalism and particularism by affirming both: an 'equal dignity' for all citizens, and a 'unique identity' for each group. Such pluralism must be founded on a deep and comprehensive understanding of tolerance, as the basis of a workable 'politics of recognition', that includes the 'politics of universalism' and the 'politics of difference'. (Taylor 1992) But then again only to the extent that such identities are defined positively is any reconciliation for real tolerance possible. This is really the only viable option in a society as resiliently diverse as ours.

Dealing with plurality and difference within the politics of recognition of Charles Taylor (Taylor 1992: 25) involves both the politics of universalism and the politics of difference. The first is premised on human rights and equal dignity of all citizens, and therefore is committed to enforcing equal rights for all. The second is premised on cultural rights, and is responsible for ensuring the unique identity of each cultural group. In the first, individual rights are privileged, and in the second, collective rights. Such pluralism must be founded on a deep and comprehensive understanding of tolerance as the basis of a workable 'politics of recognition', that includes the 'politics of universalism' and the 'politics of deference'. (Taylor 1992)

In our world today pluralism is an inescapable necessity, whether ideological, religious, or otherwise. We have, moreover, evolved a whole doctrine of human freedom and the dignity of the human person. In other words, pluralism today should not be isolated as an unnecessary evil to be repressed, before it engulfs us further; or merely tolerated and seen as something to be distanced, since it cannot be dismissed. Rather it is a challenge which will not go away. It must be constructively and creatively met or it will exhaust, if not destroy us.

New Scenario

The need for a genuine pluralism and an active civil society cannot be overestimated, as also the urgency of practical strategies for effectively dealing with the upstream causes of such violence. What we really need is our own equivalent of the Truth and Justice Commission that will heal the wounds of the past, sublimate historical memories that have simmered in our collective unconscious, and inspire hope for our future together. And if this seems too utopian a dream to strive after then the alternative is a collective hell from which there will be no escape. But we must first heal the past, if we are to recover our future.

Modernity and the rapid changes it brings are shaking down the old hierarchies in which people had their place, their status and role, their niche in the social ecosystem. But we cannot simply jettison the old even before the new is born. On the other hand, romanticizing our own traditions and isolating ourselves in them is an inadequate and defensive response. Gandhi's metaphor of a house with 'open windows' could be an important idea here. (*Young India*, June 1921, p170) We need to critique our traditions radically and draw on them as resources to understand and respond creatively and constructively to our present crisis, not simply negate our traditions to ease the weight of the past on our present situation.

We are not here to discuss whether traditional India was tolerant or not. Our concern is that contemporary India is increasingly intolerant of difference and dissent. And this is clearly being politically promoted. But alarmingly so, it is being popularly accepted even by once committed moderates, while the political right is pleased, the political left is disillusioned and disoriented. Feeling the majoritarian threat, minorities react defensively and this becomes a self-fulfilling prophecy that only confirms the hostility of the protagonists.

In our Indic tradition we have a rich inspiration for tolerance, but not without its very real ambiguities. We have the Jaina concept of anekantavada (the many-sidedness of truth) and syadvada (the interrelatedness of all things); the Buddhist outreach in sarvabhutadaya, (universal compassion); the advaitic relativizing of mayavada and avidya; the Upanishadic ideal of vasudhaiva kutumbakam, (the universal family); the materialistic rationalism of Charvaka philosophy; the religious pluralism of the sarva dharma sama bhava, of the Sufi-bhakti heritage of our sant-kavis, etc. But there is also the intolerance of caste, regional stereotyping and our racial prejudices.

Gandhi drew on the best in our tradition to develop a non-violent mass movement through his praxis of ahimsa and satyagraha and his numerous 'experiments with truth' (1927). However, such a construction of tradition is already being contested by an uninhibitedly ethnocentric and chauvinistic religious majoritarianism. We must challenge this not by denying our past ambiguities but by critiquing them; not by a flight from the present crisis but by encountering them; not by escaping into an imagined utopia, but by giving a realistic provision for our future.

Our point of departure must be a radical acceptance of the reality of our plural society, in all the multi-faceted dimensions of its religious cultures and the unevenness of its political economy. We need a critical modernity to interrogate our taken-for-granted populist traditions. We must face up to modern pathologies to find, for our times, an alternate understanding of the 'normal'. (Saran 1989)

Ultimately, pluralism is about difference, especially differences that are challenging and take us out of ourselves. When the different other is encountered in openness and transparency the encounter can be enriching and celebratory. But when the other is perceived as a threat then the encounter will be counter-productive, reinforcing differences and divisions. Collective violence cathects along these faultlines and gets embedded into traditions and culture. This destroys mutual trust and confidence. In the wake of such destructive consequences, reconciling the parties will be impossible without an appreciation of pluralism and tolerance as enriching and humanizing.

It is our contention that in the final analysis the trajectory of our response to pluralism must begin with acceptance of difference and respect for other identities and then reach out to live and celebrate diversity as parts of a larger organic whole. (Kothari 1989: 20) In other words, our tolerance must reach across the polarities to embrace the hostile and unreconciled opponents on all sides of the conflict as parts of a larger integral whole.

Levels of Tolerance

The Enlightenment understanding of 'tolerance' is multi-vocal, from passive endurance to active endorsement and even celebration. As we have seen, Doniger argues that tolerance is not merely the absence of intolerance but something more encouraging and proactive. It is her contention that the idea of Indic tolerance stems from 'the intellectual rather than the political history'. (Doniger 2014: 126) The idea of India grounds the acceptance of Indic pluralism.

Tolerance is a commonly used word which covers a wide range of meaning from the passive forbearance of the long-suffering victim to the paternal indulgence of the benefactor. A more refined and elaborated spectrum of the 'levels of tolerance' is helpful in locating our own level of tolerance in our response to the different other. (Panikkar 1983: 20–36)

Here, Panikkar distinguishes four levels of tolerance. The first is tolerance as a practical necessity, i.e., bearing with a lesser evil for the sake of a greater good. This amounts to passively accepting necessary evils, and is little more than political pragmatism. The second is based on the realization that the human grasp of any truth is always partial and never complete. From such philosophically founded tolerance will come respect.

At the third level, ethical or religious tolerance derives from the moral responsibility to love and care for others, especially those different from us, even our enemies. Yet the different 'other' here is still the 'object' of one's love; it can celebrate our differences, but cannot overcome and transcend them completely in a higher unity.

Overcoming this objectification of the other is 'a mystical experience of tolerance'. It is 'the way one being exists in another and expresses the radical interdependence of all that exists'.

(Panikkar 1983: 23) Only this kind of mystical tolerance can overcome and transcend the contradictions and conflicts between religious traditions, bringing them into a higher communion.

There is, here, a continuous spectrum in the various levels of tolerance: from calculating the pragmatic limits of intolerance, through an intellectual realization for the need, and an ethical obligation for the practice of tolerance, to a spiritual celebration of the enrichment of diversity. Yet in a given context, one or the other perception will be the more operative, and so we need to limit the level of tolerance correspondingly.

This is still the form relationships of tolerance can take. What about the substantive content of our tolerance? If we are instrumentalizing practice of tolerance as a mutually beneficial complimentary exchange, we yet must ask: what is to be tolerated and what not? How do we set limits to intolerance without abandoning our own tolerance and becoming intolerant ourselves? This is indeed a delicate paradox that brings us to the necessity of dialogue as the sine qua non of tolerance.

Any understanding of tolerance that does not consider how limits must be set to intolerance would be impractical and naive. Hence we must set the social context within the pertinent level of tolerance, if indeed we are to cope with intolerance. For this some defining parameters must be effective both for individuals and for groups, if tolerance is to be a viable social option in a plural society and not hijacked by cynical and intolerant chauvinists. The following are basic for a just and decent society: social equality for all; distributive justice across every social divide; fundamental freedoms—political, religious, cultural, and peoples' participation. (Heredia 1996: 255–264)

We need to articulate an ideology of tolerance, a systematic statement of cohesive and convincing ideas in more than the vague generalities and pious sound bites. It must be reflected in laws that are not bureaucratically misapplied or politically misused or subverted by vested interests. We need a new determination to counter the politics of hate, which is compartmentalizing us into hostile communities.

But a tolerant society is less a matter of laws than of culture, though together they would be most effective. A culture of tolerance is a matter of empathy and compassion, and we have rich resources to draw on. However, there is no point in glorifying our past tolerance when it is being betrayed by present violent hostilities. For, tolerance in society must be more than a personal virtue, it must be a cultural characteristic, embedded in our social psyche. It must be a continuing socialization process that begins early at home and the school and is on-going in the public domain with the help of the media, something that amounts to a pedagogy of tolerance for a culture of tolerance.

Ideology and Myth

Panikkar distinguishes two dimensions of comprehension: ideological and mythic. 'Myth' here is not understood in the pejorative sense as opposed to fact, but rather as the 'horizon of intelligibility' (Panikkar 1983: 101) and hence a form of consciousness. It is the taken-for-granted, unquestioned, pre-understanding, something that is accepted in 'faith'; not an irrational, blind faith, but a non-rational, pre-articulate understanding. In *The Power of Myth* (1991) Joseph Campbell describes it as a collective dream that expresses the unarticulated depths of a people's unconscious, their deepest longings that they themselves may not be consciously aware of. More than ever, we need such collective dreams for our societies today. For 'myth' is a story, a narrative that poetically, not conceptually, points to an eternal truth. It is an imaginative, not merely rational, grasp that can only be expressed in symbol and metaphor.

Panikkar describes 'ideology', in this context as: 'the more or less coherent ensemble of ideas that make up critical awareness, i.e., the doctrinal system that enables you to locate yourself rationally…a spacio-temporal system constructed by the logos as a function of its concrete historical moment.' (Panikkar 1983 21)

An ideology for tolerance puts together systematically a set of rational ideas to justify and support the meaningfulness and practice of tolerance. In the Panikkarian sense, 'myth' is a heuristic construct 'against which any hermeneutic is possible'. It is taken for granted, unquestioned, a part of our pre-understanding, something we accept in 'faith'.

Ideologies appeal to the rational in us. We need open-ended ideologies ready to give an account of themselves, and which can be questioned and challenged. These have an affinity to non-violence and tolerance when they make ground. Close-ended ideologies are total products, rigid, dogmatic and unwilling to change. These have an affinity to violence and intolerance when they are aggressive and self-serving.

Myths use symbols and images and their appeal is non-rational, but not irrational, more intuitive and imaginative. Myth touches the places in our consciousness where reason does not enter and are the more powerful for that. Ideologies lend themselves to debate, but only an open, honest debate will be constructive. Ideologies can be liberating or disempowering and oppressive. Debate can sift the wheat from the chaff. Myths are an imagined universe. They are best shared with appreciation and understanding and a readiness to enter and discover new worlds though here too myths can be humanizing and ennobling or dehumanizing and belittling.

An ideology of tolerance will require a real change of heart to free us from our paranoia. Then the self-other difference can bring a higher-level unity in a more integrated whole. And sharing positives myths can bring a metanoia of our myths to liberate us from the paranoia of our ideologies. More explicitly, Gandhi's *Hind Swaraj* (1908) represented his core thinking though many then did not understand his stance; Hindutva (1989) is the essential ideological thinking of Savarkar, and its implications are now unfolding. It was Gandhi's endeavour to popularize 'Ramrajya' as a myth for an ecumenical future for all, a mythic utopia. It is contrary to the Hindu Rashtra of Hindutva, where the Ram Maryada, the Uttam Purush of Valmiki and Tulsidas evolves into Ram Rudra, the angry god.

This is not the place to develop an ideology of tolerance, but we have indicted resources to draw on and generate a discussion in the public domain, where public opinion is formed. For it is only in the mutual encounter of myths that they are deepened and enriched, and in the reciprocal exchange among ideologies that these become more open and refined and where the media should be playing a far more proactive role.

Distinguishing ideology and myth makes possible in our praxis, as an action-reflection-action process, a dialectical interaction between theory and practice, of imaginative mythic reflection and ideologically inspired action. It is our conviction that the constructive potential of such a dialectic can be fully realized only in a creative dialogue for both myth and ideology.

Pluralism and Tolerance

All pluralism implies difference. In society, difference between members is eventually founded on the polarity between the 'self' and the 'other' among different persons and diverse groups. The 'other' cannot simply be wished away, but always poses a question to the 'self', one that will not just go away. One can ignore the question only for a while, but the questioning cannot be so easily negated, unless one destroys the questioner. History bears witness to how dominant persons and groups have eliminated subordinate ones in massacres and genocides, or forcibly assimilated them in miscegenation or ethnocide. But where such brutal solutions cannot be attempted, either because of the realities on the ground or the ethical outrage it might cause, then tolerance can be our only viable human response. Certainly, it is for the multicultural, pluri-religious Indic society.

Moreover, it is important that this encounter between groups, between the self and the other, ego and alter, be facilitated and mediated by a third party—especially when 'communicative rationality' of Habermas (1991), which he defines as: 'oriented to achieving, sustaining and reviewing consensus—and indeed a consensus that rests on the intersubjective recognition of criticisable validity claims'—(Habermas 1984: 17) is conspicuous by its absence in the encounter. Hence the need to extend the dyad to a triad, with a third party as a reference point for a reality check, lest the powerful resolve differences in their own favour. Whether this be a more specific agency, like 'the nation-state, or simply the government', (Gupta 1996 :11) or a more general frame of reference.

For us, in the Indian scenario the most significant referent for the mediating state function is our Constitution which recognizes 'the principle of equality between groups *qua* group'. (Sheth 1989:8) This is the foundation for collective rights with special provision for the more vulnerable sections of our society, such as linguistic and religious minorities and socially and economically backward classes. And yet today there are powerful movements for homogenization within the same body-politic.

In a plural society with the many divides and differences, an understanding of tolerance must be correspondingly elaborated to match this complexity. There is also need for a dialogue between the 'self' and the 'other', one that moves through these dimensions and across these levels of tolerance to a fulfilling and enriching encounter of the 'self' and the 'other'. Obviously, an understanding of tolerance, especially in a pluralist society, must elaborate its many dimensions and distinct levels. Hence the need for a dialogue between the 'self' and the 'other', one that moves through these dimensions and across these levels of tolerance to a fulfilling and enriching encounter of the 'self' and the 'other'.

Pedagogy for Pluralism

Any pedagogy premised on tolerance must be non-violent and a negation of the 'pedagogy of violence' (Lele 1995) that promotes a politics of hate. Moreover, it will be a tolerance founded on a culture of dialogue as opposed to the 'culture of silence' (Freire 1972) that results from the politics of domination; we would need 'communicative rationality' to understand the other. (Habermas 1984) Non-violent pedagogies of tolerance can be spread across the spectrum of the various levels of tolerance that have been distinguished earlier. If these are to foster tolerance, then in a multicultural, pluri-religious society like ours it must necessarily be a pedagogy for pluralism. Indeed, it is the only viable alternative for the scale and depth of diversity in a society such as ours. Obviously such pedagogies have to be worked out in detail, only general indications are given here. Unfortunately, so far little official thinking has been done on pedagogic processes of relating to the different other.

At the pragmatic level it would be a pedagogy of adaptive coping and creative enabling. This would have to include intellectual skills and emotional discipline. At the intellectual level it would be a pedagogy of enquiry and discovery. The scientific methodology and the rationality it implies is a good illustration of this. Ethically and religiously it could be a pedagogy of freedom and responsibility, of love and commitment. Interpersonal encounter and social involvement can provide the context here. Spiritually and mystically it would be a pedagogy of love and union, an 'I-thou' celebration of our final destiny together. At all four levels our rich cultural and spiritual heritage can be drawn on and adapted for a contemporary context.

Culture of Tolerance

Unity in diversity is so intricately woven over centuries into the fabric of our societies in the Indian subcontinent, that a threat to diversity could have unintended and undesirable consequences as witnessed in the imposition of an ethno-religious nationalism in Sri Lanka, Pakistan and Myanmar. To feel a sense of belonging to the larger whole of the nation, a people's identity must be acknowledged and respected, or else they remain outsiders. In India, Hindu nationalism seems to have learned no lessons as they proceed to polarize the country between the majority and the default categories of the minorities and marginalized. Hegemonic impositions do not give people a sense of belonging, nor does it contribute to a culture of tolerance but rather undermines it. It creates a 'culture of silence', (Freire 1972) which eventually morphs into a culture of suspicion.

In our world today, plurality is an inescapable given, whether political-economic or socio-religious or ethno-linguistic or otherwise. For, the complexity of an imploding globalization in our modern world cannot be contained in any single worldview, (Rahner 1969: 26) nor can a dominant one be imposed on people without destroying their freedom and openness. In our multi-cultural and pluri-religious society, pluralism is a psychological challenge, a cultural imperative, an economic political necessity, a theological given. We need a pluralism inspired by a humanist, liberating and this-worldly ethic, premised on tolerance and sustained by dialogue. For a genuine pluralism is possible only within such a context. However, plurality necessarily implies difference. And how communities in a society deal with this different other is defining.

Communities could fall into indifference and distance each other, which may eventually lead to fragmentation of society, each community going its own way. Or a hostile and violent relationship between communities could polarize society, spilling over into collective violence and even civil war. But mutual affirmation and appreciation of difference can open into ever deeper levels of tolerance and broader dimensions of engagement. An enriching 'communion' or common union can inspire us not just to a 'unity in diversity', that accepts and respects differences, but rather a 'diversity in unity', that appreciates and celebrates difference. (Kothari 1988: 20) However, we must both interrogate and critique all those involved. For this, a culture of tolerance is imperative, and what we all most need, especially today is a conversion to tolerance.

Tolerance is more than a matter of mere endurance of, and resignation to differences, conflict resolution and emancipation. As a constructive and creative response to pluralism, it must include something more positive: the active acceptance of, and even the celebration of plurality. It must be as multifaceted as the broad spectrum of social pluralities it responds to: from political ideologies to economic systems; from intellectual worldviews to ethical values; from religious beliefs to cultural patterns; and from ethnic divisions to geographic regions. Moreover, we must celebrate our difference together in dialogue, not in isolation from others, for an inwardly directed dialogue becomes a monologue. This is true for individuals and groups. It is the kind of in-breeding that leads to a decline of the group's cultural and intellectual DNA.

As a response to pluralism we can distinguish progressive levels in our understanding, all deriving from a deepening realization of the reality, truth, satya, underlying our human situation; a reality that is radically pluralist and ultimately uniting, a truth that is essentially non-violent. These are not exclusive but rather overlapping dimensions and interpenetrating levels that form a continuous progression. This is the common ground we must seek to meet on and then move together to higher ground.

At times of rapid change and consequent tensions, collective pathologies of alienation and anomie are not uncommon. To break through to a sane and healthy social ethic as the old gives way to the new, we need a radical change of our collective myths, to escape the delusions of the old ideologies, whether religious, political or otherwise, and construct new ones. Cultures are socially constructed and so can be deconstructed. If we can accept religious affiliation to be a matter of freedom of conscience that can be informed and responsible, then the common concerns that bind the human community together can be brought back to centre stage in our shared lives to reverse the spiralling violence, to heal old wounds, to create a new future. The World Social Forum believes 'another world is possible'. But it is up to us to make it a better world than the one we inherited. This is a utopian ideal for any society, but it is still an ideal we can reach out to even if it remains beyond our grasp.

Unfortunately at present, majoritarianism is the dominant ideological response to the crises of plurality and polarization today, whereas pluralism as an ideological response addresses issues of diversity and difference with democratic equality and freedom. This requires some minimal orientation towards cooperation rather than conflict and finding some common ground where communication without recrimination is possible. This could be shared histories and values, overlapping identities and interests. Unfortunately, politicized religion and religionized politics is being used to whip up a culture of hate which is unbalanced and uncontrolled.

It confirms identities that are negative and exclusive, singular and solidary, rather than inclusive, multiple and fluid. Faultlines between communities get hardened and mutual hostility becomes embedded. A re-socialization process will be needed to create a climate of social tolerance and reciprocal acceptance once again. This is a precondition for a safe and stable multicultural society.

For we must realize now more than ever, tolerance and dialogue are defining ways of being human in our pluralist world. This demands a conversion of heart, an atmaparivartan, lest our world self-destructs.

Hermeneutics of Dialogue

Tolerance creates the space for communication between people. It is the necessary condition for any dialogue. This tolerance must have some measure of reciprocity or the more tolerant partner is disadvantaged and the encounter itself becomes problematic, unequal, and unstable. If tolerance is the sine qua non for dialogue, dialogue in turn facilitates the conditions for tolerance. However, there must be a minimal reciprocity between the parties involved.

Moreover, the level of tolerance sets the context for the depth of dialogue. Thus, corresponding to the levels of tolerance indicated earlier we can either have a pragmatic political dialogue, an intellectual philosophic one, an ethical religious one or a spiritual mystical one. This requires that we exorcise the negative sentiments, prejudices, stereotypes, which are so embedded in the myths we live by and the ideologies we act from. Such a constructive engagement across the levels of tolerance can deepen and enrich our myths and open up and refine our ideologies.

However, even in favourable conditions:

> Dialogue is a difficult art. It means engaging in conversation with the intention of jointly clarifying the issues, rather than having them one's own way; of multiplying voices, rather than reducing their number; of widening the set of possibilities, rather than aiming at a wholesale consensus (that relic of monotheistic dreams stripped of politically incorrect coercion); of jointly pursuing understanding, instead of aiming at the others defeat; and all in all being animated by the wish to keep the conversation going, rather than by a desire to grind it to a halt. (Bauman 2011: 172)

The focus here is on rationality and rational meaning. The nature of dialogic communication focuses less on these than on interpretive meaningfulness. Dialectics is based on a difference of opposites, on thesis and anti-thesis, from which the synthesis emerges. Dialogue is premised on differences as complementary, brought together in a conversation, awaiting the moment of coherence, of fulfilment, of a 'fusion' of different horizons that will bring a new and more enriching perspective to each other's truths, harmonizing and enhancing, relativizing and contextualizing them.

For Panikkar, 'dialogue' is a most fundamental condition of our existence. It is our way of being. 'Dialogue is, fundamentally, opening myself to another so that he might speak and reveal my myth…Dialogue is a way of knowing myself and of disentangling my own point of view from other viewpoints and from me.' (Panikkar, 1983: 242)

In dialogue the 'self' and the 'other' are both discovered and enriched; so are the cultural 'other' and especially the 'counter-cultural other', within my own culture and across cultures too. For as we unveil our 'self' in the 'other', and the 'other' in our 'self', we will find that our deepest identity and bonding transcends all differences in an immanent I-thou communion. It this that makes a dialogue pedagogic: learning together and from each other. Indeed, dialogue is the most constructive and creative practice of tolerance, the only effective way to really cope with the bewildering diversity that challenges and confounds us, as a precarious legacy and a precious treasure.

However, self-transparency requires an internal dialogue within as the condition for an external one without. Only such openness overcomes our prejudgments, our prejudices, the unconscious ideologies and mindsets, which eventually can only bring a 'clash of civilizations'. Thus an intrapersonal dialogue is the pre-condition for an interpersonal one: openness within the self so that one is open to other and not locked in a 'walled-in consciousness'. So too is an intracommunity dialogue imperative for an intercommunity one. If dialogue is to be pedagogic then there must be a 'fusion of horizons', each side learning from the other and meeting on common ground to journey together to higher ground.

But genuine dialogue is not possible where identities are exclusive, singular and solidary, rather than inclusive, multiple and fluid. For without tolerance and openness such conversations become recriminatory debates that further harden faultlines and embed mutual hostilities, making reconciliation ever more distant. Sadly our social tradition of tolerance seems to be increasingly displaced from public life.

A majoritarianism is uniformizing our diversity, with an ethnic Hindu nationalism. Thus alienating the minorities and marginalized and creating hostility and even violent conflict between groups and communities, including Hindus who want to retain their distinctiveness. The present crisis of intolerance and violence has to be reversed into a culture of tolerance that opens to a culture of dialogue, as the normal way of coping with difference, whether religio-cultural or eco-political. More recently, on 4 February 2019 in Abu Dhabi in the troubled Middle East, the Al Azhar Grand Imam and Pope Francis affirmed 'Human Fraternity for World Peace and Life Together': 'the adoption of a culture of dialogue as the path; mutual cooperation as the code of conduct; reciprocal understanding as the method and standard'. (https://www.laciviltacattolica.com/human-fraternity-for-world-peace-and-life-together/) It will take vision and leadership for South Asian leaders to do likewise.

Domains of Dialogue

In dialogue, transparency between the self and the other can lead to a transformative experience for both sides. Human beings are meant to be interrelated and interactive, not isolated and alone. That is why solitary confinement is such an inhuman punishment. Dialogue and conversation, then, are intrinsic to the human condition, the very language of our existence, the necessary site for interpreting all our experience. For we are constructed and deconstructed in dialogue with ourselves and others, as the German philosopher, Hans Georg Gadamer (1900–2002), insists, 'the conversation that we are is one that never ends'. (Gadamer 1989: 95) Human beings are social beings. For better or worse, growth and development is always in the context of the interactions with others in society, for both the personal and the social: positive interactions produce positive growth, negative ones are diminishing and can even be dehumanizing.

Thus at the psycho-socio level, to be an authentic human person one must be interpersonal or risk a dangerous neurosis or even a psychosis. At the socio-cultural one, to truly assimilate one's own culture one must be inter-cultural, and a really cultured society would have to be inter-cultural as well. At the eco-political level, it is only through egalitarian participation and equitable exchange that a progressive economic and political development is possible for individuals and communities, for societies and nations. Finally, at the socio-religious level, to be authentically religious in one's own tradition one must be inter-religiously involved in others, for to be to be true to itself and discover its own religious depths, a religious tradition needs to reach out to other religious traditions in concord, not confrontation.

Here are a few pertinent sutras on human interactions as the basis for dialogue:

to be a person is to be interpersonal;
to be cultured is to be inter-cultural;
to develop is to participate and exchange;
to be religious is to be inter-religious;

Psychologists have convinced us of the first; sociologists are trying to teach us the second; political economists are promoting the third; theologians are coming to realize the fourth.

Dialogue is surely more than a verbal exchange, as is all human communication. The Pontifical Council for Inter-Religious Dialogue (1991: no. 42) listed four pertinent domains which are slightly nuanced for our purpose here:

1. '*the dialogue of life*, where people strive to live in an open and neighbourly spirit…'
2. '*the dialogue of action*', in which we 'collaborate for the integral development and liberation of people'.
3. '*the dialogue of experience*, where persons, rooted in their own religious traditions, share their spiritual riches…'
4. '*the dialogue of intellectual exchange*, where specialists seek to deepen their understanding of their respective religious heritages…'

These are distinct but not separated domains, they interact and overlap and allow a multiplicity of diverse dialogues with a variety of different partners. Moreover, the reciprocity between the 'self' and the 'other' in dialogue between the dialogic partners will correspond to the levels of tolerance they bring to it, and on their differing understandings of the self and the other.

Thus at the pragmatic/political level of tolerance, the other is perceived as the limitation of the self. Here dialogue becomes a practical way of overcoming differences and keeping one's integrity, rather than confrontation which could end in the assimilation or in elimination of the other. At the intellectual level, the other is seen as complementary to the self, dialogue seeks to mutually overcome the limitations of the self with help of the other, rather than instrumentalize the other in the pursuit of self-interest. At the ethical/religious level, the self, in accepting moral responsibility for the other, reaches out to establish relationships of equity, which are reciprocated in their interactions. Here dialogue becomes a sharing of mutual responsibilities. At the mystical/spiritual level, the other is perceived beyond a limitation of need, complement or obligation, but as the fulfilment of the self in the other and finally in the Ultimate Other. Here dialogue calls for a celebration of one another.

In this perspective, the dialogue of life, living in peaceful co-existence implies sharing and the common myths we live by, which is then deepened in the dialogue of life-experiences. There can be an even deeper level of not just sharing mythic communication but mystical experience as well. Collaborative action requires some level of ideological and political consensus, which can be built by an ideological exchange. Thus, life and experience are at the level of 'myth' and mysticism; action and articulation at that of 'ideology' and politics.

All this will demand a more liberal and humanist approach within each tradition. Hence, an intra-religious dialogue is a necessary condition for an inter-religious one, otherwise we will have a debate not a dialogue, a controversy not complementarity. Panikkar has described the intra-religious dialogue at the personal level thus:

> An inner dialogue within myself, an encounter in depth of my personal religiousness, having met another religious experience on that very intimate level. In other words, if *interreligious* dialogue is to be real dialogue, an *intrareligious* dialogue must accompany it, i.e., it must begin with my questioning myself and the relativity of my beliefs (which does not mean *relativism*), accepting the challenge of a change, a conversation and the risk of upsetting my traditional patterns. (Panikkar 1978: 40)

Dialogue for Reconciliation

All unequal exchange, whether between classes, castes, genders or even between communities, regions, etc., eventually becomes exploitative and oppressive. To be truly creative, dialogue must be equal and open, committed and free, beginning with mutual respect and continuing in reciprocal enrichment.

If friendship must find or make equals, as Aristotle argues in his *Nicomachean Ethics*, (Book Eight), so must fair exchange in dialogue find or make equal partners. For any dialogue that starts with assumptions of superiority on one side, or has a hidden agenda can never be an equal, open exchange. The challenge is for the partners in the dialogue to give up their insider perspective and take an outsider one, by positioning themselves on common ground, a level playing field, where all the partners to the dialogue can be equal and free and open.

Only on such a common ground can all engage as equal partners and set the conditions for a deeper inter-community dialogue. To clear a common ground for an equal dialogue demands a reciprocity of perspectives, i.e., seeing ourselves as others see us and vice versa. This a necessary exercise for all the partners in the dialogue, individuals and groups, for communities and other agents as well. But given the communal polarities and sharp divides, building a consensus for the common ground will be a difficult and delicate task, and yet it is really the place to begin a reconciliation with some common minimum programme.

This requires that we do not bring the baggage of our past negativities to the table; it will only revive and revitalize them. Rather we bracket all this away, not to abandon or betray our own convictions and commitments, but to hold them in abeyance as we reach out to each other, as in any attempt at resolving differences. This is a pragmatic approach to conflict resolution. It need not be a great leap of faith in the other, but a step by step process towards a common goal of conflict-resolution and bringing a fair reconciliation and a just peace.

Given the right conditions, dialogue is a powerful process for reconciliation, just as reconciliation is a potent initiator of dialogue. For both processes timing and persistence are critical, or they may well degenerate into contestation and recrimination, and become not reconciliatory but inflammatory. Many efforts at dialogue and reconciliation fail because the preconditions, like tolerance and openness, are not in place or when the level of tolerance and degree of dialogue are mismatched. For the level of mutual tolerance sets the context for the degree of dialogue. Furthermore, an 'indispensable prerequisite' or such openness is 'a deep human honesty in searching for the truth wherever it can be found; a great intellectual openness in this search, without conscious preconceptions or willingly entertained prejudices; and finally a profound loyalty towards one's own tradition'. (Panikkar 1978: 34)

Thus for a dialogue of life there must be at least pragmatic tolerance or else peaceful co-existence becomes problematic, and reconciliation precarious. This is the minimum requirement for reconciliatory dialogue. Tolerance founded on the mutual acceptance of the complementary other is the basis for a dialogue of action, which can be mutually beneficial and open to reconciliation. Tolerance that accepts ethical responsibility opens us to a dialogue to clarify values and norms for a reconciliatory process. When tolerance seeks spiritual-mystical union, the dialogue can be a sharing of experiences, which reaches out beyond anomalies and contradictions. This can set off a healing process of reconciliation and peace.

However, in all dialogues for reconciliation there must be a reference point that orients the process purposefully. In a family quarrel, the common good of the family grounds the appeal for harmony; in gender debates, our common humanity must be the accepted point of reference. Similarly, in inter-community exchanges it must be the over-riding priority of the common good of all, not partisan vested interests.

Multiple Belongings

Inclusive, flexible and multiple identities allow for multiple belongings. Such groups have soft and porous boundaries. Conversely, exclusive, rigid and totalizing identities demand a commitment to a singular group. These groups harden group borders and do not approve of cross-border relations; they may even penalize members for transgressions.

If exclusive and rigid religious identities of individuals and communities yield to more inclusive and flexible ones, then multiple belongings are possible—and indeed necessary in a pluralist society like ours, where boundaries overlap. We can and do belong to more than one group without compromising ourselves, and find room enough to adjust to their various claims, e.g., one's family by birth, by marriage, by adoption.

When group boundaries overlap, dialogue can open social and community space for multiple belongings. However, if the identity of the community is exclusive and totalizing, its interaction in society becomes problematic, for a change of identity and allegiance will be a threat to this community, and disruptive in that society. Panikkar's experience is so reaffirming: 'I "left" as a Christian, "found myself" as a Hindu, and I "return" as a Buddhist, without having ceased to be a Christian.' (Panikkar 1978: 2)

Multi-lingualism can provide a deeper insight into multiple belongings. We speak different languages in different contexts. Learning a new language does not demand that we abandon the old one, rather it enriches our understanding and facility in both. Each new language represents a whole other universe, a worldview of its own. We must enter into this to really absorb the deep structures of its syntax and access the hidden treasures of its symbolic universe and worldview, without abandoning the earlier ones. This is an apt metaphor for dialogue across our multiple worlds of culture and religion.

Culture of Violence

For all the progress we might congratulate ourselves on, violence is still the final arbitrator to conflicts and divisions that increasingly riddles our societies and our world. A catalogue of the violence of these last years—genocides, atrocities, riots, terrorism, murders, rapes—is merely the external evidence of the constant social tension between countries, regions, communities, groups, individuals that never go away but too easily escalate out of control. We must reverse the spiral of violence that engulfs us like a cyclonic tidal wave, and reflect together on what peace and harmony today might mean for us.

Collective violence in India must be addressed in its upstream origins and in its downstream impact. In a polarized society like ours, ending overt physical violence is a necessary first step. It is the political culture that legitimizes and supports such violence with its politics of hate, fuelled by a rhetoric of vengefulness for historical wrongs—more imagined than real but narrated to inflame collective political passions. It is a dangerous way of mobilizing political support and consolidating vote banks. As long as there is a payoff for such identity politics, the violence it precipitates will continue, finding new ways of expression: whether it be 'love-jihad' (interreligious marriages) or the gau rakshaks (cow vigilantes), or filing FIRs (First Information Reports) on dubious charges with police connivance—in other words an institutional prejudice against the minorities and marginalized.

The citizen must resist the manipulations of such identity politics and focus on a politics of interest. They must hold the politicians they elect responsible for fulfilling their public obligations, punishing non-performing ones at the hustings. Unfortunately, cynical leaders can manipulate unwary citizens into extraordinary violence. The Sangh Parivar have propagated a Hindu nationalism, which has become Tocqueville's classic 'tyranny of the majority'. (Tocqueville 1862) We need a counter-narrative to this rhetoric of hate and its agenda of communal polarizing and political consolidation.

To recall the Preamble of the UNESCO Constitution quoted in chapter one: 'That since wars begin in the minds of men, it is in the minds of men that the defences of peace must be constructed.' It is within our minds and in their hearts, that evil is first born and nurtured and then set off on a rampage without. (http://www.unesco.org/education/pdf/UNESCO_E.PDF) A cessation of violence will not change the mindset of people, if there is no reconciliation between communities and groups, no healing within them, then the tensions between the alienated communities will invite a repetition of the violence which might well be more intense for having been suppressed. This could be deliberately provoked or triggered by something trivial. So many communal conflagrations have been manipulated thus by vested political interests in the background.

Majoritarian Hindu nationalism is politicizing Hindu traditions, and sacralizing the nation. We have not learned from our neighbours and other states around the world that when religion is espoused by the state, it compromises, if not terminates, liberty, equality and fraternity for all its citizens, beginning with scapegoating the other and the vulnerable.

This is in complete contradiction to our Constitution and so very out of sync with the expansive capaciousness of the sanatan dharma. We must exorcise this culture of violence and hate, which is alien to our traditions and has overtaken our country more recently. But the discontents of disorienting rapid change has made people feel insecure and apprehensive, and the hapless become scapegoats for collective violence.

We need to recall that non-violence and satyagraha were once integral to the mass movement of our freedom struggle and re-socialize our people once again into the culture of peace as the foundation of our constitutional democracy. Non-violence is not an idea whose time has passed, rather it is more relevant than ever in our time. For, while the will to power remains one of our most insidious human temptations, the longing for peace is part of our deepest human yearnings.

Peace and Power

In common parlance peace is often understood as the opposite of war and conflict. These necessarily imply the use of force, which is legitimated as a means to the end pursued, as happens with what has been called a just war or a justifiable conflict. All too often such use of force is seen as a preamble to peace, a war to end all wars, a conflict now to minimize greater conflict later. This amounts to a negative perception of peace through its opposite. But it does give us one crucial element in our understanding of peace, namely, that as a minimum, peace is not compatible with the continuing use of force. However, the problem of a peace founded on the use or threat of force remains. This was the basis of the Pax Romana, '*Si vis pacem, para bellum*' (If you want peace, prepare for war).

When peace is not reconcilable with violence and certainly not with violation, peace founded on violence is an anomaly. Such violence can only be thought of as a preliminary for peace, not something compatible with it, for any peace brought about by violent or violating means would itself be an unjustifiable peace. However, if peace implies the absence of force and violence, it does not mean a negation or the absence of power. But we need to understand what kind of power is compatible with a stable peace.

The classic definition of Max Weber (1947) of power as the capacity to impose one's will against resistance, is an understanding of power as domination, as 'power *over*', that implies a zero-sum game in which there must be losers in order that they may be winners. This is a political understanding of power. Here violence is necessarily implicated in any exercise of power, in fact 'violence is nothing more than the most flagrant manifestation of power'. (Arendt 1970: 35) C. Wright Mills draws the logical consequence: 'all politics is a struggle for power; the ultimate kind of power is violence.' (Mills 1956: 171)

Here the fundamental principle of societal integration assumed is coercion, and competition and conflict is an on-going social process. It is precisely this power as domination which corrupts, and when absolute, corrupts absolutely. Moreover, an imposed peace can never be free and is not likely to be fair either. It is a balance of power, which all too readily becomes a balance of terror, very far from the peace we long for.

A more functional understanding of 'power' articulated by Talcott Parsons is that of efficacy or capacity to achieve or effect something. (Parsons 1963) Here, the principle of societal integration is consensus, which makes possible cooperation and collaboration between persons and groups rather than competition or conflict. Such multiple capacities need not be in any inherent contradiction with each other, though they may well need to be controlled and coordinated, if they are to complement, and not conflict with each other.

However, no society is integrated exclusively by consensus or coercion, and in no society would power be premised on just one or the other principle. For even where there is coercion and competition there can still be a coincidence of interests, that make for some measure of cooperation, just as when there is consensus and cooperation there still could be a conflict of interests that makes for competition or worse.

For any viable social order there must be control and coordination. This cannot be done by mere coercion and shear force, but must be based on some level of consent, that legitimates power, and stabilizes it. This is what Weber called 'authority'. However, legitimacy can still be questioned and subverted, particularly by those under this authority, as would happen when power is dominating and not enabling.

But such authority is always open to realignment because it requires the consent of the governed. This makes power over others, even when 'legitimated', inherently unstable. As also the peace premised on it. However, power as enabling efficacy and enhancing capacity, implies not a balance but rather a complementarity of powers that requires coordination more than control. It is not only compatible but can be very much the foundation of a sound and stable peace, precisely because it is not premised on domination but on complementarity. But all power is always a means. If it becomes an end in itself it inevitably violates the ends it is meant to serve.

A sound and stable peace must be founded on such complementarity, on enabling power not on domination. Following Panikkar we shall attempt to give some content to such a longing for peace. (Panikkar 1995) After the Romans, St Augustine defined peace as 'the tranquillity of order'. But tranquillity is still a rather passive understanding, and surely peace must have a more positive content. Thus besides justice, which is implied by order, there must be freedom, if this just order is to be compatible with human dignity.

Peace must be 'the fruit of justice'. A just social order necessarily implies freedom if it is to be compatible with human dignity. Moreover, if the dialectical tension between justice and order is effectively and constructively resolved, then we would have a third element in our understanding of peace which is harmony. This is a treasured Asian value. Each of these three elements—justice, freedom and harmony—can be described, but we still need to put them together in a collective 'myth of peace'. (Heredia 1999) In fact this is what most salvation myths are intended to express. This is the peace that is reflected in popular greetings: pax vobis, shalom alaikum, As-salāmu ʿalaykum, shanti om, etc. This is the promise of peace that needs to be explored as a foundation for creating a brave new world.

Sri Aurobindo once said, 'All problems of existence are essentially problems of harmony.' (Aurobindo 1965, Vol. 2) Indeed, for most religious traditions harmony is the ultimate structure of the universe. But in our pluralist human world, harmony must be not just a 'coincidence of opposites', it must make space and place for all, without repression, without violence. Such harmony, then, can only prevail when it is inclusive of the other two elements—freedom and justice. This is precisely why the harmony we speak of must be a continuous creation.

The ultimate subject of this peace is not the isolated individual, it is the person in community, or a community of persons. Hence the freedom we want is not just a freedom *from*, it must also be a freedom *for*. It cannot be merely an individualist liberty that so easily regresses into license. Rather freedom must be inclusive of both: a more universal harmony and a more compelling justice. So also the justice we seek is not retributive but restorative justice, one that brings reconciliation and forgiveness, and includes harmony and freedom. This is precisely why such justice cannot contradict love. And the harmony this fructifies into must be creative and fraternal, not a default option. Finally peace must be grounded in reality as the truth, the satya, that can make us really and truly free.

Moreover, this peace and harmony we long for and dream of must be a continuing quest, perhaps the most relevant and deepest quest for the new millennium, a quest that not only bonds us each to the other, but encompasses the whole of the world in its embrace, in one inclusive human community, beginning with our families and our neighbourhoods, in ever widening oceanic circles to include all peoples and countries, and indeed the whole cosmos. Such an inclusive community of solidarity would inevitably be a counter-cultural one today.

Furthermore, this solidarity must include the environment. We cannot keep degrading it and expect to live peaceful, dignified lives. The environment represents the cosmic dimension of peace and as Panikkar insists, 'human peace is bound up with the cosmic order, the human peace is our share of that order'. (Panikkar 1995) Indeed, this the Vedic concept of 'rta'.

Ecology has taught us that collective problems can only be resolved by the corresponding collective community: global ones by the global community, local ones by local communities. So too collective violence demands a correspondingly collective response in this sea of the violence. However, there are commonalities across these incidents that demand a common counter narrative, which will respond to our longing for peace, expressed in an inspiring myth of peace.

Tragically, we have too few creative and inspiring myths to live by and too many fads and fashions to distract us. In desperation we revive and cling to images and symbols that draw on the darkest recesses of our destructive potential. Thus we seek redress in violence for our injured psyches, both individual and collective; we seek redemption in revenge for our traumatized memories both personal and social. Apologies are demanded but forgiveness is forgotten, revenge seeks satisfaction while reconciliation becomes alien, power is glorified and weakness is belittled. Yet all this is ultimately a violation of our truest selves and a betrayal of our deepest dreams. Such violence cannot but alienate us from ourselves and each other, and terrorize us in a nightmare without hope.

Gandhi did try to express such an ideal of peace with his

secularized myth of 'Ramraj'. But this could not quite free itself from its religious context and so was not as universal in its appeal as Gandhi intended. Now it has been misappropriated to sanction the very opposite of what Gandhi stood for, Ram Rudra, the war-like and not Ram Saumya, the gentle.

But if Gandhi does not leave us with an effective myth of peace he does give us an image of society that can point us towards a deeper mythical foundation for this peace. Gandhi's vision of the oceanic circles, centring on little communities and neighbourhoods, ever widening and overlapping, reinforcing and inclusive, reverses the pyramidal image of a society stratified by class and/or segmented by caste hierarchies. It gives us a commanding image and symbol for peace on which we can hope to base our new foundational social myth, our deep collective dream of peace. This will not be so much part of the logic we reason with, as part of the myth we live by, i.e., our non-rational or rather trans-rational grasp of reality we live by and live for.

Bridging the Divides

This nation was born in the trauma of the Partition. Since then the Hindu-Muslim divide on the subcontinent has still not been resolved. 'In terms of group relations, the Hindu-Muslim coexistence of the nineteenth century has never been fully re-created, except at a very upper-class level.' (Nussbaum 2025: 332) Rather, the country's commitment to secularism, whether Nehruvian or Gandhian, has eroded. Hindu ethno-nationalism has now come to the fore and its political dominance has been established in the last two general elections.

The need for a genuine pluralism and an active civil society cannot be overestimated, as also the urgency of practical strategies for effectively dealing with the upstream causes of such violence. What we really need is our own Truth and Justice Commission that will heal the wounds of the past, sublimate historical memories that have simmered in our collective unconscious, and inspire hope for our future together. And if this seems too utopian a dream to strive after then the alternative is a collective hell from which there will be no escape. But we must first heal the past, if we are to recover our future.

Today religious extremism and fundamentalism is whipping up a wave of terror that seems unbalanced and uncontrolled. In a multicultural society like ours continuing and intense cultural conflict often reaches an impasse. With new technologies of massive social communication and collective mobilization in which competing groups clash and conflicting interests implode, this can become a point of no return and no advance.

The communal divides in India are reaching this point, if they have not already. The weak and vulnerable are being pushed to the brink. Hindu extremism is indulging in politics of hate against other religious minorities, especially demonizing Muslims; the upper-caste atrocities are forcing the SCs and STs to the margins; the upper and middle classes have little consideration for the poor when it comes to privileging growth over equity. Identity politics has constructed a Hindu majority vote bank that has swept the Hindutva committed government to power a second time by even bigger margins.

In the aftermath of years of collective violence, governments have made very little attempt at reconciliation and healing. The basic tolerance needed for this is woefully lacking. Communal relations have been politicized to the point where there's little communication between communities, trapped in their prejudices and ideologies. The consequent polarization between hostile communities crowded into a restricted space, with limited opportunities of escape, makes collective conflict so much the more likely. Furthermore, the government treats dissent as anti-national and subversive.

Yet these groups cannot remain in hostile isolation from each other when they share so much in common, but polarizing the differences can override this. So when the government fails to be the third-party mediator, civil society must step in to work at the slow process of changing the mindset of the people to whom governments are finally accountable. For as John Locke (1632–1704) insisted in his second treatise: 'The government is not legitimate unless it is carried on with the consent of the governed.' (Locke 1690)

To break the impasse in our polarized society we need a people's movement with a narrative to counter the majoritarian Hindu nationalism starting at the grass roots and scaled up to the highest levels of governance. It might seem a disheartening task, but RSS, founded in 1925, began its movement for Hindu Rashtra almost a century ago. Playing on the 'hurt sentiments' of the upper caste Hindus, it built itself shakha by shakha, into a national movement, estimated to be of some 5-6 million volunteers in 56,859 shakhas by 2016. There are no official figures available. (Anderson W. 1984) The *Hindu* estimates the number of shakhas have doubled over in the last ten years. Its extended family, the Sangh Parivar, includes a wide spectrum of hundreds of organizations with millions of members, covering most areas of society. (See list of affiliate Parivar_members (https://en.wikipedia.org/wiki/Sangh_Parivar#Sangh)

However the nationalism it propagates in its political rampage is exclusive and marginalizes the other, even demonizes the Muslims as the largest minority and so particularly threatening. Its inspiration is based on othering difference not on foregrounding complementarity, whereas Hinduism is expansive in its teachings and inclusive within its structure. Our freedom movement, in which the RSS had little if any part, culminated with a liberal republican Constitution for an inclusive transformative revolution, a Fabian gradualism towards a social democracy.

The BJP's quest for a Hindu Rashtra has morphed into saffron neoliberalism, with authoritarian characteristics. The tyranny of the majority shows little respect for a constitutional regime of rights. Eventually such tyrannies turn inward on their own people. For a majoritarianism without law and minority rights is not democracy, rule of the people, but mobocracy, rule of the mob. The many lynchings reported are a presage of this.

Points of Engagement

Collective violence must be comprehended and responded to at multiple levels of discourse and analysis. The psychopathology of individuals that support such conflict must be considered, but because it is 'collective', such violence must be understood in terms of group interactions and social structures. Hence besides the socio-psychological one, we must consider other dimensions of discourse as well: the socio-political, the socio-cultural and the socio-religious.

Already in 1994, the UNESCO International Conference on Education in Geneva, presented 'Proposals for a Culture of Peace'. These represent pertinent suggestions for a rather comprehensive reform agenda, quoted here in full:

> Proposals for a Culture of Peace
> Presented to the International Conference on Education.
> (Geneva. October 1994)
>
> (a) Training and practice of conflict resolution and mediation in school systems, among staff and students, and extension through community involvement to the rest of society.
>
> (b) Linkage of school activities to ongoing activities in the community which promote participation by all in culture and development.
>
> (c) Incorporation into curricula of information about social movements for peace and non-violence, democracy and equitable development.
>
> (d) Extension of the sense of community not only to all peoples but also to all life on the planet, with the aim of preserving both the world's cultural diversity and its ecology for future generations.
>
> (e) Systematic review and renovation of curricula to ensure an approach to ethnic, racial and cultural differences which emphasizes their equality and unique contributions to the enrichment of the common good.
>
> (f) Systematic review and renovation of the teaching of history, to give as much emphasis to non-violent social change as to military aspects of history, with special attention given to the role of women in history.
>
> (g) Teaching of science in terms of its relation to culture and society, as a tool which can be used for war or for peace, for exploitation or for co-operative development.
>
> (UNESCO 1995: 48)

The only long-term way of dealing with collective violence in our country is effective and firm mediation by the state as a neutral and just third party that is acceptable not necessarily to the extremists across the divide but to the vast masses of moderate and sensible citizens that are waiting for a cessation of this communal madness to get on with their real lives. Dipankar Gupta's (2002, 2004) insights into social pathology provide some effective ways of dealing with riots and containing the violence. The most important thing, he urges, is for the state to make sure the perpetrators are made accountable to the law so that their risk of precipitating any future violence becomes greater than any anticipated gain from joining the mayhem. The state must also uncompromisingly guarantee and protect its citizens' rights.

This will require effective political will which in fact some states in the Union have demonstrated. It must be noted that communal violence plays a much-reduced role in the electoral politics of these states. As long such violence yields electoral returns, politicians will use them to their own advantage. Enacting laws to prevent and penalize communal riots must also focus on post-riot remedial measures as also on pre-riot preventative ones. However, such measures address the problem at the socio-political level only.

At the cultural level we must eschew the kind of homogeneity, such as projected by 'cultural nationalism': Hindi, Hindu, Hindustan; one language, one religion, one nation. This can only result in alienation and worse for our culturally diverse communities, not to mention the awful impoverishment of our rich and plural heritage. Rather we need a certain cultural autonomy for all our diverse communities, one that expresses constructive interdependence rather than subservient dependence or subversive independence. In other words, we need an interculturality to construct a community of communities all the way from the grass roots up to our federal polity. The Gandhian ideal of inclusive 'oceanic circles' has much relevance here.

All this will demand a further commitment to promote cultural and religious pluralism, which can only be done by strengthening civil society so as to privilege positive and inclusive identities. This will further require a transformation of the family and a reorientation of community, something that can be done by civil society initiatives better than by state intervention. Moreover, a true religious pluralism will need as a minimum an acceptance of the secular state as the neutral mediator among religious traditions and between their followers. But more positively inter-community dialogue becomes imperative, if mutual understanding and inter-community harmony is to pre-empt inter-communal conflict and collective violence.

We need other strategies at the socio-psychological level too. Within families, the encouragement of competition and consumerism can only add to the kinds of alienation and anomie that perpetuate the identity crisis on which identity politics of the most regressive kinds feed. We must develop positive not negative identities, inclusive not exclusive ones. And the family and the school are the best place to begin such initiatives. This will mobilize identities not in the direction of perpetuating divisions and tensions, but rather towards addressing common interests and concerns.

Beginning with a minimum of at least pragmatic tolerance, a dialogue of life, peaceful co-existence can be an opening to further tolerance and dialogue, eventually opening to reconciliation and peace, as has been effectively demonstrated by the mohalla committees and the committed citizens for peace groups. This becomes a multi-pronged practical strategy in addressing the issue of collective violence on a long-term basis.

These are localized strategies. They can be multiplied and generalized to higher levels, to national and even international ones as well, once this gets the momentum of a people's movement. However, all this will demand an 'alternative politics', one that is more participative and accountable, and with this an 'alternative development', which is less consumerist and more egalitarian as well. In other words, constitutional, not populist politics, focused more on substantive than electoral democracy.

Cultural Disarmament

Tragically modern man with his loss of innocence in a disenchanted world has no longer any abiding myths. Today more than ever we need such bonding myths to sustain our world. Now myths are collective imaginaries, never individual projects, and the 'myth of peace' is one in which we can all share. Certainly it is one whose time has now come in our tired and torn, broken and bruised world. But as yet we have no such common myths. Even the symbols and images we use for peace are quite inadequate or needlessly divisive. The tragedy of modern humanity seems to be that it has too few creative and inspiring myths to live by and too many competing ideologies to die for. And so in desperation, we revive and cling to images and symbols that draw on the darkest recesses of our destructive potential, like the trishul and the talwar as symbols of peace-keeping.

The myth of peace must express our collective dream of a free, just, harmonious world. If it is to redeem us from a destructive future, it must become the common ground for our dialogues. At this profound level of myth, peace can be an end in itself, as in fact is so universally expressed in religious traditions, and utopian ideologies of various political persuasions.

If this dream of peace is to become a reality, we must divest ourselves of a great deal of the presumptions and pre-options we have been, and still are being, socialized into by exclusive communal identities and religious fundamentalisms, national extremists and radical rationalism. Reaching out across group boundaries and overcoming our prejudices and stereotypes is no easy task. For negative community perceptions and consequent interrelationships may well have deep historic origins. However, we must not allow our history to control our destiny, or our negative inheritance to become our fate. For, 'even if history cannot be rewritten, an apology could set the ball rolling to heal festering wounds, trigger rapprochement and, in turn, promote better relations between communities in a world that is engulfed by many of the conflicts nurtured on the bedrock of past wrongs.' (Desai and Siddhu 2019: 85)

There are numerous examples of the reconciliatory effect of such honest apologies on hostile communities, especially when made by the appropriate authority at an appropriate time. Eventually we must come to terms with our collective memories and allow our wounded psyche to heal, or these will fester within.

Hence before we can begin a dialogue at any level, in any domain, we must first dialogue among ourselves and even within our self. For the myth of peace must first be rooted, individually and collectively, in our hearts and minds, our cultures and religions. The more open and egalitarian a society is the more fruitful the dialogue will be. A society divided by caste and class, compartmentalized by culture and religion stymies dialogic communication and may actually be counter-productive in bridging the distance between groups and communities.

Strange as it may seem there are vested interested in conflict and violence. These feed of the spoils of human oppression and suffering, neutralizing, or terminating a threatening or otherwise dispensable opponent. Some of these are ideologically committed extremists, like terrorists. But there also others whose interest is in the political advantage social conflict can bring. Peace promoters are hated and opposed by such people. Consequently, communal conflict can become an on-going process, whose origins are lost in the past, and whose future has no end in sight.

In such long-term battles, a cultural community can dig itself into a kind of cultural trench warfare. In such a war of attrition the only contemporary alternatives seem to be to retreat, which would be dangerous and even unviable, or to mobilize for total conflict and mass destruction, which would be an inhuman price to pay even for survivors.

Panikkar's radical solution for such a situation is a 'cultural disarmament'. It involves stepping back from our cultural entrenchments to seek common ground for an inter-cultural dialogue as a way to deeper understanding of peace and harmony. Panikkar understood this 'as the abandonment of the rut' in which we have entrenched ourselves; such 'a disarmament is to make oneself vulnerable and must be realized slowly, but forms an essential condition for being able to establish a dialogue in parity with all the cultures of the earth' (Panikkar 1995) on equal and open ground for inter-culturality. Against Huntington's 'clash of civilisations', (Huntington 1996) Panikkar proposes an inter-cultural dialogue.

Similarly in a pluri-religious society already exploding in

violence, we need to disarm religious fundamentalisms of all hues, and open ourselves to finding common ground in values and commitments we can all share so that an inter-religious dialogue can enrich us and the religious traditions to which we belong. This requires a radical change of heart, from a history of violence to a commitment to non-violence, from the pursuit of power to the quest for peace, from a pragmatic to a deeper level of tolerance, from a self-righteous monologue with ourselves to a truly open inter-religious dialogue. Cultural disarmament has the potential of transforming the clash of communities with different civilizational traditions into mutually profitable dialogues of cultures and peoples.

In our society today, the myth of violence as empowering and effective is predominant over the myth of peace and ahimsa. This cult of violence must be deconstructed and disarmed for a viable peace process. The first step would be a pragmatic tolerance for a dialogue of life, living together in peaceful co-existence and discovering together our common humanity, deconstructing stereotypes, rejecting prejudices and building the ground for deeper engagement. For ultimately, Panikkar insists: 'Peace is not something that is imposed, that one gives or merits: peace is a gift that is received by grace, freely. This attitude of receptivity is the foundation to peace.' (Panikkar 1995)

In the context of violence, collective religio-cultural disarmament is thus the metaphor for such tolerance and dialogue. It is not to dismiss or denigrate culture or religion, but to disarm and discard the aggression and violence of those who indulge in, and those who inspire such madness. We must demythologize this 'myth of violence' and re-enchant the 'myth of peace'.

Panikkar sketches his 'myth of peace' in nine sutras that brings this discussion together:

1. Peace is participation in the harmony of the rhythm of being.
2. It is difficult to live without outer peace; it is impossible to live without inner peace.
3. Peace is neither conquered for oneself nor imposed on others. Peace is received, as well as discovered, and created. It is a gift (of the Spirit).

4. Victory never leads to peace.
5. Military disarmament requires cultural disarmament.
6. In isolation, no culture, religion, or tradition can resolve the problems of the world.
7. Peace pertains essentially to the order of mythos, not to that of logos.
8. Religion is a way to peace.
9. Only forgiveness, reconciliation, and ongoing dialogue lead to peace and shatter the law of karma.

(Panikkar 1995: 15)

Beyond the Horizon

Our democracy was born poor and illiterate. Ninety per cent of India was below the poverty line and 88 per cent were illiterate. On 26 January 1952, 'independent India became the first country in the non-Western world to choose a resolutely democratic constitution, it not only used what it had learned from the institutional experiences in Europe and America (particularly Great Britain), it also drew on its own tradition of public reasoning and argumentative heterodoxy'. (Sen 2005: 12–13)

Many thought it would be a failed experiment. Will India survive, they wondered. Seven decades later, except for the years of the Emergency (1975–77), Indian democracy can still claim to be the largest in the world. It is 'the first time in human history, a poor nation has practiced universal franchise for so long' (Varshney 2013: 3–4). Amartya Sen's *Argumentative Indian* (Sen 2005) makes all the difference. Bhikhu Parekh points out that 'the tradition of public debate has a long history in India going back to around 1000 BC'. (Parekh 2015: 3) However, in our Republic, electoral democracy prevailed over substantive democracy. Winning elections is the overriding objective of politicians and their parties, thus creating vote banks and network of patronage, politicizing cultural and religious identities.

Ambedkar had warned us of the emptiness of political democracy without economic democracy, and I would add, social and cultural democracy too: 'one man one value'. (Ambedkar 1978: 47) This is the substance of democracy; elections are but a means to these ends. If we fail here, authoritarianism would be ever more attractive and eventually even irresistible to our people, whether of the political right or of the left, the religious chauvinists or the secular rationalists.

As mentioned in Chapter 2, Ambedkar's last speech to the Constituent Assembly on 25 November laid out final three cautions:

> If we wish to maintain democracy not merely in form, but also in fact, what must we do? The first…hold fast to constitutional methods of achieving our social and economic objectives….
>
> The second…observe the caution which John Stuart Mill has given… not 'to lay their liberties at the feet of even a great man, or to trust him with power which enable him to subvert their institutions.
>
> The third…not to be content with mere political democracy.…Political democracy cannot last unless there lies at the base of its social democracy. (Constituent Assembly Debates 1989: VII: 336)

Once our republic leaned towards a social democracy; it began to be liberalized in the 1990s. Today the dominant ideology of the BJP is an unabashed saffron neoliberalism, emphasizing free-market-led growth and Hindutva priorities. What we have now is a majoritarian government that has little consideration for minorities, especially the single largest minority, the Muslims; it is an authoritarian administration that constantly projects its leader as saviour; a monolithic party with little patience for criticism and dissent; a neoliberalism that has little consideration for the poor and oppressed. This present situation is so very out of sync with our capacious and expansive Indic traditions that it is sustainable only by undemocratic force and fear.

So even as we celebrate the 'dance of democracy' with our elections, we cannot be unaware that the very idea of India as projected in the constitutional vision in now under strain, and we must draw on the historical roots of our tradition of public reasoning to rescue our democracy. For the only remedy for a failing democracy is more real democracy, and for a multicultural, multilingual, pluri-religious civilization like ours, there can be no other route to fulfilling our 'tryst with destiny' than in an egalitarian, pluralist, secular, democratic state.

In the communal polarization plaguing our society and spilling over into collective violence, a saffron neoliberal state is unlikely to play a neutral mediating role. It is not in the interest of such politicians to defuse the tensions that consolidate their voter base of Hindu ethno-nationalism. However given the large population of minorities, we cannot have an authentic democracy or stable government for long if the minorities are alienated. A democratic nation most essentially means equal citizenship in an egalitarian society, not a graded hierarchy of its subjects. Or else we will have a *Nationalism without a Nation in India*. (Aloysius 1997)

Taking Back Democracy

With a decimated opposition in Parliament constantly put on the defensive, it is now for civil society to foster a critical and alert citizenry to take back our democracy to its constitutional roots and to devise practical strategies for this. The basic principle of democracy was expressed in Roman Republican law: 'What touches all must be decided by all' *(Quod omnes tangit, ab omnibus approbetur)*. But operationalizing this is a complex and fragile task. Constitutional patriotism visualizes this as a contest between parties with different agendas for the people's common good. An ethno-nationalism makes democratic politics a struggle for dominance of diverse identity communities, and in the struggle for dominance, the numbers game favours the majority.

Without an effective opposition, such majoritarianism is easily corrupted by its monopoly of power and becomes a tyranny for minorities and marginalized. This hollows out the very substance of democracy, only the formal procedures are left. The history of ethno-nationalism in many counties is evidence of this. Our Constitution set our democracy within a regime of rights, including protective rights, for linguistic and religious minorities, affirmative action for the vulnerable, and a set of protective statutory institutions for the new republic. A government that compromises or abbreviates our constitutional democracy eventually falls into the populist trap, claiming a people's mandate, using electoral victories to legitimize questionable policies.

Such majoritarian ethnic politics thrives on polarizing communities, finding or making enemy scapegoats for their politics of hate and does not hesitate to use collective violence to up the ante into a spiral of vengeance. There is no tolerance that could begin a breakthrough to a reconciliation, for peace and harmony. This is a disharmonious society and dysfunctional for the common good of all. For there can be

no harmony without peace,
no peace without justice,
no justice without fairness,
no fairness without reconciliation,
no reconciliation without forgiveness,
no forgiveness without love, that brings harmony.

The story of Joseph and his brothers in the Bible and the Quran is precisely about breaking the cycle of revenge. His brothers who first tried to kill him and then sold him into Egypt, eventually had to come to him for grain when famine struck the land. Joseph, now a high official in Pharaoh's court, could have had them executed for their attempted murder and it would have been seen as the just and honourable thing to do. But not only does he pardon them, he reconciles with his whole family and supports them in their new country.

Seagren (1993) helps us to understand forgiveness in ten points:

Forgiveness can be a long process.
Forgiveness is not dependent upon confession…
Forgiveness does not require an agreed version of the past…
Forgiveness means letting go of my natural right to revenge…
Forgiving does not mean forgetting…
Forgiveness means not bringing it up again…
Forgiveness does not mean excusing the behaviour of the other person…
Forgiveness does not always mean re-trusting…
Forgiveness is incomplete until love replaces anger.

Anthony Giddens indicates four possible ways of dealing with a 'clash of values': through geographic segregation, active exit, positive dialogue and finally force or violence. (Giddens 1994: 19) The first two are not viable in a globalizing world today. There is no safe haven now, no exit from the global cauldron, in which we are all being churned. Force and violence even as options of last resort are hardly viable any more, as the means of such violence have escalated to impossible levels of horror. This leaves us with dialogue as a means to both resolve and celebrate 'difference' as a way of being more richly human.

In the polarized hostility between communities in our multicultural, pluri-religious society a genuine reconciliation will be a generational affair. Yet only reconciliation arrives at peace. Dialogue is the only possible road to reconciliation and a minimum of mutual tolerance and openness is the first step as a necessary condition. This must be a priority. On the UN sponsored Dialogue Among Civilizations, 2001, Kaveh L. Afrasiabi, writes:

> The premise is that through dialogue we will cultivate deeper and more direct experience of cultural traditions other than our own, a belief which becomes a *sine qua non* for moral agency in intercultural discourse.
>
> But if intolerance is to be reduced and the tide of ethnic violence stemmed, there must be a commitment by governments to make the elimination of intolerance a priority.
>
> Making civilisational dialogue operational implies a collective willingness by the world's discrete 'cultural forces' to promote dialogue as a common problem-solving approach to the global sources of war and conflict. It remains to be seen whether the United Nations can fulfil the deluge of expectations that this initiative has generated worldwide. (Afrasiabi 2001)

Our deep longing is for a peace that is just, free, and harmonious to liberate us all from the violence and hate our polarized society has trapped itself in, mobilized and motivated by a majoritarian ethno-nationalism, not unlike many developing new nations, whose nationalism became an expression of the ethnicity of their historical societies. The experience of such nations has been an increasing exclusive ethnocentricity, authoritarian majoritarianism, and the hollowing out of democracy. 'Yet democracy is one of those elusive things—happiness is another—whose promise, even if perpetually deferred, is more important than its actual existence. We may never get it, but we cannot afford to stop dreaming of it.' (Bradatan *New York Times* 5 Jul 2019)

We need to deconstruct this ideology of exclusion and its politics of hate. We need a struggle, a 'jihad', a 'crusade', a 'padayatra' for the idea of a sovereign, democratic, secular socialist India. We need to sow the good seed of meaningful, relevant, liberating, humane cultural and religious traditions for a hundredfold harvest of a harmonious peace, premised on tolerance and justice, forgiveness and reconciliation. For if we stop dreaming peace, we will stop dreaming India.

ACKNOWLEDGEMENTS

I owe an enormous debt of gratitude to all those who supported me in writing this book: my Jesuit brothers at ISI and other friends in Delhi and Mumbai, most especially to Jerry Pinto for his generous help in editing and finalizing the draft manuscript, and finally to Speaking Tiger for publishing the book in very good time: copy editing and proof reading the text, and designing the cover.

In this discussion in the book, I have fallen back on my earlier work and drawn on it where pertinent. Many of the topics and themes, issues and problems, recommendations and responses are similar, if not the same. Hopefully, this has helped to make the discourse here more continuous and coherent in our present situation.

ACKNOWLEDGEMENTS

BIBLIOGRAPHY

Abraham, Itty, Edward Newman and Meredith L. Weiss, Eds., 2010. *Political Violence in South and Southeast Asia: Critical Perspectives.* UN University, Tokyo, NY, Paris.

Adler, Nanci, Mary Chamberlain, Leyla Neyzi, Eds., 2009. *Memories of Mass Repression: Narrating Life Stories in the Aftermath of Atrocity.* Francis Taylor, London.

Adorno, T.W., E. Frenkel-Brunswik, D.J. Levinson & R.N. Sanford, 1950. *The Authoritarian Personality.* Harper and Row, New York.

Afrasiabi, Kaveh L., 2001. 'The United Nations and the Idea of Dialogue Among Civilisations', *Global Dialogue* Vol. 3, No. 1, Winter.

Aloysius, G., 1997. *Nationalism Without a Nation in India.* Oxford University Press, Delhi.

Anderson, Benedict, 1983. *Imagined Communities: Reflections on the Origin and Spread of Nationalism.* Verso, London.

Anderson, Michael R., and Sumit Guha, Eds., 1998. *Changing Concepts of Rights and Justice in South Asia.* Oxford University Press, Delhi.

Ahmad, Imtiaz, 2002. 'Urdu and Madrasa Education', *Economic & Political Weekly*, Vol. 37, No. 24. https://www.epw.in/system/files/pdf/2002_37/24/Urdu_and_Madrasa_Education.pdf.

Alavi, Hamsa, 2002. 'Social Forces and Ideology in the Making of Pakistan', *Economic & Political Weekly*, Vol. 37, No. 51, pp. 5119-5124.

All India Reporter, (AIR), Supreme Court 1986.

All India Reporter, (AIR), Supreme Court, 2002, 8 SCC 481.

Allen, Douglas, Ed, 2006. *Comparative Philosophy and Religion in Times of Terror.* Rowman and Little, NY, Lanham, Boulder.

Alliance for Justice & Accountability, *Minority Rights Violations in India: A Report*, 2017. South Asian Solidarity Initiative, Washington, D.C. (http://www.indianet.nl/pdf/MinorityRightsViolationsInIndia-2017.pdf)

Ambedkar, Bhimrao Ramji, 1957. *The Buddha and His Dhamma.*

———1978. *States and Minorities.* Buddha Vihar, Lucknow.

———1995, (1st 1944). *Annihilation of Caste*, Bheem Patrika Pub., Jalandar.

Ardent, Hannah, 1951. *The Origins of Totalitarianism.* Schocken Books, New York.

———1970. *On Violence.* Harvest Book, NY.

———1977. *Eichmann in Jerusalem: A Report of the Banality of Evil*, Penguin Books, revised and enlarged edition, New York.

Aristotle, 1925. *The Nicomachean Ethics*, trans. William David Ross, J. L. Ackrill, J. O. Urmson. Oxford Univ. Press, Oxford.

Armstrong, Karen, 2000. *The Battle for God.* Alfred A. Knopf, New York.

———2014. *Fields of Blood: Religion and the History of Violence.* Bodley Head, London.

———2014. 'Karen Armstrong on Sam Harris and Bill Maher', http://www.salon.com/2014/11/23/karen_armstrong_sam_harris_anti_islam_talk_fills_me_with_despair/

Arnold, Dan & Alicia Turner, 'Why Are We Surprised When Buddhists Are Violent?', *New York Times*, 5 Mar 2018. https://www.nytimes.com/2018/03/05/opinion/buddhists-violence-tolerance.html?action=click&pgtype=Homepage&version=Moth-Visible&moduleDetail=inside-nyt-region-4&module=inside-nyt-region&region=inside-nyt-region&WT.nav=inside-nyt-region

Austin, Granville, 1966. *The Indian Constitution Cornerstone of the Nation.* Oxford U. Press. Oxford.

Bauman, Zygmunt, 2011. *Collateral Damage: Social Inequalities in a Global Age.* Polity Press, Cambridge, UK.

Balch, Elliott, 2015. 'Myth Busting: Robert Pape on ISIS, Suicide Terrorism, and U.S. Foreign Policy', *Chicago Policy Review*, 5 May 2015. http://chicagopolicyreview.org/2015/05/05/myth-busting-robert-pape-on-isis-suicide-terrorism-and-u-s-foreign-policy/

Ball, Terence, 2005. 'James Mill', *Stanford Encyclopedia of Philosophy*, Stanford, CA, USA, 30 November. https://stanford.library.sydney.edu.au/archives/fall2008/entries/james-mill/ ??

Barrier, N. Gerald, 1968. 'The Punjab Government and Communal Politics, 1870-1908', *The Journal of Asian Studies*, Vol. 27, No. 3, May, pp. 523-539.

Basham A. L., 1975. *A Cultural History of India*. Clarendon Press, Oxford.

Barve, Sushobha, 2003. *Healing Streams: Bringing Back Hope in the Aftermath of Violence.* Penguin Books, New Delhi.

Bayley, Susan, 1989. *Saints, Goddesses and Kings: Muslims and Christians in South Indian Society, 1700–1900.* Cambridge Univ. Press, Cambridge, UK.

Belloc, Hillaire, 1992, (1st 1920) *Europe and the Faith***.** Tan Books**,** Charlotte, North Carolina, USA.

Bentham, Jeremy, 1962. *The Works of Jeremy Bentham*. Published under the superintendence of his executor, John Bowring, 11 Vols, Russell *&* Russell, New York.

Béteille, Andre, 1999. 'Citizenship, State and Civil Society', *Economic & Political Weekly*, Vol 24, No. 36, pp 2566-91.

_______2008. 'Constitutional Morality', *Economic & Political Weekly*, Vol. 43, No. 40, pp. 35-42.

Bhargava, Rajeev, 2013. 'Reimagining Secularism Respect, Domination and Principled Distance', *Economic & Political Weekly*, Vol. 48, No. 50, pp. 79-92.

Bhattacharjee, Manash, 2015. 'Nehru and the Question of National Identity', *Economic & Political Weekly*, Vol. 50, No. 16, pp. 20-23.

Bhattacharya, Sabyasachi, 2016. 'Antinomies of Nationalism and Rabindranath Tagore', *Economic & Political Weekly*, Vol. 51, No. 6, pp. 39-45.

Bloomfield, David, Teresa Barnes, Luc Huyse, Eds, 2003. *Reconciliation After Violent Conflict: A Handbook*. International IDEA, Stockholm Sweden.

Bondurant, Joan V., 1988. *Conquest of Violence: The Gandhian Philosophy of Conflict,* new revised edition. Princeton University Press, Princeton, NJ.

Bouillier, Veronique, 2003. 'The Violence of the Non-Violent, or Ascetics in Combat', in op., cit., Denis Vidal, Gilles Tarabout and Eric Meyer, pp., 27-28, Manohar, New Delhi.

Boswell, James, 1986. Hibbert, Christopher, Ed., *The Life of Samuel Johnson.* Penguin Classics, New York.

Bradatan, Costica, 2019, 'Democracy Is for the Gods' *New York Times*, 5 Jul. https://www.nytimes.com/2019/07/05/opinion/why-democracies-fail.html?fbclid=IwAR1eGI6Oi2tbmLd2eae1Fg1LWNPMnippSoGYHI_cmAx2MHELwvJMssxZxx8

Brass Paul R., Achin Vanaik, Eds, 2002. *Competing nationalisms in South Asia: Essays for Asghar Ali Engineer*. Orient Longman, New Delhi.

Brass, Paul, 2003. *The Production of Hindu-Muslim Violence in Contemporary India*. University of Washington Press, Seattle.

Bryant, Christopher, G. A., Jary, David 2003. 'Anthony Giddens', Chapter 10, *Anthony Giddens*. Wiley, New York. pp. 247–273.

Bufacchi, Victorio, 2005. 'Two Concepts of Violence', *Political Studies Review*, Vol. 3, Sept, pp. 193–204. https://www.scribd.com/document/326350251/Two-Concepts-of-Violence

Burns, John F., 2016. 'A Case of Deadly Delusions', *New York Times*, 26 Mar. https://www.nytimes.com/2016/03/27/opinion/sunday/a-case-of-deadly-delusions.html

Bush, George W., 2001. 'A Nation Challenged', President's Address on Terrorism Before a Joint Meeting of Congress, *New York Times*, 21 Sept.

Brzezinski, Z., 1993. *Out of Control: Global Turmoil on the Eve of the Twenty-first Century*. Simon & Schuster, New York.

Borradori, Giovanna, Ed., 2003. *Philosophy in a Time of Terror: Dialogues with Jurgen Habermas and Jacques Derrida*. Univ of Chicago Press, Chicago.

Buchanan, James, M., 1954. 'Social Choice, Democracy, and Free Markets', *Journal of Political Economy*, Vol. 62, pp 114-123.

Cantwell Smith, Wilfred, 1964. *The Meaning and End of Religion*. Macmillan, New York.

Campell, Joseph, 1991. *The Power of Myth*. Anchor Books, New York.

Cantacuzino, Marina, 2015. 'A Move Beyond Old Wounds', *The Tablet*. 5 May. http://www.thetablet.co.uk/features/2/5603/a-move-beyond-old-wounds

Carr, E. H., 1990. *What Is History*. Penguin, England.

Cavanaugh, William T., 2009. *The Myth of Religious Violence: Secular Ideology and the Roots of Modern Conflict*. Oxford University Press, New York.

Chancel, Lucas, Thomas Piketty, 2017. 'Indian Income Inequality 1922-2014', WID http://wid.world/wp-content/uploads/2017/12/ChancelPiketty2017WIDworld.pdf

Chandra, Bipin, 1984. *Communalism in Modern India*. Vikas, New Delhi.

———1988. *Indian National Movement: The Long-term Dynamics*. Vikas, New Delhi.

Chandra, Bipan, et. al., 1988. *India's Struggle for Independence, 1857-1947*. Viking, New Delhi.

Chandra, Sudhir, 2017. *Gandhi: An Impossible Possibility*. Routledge, India.

Chandramohan, C.K., 2002. 'We Are No Longer Bound by Promise on Ayodhya: VHP', *The Hindu*, 23 January. https://www.thehindu.com/2002/06/23/stories/2002062304570100.htm.

Charlesworth, James H. et al., Eds, 2007. *Jesus Research: New Methodologies and Perceptions—The Second Princeton-Prague Symposium on Jesus Research, Princeton*. Wm. B. Eerdmans & Co., Grand Rapids, Mi., USA.

Chatterjee, Partha, 1997. *A Possible World: Essays in Political Criticism*. Oxford University Press, Delhi.

Chitralekha, 2012. *Ordinary People, Extraordinary Violence*. Routledge, Taylor & Francis, London, New York, New Delhi.

Chong, Jane, 2015. 'White Hate But Islamic Terror? Charleston, Hate Crimes and Terrorism Per Quod', *Lawfare*, 21 June. https://www.lawfareblog.com/white-hate-islamic-terror-charleston-hate-crimes-and-terrorism-quod

Coll, Steve, 2017. 'The Strongman Problem, from Modi to Trump', *The New Yorker*, 18 January. http://www.newyorker.com/news/daily-comment/the-strongman-problem-from-modi-to-trump?mbid=nl_January%2016th%202017%20(4)&CNDID=31738503&spMailingID=10253883&spUserID=MTMzMTgzMjE0NDgxS0&spJobID=1081488782&spReportId=MTA4MTQ4ODc4MgS2

Constitutional Assembly Debates: Official Report, (CAD) 1948. 7 Vols, Government of India Manager of Publications, Delhi.

Corbridge, Stuart, John Harris, 2000. *Reinventing India: Liberalization, Hindu Nationalism and Popular Democracy*. Polity Press, Cambridge, UK.

Crawford, James, Ed., 1988. *The Rights of Peoples*. Oxford University Press, Oxford.

Dalmia, Vasudha & Heinrich Von Stietencron, 1995. *Representing Hinduism: The Construction of Religious Traditions and National Identity*. Sage Publication, New Delhi.

Dalrymple, William, 2004. *White Mughals: Love and Betrayal in Eighteenth-Century India*. Penguin, India.

_______2007. *The Last Mughal: The Fall of a Dynasty*. Penguin, India.

Dalton, Dennis, 1963. *Mahatma Gandhi: Nonviolent Power in Action*. Columbia University Press, New York.

Das, Durga, Ed., 1973. *Sardar Patel's Correspondence 1945-50*, Vol. 6. Navajivan Press, Ahmedabad.

Das, Veena, Ed., 1992. *Mirrors of Violence: Communities, Riots and Survivors in South Asia*. Oxford University Press, Delhi.

David, Kumar & Santisilan Kadirgamar, Eds, 1989. *Ethnicity, Identity, Conflict and Crisis*. ARENA Press, Hong Kong.

Davis, Richard H., 1993. 'Indian Art Objects *as* Loot', *Journal of Asian Studies*, Vol. 52 No. 1, pp. 22-48.

Dawson, Christopher, 1965. *The Dividing of Christendom*. Sheed and Ward, London.

Deegalle, Mahinda, 'Sinhala Ethno-nationalisms and Militarization in Sri Lanka', in Tikhonov, Vladimir and Torkel Brekke, Eds., op.cit. pp. 15-36.

Desai, Bharat & Siddhu Balray K., 2019. 'Healing Touch', *Economic & Political Weekly*, 27 Aug, Vol. 51, No. 35. http://www.epw.in/system/files/pdf/2016_51/35/PS_LI_35_270816_Postscript_Bharat_H_Desai.pdf

Devji, Faisal, 2008. *The Terrorist in Search of Humanity: Militant Islam and Global Politics*. Hurst, London.

Dewey, J., 1980. 'Force, Violence and Law' and 'Force and Coercion', in Jo Ann Boydston, Ed., 1980. *John Dewey, The Middle Works, 1899–1924, Volume 10: 1916–1917*. pp. 211–15 and pp. 244–51, Southern Illinois University Press, Carbondale IL, USA.

Dhar, Anup & Anjan Chakrabarti, 2017. 'Sriniketan Encounters Ambedkar Whither the Political?', *Economic & Political Weekly*, 13 May, Vol. 51, No. 53, pp. 56.

Doniger, Wendy, 2010. *The Hindus: An Alternative History*. Penguin Books, India.

_______2014. *On Hinduism*. Oxford University Press, Oxford.

Drèze, Jean, Amartya Sen, 2002. *An Uncertain Glory: India and Its Contradictions*. Princeton University Press, New Jersey.

Durkheim, Emile, 1997, (1st 1893). *The Division of Labour in Society*. Trans. W. D. Halls, Intro. Lewis A. Coser, Free Press, New York.

Eaton, Richard M., 2000. 'Temple Desecration and Indo-Muslim States', *Journal of Islamic Studies*, Vol. 11, No. 3 (September 2000), pp. 283-319.

Economic & Political Weekly, 2018. Editorial, "Missing the Point", Vol. Liii, No. 29, 21 Jul. https://www.epw.in/system/files/pdf/2018_53/29/ED_LIII_29_210718_Missing_the_Point.pdf

The Economist, 1999. 'A Survey of India and Pakistan: The most Dangerous Place on Earth?', https://www.economist.com/node/205889

The Economist, 2018. 'The Wealth of the 1% May Have Peaked', 25 Oct. https://www.economist.com/finance-and-economics/2018/10/27/the-wealth-of-the-top-1-may-have-peaked?cid1=cust/ddnew/email/n/n/20181026n/owned/n/n/ddnew/n/n/n/nap/Daily_Dispatch/email&etear=dailydispatch&utm_source=newsletter&utm_medium=email&utm_campaign=Daily_Dispatch&utm_term=20181 026

The Economist, 2018. 'Growth Can Overcome Loss of Faith in Global Co-operation', 19 Sept. https://www.economist.com/open-future/2018/09/19/growth-can-overcome-the-loss-of-faith-in-global-co-operation?fsrc=gp_en&cid1=cust/ddnew/email/n/n/20180919n/owned/n/n/ddnew/n/n/n/nap/Daily_Dispatch/email&etear=dailydispatch&utm_source=newsletter&utm_medium=email&utm_campaign=Daily_Dispatch&utm_term=20180919

The Economist, 2019. 'Political Savagery Makes Government Impossible', 8 Mar. https://www.economist.com/open-future/2019/03/08/political-savagery-makes-self-government-impossible?cid1=cust/dailypicks/n/bl/n/2019038n/owned/n/n/dailypicks/n/n/ap/212415/n

Edward, David, 2001. *The Compassionate Revolution: Radical Politics and Buddhism.* The Viveka Foundation, New Delhi.

Eliot, T. S., 1934. *The Rock*. London: Faber & Faber.

Elst, Koenraad, 2001. *The Saffron Swastika: The Notion of Hindu Fascism.* New Delhi.

_______2015. *Return of the Swastika: Hate and Hysteria Versus Hindu Sanity*. Arklos, Budapest.

Eze, Michael, Onyebuchi, 2010. *Intellectual History in Contemporary South Africa*. Palgrave Macmillan, New York.

Fanon, Franz, 1961. *The Wretched of the Earth*. Grove Publishers, Random House, New York.

Falk, Richard, 1988. 'Rights of People (in Particular Indigenous Peoples)', in James Crawford, Ed., op.cit., pp. 17- 37.

Fairouz, Mohammed, 2011. 'After Tahrir, New Voices in a Global Fugue', *New York Times*, 6 Jul.

Ferrándiz, Francisco, Antonius C.G.M. Robben, Eds, 2007. *Multidisciplinary Perspectives on Peace and Conflict Research: A View from Europe*. Univ of Deusto, Bilbao. http://digital.csic.es/bitstream/10261/21564/3/EDENFerrandizRobbenBook07.pdf

Fernée, Tadd, 2014. *Enlightenment and Violence: Modernity and Nation-Making*. Sage, India.

Financial Times, 2018. 'Thousands of Migrant Workers Flee Gujarat After Alleged Hate Attacks', 9 Oct. https://economictimes.indiatimes.com/news/politics-and-nation/thousands-of-migrant-workers-flee-gujarat-after-alleged-hate-attacks/articleshow/66138037.cms

Ford, Franklin L., 1985. *Political Murder: From Tyrannicide to Terrorism*. Harvard University Press, Cambridge, Mass. USA.

Freire, Paulo, 1972. *Pedagogy of the Opressed*. Penguin, England.

Freitag, Sandra, 1990. *Collective Action and Community: Public Areas and the Emergernce of Communalism in North India*. Oxford University Press, Delhi.

Frydenlund, Iselin, 2013. 'Canonical Ambiguity and Differential Practices: Militarism in Contemporary Sri Lanka', pp 95-119, in Tikhonov, Vladimir and Torkel Brekke, Eds., op.cit.

Frykenberg, Robert Eric, 2003. *Christian Missionaries in India: Cross-Cultural Communication Since 1500 with Special Reference to Caste, Conversion and Colonialism*. William B. Eerdmans Publ., Grand Rapids, Michigan & Cambridge, UK.

Galbraith, John Kenneth, 1963. *An Ambassador's Journal*. Hought, Mifflin, Boston.

Galtung, J., 1969. 'Violence, Peace and Peace Research', *Journal of Peace Research*, 3, 167–91.

Gandhi, M.K., 1909 (1st Gujarati, 1908). *Hind Swaraj, or Indian Home Rule*. Navjivan Press, Ahmedabad.

______1927. *The Story of My Experiments with Truth*. Translated by (from Gujarati) by Mahadev Desai, Navajivan, Ahemdabad.

______1935. *From Yeravda Mandir: Ashram Observances*. Jivanji Desai, Ahmedabad.

______*Collected Works*, 1958-89, 100 vols. Government of India, New Delhi.

______2007, (1st 1941). *Constructive Programme: Its Meaning and Place*. Navjivan, Ahmedabad.

______undated, *India of My Dreams*. Compiled by R.K. Prabhu, Navjivan, Ahmedabad.

Gandhi, Rajmohan, 2004. *Ghaffar Khan: Nonviolent Badshah of the Pakhtuns*. Penguin (Viking) Books, India.

Geertz, Clifford, Ed., 1963. *Old Societies and New States: The Quest for Modernity in Asia and Africa*. The Free Press of Glencoe, London.

Gellner, Ernest, 1964. *Thought and Change*. Weidenfeld and Nicolson, London.

______1983. *Nations and Nationalism*. Basil Blackwell, Oxford.

Giddens, Anthony, 1994. *Beyond Left and Right: The Future Radical Politics*. Polity Press, Cambridge, UK.

Golwalkar, M.S., 1939. *We, or Our Nationhood Defined*. Bharat Publications, Nagpur.

______1966. *Bunch of Thoughts*. Sahitya Sindhu Prakashana. 3rd ed. http://rss.org/Encyc/2015/4/7/334_03_46_30_Bunch_of_Thoughts.pdf

Goodin, Robert E., 1985. *Protecting the Vulnerable: Reaanlysis of Our Social Responsibilities*. University of Chicago, Chicago.

Gooptu, Nandini and Jonathan Parry, Eds, 2014. *Persistence of Poverty in India*. Social Science Press, Delhi.

Gore, M.S., 1993. *The Social Context of an Ideology: Ambedkar's Political and Social Thought*. Sage, New Delhi.

Gottschaulk, Peter, 2007. 'A Categorical Difference: Communal Identity in British Epistemologies', in Hinnells, John R. and Richard King, Eds, op.cit, pp: 185-199.

Government of India, Ministry of Statistics, 2018.

Gramsci, Antonio, 1996. *Selections from the Prison Notebooks*. Eds and Trans Hoare, Quintin and Geoffrey Nowell Smith, Orient Longman, Hyderabad.

Gray, John, 2007. *Black Mass: Apocalyptic Religion and the Death of Utopia*. Penguin, Delhi.

Grey, Mary, 2010. *A Cry for Dignity: Religion, Violence and the Struggle of Dalit Women in India*. Quinox, UK.

Gregg, Richard, 1935, 1959. *The Power of Nonviolence*. James Clark, London.

Gupta, Dipankar, 2001. *Culture, Space and the Nation-State–From Sentiment to Structure*. Sage, New Delhi.

______2002. 'Autopsy of a Riot: Social Science to Social Forensic', *Times of India*, 14 March, p. 8.

______Ed., 2004. *Caste in Question: Identity or Hierarchy?* Sage, Delhi.

Habermas, Jürgen, 1984 (1981). *Theory of Communicative Action, Volume One: Reason and the Rationalization of Society*, Translated by *Thomas A. McCarthy*. Beacon Press, Boston.

______1987 (1981). *Theory of Communicative Action, Volume Two: Lifeworld and System: A Critique of Functionalist Reason*, Translated by *Thomas A. McCarthy*. Beacon Press, Boston.

———1991. *Theory of Communicative Action*, 2 Vols. Polity Press, UK.

———2003. 'Reconstructing Terrorism', in *Philosophy in a Time of Terror: Dialogues with Jurgen Habermas and Jacques Derrida*, Giovanna Borradori, Ed. University of Chicago Press, Chicago, pp. 45-80.

Hansen, Thomas Blom, 2008. 'Political Theology of Violence in Contemporary India', *South Asia Multidisciplinary Academic Journal*, No. 2, Art nos, 2-47. https://journals.openedition.org/samaj/1872

Hardin, Garret, 1986. 'The Tragedy of the Commons', *Science*, Vol. 162, Dec, pp. 1243-48.

Hardiman, David, 2003. *Gandhi in His Time and Ours: The Global Legacy of His Ideas*. Hurst & Company, London.

———Ed., 2007. *Nonviolence in Modern Indian History*, Orient Black Swan, Hyderabad.

Heredia, Rudolf C., 1996. 'Pluralism, Tolerance and Dialogue', *Vidyajyoti Jornal of Theological Reflection*, Vol. 60, No. 4, Apr, pp. 255-64.

———1999. 'Gandhi and the Myth of Peace', *New Quest*, No. 136, Jul-Aug, pp. 231-239

———2007. *Changing Gods: Rethinking Conversion in India*, Penguin, India.

———2008. 'Development as Liberation: An Indian Christian Perspective', *Vidyajyoti*, Vol. 72, No. 7, Jul, pp. 502-522. Later in *Religion, Community and Development: Changing Contours of Politics and Policy in India*, Gurpreet Mahajan & Surinder S. Jodhka, Eds, Routledge Taylor & Francis Group, New Delhi, 2010, pp, 129-150.

Hindustan Times, 31 May 2018. 'Warrior Cop Got So Many Calls That He Had to Switch Off His Mobile'.

Hinnells, John R. & Richard King, Eds, 2007. *Religion and Violence in South Asia: Theory and Practice*. Routledge, London, NY.

Hirst, Paul, 1988. 'Carl Schmitt—Decisionism and Politics', *Economy and Society*, Vol. 17, Issue 2, May, pp. 272-282.

Honderich, T., 2003. *Terrorism for Humanity: Inquiries in Political Philosophy*. Pluto, London.

Horowitz, Donald L., 1985. *Ethnic Groups in Conflict*. University of California Press, Berkeley, LA.

Horowitz, Donald L., 2001. *The Deadly Ethnic Riot*. Oxford University Press, Delhi.

Hsu-Ming Teo, 2012. *Desert Passions: Orientalism and Romance Novels*. Univ Texas Press, Austin.

Huntington, Samuel P., 1996. *The Clash of Civilizations and the Remaking of World Order*. Simon and Schuster, New York.

Indian Express, 23 May 2018, 'Uttarakhand: VHP Workers Beat Up Two Muslim Youths After Spotting Them with Hindu Girl'. https://indianexpress.com/article/india/uttarakhand-vhp-workers-beat-up-two-muslim-youths-for-being-spotted-with-hindu-girl-5190888/

Indian Express, 3 January 2017 'Why, 22 Years on, the SC's "Hindutva Judgement" Remains Elephant in Room'. http://indianexpress.com/article/explained/gujarat-riot-nhrc-religion-elections-vote-bank-supreme-court-why-22-years-on-the-scs-hindutva-judgment-remains-elephant-in-room-4456258/

Jaffrelot, Christophe, 1996. *The Hindu Nationalist Movement and Indian Politics*. C. Hurst & Co. Publishers, London.

______2018. 'Moment of Strongman", *Indian Express*, Dec 26. https://indianexpress.com/article/opinion/columns/strongman-coalition-modi-rahul-gandhi-narsimha-rao-2019-elections-5508179/

James, S., 2003. 'Passion and Politics', *Royal Institute of Philosophy Supplement*, No. 52, pp. 221–34.

Jenkins, Stephen, 2010. 'On the Auspiciousness of Compassionate Violence', *Journal of the International Association of Buddhist* Studies, Vol. 33, No. 1–2, pp. 299–331. http://journals.ub.uni-heidelberg.de/index. php/jiabs/article/view/9284

Jerryson, Michael K., 2018. *If You Meet the Buddha on the Road: Buddhism, Politics, and Violence*. Oxford University Press, Delhi.

Jinnah, Mohammed Ali, 1948. *Speeches of the Quaid-i-Azam Mohammed Ali Jinnah as Governor General of Pakistan*. Sind Observer Press, Karachi.

Juergensmeyer, Mark, 2000. *Terror in the Mind of God: The Global Rise of Religious Violence*. Oxford University Press, Delhi.

Kakar, Sudhir, 1995. *Colours of Violence*. Viking, Penguin Books, New Delhi.

Keane, J., 1996. *Reflections on Violence*. Verso, London.

Khan, Yasmin, 2007. *The Great Partition: The Making of India and Pakistan*. Yale University Press, New Haven, USA.

King, Richard, 2007. 'The Association of "Religion" with Violence: Reflections on a Modern Trope', Hinnells & King, Eds, op. cit. pp. 226–257.

Kosambi, D.D., 1962. *Myth and Reality: Studies in the Formation of Indian Culture*. Popular Prakashan, Mumbai.

Kothari, Rajni. 1988, 'Integration and Exclusion in Indian Politics', *Economic & Political Weekly*, Vol. 23, No. 43, 22 Oct, pp. 2223-27.

______'Ethnicity', in David and Kadirgamar, Eds, pp. 15-44.

Kripalani, J.B., 1938. *Non-Violent Revolution* (India day to day pamphlets series). Vohra, India.

Krishna, Kumar, 2007. *Battle for Peace*. Penguin, Gurgaon, India.

Kurtz, Lester R., Ed., 2018. *The Warrior and the Pacifist: Competing Motifs in Buddhism, Judaism*. Routledge, New York.

Kymlicka, Will, 1995. *Multicultural Citizenship: A Liberal Theory of Minority Rights*. Clarendon Press, Oxford.

Lele, Jayant, 1995. *Hindutva: The Emergence of the Right*. Earthworm Books, Madras.

Lele, Jayant, 1995. 'Saffronization of the Shiv Sena: Political Economy of City, State and Nation', *Economic & Political Weekly*, Vol. 30, No. 25, 24 Jun. pp.1520-28.

Malraux, Andre, 1968. *Antimemoirs*. Penguin, England.

Lewis, Bernard, 1990, 'Roots of Muslim Rage', *The Atlantic*. https://www.theatlantic.com/magazine/archive/1990/09/the-roots-of-muslim- rage/304643/

Lijphart, Arend, 1984. *Democracies: Patterns of Majoritarian and Consensus Government in Twenty-One Countries*. Yale University Press, New Haven, USA.

Langworth, Richard, 2012. *Churchill in His Own Words*. London, Ebury Press.

Lewis, Michael L., 2003. *Inventing Global Ecology: Tracking the Biodiversity Ideal in India, 1947–1997*. Ohio University Press, USA.

Locke, John, 1988 (1st 1690). *Two Treatises of Government*, P. Laslett, Ed. Cambridge University Press, Cambridge, UK.

Madan, T.N., 1997. *Modern Myths, Locked Minds: Secularism and Fundamentalism in India*. Oxford University Press, New Delhi.

Mander, Harsh, John Dayal, Natasha Badhwar, Eds, 2018. *Reconciliation: Karwan-e Mohabbat's Journey of Solidarity through a Wounded India*. Westland, Chennai.

Maine, Henry Summer, 1889. *Village-communities in the East and West*. H. Holt and company, New York.

Mamdani, Mahood, 2001. *When Victims Become Killers: Colonialism, Nativism and Genocide*. Princeton Univ Press, Princeton, NJ.

______2015. 'Beyond Nuremberg: The Historical Significance of the Post-Apartheid Transition in South Africa', Makerere Institute of Social Research, Uganda. https://idl-bnc-idrc.dspacedirect.

org/bitstream/handle/10625/55811/IDL-55811.pdf?sequence=1&is Allowed=y

Marchman, Kendall, 2016. 'Buddhism and Violence: Militarism and Buddhism in Modern Asia', *Journal of Buddhist Ethics*, Vol. 23. https://pdfs.semanticscholar.org/f402/f4b80b3377630e59dc5e86bafda5d6622feb.pdf

McKean, Lise, 1996. *Divine Enterprise: Gurus and the Hindu Nationalist Movement*. University of Chicago, Chicago.

McMillan, Alistair, 2005. *Standing at the Margins Representation and Electoral Reservation in India*. Oxford University Press, Delhi.

McGregor, R. S., 1993. *The Oxford Hindi-English Dictionary*. Oxford University Press, Oxford and Delhi.

Metha, Pratap Banu, 2018. 'At Red Fort, PM Modi's Hope and Fear', *Indian Express*, 16 Aug.

Menon, Nivedita, 2004. 'Citizenship and the Passive Revolution: Interpreting the First Amendment', *Economic & Political Weekly*, Vol. 39, No. 18, 1 May, pp. 1802-1819.

Michels, Robert, 1915. *Political Parties: A Sociological Study of the Oligarchical Tendencies of Modern Democracy*, Translated into English by Eden Paul and Cedar Paul. The Free Press, New York.

Mill, James Stuart, 1817. *The History of British India*, Baldwin, Cradock and Joy, London.

Mill, John Stuart, 1867. 'Inaugural Address Delivered to the University of St Andrews', Longmans, Green, Reader, and Dyer, London, pp.1-84.

Mills, C. Wright, 1956. *The Power Elite*. Oxford University Press, NY.

Mishra, Pankaj, 2014. 'Modi and the New Face of India', *The Guardian*, May 16. http://www.theguardian.com/books/2014/may/16/what-next-india-pankaj-mishra

______2017. 'Hindu Nationalism Is More Italian and Christian Than Sonia Gandhi', *Times of India*, Mumbai, 22 Jan, p. 22. http://timesofindia.indiatimes.com/home/sunday-times/all-that-matters/hindu-nationalism-is-more-italian-and-christian-than-sonia-gandhi/articleshow/56711905.cms

______2017. 'Modi's Real Mission Development and Reforms Are Just a Means to an End', *Bloomberg*, Mar 21. https://www.bloomberg.com/view/articles/2017-03-21/politics-wins-out-over-economics-for-india-s-modi

______2018. 'A Gandhian Stand Against the Culture of Cruelty', *New York Review of Books*, 21 Mar. https://www.nybooks.com/daily/2018/05/22/the-culture-of-cruelty/

Monier-Williams, M., 1899. *A Sanskrit-English Dictionary: Etymologically and Philologically Arranged with Special Reference to Cognate Indo-European Languages*. Clarendon Press Oxford.

Moon, Vasant, Ed., 1987. *Revolution and Counter-Revolution in Ancient India*, in *Dr. Babasaheb Ambedkar: Writings and Speeches*, 1987(a), Vol. 3. Dept. of Education, Govt. of Maharashtra, Mumbai.

Muralidharan, Sukumar, 2019. 'The Majoritarian Challenge and an Ambedkarite Remedy', *Economic & Political Weekly*, 23 Feb, Vol. 54, No. 8, pp. 34-39.

Nampoothiri, P.G.J. & Gagan Sethi, 2012. *Lest We Forget History: Tracing Communal Violence in Gujarat 2002*. International Publ. House, Bangalore.

Nanda, B. R., 1985. *Gandhi and His Critics*. Oxford University Press, Delhi.

Nandy, Ashis, 1980. *At the Edge of Psychology: Essays in Politics and Culture*. Oxford University Press, Delhi.

______1983. *The Intimate Enemy: Loss and Recovery of Self Under Colonialism*. Oxford University Press, Delhi.

______1986. 'From Outside the Imperium: Gandhi's Cultural Critique of the West', in Ramashray Roy, Ed., *Contemporary Crisis and Gandhi*, op. cit., pp. 89-126.

______1992. 'The Politics of Secularism and the Recovery of Religious Tolerance', in Veena Das, Ed., op. cit., pp. 69-93.

______1994. *The Illegitimacy of Nationalism: Rabindranath Tagore and the Politics of Self*. Oxford University Press, Delhi.

______2012. 'Nationalism, Genuine and Spurious: A Very Late Obituary of Two Early Postnationalist Strains in India', *Occasion: Interdisciplinary Studies in the Humanities*, Vol. 3, March 1. http://occasion.stanford.edu/node/105.

______2013. *Regimes of Narcissism, Regimes of Despair*. Oxford University Press, New Delhi.

National Crime Records Bureau, *Crime in India*, www.ncrb.gov.in.

Nehru, Jawaharlal, 1946. *Discovery of India*. Signet Press, Calcutta.

______1958. *A Bunch of Old Letters*. London.

______1985 (1st 1946). *The Discovery of India*. Oxford University Press, Oxford.

Noorani, A. G., Ed., 2001. *The RSS and the BJP: A Division of Labour*, with updated epilogue. Left Word, New Delhi.

Nussbaum, Martha C., 2007. *Frontiers of Justice: Disability, Nationality, Species Membership*. Oxford University Press, New Delhi.

______2015. *Political Emotions: Why Love Matters for Justice*. Harvard, Cambridge, MA.

O'Dea, Thomas, 1969. *Sociology of Religion*. Prentice-Hall, New Delhi.

Olson, Mancur, 1965. *The Logic of Collective Action: Public Goods and the Theory of Groups*. Harvard Univ Press, Cambridge.

Omvedt, Gail, 1994. *Dalits and the Democratic Revolution: Dr. Ambedkar and the Dalit Movement in Colonial India*. Sage, New Delhi.

______1995. *Dalit Visions: The Anti-caste Movement and the Construction of an Indian Identity*. Orient Longman, New Delhi.

______2003. *Buddhism in India: Challenging Brahmanism and Caste*. Sage, New Delhi.

Otto, Rudolf, 1970, (1st 1923). *The Idea of the Holy,* Trans. J.W. Harvey. Oxford University Press, New York.

Ostergaard G., M. Currell, 1971. *The Gentle Anarchists: A Study of the Leaders of the Sarvodaya Movement for Non-violent Revolution in India*. Clarendon, Oxford.

Overy, Bob, 1982. 'Gandhi as Political Organiser: An Analysis of Local and National Campaigns in India 1915-1922', unpublished PhD thesis, University of Bradford, Bradford.

Oxfam India, 2018, 'Widening Gaps: India Inequality Report, 2018'. https://www.oxfamindia.org/sites/default/files/WideningGaps_IndiaInequalityReport2018.pdf

Pandey, Gyanendra, 1990. *The Construction of Communalism in Colonial North India*. Oxford University Press, Delhi.

Pandian, M.S.S., Satyaki Roy, 2014. 'Decisionism and the Cult of Narendra Modi', *Economic & Political Weekly*, Vol. 49, No. 3, pp. 30-31.

Panikkar, Raimon, 1978. *The Intrareligious Dialogue*. Paulist Press, New York.

______1983. *Myth, Faith, and Hermeneutics*. Asian Trading, Bangalore.

______1987. 'Towards a Dialogical Dialogue', *Inter Culture*, Vol. 20, No. 4, Oct., pp. 21-26.

______1995. *Cultural Disarmament: The Way to Peace*. Westminster/John Knox Press, US.

Parekh, Bhikhu, 1995. *Gandhi's Political Philosophy: A Critical Appreciation*. Ajanta, Delhi.

______2003. 'Some Reflections on the Hindu Theory of Tolerance', *Seminar*, No. 527, pp. 48-53. http://www.india-seminar.com/2003/521/521%20bhikhu%20parekh.htm

______2015. 'Indian Traditions of Public Debate', in *Debating India: Essays on Indian Political Discourse*. Oxford University Press. pp. 3-33.

Parel, Anthony J., Ed., 1997. *Gandhi: Hind Swaraj and Other Writings*. Foundation Books, New Delhi.

Pareto, Vilfredo, 1966. *Sociological Writing*, Selected and Introduced by S.E. Finer, trans. Derick Mirfin. Fredrick Praeger, New York.

Parsons, Talcott, 1963. 'On the Concept of Political Power', Proceedings of the American Philosophical Society, Vol. 107, No. 3, pp. 232-262.

Paz, Octavio, 1967. *Nehru: Man of Two Cultures and One World*. Indian National Commission for Cooperation with UNESCO, New Delhi.

Phillips, Charles, Axelrod, Alan, Eds, 2004. *Encyclopedia of Wars*, 3 Vols. Facts on File Inc, New York.

Perera, Anoli, 1998. 'After a Dialogue with Two Artists', *Daily News*, 28 Jan, Lake House, Colombo.

Perera, Sasanka, 2015. *Violence and the Burden of Memory: Remembrance and Erasure in Sinhala Consciousness*. Orient Blackswan, Hyderabad.

Pinker, Steven, 2011. *The Better Angels of Our Nature: Why Violence Has Declined*. Viking Books.

Piketty, Thomas, 2014. *Capital in the Twenty-first Century*. Harvard University Press, Cambridge, Massachusetts.

Pontifical Council for Inter-Religious Dialogue, 1991. 'Dialogue and Proclamation', Vatican City. *Vidyajyoti: Journal of Theological Reflection*, Vol. 70, No. 8 Aug. 2006: pp. 625- 628.

Radhakrishnan, Sarvepalli, 1927. *The Hindu View of Life*. George Allen and Unwin, London.

______1939. *Eastern Religions and Western Thought*. Oxford University Press, Oxford.

Rahula, Walpola, 1974. *The Heritage of the Bhikkhu*. (1946 Bhiksuvage Urimaya Sinhalese) Grove Press, USA.

Rahner, Karl, 1969. *Theological Investigations*, Vol. VI. Payton, Longman and Todd, London.

Ramadan, Tariq, 2010. *The Quest for Meaning: Developing a Philosophy of Pluralism*. Allen Lane, London.

Randle, Michael, 1994. *Civil Resistance*. Fontana, London.

Regamey, O.P., 1996. *Non-Violence and the Christian Conscience*. Darton, Longman & Todd, London.

Reuters, 28 June 2017. 'Protests Held Across India After Attacks Against Muslims'. https://in.reuters.com/article/india-protests/protests-held-across-india-after-attacks-against-muslims-idINKBN19J2C3

Rigby, Andrew, 2007. 'The Nonviolent Activism of the Radical Gandian Jaganathanji (1912-2013)', in Hardiman, Ed., op. cit, pp. 179-201.

Robinson, Francis, 2001. 'On the Islamic Background to the Events of 11 September', Yale Conference: Historical Perspectives on the September 11 Crisis, 19 October, New Haven, USA.

Robinson, Rowena. 2013. *Boundaries of Religion: Essays on Christianity, Ethnic Conflict, and Violence*. Oxford University Press, Delhi.

Robinson, Rowena, Sathianathan Clarke, Eds., 2003. *Christians of India*. Oxford University Press, Delhi.

Roy, Arundhati, 2013. 'The Hanging of Afzal Guru Is a Stain on India's Democracy', *The Guardian*, 2 Feb. https://www.theguardian.com/commentisfree/2013/feb/10/hanging-afzal-guru-india-democracy

Roy, Oliver, 2002. *Globalised Islam: The Search for a New Ummah*. Hurst and Co., London.

Roy, Ramashray, Ed., 1986. *Contemporary Crisis and Gandhi*. Discovery Pub. House, Delhi.

______1986. 'Modern Predicament and Gandhi', in *Contemporary Crisis and Gandhi*, op. cit., pp. 44-88.

Ruskin, John, 1921, (1st 1862). *Unto This Last*. J.M. Dent & Sons, London.

Sacks, Jonathan, 2002. *The Dignity of Difference: How to Avoid the Clash of Civilizations*. Continuum, London.

Sahni, Varun & Shamuel Tharu, 2013. 'Subversion, secession and the state in South Asia: Varieties of violence', in *Political Violence in South and Southeast Asia: Critical Perspectives*, UN, New York.

Sainath, P., 1996. *Everybody Loves a Good Drought: Stories from India's Poorest Districts*. Penguin, New Delhi.

Saran. A.K., 1989. 'Gandhi and the Concept of Politics: Towards a Normal Civilization', *Gandhi Marg* (1), 675-727.

Savarkar, V.D., 1964. *Hindu Rastra Darshan*, in *Samagra Savarkar Wangmaya*, Vol. 6. Maharashtra Prantik Hindusabbha, Pune.

______1970 (1st 1908). *The Indian War of Independence, 1857*. Rajdhani Granthnagar, New Delhi.

———1989. *Hindutva: Who Is a Hindu?* Bharati Sahitya Sadan, 6th ed., New Delhi, 1st ed. 1923.

Schultz, David, 2018. 'Neo-Liberalism and the Retreat of Democracy', Counterpunch, 28 June. https://www.counterpunch.org/2018/06/28/neo-liberalism-and-the-retreat-of-democracy/

Seagren, Barry, 1993. 'Forgiveness: Joseph and His Brothers', L'Abri Papers #BS01. http://www.labri.org/england/resources/05052008/BS01_Forgiveness.pdf

Sethi, J.D., 1979. *Gandhian Values and 20th Century Challenges*. Gvt. of India Pub. Div., New Delhi.

Sen, Amartya, 1977, 'Rational Fools: A Critique of the Behavioral Foundations of Economic Theory', *Philosophy and Public Affairs*, Vol. 6, No. 4, pp:317-344.

———2005. *The Argumentative Indian: Writings on Indian History, Culture and Identity*. Penguin Books, London, 2005.

———2006. *Identity and Violence: The Illusion of Destiny*. Penguin Books India, New Delhi.

Sinha, Rakesh, Suruchi Prakashan, 2006, http://www.thehindu.com/todays-paper/tp-national/BJP-to-focus-on-cultural-nationalism-oppose-appeasement/article14742877.ece

Shackle, Christopher & Javeed Mujeed, 1997. *Islam and Global Dialogue: Religious Pluralism and the Pursuit of Peace*. Oxford University Press, Delhi.

Shah, Ghanshyam, Mario Rutten, Hein Streefkerk, Eds, 2003. *Development and Deprivation in Gujarat*. Sage Publications, New Delhi.

Sharma, Vivek Swaroop, 2016. 'Secularism and Religious Violence in Hinduism and Islam', *Economic & Political Weekly*, Apr 30, Vol. 51, No. 18, pp. 19-21.

Sharp, Gene, 1973. *The Politics of Nonviolent Action*. Porter Sargent, Boston.

———1979. *Gandhi as a Political Strategist*. Porter Sargent, Boston.

Sheikh, Salman Rafi, 2019. *The Genesis of Baloch Nationalism: Politics and Ethnicity in Pakistan, 1947–1977*. Routledge, India.

Sheth, D.L., 1989. 'State, Nation and Ethnicity-Experience of Third World Countries', *Economic & Political Weekly*, 25 Mar, Vol. 24, No. 12.

Siddhartha K., 2012. 'The Truth: Gujarat 2002 Genocide: Babu Bajrangi-Bajrang Dal Leader', *Tehelka*, 29 Aug. https://www.youtube.com/watch?v=UFIyMSLOC64

Skinner, B.F., 1953. *Science and Human Behavior*. Macmillan, Oxford, England.

Sluka, Jeeffery A., Ed., 2000. *Death Squad: The Anthropology of State Terror*. Universtiy of Pennsylvania, Phiadelphia, USA.

Smith, Anthony D., 1994. 'The Politics of Culture: Ethnicity and Nationalism', in *Companion Encyclopedia of Anthropology*, Tim Ingold, Ed. Routledge, London, pp. 706–733.

Sri Aurobindo, 1965, (1st 1939). *The Life Divine*, 2 Vols. The India Library Society, New York.

Som, Reba, Ed., 2009. *Rabindranath Tagore: The Singer and His Song*. Penguin India, New Delhi.

Soufan, Ali, 2011, *The Black Banners: The Inside Story of 9/11 and the War Against al-Qaeda.* W.W. Norton & Company, New York.

_______2017. *Anatomy of Terror: From the Death of Bin Laden to the Rise of the Islamic State*. W.W. Norton & Company, NewYork.

Spivak, Gayatri Chakravorty, 2004 'Terror: A Speech after 9-11', *Boundary 2*, 31(2): 81-111.

Steger, M., 2003. *Judging Nonviolence: The Dispute Between Realists and Idealists*. Routledge, London.

Stevenson, Adlai, 1974 (1st 1953). *The Papers of Adlai E. Stevenson*, Vol. 5, p. 411; 1st pub *Look*, 22 September 1953, p. 46.

Streeck, Wolfgang, 2017. *How Will Capitalism End? Essays on a Failing System*. Juggernaut Books, New Delhi.

Subrahmanyam, Sanjay, 1996. 'Before the Leviathan: Sectarian Violence and the State in Precolonial India', in Basu and Subrahmanyam, Eds., op.cit., pp. 44-80.

Suhrud, Tridip, 2002, 'In Search of Gandhi', *Seminar*, May, No. 513.

Supreme Court of India, 1980. 'Bachan Singh vs State of Punjab', May 9, (2 SCC 684). https://indiankanoon.org/doc/307021/

Supreme Court of India, 1983. 'Machhi Singh And Others vs State of Punjab', July 20, (3 SCC 470). https://indiankanoon.org/doc/545301/

Supreme Court of India, 2009. 'Rameshbhai Chandubhai Rathod vs State of Gujarat', April 27, (5 SCC 740). https://indiankanoon.org/doc/1338996/

Supreme Court of India, 2009. 'Santosh Kumar Satishbhushan … vs State of Maharashtra', May 13, (6 SCC 498). https://indiankanoon.org/doc/1312651/

Reportable in the Supreme Court of India civil original jurisdiction writ petition (civil) NO.330 OF 2018, pp 9-10, (https://www.sci.

gov.in/supremecourt/2018/3158/3158_2018_Judgement_01-Oct-2018.pdf)

Supreme Court of the United States, 1970. 'Goldberg v. Kelly', (397 US 254). https://supreme.justia.com/cases/federal/us/397/254/

Tagore, Rabindranath, 1902. *Bharatvarsher Itihas.* Bangladarshan, reprinted in Tagore, *Ithias,* Vishwa-Bharati, 1935, Calcutta, pp.1-15.

______1913. *Gitanjali* (Song Offerings). Macmillian, 96, 1st 1917.

______1950. *Crisis in Civilization.* Vishwa-Bharati, Calcutta.

______1993, (1st 1922). 'Hindu-Musalman', *Kalantar.* Visva-Bharati Pub, Calcutta.

______1996, (1st 1917) 'Nationalism', in *English Writings of Rabindranath Tagore,* Vol. II, Sisir Kumar Das, Ed. Delhi.

Tambiah, Stanley Jeyaraja, 1992. *Buddhism Betrayed? Religion, Politics, and Violence in Sri Lanka.* University of Chicago Press, Chicago.

______1996. *Leveling Crowds: Ethnonationalist Conflicts and Collective Violence in South Asia.* University of California Press, CA, USA.

Taylor, Charles, 1992. *Multiculturalism and the Politic of Recognition.* Princeton University Press, New Jersey.

______2008. 'Foreword: Politics and Passion' in R. Kingston and L. Ferry, Eds, *Bringing the Passions Back in: The Emotions in Political Philosophy.* UBC Press, Vancouver, pp. vii–viii.

Thakkar, Usha, 2004. 'Mohalla Committees of Mumbai: Candles in Ominous Darkness', *Economic & Political Weekly,* 7 Feb, pp.580-586.

Thapar, Romila, 1961. *Ashoka and the Decline of the Mauryas.* Oxford University Press, London.

______1966. *A History of India.* Penguin, England.

______1987. *The Mauryas Revisited,* Sakharam Ganesh Deuskar lectures on Indian history, K.P. Bagchi & Co, Kolkata.

______1989. 'Imagined Religious Communities? Ancient History and the Modern Search for a Hindu Indenity', in Lorenzen, Ed., op. cit. pp. 333 – 359.

______2004. *The Many Voices of History.* Penguin, New Delhi.

______2016. 'Cololinal Roots of Hindutva "Nationalism"', *Outlook* 11 Jul, p. 11. http://www.outlookindia.com/magazine/story/the-colonial-roots-of-hindutva-nationalism/297420

Teltumbde, Anand, 2014. 'Saffron Neoliberalism', *Economic & Political Weekly,* Aug 2., Vol. 49, No. 31, pp. 10-11.

Tilly, Charles, 1990. *Coercion, Capital, and European States, A.D. 990-1990.* Blackwell, Cambridge, MA, Oxford.

Tikhonov, Vladimir and Torkel Brekke, Eds, 2013. *Buddhism and Violence: Militarism and Buddhism in Modern Asia*. Routledge, New York.

Tomlinson, Hugh, 'Years of Misogyny and Religious Hatred Fuel Sexual Violence", *The Times*, 19 Apr 2018.

Tocqueville, Alexis de, 1862. *Democracy in America*. Francis Bowen, Ed., Univ. Press, Welch, Bigelow and Co., Cambridge, Mass., USA.

Toscano, Robert, 2013. 'Group Identity and Difference', *Seminar*, Sept, No. 349.

Thomson Reuters, 2018. 'The World's 10 Most Dangerous Countries for Women'. http://poll2018.trust.org/

Triyakin, Edward A., Ed., 1963. *Sociological Theory, Values and Sociological Change*. Free Press, Glencoe, London.

Tutu, Desmond, *1999. No Future Without Forgiveness*. Image DoublesT, New York.

______2004. 'Restoring Justice', *The Tablet*, 21 Feb, Vol. 258, No. 8525, p. 13-14.

Ure, Michael and Mervyn Frost, Eds, 2014. *The Politics of Compassion*. Routledge, Taylor & Francis, London and New York.

Vajpeyi, Ananya, 2014. 'Hindu Swaraj and Hinduism', *The Hindu* 12 Jul 2014.

van den Berge, Pierre L., 1969. 'Pluralism and Polity: A Theoretical Exploration', in Leo Kuper and M.G. Smith, Eds, *Pluralism in Africa*, University of California Press, Berkeley.

UNESCO, Constitution. http://www.unesco.org/education/pdf/UNESCO_E.PDF

Varshney, Ashutosh, 2002. *Ethnic Conflict and Civic Life: Hindus and Muslims in India*. Yale University Press, New Haven.

______2003. 'South Asia and the War on Terror', *Seminar*, Jan, No. 521.

______2013. *Battles Half Won: India's Improbable Democracy*. Penguin, India.

Vidal, Denis, Gilles Tarabout & Eric Meyer, Eds, 2003. *Violence/Non-Violence: Some Hindu Perspectives*. Manohar, New Delhi.

Vyas, Neena, 2007, 'BJP to Focus on Cultural Nationalism', *The Hindu*, 1 Apr. https://www.thehindu.com/todays-paper/tp-national/BJP-to-focus-on-cultural-nationalism-oppose-appeasement/article14742877.ece

Weber, Max, 1947. *The Theory and Economic Organization*. William Hodge and Co., London.

Weber, Max, 1946. *From Max Weber*, H.H. Gerth and C. Wright Mills, Trans & Eds. Oxford University Press, New York.

Windass, Stanley, 1964. *Christianity versus Violence: A Social and Historical Study of War and Christianity*. Sheed and Ward, London.

Wilkinson, Steven I., 2004. *Votes and Violence: Electoral Competition and Ethnic Riots in India*. Cambridge University Press, UK.

Wilson, E.O., 1975. *Sociobiology: The New Synthesis*. Harvard University Press, USA.

Wittgenstein, Ludwig, 1998. *Culture and Value*. Blackwell, London.

Wolf, Ernest S., 1988. *Treating the Self: Elements of Clinical Self Psychology*. Guilford Press, New York/London.

World Economic Forum (WEF), 2017. 'The Inclusive Growth and Development Report 2017'. http://www3.weforum.org/docs/WEF_Forumo_IncGrwth_2017.pdf

Young, Iris Marion, 2011. *Responsibility for Justice*. Oxford University Press, Oxford.

Zimbardo, Philip G., 2007. *Lucifer Effect Understanding How Good People Turn Evil*. Random House, New York.

Zunes, Stephen, Lester Kurtz & Sarah Asher, Eds, 1999. 'Introduction', in *Nonviolent Movements Social: A Geographical Perspective*. Blackwell, Maiden, Massachusetts.

INDEX

ALSO IN SPEAKING TIGER

SHAHEEN BAGH AND THE IDEA OF INDIA

Writings on a Movement for Justice, Liberty and Equality

Edited by Seema Mustafa

On 15 December 2019, police in riot gear stormed Delhi's Jamia Millia Islamia University and attacked unarmed students protesting against the Citizenship (Amendment) Act (CAA), which makes religion a factor in the process of granting Indian citizenship. In neighbouring Shaheen Bagh, mothers and other relatives and friends of the students came out into the streets in outrage and anguish. They sat on a main road demanding repeal of the CAA, which, twinned with the National Register of Citizens (NRC), could make Indian Muslims aliens in their own homeland. Within days, similar protests broke out across the country. Free India had never seen anything like it.

Shaheen Bagh and the Idea of India examines how the sit-in by a small group of Muslim women—many of whom had stepped out of their homes alone for the first time—united millions of Indians of different faiths and ideologies in defence of the principles of liberty, equality and secularism enshrined in our Constitution. It also throws up many important questions: Can the Shaheen Bagh protests reverse the damage done to our democracy in recent years? How did the non-violent movement sustain itself despite vilification, threats and persecution by the establishment? Is this movement the beginning of new solidarities in our society? Will it survive the aftermath of the communal violence that devastated northeast Delhi in February 2020, and the witch-hunt that has now been launched under cover of the Covid-19 pandemic and lockdown?

This necessary collection comprises interviews with some of the brave women at the core of the protests; ground reports and photographs by journalists like Seema Mustafa, Seemi Pasha, Nazes Afroz and Mustafa Quraishi; and essays by thinkers, writers, lawyers and activists, including Nayantara Sahgal, Harsh Mander, Subhashini Ali, Nandita Haksar, Zoya Hasan, Apoorvanand, Enakshi Ganguly, Sharik Laliwala and Nizam Pasha. It is a book that must be read by everyone who cares about India's democracy and its future.

ALSO IN SPEAKING TIGER

THE DISOBEDIENT INDIAN

Towards a Gandhian Philosophy Of Dissent

Ramin Jahanbegloo

In this original and timely book, Ramin Jahanbegloo, one of the world's leading political philosophers, engages with the most pressing question facing all of us today: is it not our duty, as free and autonomous citizens of democracy, to question and speak out against all authority? Should we not take back the power from self-interested political actors in the true spirit of Gandhi, for whom Swaraj was more than mere freedom from oppression?

The core idea of Gandhi's philosophy of resistance, Jahanbegloo argues, is his unshakeable conviction that it is no longer possible to organize political action without disobedience. Democracy, to be worthy of obedience, he says, must be structured so that every citizen can question and disobey unjust laws and institutions. This is what Mahatma Gandhi still tells us, more forcefully than any other thinker of the twentieth century.

The Disobedient Indian is a compellingly argued, persuasive handbook about the history, philosophy and necessity of disobedience. It is a vital tract for our times.

ALSO IN SPEAKING TIGER

LOOKING AWAY

Inequality, Prejudice and Indifference in New India

Harsh Mander

In the two decades since the early 1990s, when India confirmed its allegiance to the Free Market, more of its citizens have become marginalized than ever before, and society has become more sharply riven than ever. In *Looking Away*, Harsh Mander ranges wide to record and analyse the many different fault lines which crisscross Indian society today.

There is increasing prosperity among the middle classes, but also a corresponding intolerance for the less fortunate. Poverty and homelessness are also on the rise—both in urban and rural settings—but not only has the state abandoned its responsibility to provide for those afflicted, the middle class, too, now avoids even the basic impulses of sharing. And with the sharp Rightward turn in politics, minority communities are under serious threat—their very status as citizens in question—as a belligerent, monolithic idea of the nation takes the place of an inclusive, tolerant one.

However, as Harsh Mander points out, what most stains society today is the erosion in the imperative for sympathy, both at the state and individual levels, a crumbling that is principally at the base of the vast inequities which afflict India. Exhaustive in its scope, impassioned in its arguments, and rigorous in its scholarship, *Looking Away* is a sobering checklist of all the things we must collectively get right if India is to become the country that was promised, in equal measure, to all its citizens.